Capturing the South

Capturing the South

Imagining America's Most Documented Region

Scott L. Matthews

Published by the University of North Carolina Press, Chapel Hill,
in association with the Center for Documentary Studies
at Duke University

This book was sponsored by the postdoctoral fellows program at the Center for the Study of the American South, University of North Carolina at Chapel Hill.

Set in Merope Basic by Westchester Publishing Services
Manufactured in the United States of America

The University of North Carolina Press has been a member of the Green Press Initiative since 2003.

Library of Congress Cataloging-in-Publication Data
Names: Matthews, Scott L., author.
Title: Capturing the South : imagining America's most documented region / Scott L. Matthews.
Description: [Chapel Hill, North Carolina] : Published by the University of North Carolina Press, Chapel Hill, in association with the Center for Documentary Studies at Duke University, [2018] | Includes bibliographical references and index.
Identifiers: LCCN 2018017918| ISBN 9781469646442 (cloth : alk. paper) | ISBN 9781469646459 (pbk : alk. paper) | ISBN 9781469646466 (ebook)
Subjects: LCSH: Social sciences—Research—Southern States—History—20th century. | Social scientists—Southern States—History—20th century.
Classification: LCC H62.5.U5 M383 2018 | DDC 975/.043—dc23
LC record available at https://lccn.loc.gov/2018017918

Cover illustration: Photograph of Dora Mae Tengle, 1936, by Walker Evans. LC-USF3301-031301-M4, FSA/OWI Collection, Prints and Photographs Division, Library of Congress.

This book includes previously published material, used here with permission. An earlier version of chapter three appeared as "John Cohen in Eastern Kentucky: Documentary Expression and the Image of Roscoe Halcomb during the Folk Revival," *Southern Spaces* (August 2008), doi:10.18737/M74W3W. An earlier version of chapter five appeared as "Protesting the Privilege of Perception: Resistance to Documentary Work in Hale County, Alabama, 1900-2010," *Southern Cultures* 22, no. 1 (Spring 2016): 31-65.

DOCUMENTARY ARTS AND CULTURE

Edited by Alexa Dilworth, Wesley Hogan, and Tom Rankin of the Center for Documentary Studies at Duke University

In a time when the tools of the documentary arts have become widely accessible, this series of books, published in association with the Center for Documentary Studies at Duke University, explores and develops the practice of documentary expression. Drawing on the perspectives of artists and writers, this series offers new and important ways to think about learning and doing documentary work while also examining the traditions and practice of documentary art through time.
Center for Documentary Studies at Duke University
https://documentarystudies.duke.edu

Contents

Illustrations

Acknowledgments

This book exists because I was fortunate enough to cross paths with people who took the time to recognize my passions and push me along when I doubted my way. At the University of Virginia (UVA), Ed Ayers listened one day as I wondered whether I belonged in the graduate program in history. He reassured me and affirmed my research interests by giving me a book from his shelf, *After Freedom: A Cultural Study in the Deep South*, written in the 1930s by anthropologist Hortense Powdermaker, and by recommending another, *Tenants of the Almighty*, by sociologist Arthur Raper with photographs by Farm Security Administration photographer Jack Delano. Ed's support and generosity lit the first path that led me to write *Capturing the South*.

While at UVA, I had the great fortune of having Grace Hale as an advisor. She championed my writing and teaching at every turn while also consistently pushing me to become better at both. I had the honor of serving as a teaching assistant for her courses on the twentieth-century South and poverty in America: Grace encouraged me to develop classes that revolved around our shared interests in documentary work; ill advisedly allowed me to give rambling lectures on John Lomax's field recordings from Sumter County, Alabama; and, most importantly, provided me with a model of innovative and inspiring teaching. Grace's books and essays are also touchstones of cultural history. Her influence is evident throughout this book.

I was also fortunate to work as a teaching assistant with the late Julian Bond for a number of semesters. He encouraged me to carve out class time to teach my own interests, including civil rights movement photography. One of the first times I met him I told him about my love of the photographs Danny Lyon made for the Student Nonviolent Coordinating Committee in the 1960s. He then spent an hour with me turning the pages of one of my favorite books, Lyon's *Memories of the Southern Civil Rights Movement*, and telling me the backstories of many of the photographs, which he knew well because of his role as SNCC's communications director. Over the years, he also regularly passed along books and films he thought I would like, including rare documentary films made for SNCC during the 1960s. I wish I could hand him a copy of this book.

I am extraordinarily grateful for the financial and institutional support I received while writing *Capturing the South*, including fellowships at the Smithsonian Institution's Museum of American History and at the University of North Carolina-Chapel Hill's Center for the Study of the American South (CSAS). At the Smithsonian, I had the pleasure of working with historian Pete Daniel and curator of photography David Haberstich. The year I spent as a fellow at CSAS almost seems like a dream now. I can never adequately thank Bill Ferris for his encouragement and support of my book project and his willingness to allow me to sit in on two of his classes on southern literature and music. I am also grateful to Tom Rankin for allowing me to sit in on his class "Documenting the Sacred South." There were many others who worked at CSAS who became great colleagues during my time in Chapel Hill, including Ayse Erginer and Emily Wallace, the superb editors of the journal *Southern Cultures*; the CSAS director Harry Watson; and my fellow "fellow" that year, Tammy Ingram. I also received a generous research fellowship from the Frances S. Summersell Center for the Study of the American South at the University of Alabama. I am particularly grateful to the librarians and archivists at the Wilson Library, Southern Historical Collection, and Southern Folklife Collection at UNC, as well as at the W. S. Hoole Special Collections Library at the University of Alabama, for diligently fulfilling my requests.

The fellowship at CSAS brought with it an opportunity to publish my book with the University of North Carolina Press and its Documentary Arts and Culture series in association with the Center for Documentary Studies (CDS) at Duke University. In college I had developed an abiding interest in the evocative sociological and ethnographic studies published by UNC Press during the 1920s and 1930s. It seems incredible to me that I am now publishing a book about some of those studies with that fabled press. I am eternally grateful to the people at UNC Press who have helped make this possible. David Perry and Joe Parsons were early editors who guided me through the manuscript's first stages. Since then, I have had the pleasure of working with Lucas Church, who has helped make this book immeasurably better. Mark Simpson-Vos, editorial director at the press, and Tom Rankin, editor of the Documentary Arts and Culture series and documentary studies professor at CDS, have also supported and championed this book at every stage. They have been exceedingly patient over the years as parenthood and large teaching loads slowed the revision process to a crawl.

Other friends and colleagues read portions of the manuscript in various forms over the years. I owe particular thanks to Allen Tullos and the editors at *Southern Spaces* at Emory University for publishing an early version of chapter 3 on John Cohen and Roscoe Holcomb. A number of years ago, Allen also graciously read a very long and bloated version of chapter 5 on Hale County, all the while balancing his own research and teaching obligations. Ayse Eringer and Emily Wallace provided indispensable editorial insight and assistance when I published an early version of the Hale County chapter in the "Documentary Arts" issues of *Southern Cultures*. Ted Hutchinson read through the entire manuscript and offered incisive commentary, despite facing his own deadlines as editor of a law journal. I am also grateful to the anonymous readers who submitted penetrating and instructive reports to UNC Press that helped make this a stronger and more nuanced book.

My friends in Charlottesville provided invaluable camaraderie, and occasionally commiseration, during the early stages of writing. I am glad to still count Julian Hayter, Dan Holt, Ted Hutchinson, Chris Loomis, and Chris Nehls as friends. While working at Georgia State University, I had the pleasure of befriending eminent scholars whose work and ideas inspired my own. Special thanks go to Christine Carter, Larry Grubbs, Brian Ingrassia, the late Cliff Kuhn, and Mary Rolinson. At my current school, Florida State College at Jacksonville, I have been very fortunate and grateful to have the assistance of smart and resourceful librarians, including Sheri Brown, Jennifer Grey, and Amber Strickland. They have happily filled innumerable interlibrary requests for me and are ideal coworkers. I have also benefited immensely from conversations with a fellow southern historian and friend, JoAnn Carpenter.

I found it a little daunting at times to write a historical study about people who are still alive. History, of course, is its own kind of documentary representation that raises questions about how to faithfully render another's life and art. My hope all along has been that the people I wrote about would find my history of their documentary work compelling, even if they did not always agree with my conclusions. I can never thank John Cohen enough for his willingness to open his home and his personal archive to me. He patiently listened to my questions and provided me with extensive, almost cinematic, recollections of his extraordinary life as a musician in the folk revival and his work as a documentary artist. He allowed me to use some of his unpublished photographs from eastern Kentucky in my article about him for *Southern Spaces* and to read and copy his correspondence with Roscoe Holcomb. "Since my first drive through eastern Kentucky," he wrote in the 1970s, "I have viewed traditional culture as a hidden spiritual resource, and my only aim throughout has been to share it with others, an enterprise which is its own reward." I am especially thankful to have been a beneficiary of John's generosity.

I am also grateful to friends, family members, and neighbors of Roscoe Holcomb who took time to tell me their stories about him and their lives in eastern Kentucky. They include Danny Dixon and many members of the region's Old Regular Baptist churches, Odabe Halcomb, Lee Sexton, Junior Shepherd, and Dickie Williams. Special thanks go to Odabe Halcomb who gave me a photo of Roscoe, which appears in this book, soon after meeting me for the first time.

I trace part of the inspiration for this book to my childhood when I discovered my family's own documentary tradition. The form it took was ordinary: bounded albums of carefully curated family photographs, shoeboxes full of stray snapshots, life histories in longhand, Bible records, and VHS recordings. But what I saw—photographs of ordinary lives lived on the distinctive landscapes of northeast Florida and southeast Georgia—nurtured a unique sense of familial and regional identity. I am grateful to my mother Carolyn Ettlinger for painstakingly preserving the written and photographic records of our family. No words can convey my love for her and my thankfulness for her encouragement and support. My father's side of the family, particularly my Great-Aunt Virginia Taylor, also lovingly maintained the photographic record of the Matthews, Pender, Taylor, and Barnes families of eastern North Carolina. Aunt Virginia sat with me many nights telling stories about the people who appeared in yellowed photographs looping tobacco, chopping barbeque, hunting foxes, or posing in photo studios in Wilson, Elm City, and Tarboro. So many others in my family also gave of their time, finances, food, spare rooms, photographs, and patience while I worked on *Capturing the South*. I can only offer them my thanks, love, and a physical copy of "The Book" that many, I'm sure, justly assumed might only ever exist in my imagination.

My wife Meredith and my daughter Leighton have lived with this book the entire time we have been a family. They have shown nothing but patience and hospitality toward it, despite its resembling a lingering houseguest who took over shared rooms, left behind messes, and long ago wore out its welcome. Through it all, Meredith managed my doubts and frustrations with grace, celebrated my successes with unalloyed joy, and improved my book with her keen editorial and artistic judgment. She and Leighton are the lights and loves of my life.

Capturing the South

Introduction

The Most Documented Region

In the early 1940s, social scientists in the South began making bold pronouncements about the unparalleled amount of documentary work conducted in the region throughout its history. In a series of superlatives, they spoke of the South as the "best documented" and the "most documented" region. What made the South distinct, it seemed, was not simply a list of cultural traits or social or economic indices, but the sheer volume of fieldwork conducted within its broadly construed and frequently debated borders. "It has been said that the South is the best documented region of the United States," wrote Harriet Herring, a social scientist at the University of North Carolina at Chapel Hill. "For a long time much of this writing was done by other regions. But the South has for some time been busy examining itself."[1]

Two years later, one of the people most responsible for the South's documentary self-examination echoed Herring's assessment. Howard Odum, a sociologist at the University of North Carolina (UNC) and founder of its Institute for Research in the Social Sciences (IRSS), made similar statements in a series of articles he wrote for the *Saturday Review of Literature*. "It has often been said that the South is the best documented region of any of the major regions of the United States of America," he wrote. "This is meant to indicate that it has been studied and explored, criticized and praised, and documented as a problem area more than any other division of the land." He later wrote an article in the *Saturday Review* highlighting the region's diversity, including the unique characteristics and histories of its various subregions, and argued that such a regionalist perspective "provides an excellent framework for the better understanding of the most documented and described of all the American regions."[2]

Recognition of the South's distinguished standing in the history of documentary work, in part because of the firsthand studies conducted by social scientists like Odum and Herring throughout the twentieth century, continues into the current century with even more expansive claims being made by their successors at UNC: it seems that the South not only stood out nationally but also globally for the amount of documentary attention it received in its history. "Southern sociologists contributed greatly to making the South of the interwar years probably the best documented society that has ever existed," wrote UNC sociologist John Shelton Reed in 2002. Nine years later, I sat in on a class at UNC, "Southern Literature and the Oral Tradition," taught by folklorist William Ferris, who, since the 1960s has created his own remarkable body of documentary work, including films, photographs, and music recordings of the South's vernacular cultures and landscapes, particularly those of his native state of Mississippi. Of the many sentences he spoke that semester that I dutifully tried to take down verbatim because of their elegance and insight, one stood out and I starred it in the margin: "The American South is the most documented place on earth."[3]

This book does not make a case for or against these claims about the South's status as the "best" or "most" documented region. Such superlatives, however, do testify to the significance of documentary work in the region's history and to the cultural construction of "The South" itself. What Odum called the "realistic South" seemed summoned into existence, particularly during the twentieth century, by the evocative realism of photographs taken by renowned artists such as Doris Ulmann, Walker Evans, Margaret Bourke-White, Jack Delano, Danny Lyon, Roland Freeman, and William Christenberry; films shot by Robert Flaherty, John Cohen, Alan Lomax, Harvey Richards, Bill Ferris, and Les Blank; field recordings made by John and Alan Lomax, Robert Winslow Gordon, John W. Work III, Frederic Ramsey, and George Mitchell; and innovative sociological, anthropological, folkloric, and journalistic fieldwork carried out by W. E. B. Du Bois, Howard Odum, Cecil Sharp, Zora Neale Hurston, Arthur Raper, James Agee, Hortense Powdermaker, and many others. This book explores a small but representative portion of the history of documentary work *in* and *of* the South during the twentieth century. It examines why the South became and remained such an important site of representation—a place where social scientists, photographers, filmmakers, journalists, and travel writers carried out firsthand documentary fieldwork. It also examines how they made the South into another kind of site of documentary representation—a place imagined and defined by these documentarians' realist descriptions, photographs, films, and recordings of mostly rural and poor black and white southerners whose physical appearance, vernacular architecture, life histories, folklore, and songs seemed most representative of a premodern and, therefore, authentic regional and racial essence that needed preservation before modernity wiped it away.[4]

At the same time, documentary representations often transposed these romantic images with ones that emphasized the "problem South," a place beset with unique plights that grew out of the region's racial caste system and exploitive labor practices, including sharecropping and convict labor, that also seemed to set it apart from the nation. The South's apparent temporal difference, which made it an alluring site for documenting enduring folk cultures, also made it another kind of site, reflecting various forms of what Howard Odum called "lag"—social, cultural, and chronological—that produced what appeared to be distinct regional and racial pathologies. The South thus served as a site of representation in two interrelated ways: a place to document and diagnose social problems that set it apart from the nation and a place defined by the countless documentary representations of those problems that circulated widely in books, journals, magazines, photographs, and films. These images of enchanting primitivism and endemic pathology often blurred together, neutralizing the aims of documentary work carried out in the region in the name of social reform. While the social, economic, and cultural forces that brought fieldworkers into the South changed throughout the twentieth century, their representations of the region shared these common themes despite differences in modes, styles, and purposes.[5]

In his 1981 essay, "Documenting a Culture," historian F. Jack Hurley laid out the social and cultural qualities that lured photographers and other documentarians to the South during the twentieth century, making it the "most" and "best" documented region, and also highlighted how their representations of the region blended romance and recrimination:

> Since the turn of the present century, the southern region of the U.S. has attracted photographers in the documentary tradition. Perhaps it is partly because we have been so poor; our social problems must lie right out in the open for all to see because, until recently, we have lacked the money to hide them decently. The poverty, which was endemic until after World War II, also kept our human relationships on an intimate scale and our agricultural and urban technology relatively simple, all of which is an advantage to the photographer. People who live much of their lives on their front porches, who plow with mules, and spend Saturday in town trading with their neighbors are simply much more accessible than people who live in high-rise apartments and conduct their business in huge steel and glass buildings. And so nearly all the really great documentarians have, sooner or later, come South. They have come because they believed their images could help the region with its social problems, or because they found the people picturesque or romantic or strong or admirable or appalling.[6]

Poverty made the region ripe for documentary work. It sustained premodern ways that left poor southerners more "accessible" to documentarians compared to wealthier urbanites leading more cloistered lives. It generated "appalling" scenes that enticed the voyeuristic reformer and molded a "picturesque" people that inspired the romantic artist. Such an alluring contrast ultimately drew "all the really great documentarians" into the region. "Alternately a utopia and a dystopia, the South is subject to powerful representational tides, pulling it both ways," argues musician and scholar Warren Zanes. "As with exoticism of any kind, the exoticism of the region is open-ended, fluid. . . . There is a stunning ambivalence to the imagined South—the place inverts, always potentially its own opposite." According to Odum, what the nation saw as the "realistic South" blended images made by the "romanticist" and the "photographers of pathology." The fluidity that characterizes documentary images of the South explains the apparent paradox Odum identified in 1942: the "most" and "best documented region" is also the "least understood."[7]

The appeal of the South as a place to do documentary work links the fieldwork tradition in the region with the broader history of travel writing, anthropology, and ethnography throughout the world. Like the history of European travel writing and, later, of professional anthropology, documentary work in the South during the twentieth century focused its field of view on "the most *other* of others," those most isolated from the centers of cultural, economic, and political power and "most authentically rooted in their 'natural' settings," as anthropologists Akhil Gupta and James Ferguson argue about the global history of ethnographic fieldwork. Going into "the field"—like the South imagined by documentarians—"suggests a trip to a place that is agrarian, pastoral, or maybe even 'wild.' . . . What stands metaphorically opposed to work in the field is work in industrial places: in labs, in offices, in factories, in urban settings—in short, civilized spaces that have lost their connection with nature." Gupta and Ferguson argue that there exists a "hierarchy of purity" among field sites, places that are more "'anthropological' than others (e.g., Africa more than Europe, southern Europe more than northern Europe, villages more than cities) according to the degree of Otherness from the archetypal anthropological 'home.'" Among documentarians working in the United States, the American South, long imagined and defined against the modern industrial nation, ranks near the top in the "hierarchy of purity" because of its perceived Otherness.[8]

The perception of the South as a pure place—an exotic cultural eddy cut off from the rest of the nation because of its historically agrarian way of life, which in turn nurtured folk cultures—made the region a central site for documentary fieldworkers eager to encounter and record ways of life that seemed more authentic than cities. The Black Belt of Alabama and Georgia, the Delta of Mississippi and Louisiana, the mountains of eastern Kentucky and western North Carolina, primitive churches and rural penitentiaries—all seemed like sealed incubators of premodern purity and folk authenticity. In his book, *Dusty in Memphis*, Warren Zanes writes that the appeal of the South as a place for documentary or ethnographic work is based on its perceived "authenticity." His book is an account of how he, as a native of New Hampshire, fell in love with the South because of his obsession with a record from 1969, "Dusty in Memphis," by Dusty Springfield, a white English singer who borrowed the rhythm and blues sounds of black musicians from the South. For Zanes, like so many others with similar backgrounds, the South became the "ultimate fantastic elsewhere" because it seemed like an "almost pre-modern entity, certain pockets of which know a life that is raw and without effect." For documentarians, doing fieldwork in this "fantastic elsewhere" allayed anxieties about the imminent loss of people, places, and cultures threatened by modernity. Going into "the field," traveling into the rural South, allowed one to see, experience, and document with a camera or a sound recorder a place where the raw and the real still existed, where people made art, architecture, and music out of "instinct" and "impulse," unmediated by modern influences from the outside world.[9]

By seeing the South as a haven for premodern holdouts, a perfect place in Zanes's words to do "a little ethnography," documentarians created an image of the region as not only geographically and culturally distinct but also temporally distant. And as for the ethnographers who traveled to non-Western locations such as the South Pacific or Africa during the first half of the twentieth century, going into the American South to do documentary work seemed like a journey in space and in time. In the Western world, where culture, particularly beginning in the early twentieth century under the influence of anthropologists like Franz Boas, became understood as something that existed in discrete communities and contexts across the globe, an evolutionary classification system developed that placed cultures on a continuum from primitive to modern. Ethnographers saw primitive or premodern cultures as the inevitable casualties of human and technological advancement. This was especially so in the South, where the last vestiges of a unique regional culture seemed perpetually on the verge of vanishing, and documentarians often consciously viewed their work as a form of preservation or "salvage ethnography." By recording an old banjo tune or hymn, photographing a former slave or a segregation sign soon to fall, or filming a fading river baptism ritual, documentarians preserved important parts of a culture that seemed otherwise doomed by the inevitable march of progress and time. This form of salvage, like documentary work itself, constitutes a form of power and operates under the assumption that "the other society is weak and 'needs' to be represented by an outsider (and that what matters in its life is past, not present or future)," argues anthropologist James Clifford. Cycles of ethnographic salvage occurring year after year, decade after decade, such as the recording of folk songs, have resurrected and reinscribed "The South" as a real and distinct cultural region, a place still retaining unique vernacular cultures for the next generation of fieldworkers to seek out and bring back, once again, from the brink of extinction.[10]

In addition to demonstrating why and how the South became an important site of documentary representation, I also emphasize how it became a site of resistance to the power, privilege, and the supposed authority of mostly middle-class white fieldworkers to do documentary work in mostly poor black and white communities in the rural South. Throughout, I highlight what literary critic Mary Louise Pratt calls the "interactional history" of documentary representations, which, she suggests, often turns up only in "traces." In the history of documentary work in the South, the region became what Pratt refers to in her discussion of European travel writing as a "contact zone," where people from different social, economic, and racial backgrounds encountered one another and negotiated the terms of the documentary process. In some cases, these interactions transformed sites of representation into sites of resistance where the documented refused requests by social scientists for interviews or songs, rebuffed the efforts of photographers or filmmakers to take their pictures, or sabotaged these images by glowering or closing their eyes. "There is an enormous gap in all histories of fieldwork: the indigenous 'side' of the story," Clifford writes. "How was the research process understood and influenced by informants . . . by those who did not cooperate?" While in recent years, the self-reflexive turn in postmodern ethnography has helped fill in some of these gaps in the interactional history of fieldwork, histories of what critics Patrick Holland and Graham Huggan call "resistance anecdotes" remain mostly "traces" in scholarship on documentary work. This work tends to focus more on the content and messages of photographs, films, writings, and recordings than on the human encounters and power struggles that preceded them. I also highlight in each chapter how the documented, both black and white, often wrote back, or spoke back, against mostly white middle-class documentarians, challenging their images of race, class, and region and disputing their authority to represent them in the first place.[11]

Sites of representation are primed to become sites of resistance, since documentary work constitutes a form of social, cultural, and, therefore, political power. The documentarians I discuss in this book all operated from a position of power and privilege compared to the people and places they documented. They were mostly white, male, and middle class and from northern cities; some were professional social scientists. Their pedigrees gave them the power to gain access to people from poorer communities, both black and white, and to document their lives and cultures for a wide public audience. Their representations possessed another kind of symbolic power: the power to produce knowledge and identities about the people and places they encountered, observed, and recorded that documentary realism made convincing. When set amid the South's history of racial and class conflict, sites of representation can become not only sites of resistance but also battlegrounds over who gets to determine another's identity and, potentially, fate.[12]

Throughout *Capturing the South* I demonstrate how poor southerners, especially black southerners, often resisted the authority of mostly middle-class white documentarians. I try to bring to life the "interactional history" of the documentary process, including the negotiations and concessions each side often made, and the forms of resistance the documented often used against the power and authority of the documentarian. These forms of resistance often resembled what James C. Scott has referred to as "infrapolitics." As the word implies, infrapolitics often eludes official or public notice. It operates subtly, even "cryptically," as Scott notes, out of social and political necessity. Robin D. G. Kelley has used Scott's concept of infrapolitics to spotlight the radicalism of the black working class in the Jim Crow South, who regularly resisted white supremacy outside the realm of traditional political activism. Black southerners used acts of dissimulation, grumbling, grimacing, songs, and other forms of signifying to mock the pretensions of white documentarians and resist their intrusions into their lives. These challenges to white authority in the field, which could also include polite forms of refusal, make up what Zora Neale Hurston has called the "feather bed of resistance" that stopped just short of insubordination. They created new identities for the documented, ones that turned them from icons into actors in the documentary process.[13]

IN A 1971 INTERVIEW, photographer Walker Evans expressed the difficulty of defining the word "documentary." "Documentary? That's a very sophisticated and misleading word. And not very clear. You have to have a sophisticated ear to receive that word," he said. Part of the difficulty in defining it is due to its use both as a noun and an adjective, often in the same sentence. Evans, for instance, preferred to speak of a "documentary style," rather than simply documentary, while describing his own style as "lyric documentary." And, then, like many words, documentary's meaning and use have also changed over the past century, making a single, accepted definition elusive. Filmmaker John Grierson famously used "documentary" as an adjective in his 1926 review of Robert Flaherty's film, *Moana*, which, he wrote, "being a visual account of events in the daily life of a Polynesian youth, has documentary value." Grierson, who perhaps chose "documentary" because of the wide use of the French word *documentaire* to describe early twentieth-century travel and vernacular films or because of its use among sociologists at the time, later described documentary as "the creative treatment of actuality," distinguishing it from a strictly fictional film. Like Evans's "lyric documentary," Grierson seemed to suggest that the essence of documentary existed somewhere in the spectrum between mimesis and artifice.[14]

Later scholars defined documentary as a genre with specific formal conventions and affective qualities that relies on realism and often emotion to persuade its audience about a particular subject or cause. In his foundational book published in 1973, *Documentary Expression in Thirties America*, historian William Stott emphasized the "primacy of feeling," the use of emotion as a persuasive force in social documentaries about Americans enduring the Great Depression. "Documentary expression" has since become a common descriptor of documentary work in general. Others see documentary as a product of history and not simply aesthetic or stylistic traits. "We must begin with it as a historical phenomenon, a practice with a past," writes photographer and critic Martha Rosler about documentary photography in particular. As Robert Coles, psychiatrist and founder of Duke University's Center for Documentary Studies (CDS), has written, documentary is a "tradition" that "has itself been documented" by historians who have given their own influential definitions of it as a genre and a "practice with a past." As in the case for Stott's book, histories of documentary work in America tend to focus on it as a strategy central to social movements, including Progressive reform, New Deal liberalism, and various forms of political radicalism.[15]

The difficulty of defining, and delimiting, documentary's essence and purpose only increased soon after Evans pointed out the word's ambiguity. During the 1970s and 1980s, postmodern critiques of documentary forms of representation, like ethnography and photography, influenced by theorists such as Roland Barthes, Jean Baudrillard, Michel Foucault, and others, threw into question, or simply exploded, documentary's claims to reveal unmediated reality and its ability to bring about social change. Drawing on semiology, linguistic theory, and hermeneutic philosophy, as well as other forms of cultural criticism, scholars challenged documentary's realist claims and authority, emphasized its status as a "text" to be decoded, called attention to how it culturally constructs its subject rather than reveals a preexisting reality, and highlighted how it operates as form of knowledge, power, and control in society. Other postmodern critics, like Trinh T. Minh-ha, tried to clarify—or, perhaps, confuse—the matter by arguing, "There is no such thing as *documentary*—whether the term designates a category of material, a genre, an approach, or a set of techniques."[16]

While acknowledging all of its contingent and contested meanings, I define documentary in a way that all of the documentarians I write about, particularly those who conducted fieldwork in the South from the early 1900s through the 1960s, would have recognized. During that era, a "realist mode" dominated ethnographic and documentary work before the influence of postmodern and anticolonial critiques undermined that work's authority and ability to accurately represent the Other. In this book, documentary means a representation of people and places based on firsthand fieldwork that uses written, visual, and aural modes to convey a perceived reality intended for a public audience. I also define documentary fieldwork broadly, rather than focusing on a particular professional discipline or representational style, so that it encompasses sociology, ethnography, photography, filmmaking, song recording, journalism, and travel writing. Despite their methodological and stylistic differences, these forms of documentary fieldwork, during the time period I cover in the book, all make claims to what James Clifford calls "ethnographic authority" based on experience in the field that allows one to say, "You are there, because I was there." Essentially, documentary work tries to convince its audience that they would have felt, seen, heard, and even concluded the same things as the documentarian.[17]

Over time, because of documentary's claims to represent the real, the repetition and layering of documentary texts generated an overdetermined image of "The South," one that stood out from other cultural representations of the region found in fiction, popular culture, and movies. In her book, *Dreaming of Dixie*, Karen Cox shows how the entertainment industries—film and publishing, notably—in the late nineteenth and early twentieth centuries portrayed the region as an Old South idyll, a place that retained its plantation past. If the Old South was born amid the tumults of the New South, as

C. Vann Woodward once observed, it was commodified in the North. While documentarians during this time also represented the region as a premodern place, they based their images on observations made in the "ethnographic present" rather than in an imagined past. Their photographs, films, recordings, and books resulted from fieldwork in the South, not from the office of an advertiser or publisher in the North. Most documentarians did not create their work for marketing purposes, but as documents in the service of sociological study, liberal reform, journalism, and folkloric or ethnographic salvage. Some, like Howard Odum, saw their work as a corrective to distorted images of the region promoted by advertisers, fiction writers, and the entertainment industry. As Margaret Bourke-White wrote about the photographs she made in the region that appeared in *You Have Seen Their Faces*, they "may not be the South of song and story, but it is the South that you bring back on sheets of Panchromatic film."[18]

Many documentarians, particularly as an advertising and consumer culture spread during the twentieth century, participated in what historian Miles Orvell calls the "culture of authenticity," which came of age at the end of the nineteenth century and challenged a prior "culture of imitation." The "culture of authenticity" represented "an effort to get beyond mere imitation, beyond manufacturing of illusions, to the creation of more 'authentic' works that were themselves real things." Perhaps unsurprisingly, Orvell writes that his "interest in authenticity emerged in the 1960s" after discovering *Let Us Now Praise Famous Men*, which documented the lives of three white tenant families from Hale County, Alabama, struggling to endure in the region's collapsing cotton economy in 1936. James Agee's passionate urge to cut to the heart of reality itself and present it to the reader not as an effect but as an artifact combined with the understated lyricism of Walker Evans's photographs to produce a book that reflected, and rejected, all of the formal conventions of Depression era photo-texts. Though largely ignored or misunderstood when it was first released in 1941, *Famous Men* found a devoted readership among idealistic youth involved in the civil rights movement and postwar folk revival, and who were interested in the rural South, after the book was reissued in the 1960s. At that time, Orvell writes, "Documentary represented . . . an effort to get closer to 'reality' in a culture that seemed at times to be going in the opposite direction in its willing submission to the domination of the television image."[19]

Doing fieldwork in the South, encountering "real things"—farmers, folk singers, rural churches—and creating "real things" such as documentary books, photographs, films, and sound recordings based on that experience gave the work of documentarians a unique aura of "documentary realism" and authenticity. Thus, the realism of documentary work from the South also made the racial representations of mostly poor black and white southerners—the black convict or "creeper," the white "cracker" or "hillbilly"—particularly convincing, and potentially damaging, at the time of their creation. As such documentary images circulated in books, magazines, photographs, films, and recordings, racial essence often became linked with regional essence. Many of these images have endured, been repeated and recycled, and continue to define the region, in part because of the difficulty of seeing them not as "the thing itself," but as carefully constructed and, therefore, fictive, documentary representations of race and region.

WHILE THIS BOOK focuses on the South during the twentieth century, the issues and themes it addresses—including how the South became a prominent site of documentary representation because of the intriguing contrasts between premodern folk cultures in need of salvage and endemic social pathologies in need of reform, and how it became a corresponding site of resistance because of the power dynamics between documentarians and the documented that involved differences based on race, class, and gender—have precedents in documentary work from the region in prior centuries. For more than four hundred years, documentarians of different stripes—European explorers and colonizers, natural scientists and sketch artists, travel writers and journalists, photographers and proto-ethnographers—have observed and recorded life and landscape in the South. In their descriptions and sketches and, later, lithographs and photographs, these documentarians presented the South as a distinct, exotic, and problematic place that seemed to occupy a different order of time when compared to Europe or, later, the North.

During the late eighteenth century and particularly in the nineteenth century travel writers and sketch artists found the region's indigenous folk cultures curious and even aesthetically pleasing antidotes to the urbanization and industrialization found in Europe and increasingly in the North. The region's poor whites, once derided by famous chroniclers such as William Byrd II in his 1728 depiction of the North Carolina Dismal Swamp region, "History of the Dividing Line betwixt Virginia and North Carolina," as a degraded and wasted race, became "country crackers" who in the eyes of some were the "bone of sinew of the country"—the quintessential "common man who came to epitomize Jacksonian democracy" by the 1830s, argues historian

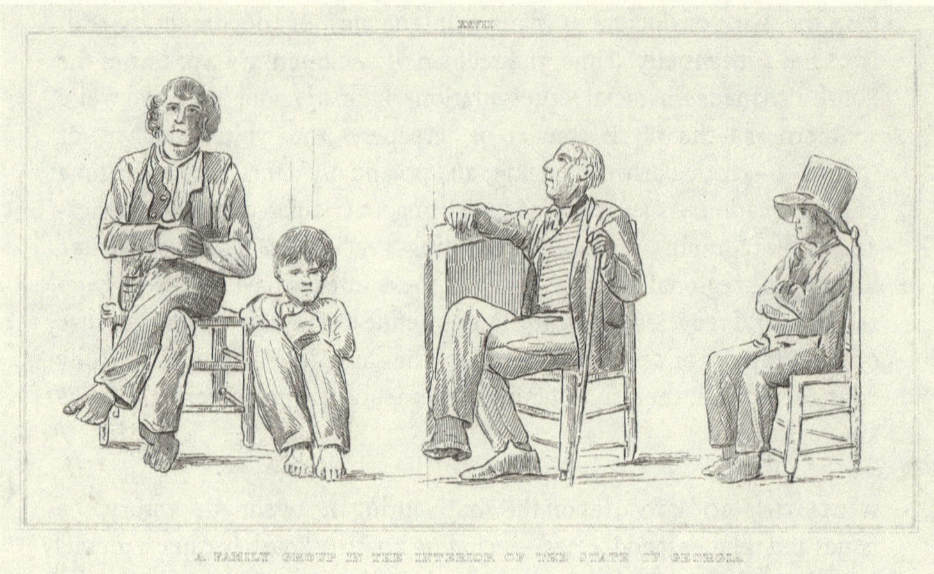

Basil Hall, *A Family Group in the Interior of the State of Georgia*, from *Forty Etchings* (1830). Rare Book Collection, Louis Round Wilson Special Collections Library, University of North Carolina at Chapel Hill.

Nancy Isenberg. In the 1820s, while traveling through the piney woods of southeast Georgia and other areas of the South, British travel writer and artist Captain Basil Hall used new technologies like the camera lucida to sketch as accurately as possible the picturesque "crackers" and "squatters" he encountered in the "wild parts of the country," including their vernacular architecture. The images he made of the rural South's architecture and residents foreshadow the photographs made more than a century later for the Farm Security Administration by artists such as Walker Evans in Alabama and Jack Delano in Georgia during the New Deal. Likewise, in 1857 a New York traveler named Ledyard Lincklaen described how encountering these apparent primitive or premodern people and places inspired travelers not only to document and record what they saw but to do so by harnessing the latest technology like photography: "I am constantly wishing that I could photograph the objects of this country, trees, buildings, especially negros . . . nothing but photographic pictures would give perfect representation of the buildings or population . . . and I have been wishing for the means of taking such pictures ever since landing on the southern side of the Potomac."[20]

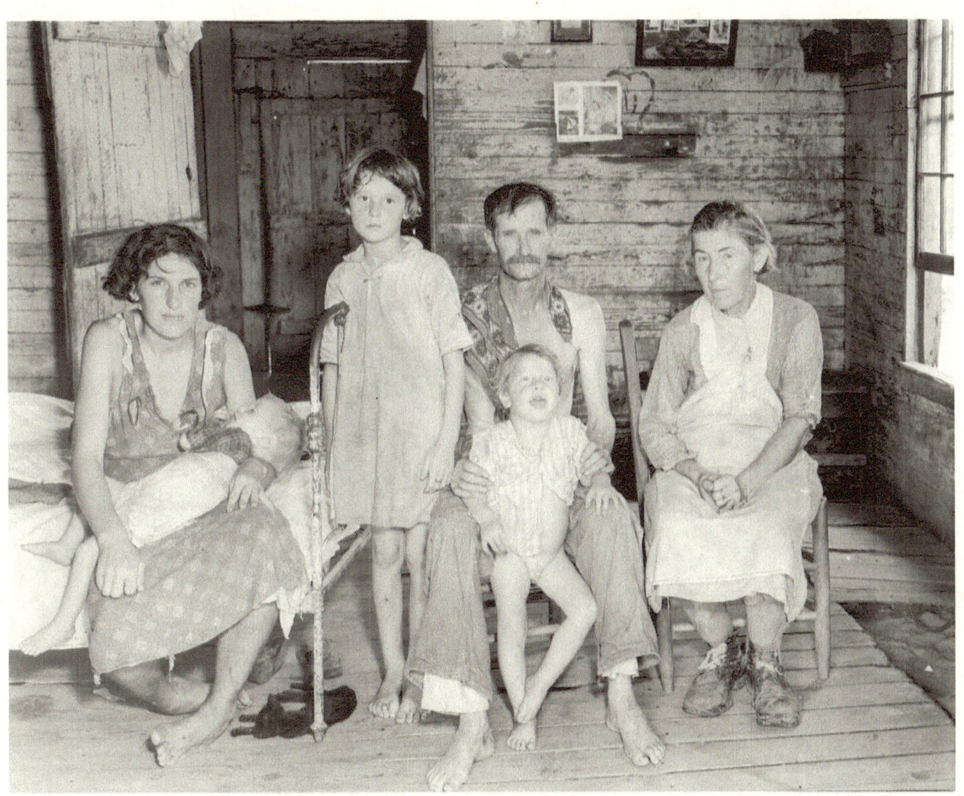

Walker Evans, *Sharecropper Bud Fields and His Family at Home, Hale County, Alabama*, Summer 1936. Courtesy of the Library of Congress, Prints and Photographs Division, FSA/OWI Collection. LC-DIG-ppmsc-00234.

During the Civil War, Union Army commanders, like Thomas Wentworth Higginson, and northern reformers associated with Port Royal Experiment in South Carolina, such as Lucy McKim Garrison, Charles Pickard Ware, and William Francis Allen, heard the shouts, hymns, and spirituals of former slaves and found in them a powerful, primitive, and emotionally resonant sound that contrasted markedly with popular music, including minstrelsy, then found in the commercialized culture of the North. The reformers' *Slave Songs of the United States* (1867) and Higginson's *Army Life in a Black Regiment* (1870) constituted early forms of folklore and ethnographic fieldwork by whites fascinated by black culture in the rural South that prefigured twentieth-century fieldwork by folklorists and sociologists such as John and Alan Lomax and Howard Odum. The work of these nineteenth century documentarians, animated by white romanticism that imagined black

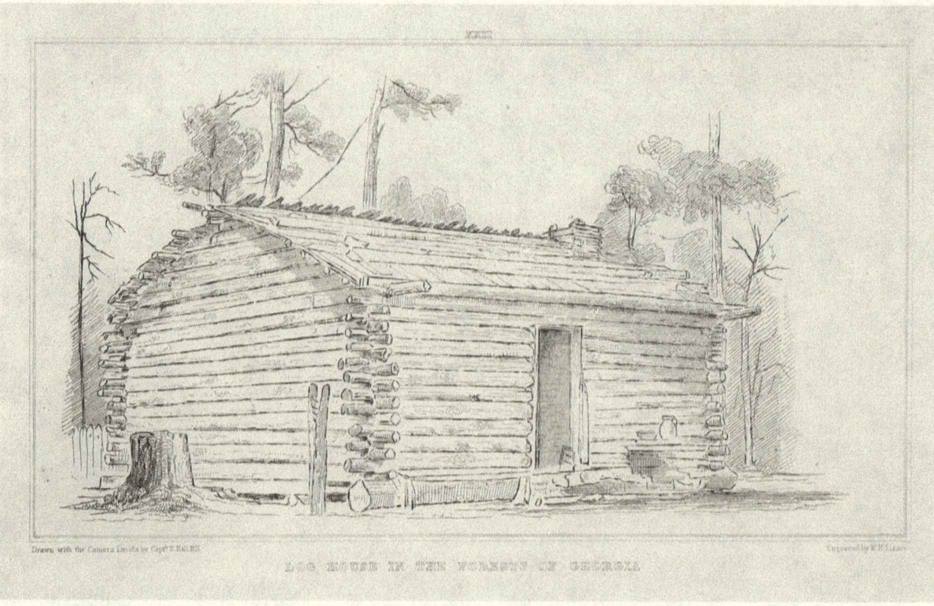

Basil Hall, *Log Cabin in the Forests of Georgia*, from *Forty Etchings* (1830). Rare Book Collection, Louis Round Wilson Special Collections Library, University of North Carolina at Chapel Hill.

people as preternatural singers and childlike primitives ("my young barbarians" as Higginson described them), transformed black oral culture and testimony with religious and political implications into a collection of aesthetic artifacts that white authors and readers could classify, analyze, and perhaps even perform in their parlors.[21]

At the same time, during the antebellum era, travel writers and journalists like Frederick Law Olmsted, who documented the South and published influential accounts such as *The Cotton Kingdom* (1860), became fixated on the reasons for regional difference and focused on the South not simply as a bastion of appealing folk or regional cultures but as a national problem, a place where a brutal and retrograde system of slavery squashed free labor and hindered economic development. Describing, diagnosing, and reforming the "problem" South continued to lure journalists, travel writers, and protosociologists to the South during Reconstruction and into the New South era of the late nineteenth century. Between 1865 and 1880, 245 books were published about the problems facing the postwar South. Northern readers clamored for descriptions of conditions in the defeated and desolated region. "The collection of knowledge by observation, classification, and differenti-

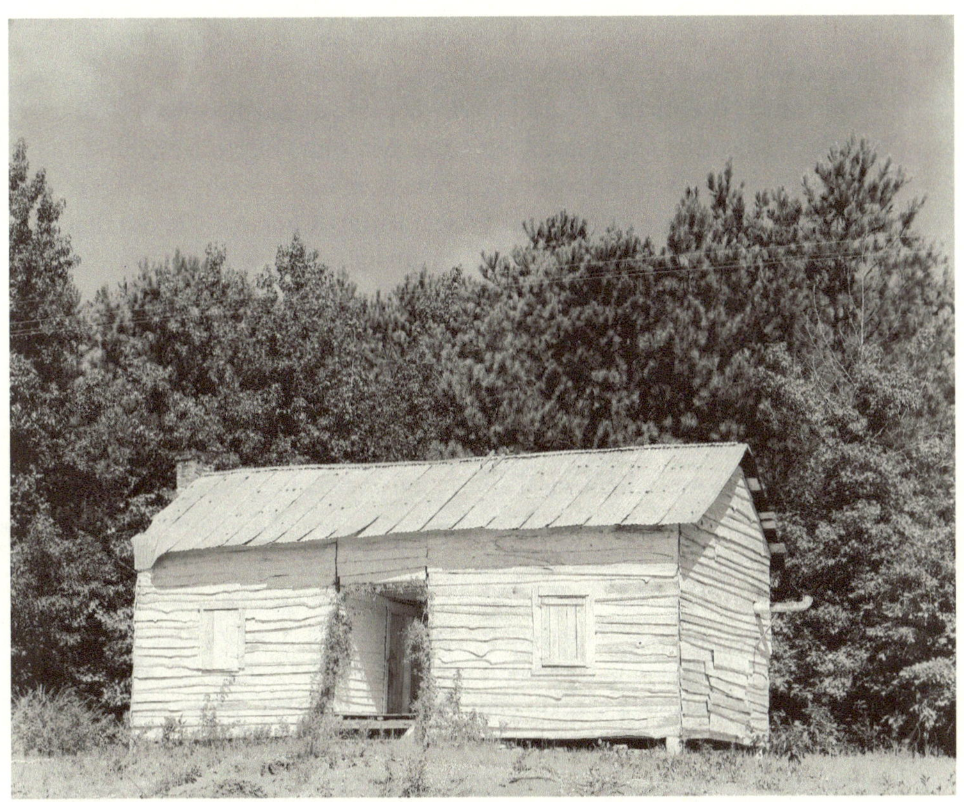

Walker Evans, *Negro Cabin, Hale County, Alabama,* Summer 1936. Courtesy of Library of Congress, Prints and Photographs Division, FSA/OWI Collection. LC-USF342-T01-008156-A.

ation was a prerequisite to reforming the region," argues historian K. Stephen Prince. During the 1880s, Union Army veteran and Unitarian minister from Massachusetts, Jonathan Baxter Harrison, published a series of articles in the *Atlantic Monthly,* "Studies in the South," that envisioned the region as a separate country, peculiar, still uncivilized, and in need of intervention and reform by enlightened white men from the North. What he called his "photographic reporting" of the region projected images of persistent southern pathologies despite a new era of national reconciliation. Historian Timothy Crimmins has argued that taken together, Olmsted's documentary work before the Civil War and Harrison's after it make them "among the forefathers of modern social science." Documenting, diagnosing, and reforming the "problem" South would become the preoccupation of professional sociological fieldworkers in the region beginning with W. E. B. Du Bois in the 1890s and continuing into the twentieth century with the work of scholars like Howard Odum and Arthur Raper, among many others.[22]

During the twentieth century, the rise of professional disciplines dedicated to fieldwork, such as sociology, combined with Progressive and New Deal reform impulses, the postwar folk music revival, and the civil rights movement to produce a floodtide of documentary work in the South that made it seem like the "best" or "most documented region in America" in the minds of social scientists like Howard Odum and Harriett Herring. Documentarians carried out their fieldwork to expose and reform the region or salvage and celebrate its folk cultures jeopardized by the growing influence of commercialism, consumerism, urbanization, and technological change. These new generations of documentarians also went into the field with the latest technological innovations, including portable cameras and sound recorders, that heightened the realism and authority of their representations of the region and its people.

By focusing on a broad sweep of the twentieth century, *Capturing the South* shows how and why documentary work remained a constant and critical form of regional representation despite changing intellectual, social, and cultural contexts, and not a phenomenon isolated in one particular historical context like the Great Depression. While documentary expression did seem to reach an apogee during the 1930s and early 1940s when the federal government sponsored projects that documented America's diverse cultures and communities; when magazines like *Life*, *Look*, and *Collier's* dedicated space to stories on the plight of the poor; when, as Alfred Kazin wrote in 1942, "the sharecropper haunted the imagination"[23] and publishing houses released documentary books, often focusing on the South, with titles such as *You Have Seen Their Faces*, *Let Us Now Praise Famous Men*, and *Forty Acres and Steel Mules*, the overwhelming historiographical focus on that era has obscured the long history of documentary work in the South that preceded and followed the decade.[24] A broader view of the documentary tradition in the South also reveals the relationships that existed between different generations of documentarians and how particular documentary texts and images inspired successive waves of documentary workers to do their own fieldwork in the name of reform, salvage, and art.

Yet *Capturing the South* is hardly a comprehensive history of the documentary tradition in the South during the twentieth century. Major figures in the region's documentary history make only brief appearances in the book or do not appear at all. There are also modes of documentary expression, such as oral history and professional folklore and anthropology, that receive limited attention. I examine a small but significant sample of documentarians, especially Howard Odum whose "folk background studies" of black communities and their secular and sacred song traditions spread powerful and controversial representations of race and region during the 1900s and again in the 1920s; Jack Delano, a Farm Security Administration photographer whose collaboration with sociologist Arthur Raper made Greene County, Georgia, the most photographed place in the South during the Depression and New Deal; John Cohen, a leading figure in the postwar folk revival who used photography, film, and song recordings to create an influential portrait of a musician from eastern Kentucky named Roscoe Holcomb, who became an icon of Appalachian tradition and authenticity; and Danny Lyon, a photographer for the Student Nonviolent Coordinating Committee (SNCC), whose evocative images mythologized SNCC's black activists, the black southerners they organized in the rural South, and the region itself during the civil rights movement. I also demonstrate how Hale County, Alabama, became not only an iconic site of documentary representation during the twentieth century but also a controversial site of resistance where poor blacks and whites questioned and challenged the right of documentarians to expose their private lives for public consumption.

Capturing the South shows how these case studies are both exceptional and representative of dominant themes in the long history of documentary work in and of the region. By focusing on mostly white middle-class documentarians, I am emphasizing how race and class often determined who possessed the power to do fieldwork in predominantly poor black and white communities throughout the South's contentious history. Their privileged social positions also provided them with opportunities to disseminate their work nationally and even internationally, which magnified its cultural influence and helped make the South seem like America's "most documented region."

CHAPTER ONE

Race, Region, and Resistance

Howard Odum's Community and Folk Background Studies, 1905–1928

In 1945, sociologist Howard Odum took stock of more than two decades of what he called "southern regional studies" that social scientists had published under his watch as editor of the journal, *Social Forces*, and director of the Institute for Research in Social Science (IRSS) at the University of North Carolina, Chapel Hill, between 1922 and 1944. In a special issue of *Social Forces*, Odum, and Katharine Jocher, the journal's managing editor, published a twenty-five-page bibliography, "Toward Regional Documentation," that detailed the breadth of these "firsthand studies and observations." They cataloged well over three hundred articles that appeared in the journal, more than two hundred manuscripts written under the auspices of the IRSS, and nearly ninety IRSS-supported books, most published by the University of North Carolina Press, which Odum helped start in 1922. A few months later, the IRSS submitted a report to the *American Sociological Review* that suggested a bibliography titled "The Documented South" would be forthcoming, along with a bibliography by geographer Rupert Vance on "Travellers in the South, 1900–1944." While Vance's bibliography eventually appeared in print, "The Documented South" was never published, although Odum did provide some suggestive evidence from it in one of his last essays, "On Southern Literature and Southern Culture," published in 1953. During the first half of the twentieth century, eight hundred books were published on "Negro Life," four hundred on "Nature and the Folk," and more than one hundred books on "Socio-economic Studies, Nature and Resources, Travel and Description." "So far as our inquiries go," Odum wrote, "none of the other regions, the Northeast, the Middle States, the Northwest, or the Far West approximate this quantitative measurement of achievements."[1]

The scope and ambition of these bibliographies testify to how the South became a central site for social scientific fieldwork conducted by scholars associated with research universities during the first third of the twentieth century. Convulsions such as the collapse of the South's cotton economy, the migration of more than a million of its black people to northern cities, lynchings, labor strife, sharecropping and soil erosion, and folk cultures threatened by modernity, among countless other topics, lured sociologists, geographers, folklorists, and ethnographers into the field in the name of social reform and cultural salvage. Academics made the South into what Odum called a "living laboratory," a place where scholars carried out fieldwork and created empirical studies that described and diagnosed, quantified and mapped the region's distinctive qualities. Their work, Odum declared yet again in 1945, made the South "the most completely documented region of any in the Nation." If there is any truth to Odum's statement, he could claim a crucial role in making it a reality.[2]

Today, Odum's legacy as a sociologist is often associated with his concept of regionalism and his culminating study on the topic, *Southern Regions*, published in 1936. It was a monumental text totaling more than 600 pages, containing more than 270 statistical tables and charts, and illustrated with 250 maps that gave "graphic expression" to regional difference and deficiency and the need for regional cooperation rather than sectional isolation. Some of his most enduring contributions came from his documentary fieldwork in the region in the 1900s and 1920s and his support of other documentary work in the South into the 1940s. In the 1900s, his early fieldwork was on black communities in the Deep South and their sacred and secular song traditions. In the 1920s, he co-conducted new fieldwork and published new collections of black folk songs from the South. He also wrote a popular trilogy of books on the life, songs, and stories of a black itinerant laborer he met in Chapel Hill and, during the New Deal, collaborated with Farm Security Administration (FSA) photographers as part of the new Subregional Laboratory for Social Research at UNC.[3]

Along with W. E. B. Du Bois, Odum began his career as part of a new generation of social scientists in the South who embraced fieldwork rather than theorizing as the basis of sociological study and professional authority. From 1905–8, he documented social conditions and institutions, as well as the "social and mental traits" of black residents living in small towns in Mississippi and Georgia. Odum described his early documentary work as "community studies" or "background community inquiries." During this time, he also documented black sacred and secular songs, including some of the earliest examples of what would become known as the blues, with pen and paper and a graphophone, the latest in sound recording technology. Documenting black folk songs allowed him to collect evidence of what he saw as "the soul of a people"—their thoughts, beliefs, and capabilities—that revealed the essence of an otherwise inscrutable race that whites such as Odum determined to be a "problem." Odum, like so many other documentarians anxious about modernity's corrosive effect on vernacular cultures, also emphasized the importance of salvaging black folk songs before they were "blown away with [the] changing environment."[4]

Odum returned to documenting and writing about black folk culture in the mid-1920s after years as a professor and administrator. He referred to his collections of black sacred and secular songs, and other similar inventories of black folk culture supported by the IRSS, as "folk background studies." Writing and publishing on black folk culture from the South in the 1920s allowed Odum to tap into elite interest in the race's cultural roots in the region. This interest was born of several factors: the Harlem Renaissance and the "New Negro" movement, the commercialization of the blues, the modernist fascination for primitivism, and perennial fears of regional folk cultures succumbing to technology and commercialism. Odum was an opportunist. He recognized that "the Negro's singing had universal appeal," and he hoped these folk background studies would spark widespread public interest in and awareness of the IRSS's work all the while generating financial support from well-heeled foundations. Odum also hoped books about black folk culture would provide cover from criticisms he faced from conservative politicians and other white southerners of more controversial work published in *Social Forces* and IRSS publications that spotlighted potentially explosive topics such as labor conflict in cotton mills, the Ku Klux Klan, the teaching of evolution in public schools, chain gangs, and lynching.[5]

Within a year of the IRSS's founding, Odum had, with his research assistant Guy Benton Johnson, published *The Negro and His Songs: A Study of Typical Negro Songs in the South*. In 1926, Odum published *Negro Workaday Songs*, which he based in part on new fieldwork he conducted at UNC's campus where black laborers lived and worked building the new, modern research university. Two years later, UNC Press, with IRSS support, published *Phonophotography in Folk Music: American Negro Songs in New Notation* by psychologist Milton Metfessel. Odum collaborated with Metfessel and his University of Iowa colleague, Carl E. Seashore, on their fieldwork in North Carolina using motion picture cameras and a new recording device designed to measure the distinctive musical qualities of black folk singing. Also in 1928, Odum published *Rainbow Round My Shoulder*, the first book in his trilogy about the life of one of the black laborers he met in Chapel Hill in the 1920s, John Wesley "Left Wing" Gordon, whom he would call, "Black Ulysses"—a man who was the embodiment of the blues in Odum's mind. These books, which Odum also filed under the heading of "folk background studies," combined ethnographic description, folkloric transcription, Whitmanesque verse, and novelistic narrative into a form of documentary writing Odum called "portraiture." By the early 1930s, Odum viewed these folk background studies as the basis for new forms of social analysis he called "folk sociology" and for regionalism, which promoted a new vision of the South as a region integrated with, instead of separate from the nation, and a place that ideally balanced indigenous regional culture (folkways) with modern bureaucracy, government, and technology. If Odum began his career as a sociologist by breaking from the discipline's focus on armchair theorizing and conducting firsthand fieldwork *in* the South to remedy racial conflict, he would end it using the fruits of those documentary studies to produce his own theory *of* the South to resolve regional conflict.[6]

Odum's impact on the history of documentary work and sociology in and of the South, while profound, was not always pioneering. W. E. B. Du Bois preceded him in nearly every facet of his career. Du Bois first called for rigorous empirical studies on the "Negro problems" in the late nineteenth century. He also was the first to conduct professional sociological fieldwork in black communities in the South and to highlight the "neglected . . . half despised . . . persistently mistaken and misunderstood" body of religious "Negro folk-song" he called "Sorrow Songs." And it was Du Bois who first used the university, in his case Atlanta University and its Sociological Laboratory, as the locus of research on racial issues. Odum's stature is due in part to institutional racism at the time that minimized and marginalized the work of black scholars like Du Bois. Odum's whiteness, when combined with his regional background and professional credentials, allowed his community and folk background studies on black culture in the South to gain wide acceptance in the academy and, later, among foundations that funded his work and the presses that published it. Du Bois, however, would challenge Odum's power and authority directly and indirectly during the first third of the twentieth century by critiquing the conclusions reached by his community studies and questioning the motives and images of white chroniclers of black life and culture, whether professional or popular.[7]

Odum stands out in the long history of documentary work in the South because he wove together a Progressive reform impulse with the imprimatur of professional social science and the modern research university to study black folk culture from the perspective of a sociologist—rather than a folklorist or anthropologist. He did so while pioneering the use of modern recording technologies, like the graphophone and phonophotography, to document folk songs in the South. His studies of black life in small towns, though distorted by Victorian moralizing and racism, sought to comprehend a people he found not only alluring because of their folk culture but also troubling because of their social pathologies, particularly those of a new generation not beholden to the racial etiquettes of the past. Influenced by the currents of Progressivism he encountered in graduate school, Odum believed that empirical studies, by professional social scientists, would lay bare the reality of the South's racial problems and inspire reform. His early community studies therefore resembled briefs for managed and enlightened, rather than violent and demagogic, white supremacy, as well as the necessity of Jim Crow laws. For Odum, social scientific fieldwork uncovered the truths about black life in the South that could be used to maintain racial order and ensure regional progress.[8]

Odum's early community studies also coincided with the rise of fieldwork as an important part of social science during the twentieth century. His repeated invocations of his work's scientific authority not only distinguished him from nonprofessionals but also later helped justify the financial support from foundations that wanted to fund rigorous academic research at the IRSS. He believed his studies of black life and folk culture represented a new, scientifically sophisticated undertaking that replaced old sentimental representations of the South and black southerners with new descriptions rooted in objective empiricism. Odum believed that the image of blacks in the South in the recent past had been based on "the picturesque portrayal of the antebellum type." He said that these "estimates have influenced the mass of opinions, and have constituted a literature of considerable wealth." Joel Chandler Harris and Thomas Nelson Page, he argued, reflected "the true character of the negro," but only in "partial instances" and of a time now past. In contrast, his work's authority and authenticity rested on fieldwork he conducted as a professional sociologist that harnessed the latest recording technology, while conducting his community and folk background studies helped reinforce the seeming authenticity and professional authority of his work.[9]

Despite his assertions of professional authority and his hopes for a more humane and realistic representation of black life in the South, Odum remained in thrall to the same romantic and essentialist racial ideas and images he tried to challenge well into the 1920s. If his early community and folk song studies portrayed black folk culture and social pathology as products of "innate race qualities," his work in the 1920s and into the 1930s, under the influence of new anthropological conceptions of culture, argued that racial "differentials" were products not of heredity but of environment, or what he referred to as the "cumulative power of the physical and folk-regional cultural environment." Odum contended that folkways—those social habits and interactions, cultural expressions, and traditions that are products of organic rather than governmental or technological forces—determined not just racial but also regional difference. For Odum, documenting black folkways in the South, because they seemed the least influenced by what he called stateways and technicways, provided an ideal opportunity to understand the region, the "development of culture patterns and areas," and the process of profound social change. "As in earlier studies of the Negro," he wrote in the 1940s, "so again it was very clear that it was the region and the folk that constituted the field of inquiry, and that the whole regional culture was the basis upon which realistic studies must be made."[10]

What also remained constant in Odum's community and folk background studies during the 1900s and the 1920s was his desire to cross the segregated South's racial boundaries, to become a kind sociological voyeur in order to see, experience, and document the culture of a race he represented as both alluringly primitive and distressingly pathological. Throughout his career, Odum used documentary work as a form of power and control that fixed those things that seemed constantly in flux: the social customs and cultural expressions of new generations of black southerners and the meaning of race itself that modernity both produced and threatened. At every stage in Odum's career as a documentarian, however, black people resisted his power and authority to represent a race. This resistance took the form of black authors, such as Du Bois and Zora Neale Hurston, writing back at Odum. Resistance also took the form of suspicion and resentment from black southerners, who challenged his efforts to observe and document their lives by dissimulating, refusing to cooperate, creating songs that mocked white academics, or demonstrating visible anger while being recorded on film.

Odum's First Folk Song and Community Studies

In 1904, at the age of twenty, Howard Odum graduated from Emory College, then in Oxford, Georgia, humiliated and depressed. Shy, self-conscious about his rural Georgia roots, and often forced during college to return to his nearby home to work on the family farm, Odum felt alienated from his seemingly more sophisticated peers. He thought he had made no lasting personal relationships at Emory nor achieved any marks of academic distinction. He left with a major in classics and without career prospects. Nothing suggested he would soon earn two PhDs under the guidance of G. Stanley Hall and Franklin Giddings, the nation's foremost social scientists at the time, and would base those degrees on intensive fieldwork in black communities in the South that resulted in the first field recordings of what would later become known as the blues.[11]

The roots of Odum's distinguished career as a documentarian reach back to the north Mississippi hill country. Despite his frustrating undergraduate experience, Odum hoped to pursue a career in education. Teaching provided him with an opportunity for social service, which, under the influence of his parents' Christian ethics, he saw as the highest calling. Finding no jobs near home, Odum took a position as an assistant principal and teacher at a rural high school in Toccopola, Mississippi. Still, he yearned for another chance to distinguish himself in higher education. In April 1905, he was admitted into the University of Mississippi as a master's student in classics. He continued teaching in Toccopola for the remainder of the term, frequently making the twenty-one mile trek to Oxford on horseback. He found the north Mississippi landscape by turns forbidding and seductive: "I remember riding an unbroken colt from Toccopola to Pontotoc, to Tupelo to New Albany in and out across swollen streams and backwoods and pine hills, often reflecting physical reality stranger than fiction," he wrote late in his life in an essay about William Faulkner. "I have been close enough to Faulkner's quicksands to sense something of its terrors and have often imagined, behind the cedars and columned houses, that anything could happen there."[12]

While at Ole Miss, Odum's passion shifted from Sophocles to social science, from Greek literature to black song. He had something akin to a conversion experience in 1906 when he took a seminar offered by Thomas Pearce Bailey Jr., a professor of psychology and education, on the "Psychology of the Negro Problem." Odum later said Bailey's class got him "hepped up over sociology and studying the South and the Negro." Bailey, who had studied under the psychologist G. Stanley Hall at Clark University, exposed Odum to sociological and psychological theories of social evolution and racial difference. He also ignited Odum's passion for research as a form of social service.[13]

A native South Carolinian, Bailey embodied all of the tensions and contradictions that characterized the elusive subspecies known as the southern Progressive. He was an academic who justified white supremacy on the then-common idea that biology and heredity determined a racial group's behavior, character, and potential. He believed blacks lagged behind whites in evolutionary development and, as a result, were "racial inferiors" who were "perfectly content . . . recognizing the overlordship of the whites." He was also a devout Protestant and believed black people possessed souls of "immeasurable worth." The animus of bigotry in the South bothered him, and he rejected the idea that black people had degenerated into beasts in the years after emancipation, as many reactionary voices suggested at the time. In his mind, lynching and other forms of racial violence constituted the "impassive and relentless murder of a people's hopes." The unanswered question was "*Should* these things be?" Social science alone offered a way forward. Like a true Progressive, Bailey believed the objective presentation of empirical facts would inspire leaders to alleviate racial tensions and promote social stability, which required the maintenance of enlightened white supremacy.[14]

Bailey passed on this passion for social scientific research to Odum and encouraged him to conduct his own "concrete" studies of the "Negro in southern towns." Once Bailey opened his eyes to the possibility of studying a supposedly primitive culture, one that possessed its own cache of romantic folk songs and stories alongside with what whites thought were troubling pathologies in need of reform, Odum jumped at the chance. After completing his master's thesis in 1906, he spent the next two years teaching Latin at Ole Miss, but "devoted all his spare time" to observing and documenting black life in and around Oxford and back near home in Covington, Georgia.[15]

Odum chose Oxford and Covington in part out of convenience, but these two small towns in the Lower South also shared demographic characteristics that made them ideal for comparison. Both towns had populations under two thousand. Oxford, Mississippi was the home of a university, and Covington was only a mile from Emory, then in Oxford, Georgia before relocating to Atlanta in 1915. Both also had similar ratios of black and white residents. Given the equivalences, they "reflected much similarity in segregation patterns and racial folkways," Odum later wrote. "Other points of resemblance in economy and culture were sufficiently numerous to establish a satisfactory homogeneity index." While Odum only conducted fieldwork in and around Oxford and Covington, he gathered data from seventy-five other small towns in the South through questionnaires and surveys sent through the mail. Like most documentary depictions of the South, Odum's images of the region and, particularly its black society and culture, were of non-urban places that retained "folkways" still rooted in the surrounding countryside, despite their budding populations and proximity to universities. The "homogeneity index" he sought ensured that his resulting conclusions about race and region contained no inconvenient evidence then readily available in a place like Atlanta with its black professional classes and their distinguished institutions and neighborhoods.[16]

Odum believed throughout his career that the fieldwork he conducted in black communities in Oxford and Covington between 1906 and 1908 constituted "the first concrete study of the Negro in southern towns." "These studies," Odum later recalled, "grew out of the observation that there had been practically no scientific studies of the Negro in the South; that the South was amazingly ignorant about the Negro; that practically no one was interested in the subject; and that nevertheless this was the distinctive field of inquiry where knowledge must be had before progress in other respects could be made." Odum's claims, however, willfully ignored the pioneering professional fieldwork carried out by W. E. B. Du Bois in the late 1890s and early 1900s in Farmville, Virginia, and in Atlanta and Albany, Georgia, as well as the work of black scholars at Atlanta University's Sociological Laboratory, which Du Bois directed from 1897–1914.[17]

While following in Du Bois's wake, Odum was part of a new generation of social scientists in the early 1900s who increasingly embraced fieldwork. America's first generation of professional sociologists in the late nineteenth century, who sought to prove the scientific and therefore professional mettle of their young discipline, often held such "practical" sociology in disdain because it resembled social work and lacked theoretical rigor. In contrast, for sociologists like Du Bois and later Odum, doing community studies in small towns and neighborhoods in the rural South or urban North allowed researchers to document patterns and problems in places defined by their unique geography and racial, ethnic, or class compositions. Fieldworkers could use census data, surveys, interviews, life histories, participant-observation, and ethnographic description to test the macro theories of sociology's founders on a micro scale.[18] "We must more and more school ourselves to the minute study of limited fields of human action, where observation and accurate measurement are possible and where real illuminating knowledge can be had," Du Bois wrote in 1904. "The careful exhaustive study of the isolated group then is the ideal of the sociologist of the 20th century—from that may come a real knowledge of natural law as locally manifest—a glimpse and revelation of rhythm beyond this little center and at last careful, cautious generalization and formulation." For Du Bois, intensive sociological study of black people in specific communities spotlighted the "evolution of a vast group of men from simpler primitive conditions to higher more complex civilization." Odum brought his own evolutionary views of racial development to bear on his studies of discrete black communities in the South. But instead of emphasizing a new generation's creation of a "complex civilization" or the historical, social, and environmental forces that contributed to black oppression, he presented a picture of evolutionary lag, of persistent "primitive conditions" and pathology that justified Jim Crow rather than justice.[19]

If Odum ignored Du Bois's groundbreaking contributions to professional sociological study of black communities in the South, he also obscured reality by claiming "that practically no one was interested in the subject," either professional or amateur. Yet, before Odum published his first article and book, sociologists at Tuskegee Institute in Alabama had joined Atlanta University in creating research centers directed by black scholars and leaders that focused on black life in the South. In 1908, Monroe Work, a black sociologist trained at the University of Chicago and the first African American published in the *American Journal of Sociology*, was hired at Tuskegee as its director of research and records. Four years earlier, Robert E. Park, a young white sociologist, took a job at Tuskegee working alongside Booker T. Washington as a publicist, writer, and researcher on racial issues in the rural South and in Africa. In 1914, he left for the University of Chicago's Department of Sociology where he would make the city into an urban laboratory for the study of black migrants from the South. Reflecting on his time at Tuskegee with Washington, Park said, "I came to believe in firsthand knowledge not as a substitute but as a basis for more formal and systematic investigation."[20]

White pseudo-scientists, amateur ethnographers, and novelists also had their say on the day's urgent "Race Problem" and conditions of black life in the South during this time. A host of polemics about black people flew off American presses "characterizing the race as degraded, bestial, or incapable of improvement," writes C. Vann Woodward. And then there were the novels of Thomas Dixon—*The Leopard's Spots* (1902), *The Clansman* (1905), and *The Traitor* (1907)—which presented sensationalized images of predatory black men and heroic Klansmen.[21]

Northern observers, including Progressive journalist Ray Stannard Baker and historian Albert Bushnell Hart, provided far more moderate depictions that recognized the humanity, if also the inherent inferiority, of blacks living in the South. Like their predecessors Frederick Law Olmsted and Jonathan Baxter Harrison, they grounded the truthfulness of their accounts in their firsthand observations from the field and their objectivity compared to white southerners. Baker's *Following the Color Line* (1908) assessed the conditions black southerners faced in a culture of segregation. Hart, the famous Harvard University historian who advised Du Bois as he completed his PhD in history, wrote another important example of documentary reportage, *The Southern South* (1910). Hart, like Odum, believed that debates about the

"Negro Problem" in the South needed dispassionate documentary studies to correct gross generalizations and distortions of pseudo-scientists and argued that novelists like Dixon could provoke violence.[22]

If a preoccupation with the "color line" and the "Negro problem" animated many social scientific and journalistic documentary projects during this time, Odum's fieldwork in southern black communities stood out because of his documentation of vast numbers of sacred and secular songs, alongside qualitative descriptions of community life, and his use of them as scientific evidence of racial character and difference. Indeed, Hart highlighted Odum's work in *The Southern South* while Odum was preparing his manuscript for publication, calling it "one of the most instructive inquiries ever made into negro life." David H. Bishop, an English professor at Ole Miss, seems to have nurtured Odum's interest in documenting black folk music. Bishop directed Odum's course work in literature that he completed as part of his master's degree, and it seems possible that Bishop's love of old ballads and his experience collecting them wore off on Odum. In contrast to many folklorists during the early twentieth century, Odum was primarily interested not in the derivation and differences of ballad texts but in what songs revealed about the defining characteristics of a race, particularly their lingering primitivism in a rapidly modernizing society.[23]

Odum was also the first documentarian to make field recordings in the South part of sociological or folkloric fieldwork. At least a year before John Lomax used a phonograph to record cowboy songs in Texas in 1908, Odum brought a graphophone into black communities in the South and made what historian Marybeth Hamilton says "seem to have been the first field recordings of African American song." The graphophone was a version of the phonograph that recorded sound through a large funnel onto wax-coated metal cylinders.[24] Like many ethnographers and folklorists in the late nineteenth and early twentieth centuries, Odum made only oblique references to his use of the graphophone in the field. "In the official tableau favored by ethnographers during the phonograph era," writes folklorist Erika Brady, "its presence in the fieldwork encounter is airbrushed out of the picture—the ghost at the banquet." Foregrounding the use of the phonograph, it was thought, would emphasize the "artificiality" of the fieldwork encounter. Performances could seem like orchestrated rather than natural occurrences. For Odum, it was the "spontaneous" nature of black "folk-song" that enabled it to reveal the reality of a race. At the same time, the new technology could resemble a crutch and call into question the fieldworker's expertise in transcription and analysis. Thus the same technology that heralded the arrival of the modern, professional fieldworker could also undermine that identity. Consequently, first-generation field recorders like Odum often discarded or packed away the cylinders after using them to transcribe songs. The pleasure of hearing and circulating the sound of the performance mattered less to this generation of fieldworkers than the value of transcribing the songs for folkloric or social analysis.[25]

The image of Odum toting his graphophone on horseback into the black neighborhoods of Oxford and Covington captures the tensions and exigencies brought on by modernity that inspired and shaped his documentary work. His early fieldwork occurred during a time when horses still outnumbered automobiles, before profound technological change had transformed the agrarian South of his youth. As he traveled on horseback, he carried with him the new ideas and instruments of a modern, professional social scientist committed to documenting the changes upending that past. "For Odum's was a special vision of the South," writes historian Daniel Singal, "one born of a particular historical moment when southern cultural life was poised on the brink of Modernism." The spread of commercialism and public education threatened to erase the folk songs that he saw as most representative of black life in the South. "That which is distinctly the product of racial life and development deserves a better fate than to be blown away with [the] changing environment, and not even remain to enrich the soil from which it sprang," he wrote in his first published article in 1909, "Religious Folk-Songs of the Southern Negro." "The changing economic and educational conditions, the increasing influence of the white man upon the negro, and the rapid progress that is being made on every hand in the South indicate that if the present-day folk-songs of the negro are to be preserved, they must be collected now." Modernity was also upsetting the old racial order in the South and ushering in a new generation of black people who seemed more independent, more insolent, more threatening to whites like Odum. "The problem of the relations between whites and blacks is far-reaching. . . . A true knowledge of actual conditions, if properly set forth, must convince the sincere observer as to the proper relations which should exist between the two races," he wrote in 1909. Doing documentary work allowed Odum to create order out of the maelstrom of modernity, to salvage and possess apparently primitive and fleeting folk songs on modern cylinders, to describe and define the problems and characteristics of a new generation of black people he found worrisome, alluring, and inscrutable.[26]

After two years of intensive fieldwork in the South, Odum took his recordings and field notes to Clark University in Massachusetts and used them to write his first dissertation under the direction of one of America's premier psychologists, G. Stanley Hall, Thomas Pearce Bailey's former mentor. Odum earned his first PhD in 1909 and published his dissertation, "Negro Folk-Song and Character," as two separate extended articles: "Religious Folk-Songs of the Southern Negroes" (1909) and "Folk-Song and Folk-Poetry as Found in the Secular Songs of the Southern Negroes" (1911). Psychology, it seemed, provided the ideas and theories needed to penetrate the mind of a bewildering race of people whom whites had deemed a "problem." If Odum hoped to document and define the social, cultural, *and* mental characteristics of black people, then he needed to tap into the currents of psychological theory flowing from William James at Harvard and Wilhelm Wundt in Germany. Wundt's writings particularly influenced Odum. In the late 1870s, Hall had studied in Germany with Wundt, who later published at the turn of the century a ten-volume treatise he titled *Volkerpsychologie* (The Psychology of the Folk). Wundt's concept of a "folk soul" (*volksseele*) found its way into Hall's pioneering 1904 study of adolescence and eventually into Odum's analysis of black folk music and character. For Wundt, the "folk soul" comprised a social group's collective "mental products"—language, traditions, myths—that evolved naturally over time from intragroup communication.[27]

Hall embraced Wundt's conception of the "soul" in his studies of adolescence and spoke of a "child-soul" and a "folk-soul" that evolved over time and therefore demanded documentation and salvage before they succumbed to modern forces, including standardized education. "Like others who felt the antimodern impulse," write historian Jackson Lears, "Hall feared that modern intellectualism was destroying possibilities for unmediated experience. . . . Hope lay in temporarily recapturing the outlook of children, medieval knights, and contemporary primitives." Salvaging those "souls," preserving vestiges of cultures uncorrupted by over-civilization and industrialization, demanded documentary work, according to Hall. "With missing links and extinct ethnic types, much, perhaps most, soul life has been hopelessly lost. . . . From this it follows we must turn to the larger and far more laborious method of observation, description, and induction," he wrote in *Adolescence* (1904). "We must collect states of mind, sentiments, phenomena long since lapsed, psychic facts that appear faintly and perhaps but once in a lifetime."[28]

Like so many others, Hall looked to the South to find "contemporary primitives"—black southerners—who still possessed the traits of the folk soul in need of salvage. Odum's collections and recordings of sacred and secular songs surely made the young scholar from Georgia seem like an ideal graduate student to mentor. In 1905, the same year Odum began documenting black songs in Mississippi and Georgia, Hall gave a talk at the University of Virginia, "The Negro in Africa and America," which, in essence, made yet another case for the innate psychological and physical differences between the "American" and the "African." In the process, Hall also acknowledged that black people had "developed a folk-lore of wondrous richness just beginning to be exploited by the white man's song and poetry." He also located the center of black social life in the church, which stood as "the truest expression of the southern negro's character." The emotionalism and mysticism of worship, the "vision and trance" of worshippers, suggested a primitive people untainted by modern rationalism. But Hall, like other white social scientists and pseudo-scientists, found just as much to fear in black people. Without the restraints of slavery, violence, sexual impulsivity, idleness, drunkenness, and other forms of dissolute behavior ran rampant, leading to, if not justifying, racial violence, including lynching. As was the case in preserving vestiges of the folk soul in modern society, solving these problems required new social scientific fieldwork. Hall announced that a "new scientific study has arisen, and is fast developing established results which are slowly placing the problem of the future of this race upon a more solid and intelligent basis." In this case, modern intellectualism was the solution to the problem rather than the problem itself. Sociologists rather than "sentimentalists," anthropologists rather than "politicians" would light the way.[29]

Odum's first publication, "Religious Folk-Songs," and its first line reflect the influence of Wundt and Hall on Odum's own ideas about the importance of documenting folk culture and how shared customs, such as songs, could reveal the "soul" of a race. "To know the soul of a people and to find the source from which flows the expression of folk-thought is to comprehend in a large measure the capabilities of that people," Odum wrote. "To obtain the truest expression of the folk-mind and feeling is to reveal much of the inner-consciousness of a race. . . . In revealing much as what he *is* rather than what he *appears to be*, the folk-songs of the Southern negro are superior to any superficial study made from partial observations." For too long scholars and other chroniclers of black life in the South, Odum argued, had "often judged peoples without having so much as a passing knowledge of their inner life, while treasures of folk-lore and song, the psychic, religious, and social expressions of the race, have been permitted to remain in complete obscurity." The rich mother lode of folk life materials found in the rural South seemed to lie hidden in plain sight. Doing documentary work, collecting and presenting black folk songs to the world, forced black and white society to reckon with a reality once obscured by neglect and provided the basis for social reform. Odum's ideas about the potential of his work to inspire social reform echo the goals of Progressive-era documentary photographers such as Jacob Riis and Lewis Hine who believed in the power of photography to sway public opinion on problems like squalor in New York City tenements or child labor in southern cotton mills. "To bring a people face to face with themselves and to place them fairly before the world," Odum wrote, "is the first service that can be rendered in the solution of race problems."[30]

Not content with a PhD in psychology, Odum left Massachusetts for New York in 1909 to pursue another doctorate, this one in sociology under the direction of Franklin Giddings, one of the founders of professional sociology in the United States. Sociology, with its connection to social work and reform, offered Odum an opportunity for a career that more explicitly embraced social science as a form of service to society. Odum's published dissertation, *Social and Mental Traits of the Negro*, expanded his field of view to incorporate not only sacred and secular song analysis but also documentation of black community life in the small-town South. For whites to truly confront and comprehend "the Negro," they must know him "in his home, in his more private activities, at his church and lodge, where, as a rule, he is not a creature of restraint in his natural actions, as well as in the common appearances of the Negro's everyday life." Giddings was renowned as a "quantitatively oriented, positivistically inclined thinker and committed evolutionist," writes sociologist Howard Winant, who saw differences in evolutionary development among various human "types" as a central problem of the modern era. Distinct racial groups possessed a "consciousness of kind" that naturally led them to gravitate to their own race and express fear or antipathy toward others. Though Odum did not incorporate quantitative methods into his early community studies in the South, he shared Giddings's evolutionary views of blacks as an inferior race naturally at odds with the more advanced white race. He hoped his qualitative descriptions of black life in the South would point toward the "improvement and development of the negro race and to the establishment of relations between the races which shall be permanently satisfactory."[31]

Despite Odum's intensive fieldwork and his pioneering recordings and transcriptions of black folk songs, the image he presented to the world of black people in the South in his first published work only confirmed the black image in the white mind, rather than resolving "race problems." Odum's depiction of black southerners' "essential qualities" emphasized primitivism and pathology. He presented a romantic fascination for the raw and unrestrained emotionalism he found in black religious expression and secular song. As they were for his former advisor, G. Stanley Hall, emotional release and spontaneity were alluring and exotic contrasts to the rational, regimented life of a professional social scientist. In this sense, Odum carried on the romantic tradition of white proto-ethnographers and folklorists who documented blacks in the rural South, such as Thomas Wentworth Higginson and other collectors of spirituals associated with the Port Royal Experiment in South Carolina during the Civil War. This form of "romantic racialism," which, according to historian George Fredrickson, had roots in the early nineteenth century, mixed condescension and admiration and romanticized the apparently primitive qualities of black folk culture that seemed missing in modern white middle-class society. Some fifty years later, Odum used sociological methods and ideas to give his "romantic racialism" scientific authority. He identified those very qualities that seemed contrary to rationalism and restraint as responsible for dissolute living. Particularly in *Social and Mental Traits,* Odum displayed a mixture of Victorian moralism and modern scientific racism that depicted black people as beset by vice and bereft of virtue. When writing about black folk culture, he cherished those things that seemed uninfluenced by whites and therefore were more authentic representations of a race's "soul." And yet he loathed the pathologies he found in black communities in the South, which he believed could only be remedied by the embrace of white middle-class habits.[32]

Echoing Hall, Odum found the heart of black life and culture in the church. The church, as he acknowledged in *Social and Mental Traits,* was "the central point around which all negro life revolves." There men and women could shed social restraints and express deep emotion through singing, praying, and preaching. At church, Odum noted, "The Negro is at ease and can give expression to his feelings among his fellows without hindrance and interruption, and without incentive to action."[33]

Time and again Odum focused on the free expression of emotions in the black church that could range from somber to ecstatic. These occasions, often of singing and prayer, moved Odum deeply and inspired his poetic style of descriptive writing that he would later call portraiture. In this passage, Odum describes the singing of lined-out hymns, also referred to as Dr. Watts or long-meter hymns:

> One can hardly appreciate the singing of the negroes at church until he has heard on a quiet Sunday from some position, say on a hill, the

> singing of four negro congregations, each clearly audible. It would appear to be the unrestrained outburst of ten thousand souls, or the rhythmical expression of deep human longing and feeling. Inside the church, one may watch the leaders as they line the hymns, and listen to their rich tremulous voices; he may see others respond and hear the music of each particular voice. The leader's voice apparently betrays great emotion as he reads the lines, and as he begins to sing. He appears literally to drink-in the inspiration from these songs, and his soul seems to be filled to overflowing as he sings the words telling of grace and redemption. . . . He is consumed with the music and the state of feeling which singing brings to him.[34]

Odum's impressionism—his nascent portraiture style—often seemed to clash with the scientific objectivity and restraint expected from serious scholarly work. Consequently, he made sure to transform such descriptions into scientific evidence of racial essence. Religious singing, he argued, "reveals so much of the negro's nature." He found similar evidence in prayers that he recorded, transcribed, and, in some instances, musically notated in *Social and Mental Traits*.[35]

The "freedom from restraint, and the gratification of impulse, and the experience of languor"—the primitivism Odum found so appealing in black worship—also became evidence for him of racial pathology. He saw faith in the black church as rooted in emotion rather than knowledge. "It is not surprising, then, that the Negro's religion is not one of practical application, and that a scarcity of thoughtfulness and will-power is everywhere predominant." The church, particularly the pastors, did not hold themselves or their congregants morally accountable. If the church generated emotion at the expense of morality, it came as no surprise to Odum that black people in the communities he observed devalued virtue in every other phase of life: "There is, generally speaking, no deep conscience in the race. The criminal instinct appears to overbalance any consciousness which makes for righteousness and the Negro has little serene consciousness of a clean record."[36]

In the segregated South of the early 1900s, Odum's status as a white southerner and social scientist gave him the power to enter black spaces and places, like churches and small-town neighborhoods, as a detached observer or even a participant-observer—a privilege unavailable to black fieldworkers who might have wanted to observe whites in their segregated sites. The influence of Odum's fieldwork and his conclusions about racial "traits" were made possible by this relative freedom and advantage. White scholars like Odum, argues historian Karl Hagstrom Miller, "began to suggest their authority as cultural commentators was based upon their ability — some argued courage — to pass into segregated black spaces to record a culture invisible to most white people." In *Social and Mental Traits*, Odum also portrayed fieldwork in black communities in the small-town South as a feat of moral and psychological endurance that tested the mettle and rigor of the social scientist. "The student finds difficulty in holding himself to the persistent, sustained, and laborious effort that a searching investigation requires. Many instances growing out of the efforts to secure his information are repulsive, not to say nauseous and gruesome. Only the hardiest scientific interest in discoverable facts can sustain the investigator," he wrote. The very impediments to fieldwork Odum mentioned suggested a race defined by moral dissipation. Having broken through the barriers and entered segregated black spaces, Odum could then assume a kind of heroic status, not unlike future European ethnographers Bronislaw Malinowski or E. E. Evans-Pritchard, who certified their depictions of the inhabitants of the Trobriand Islands or southern Sudan based on the personal trials and adversities they endured while in the field.[37]

Tellingly, however, Odum relied more on the lyrics of the secular songs he collected to pass judgment on black morality than on his own observations from the field. The descriptive qualities of the lyrics granted him entry into bedrooms and saloons, jail cells and work camps that might have been difficult even for a white social scientist to enter. "There is no better and more accurate story of the immoral and unmoral life of the Negro than is told in his songs. . . . With the life of immorality comes its expression in story and song." The songs he documented represented the reality of black life in the South in his mind, but their "pictures go far beyond the white man's conception of the real." Nevertheless, Odum thought it was the white social scientist's duty to determine their meaning. In their striking, almost photographic level of descriptive detail, they constituted "pictures for the student of the race to contemplate."[38]

Odum's overwrought revulsion to many of the songs' sexual themes betrayed his underlying romantic attraction to their physical and sonic qualities. Odum saw these songs as the products of a young and depraved generation. He said girls and boys between ten and twelve years old knew "hundreds of such songs." Their contrast with older folk songs, spirituals, and hymns represented the dangers of a new generation unbound to the etiquette of the past: "These songs come ill-harmonized to the soft, stirring melodies of a folk-life; and sadder is it to know that the song reflects his true nature." Not only did the songs confirm white ideas of unrestrained black sexuality but they also celebrated "carelessness and idleness," which whites like Odum interpreted as dangerous expressions of autonomy that were related to increases in crime: "He sings and boasts his own freedom from work and complete independence to do as he pleases. . . . In addition to the fact that the growing tendency on the part of the younger negroes to do little work as possible is making the situation more acute, it is easily seen that the criminal ranks are increasing rather than decreasing because of these worthless negroes." Odum provided the following song lyrics as evidence of the "typical character"—the idler, the vagrant, the wanderer—also known as the "creeper," the "rounder," the "eastman."

Well dey calls me a eastman if I leaves de town,
Dey calls me a eastman if I walk around,
I got it writ on de tail o' my shirt,
I'm a natch'el bohn eastman, don't have to work.

When you kill a chicken save me the whang,
When you think I'm workin' I ain't doin' a thing.
When you kill a chicken save me the feet,
When you think I'm workin' I'm walkin' de street

Ain't no use me workin' so
Cause I ain't goin' to work no mo'.[39]

Odum seemed unaware that the song's lyrics represented a version of the trickster tale, which had roots in Africa and in slavery in the Americas and continued in the black vernacular tradition well into the twentieth century. The "eastman" in the song he transcribed evokes other "bad men" he discovered in songs that he recorded, such as "Stagloee" or "Railroad Bill." The "bad man" replaced Bre'r Rabbit as a kind of folk hero in the new, modern South as a younger generation of more mobile and independent black men and women confronted and resisted new systems of white control: convict labor camps, the police, and segregation laws. Instead of seeing the eastman's idleness as a form of resistance to white expectations and demands, Odum read the lyrics as evidence of black recklessness. "Mixed with it all is the happy-go-lucky sense of don't-care and humor," Odum wrote about another "eastman" song he collected. "It is a great philosophy of life the negro has."[40]

In *Social and Mental Traits*, Odum shared evidence of black efforts to "make felt the self feeling" in aspiring middle-class communities in the South. These efforts at self-representation took a variety of visual forms:

"the letter-heads and stationary of negro leaders, teachers and preachers, with sometimes their photograph and titles of a half-dozen offices inscribed thereon, the inserting of photographs in all reports where possible. Witness a single-report from a conference which has no less than seven hundred and sixty-eight individual photographs, besides others in groups." In Odum's eyes, these examples of black visual culture reflected innate tendencies toward ostentation: "Their love of committees and honors, their eagerness to get into print, and the extravagance of their self-commendation and commendation of one another is typical." Once again, Odum read acts of representational power and resistance as evidence of black inferiority. His unwitting documentation of black uses of photography in the small-town South provides a telling, and contemporaneous, parallel with W. E. B. Du Bois's 1900 Paris Exhibition, which sought to overturn pernicious black stereotypes that circulated in scientific literature and popular culture at the turn of the century with photographs of an emergent black middle class in cities like Atlanta. Ray Stannard Baker noticed a similar example of black representational pride in an Atlanta church he visited that posted a sign inside reading "FOR PHOTOGRAPHS, GO TO AUBURN PHOTO GALLERY OPERATED BY COLOURED MEN." Baker attributed this to a "growing race consciousness" among a younger generation and a "feeling that the white man is against him."[41]

While conducting his early fieldwork in Georgia and Mississippi, Odum also encountered examples of black challenges to white representational power. Resistance to his documentary fieldwork took a variety of forms, including the refusal to sing certain songs he requested, feigning forgetfulness, and general dissimulation. Odum constantly faced such challenges to his racial and professional authority while conducting his community and folk background studies. For black southerners in the Jim Crow era, these "everyday acts of resistance" resembled what anthropologist James C. Scott calls "infrapolitics"—a form of resistance distinct from more public or official forms of political activism—that used "evasive actions" and "stifled thoughts" to challenge white attempts to control or define black life in the South. At the same time, the black people Odum encountered questioned white presumptions of unrestrained access to black communities and cultures in the name of social science or folklore. Though Odum relied on professional affiliations to give authority to his work, his early writings reveal how blacks resisted that authority and undermined his ability to make definitive statements about what he saw and heard. "The difficulties in the way of making accurate investigations into the conditions of negro life," Odum wrote in

Social and Mental Traits, "are greater than can be realized by one who has not undertaken the task. . . . The negroes are by nature and cultivation secretive." Some, though not all, even interpreted the efforts of an "investigator" like Odum to be "harmful." During a time of rampant white violence against blacks, resistance to white fieldworkers offered a less dangerous way to challenge white supremacy than protesting against Jim Crow laws and customs or disfranchisement.[42]

More often than not, Odum faced the greatest resistance from a younger generation who refused to perform on demand for a white man or resented his requests to sing old folk songs. In fact, he always seemed to need "bait"—money, food, and drink—to induce black men to sing for him. In some cases, even "bait" did not suffice. Odum's romantic attraction to the old songs was frequently met with derision by the youth. While "ragtimes," "coon-songs," and the "latest 'hits'" abounded in small towns, he lamented the loss of the "simpler negro melodies." According to Odum, young "negroes pride themselves" on the number of new songs they can sing, but "resent a request to sing the older-melodies." His attempts to document religious folk songs often faced similar hurdles. "Many of them are sung only when the white does not hear; they are the folk-songs of the negro, and the negro is very secretive." Though Odum never explained the reasons for these refusals, beyond reticence, it seems evident that such songs, and the requests for them by a white man, evoked the culture of an idealized plantation past that a younger black generation wanted to escape and a white man like Odum wanted to preserve in the face of the modern era's "Negro Problem."[43]

Resistance to Odum continued after he returned from the field and published his work. Black scholars like W. E. B. Du Bois took particular exception to Odum's descriptions of black life in *Social and Mental Traits*. Recognizing the cultural power that whites possessed in creating and spreading ideas and images of black people, Du Bois argued that Odum's book had value only as an "expression of the philosophy of the younger South" and how white southerners imagined black life. "There has been in recent years some tendency among the postbellum generation of white Southerners to study the Negro problem scientifically," he noted in an unpublished review from 1910. Du Bois took exception to two glaring issues in Odum's book. First, it lacked quantitative evidence. "The scope indicated ought to make a social study of 100,000 Negroes—the largest single study of which I ever heard. The wealth of statistical material from such a study would be large and illuminating; yet I have searched this book in vain for a single page of statistical matter relating to the fifty or the seventy towns," Du Bois wrote. Odum simply relied on U.S. Census material anyone could acquire in the mail. Odum also exaggerated his conclusions about supposed black inferiority and pathology and constantly contradicted himself. Du Bois argued that Odum's descriptions and conclusions, whether on black education, criminality, health, or mental traits, were unverifiable: "Not only is the author extreme in his statements and contradictory, but his lack of knowledge of well-known facts is extraordinary. He asserts, without any figures or statistics whatsoever of his own and in flat contradiction to the United States Census and well-known sources." Du Bois did point out that Odum's book revealed a valuable "instinct for investigation" and "the desire to be open-minded," but could not be trusted as a work of social science. "As opinion, then, it is worth reading but as science it is not."[44]

For Du Bois, grounding truth in verifiable, quantitative data—and not simply qualitative description—was necessary to establish truth and counter these dangerous distortions of black life, as well as the racial caricatures in popular culture that demeaned and dehumanized black people. Such belittling images were the handmaidens of the culture of segregation and white supremacy that dominated American public life and politics during the late nineteenth and early twentieth centuries. Racial representation then—be it blackface minstrelsy; caricatures in advertisements, comics, and fiction; or attempts at realist ethnographic description and sociological explanation—reflected the black image in the white mind, reinforcing white supremacy and legitimating laws codifying black inferiority. For these reasons, Du Bois distrusted any sociological study motivated primarily by reform, particularly, of course, those conducted by white Progressives. "The frequent alliance of sociological research with various panaceas and particular schemes of reform," he wrote in 1898, "has resulted in closely connecting social investigation with a good deal of groundless assumption and humbug in the popular mind."[45]

Du Bois would have been hardly surprised, then, to learn that some white reviewers of *Social and Mental Traits* read the book as a kind of brief for the advantages of segregation. A front-page review in the *New York Times* from 1910 claimed that Odum presented a bleak picture of black life in the South, but also thought he hinted at a growing tendency toward "race consciousness" and pride among blacks that segregation would nurture in the long run and that would lead to greater harmony between the races: "The separateness between the two races, as thus contemplated, is simply a fact recognized to which the life of each must be made to conform." Odum's book also led a reviewer for the *Baltimore Sun* to acknowledge segregation as the only conceivable policy for two races that were so inherently different. The reviewer applauded Odum for focusing not on the black elite but on the common "darky" in the South. The book seemed to confirm in the reviewer's mind an image of young black men in the South as lazy, morose and "utterly untrustworthy."[46]

For a black sociologist like Du Bois, reading Odum's work and the praise it received from white reviewers must have felt doubly damning. Reviews of Odum's work affirmed the racism Du Bois challenged in his own work while never acknowledging the trails he blazed in the literature more than a decade earlier. Unfortunately, Du Bois's competing vision of black life in the South and of the nature of race and sources of racism was largely ignored and subsumed by white social scientists at the time. As sociologists Aldon Morris and Earl Wright II have pointed out, the racism of professional academics and their institutions led to the marginalization of Du Bois and his work throughout the twentieth century. The "scientific" fieldwork and community studies of a white sociologist like Howard Odum, in contrast, continued to dominate and shape ideas and images of black life and culture in South during the early twentieth century.[47]

Odum's Folk Background Studies of the 1920s

In 1912, Odum took a position as a professor of educational sociology at the University of Georgia (UGA). While at Georgia, he continued to write on race in the South and the need for more "objective" and "concrete studies" on the "several problems of the Negro," but he no longer conducted his own community studies or collected folk songs. Instead, he turned his attention to more pragmatic ways to use sociology and harness the power and authority of the modern public university to remedy the South's social problems, including educational and rural underdevelopment.[48]

At the university, Odum met Eugene C. Branson, who would become a pivotal figure in his career at UGA and then later at UNC. Branson's community study model, which emphasized collaborative studies and was able to secure financial support from foundations, shaped Odum's vision of how the modern university could benefit the broader public through research into topics of local and regional concern. Branson, a native North Carolinian, was a professor of pedagogy at the Georgia State Normal School in Athens from 1900 to 1912 and later president of the school. In 1912, the same year Odum arrived at the University of Georgia, Branson founded the school's Department of Rural Economics and Sociology. The two soon became close colleagues. Odum would have undoubtedly found Branson's progressive ideas about rural development and community studies appealing. At the Normal School, Branson organized "Georgia Clubs" that brought students and faculty together to study and reform community life throughout the state. "Know your community, know your state," Branson declared, "through study and discussion, and see what you can do to make things better." Two years later UNC hired Branson to create a school of social science and energize the Department of Rural Economics and Sociology. World War I slowed Branson's plans for the school of social science, but he still organized a North Carolina Club, helped initiate county surveys throughout the state, and started a publication called *News Letter* that informed the university community and the general public about current social conditions across North Carolina. All the while, he went about luring Odum to UNC to help found a new research institute there.[49]

In the meantime, Odum returned to his undergraduate alma mater, Emory University, in 1919 to become a professor of sociology and dean of liberal arts. While at Emory, he discovered a talent for administrative work and helped the school make the transition to university status. A year later, UNC approved the establishment of the School of Public Welfare and the new Department of Sociology, and Odum accepted an offer from the university's president, and his former friend and peer at Clark University, Harry Woodburn Chase, to spearhead both initiatives. Once at UNC, Odum worked tirelessly to transform it from a modest southern university into one of the region's premier institutions. He also helped launch the nationally renowned Institute for Research in Social Science (IRSS) in 1924, the influential *Journal of Social Forces*, and the University of North Carolina Press in 1922, which published some of the work supported by the IRSS by scholars from a range of disciplines and regional backgrounds.[50]

A year before the founding of the IRSS, an education professor and colleague of Odum at UNC named L. A. Williams wrote an article in *Social Forces*, "The South as a Field for Sociological Research," that spotlighted the region's untapped resources awaiting documentation and sociological study. Williams's article served as a clarion call to the new generation of researchers at Chapel Hill, like Howard Odum, who would soon turn North Carolina and the South into laboratories for professional fieldwork. "Only a superficial knowledge of the South is needed to realize that there exists here a great wealth of legend, ballad, tradition and superstitious lore which has tremendous significance to the sociologist," Williams wrote. "The form and substance of this unwritten and unrecorded material present fields of research peculiar in worth since so much of it has been retained in true primitive condition due to the isolated manner of life still possible in the mountain fastnesses and on the coastal plains." Like so many other documentarians interested in the South, he saw the technological and economic changes brought on by modernity as threats to the essence of regional culture. The solution was ethnographic salvage for posterity's sake. The old customs and traditions were "rapidly passing out of our ken as tangible evidence of how our forefathers lived, worked, fought, studied, played. Such material needs to be collected, assembled and arranged, that concrete evidence of centuries old life as lived in the South, with its atmosphere of romance and adventure may be preserved for all time, accurate, authentic, objective." In this article Williams captured the essence of the documentary impulse in the modern South during the first third of the twentieth century: recognition of creeping modernization, identification of threatened cultural resources, and documentation utilizing the tools provided by modernization to preserve an "objective" record. For documentarians working in the South during this time, modernization was a double-edged sword. It not only destroyed traditional culture, which needed preservation, but also provided the conceptual and technological tools to clear away old images and ideas associated with the region.[51]

With strong institutional assistance from UNC and financial support from foundations like the Laura Spelman Rockefeller Memorial, Odum played a prominent role in establishing UNC's IRSS to create the kind of regional documentation and analysis Williams envisioned. The IRSS was the first interdisciplinary research institute in the South with its own budget and staff comprised of faculty members and research assistants whose mission was "the cooperative study of problems in the general field of social science, arising out of State and regional conditions." The first study sponsored by the IRSS examined the conditions of North Carolina's textile industry, but it quickly became apparent that documenting labor exploitation in cotton mills, which mill owners vehemently resisted, was far too controversial to sustain and promote. It did not help that some industry leaders blamed Odum for turning UNC into a "breeding place for socialism and communism." In response, Odum turned his research attention to his first love as a social scientist. "When the Institute for Research in Social Science was established at the University of North Carolina, with the specific keystone of its program that of Regional Research and Study, immediately the Negro and the folk life became a first unit," Odum later wrote.[52]

The focus on documenting black folk life in the South in the 1920s appealed to Odum for both personal and pragmatic reasons. Of course, it would enable him to return to his origins as a fieldworker and to delve again into his incomparable archive of sacred and secular song. But making the documentation of black folk culture the primary mission of the IRSS also seemed to guarantee public interest and support for the fledgling experiment in regional research. In the aftermath of World War I, modernists in Europe and America embraced the supposed primitivism of African and African American culture to create new transgressive forms of art and music. At the same time, black and white writers mined black folk culture in the rural South, albeit for different political and literary ends, in an effort to preserve an authentic black essence uncorrupted by the modern world. The popularization and commercialization of the blues as a genre in the early 1920s also gave Odum the impetus to publish his transcriptions of songs he now found for sale on 78 RPM discs. Soon, black folk culture in the South became the ballast for institutional growth at UNC and for professional advancement for Odum. By focusing on the aesthetics and relics, rather than the politics, of black folk expression, Odum, Johnson, and the IRSS could avoid the controversies inhibiting some of the documentation of the North Carolina textile industry and generate white support.[53]

Odum distinguished his folk background studies, and those carried out under the auspices of the IRSS, by emphasizing their scientific rigor and public appeal. His plan was to "present scientific, descriptive, objective studies in as interesting and readable form as possible." He hoped they would "get the South to 'look at' instead of 'feel about' the Negro." He believed these studies would usher in a new way of representing race and region. "Here is important material for the newer scientific interest which is taking the place of the old sentimental viewpoint," Odum wrote. "And here is a mine of descriptive and objective data to substitute for the emotional and subjective attitudes of the older days. It is a day of great promise in the United States when both races, North and South, enter upon a new era of the rediscovery of the Negro and face the future with an enthusiasm for facts, concerning both the new creative urge and the earlier background sources." At Chapel Hill in the 1920s, as he did in his early publications, Odum once again portrayed his documentary work as the scientific corrective to outdated images based on sentiment.[54]

Nevertheless, Odum's folk background studies, and many of those sponsored by the IRSS during the 1920s, recycled old romantic images of black racial essence rooted in a primitive culture in the rural South, albeit with the imprimatur of the modern research university. Odum for the most part had abandoned his preoccupation with black pathology and, instead, redoubled his effort to document black folk culture in the rural South to achieve a familiar end: essentializing racial difference. "Our viewpoint," he told F. N. Sondley, an independent folklorist in 1926, "is that the main field of study for Southern scholarship, with reference to the Negro, is that of actual portrayal of facts and the description of the Negro as he is. In my judgment the facts speak more eloquently of racial difference than any amount of argument." Odum also no longer made any pretense of using his documentary work to promote social reform or improve race relations. Instead, his work, and the other folk background studies published by the IRSS, later became the basis for foregrounding his theories of the folk-regional society and regionalism in the 1930s.[55]

In the 1920s, the folk background studies published by Odum and the IRSS imagined black folk culture as the elemental culture in the South because of its perceived primitivism. Documenting a supposed primitive culture tapped into Odum's romantic racial fantasies as well. Just as many writers in the late nineteenth century responded to the political and economic tensions of the "New South" by creating an "Old South" mythology of nobility and racial harmony, Odum and his white southern contemporaries found harmony and pleasure in documenting and writing about black folk culture in the 1920s. In the context of the constant upheavals stemming from modernization, industrialization, and other controversial issues, documentary work and writing was a salve for Odum. This work testified to the limits of the corrupting forces of modern change and presented blacks in the rural South as apolitical and unthreatening primitive holdouts still in possession of the raw materials of a true folk society.

Odum kicked off a remarkably productive decade for the IRSS and its studies of regional and racial culture by publishing *The Negro and His Songs* (1925) and *Negro Workaday Songs* (1926) with the University of North Carolina Press. Dozens of titles followed in quick succession, and within ten years of its founding, the IRSS had published 48 books and 142 papers on southern topics.[56]

In 1934, University of California geographer Carl Sauer wrote to Odum to congratulate him on his accomplishments and those of the IRSS in effectively mapping the contours of the South. Sauer suggested that the publications flowing out of UNC made the South into a geographic and cultural reality, one that he found immensely appealing. He told Odum,

> The South certainly has a quality of culture, vividness of problem, and historical personality that makes it an enviable ground for the social scientist. . . . I like the way you have insisted that you were dealing with the reality of the South, that life was and would be different in its problems in your part of the country from others, that it was your job to examine the personality of the South. . . . I wouldn't swap it, personally, for all the social science theory or statistics in the country, because you are documenting a distinctive part of the American scene.[57]

Odum returned to his own documentary work in the late summer of 1924 soon after Guy Johnson arrived in Chapel Hill to work for the IRSS as his research assistant. They immediately started poring over Odum's folk song collections from Mississippi and Georgia and planning the IRSS's first publication, *The Negro and His Songs*. Johnson got the job on the strength of two articles he published in 1923 and 1924 in *Social Forces*: "A Sociological Interpretation of the New Ku Klux Klan Movement" and "The Negro Migration and Its Consequences." Odum found them so compelling that he lured Johnson and his wife Guion, a historian, from Baylor Women's College to UNC. Given Johnson's research interests, Odum felt compelled to explain to his new colleague why their first order of business was to resurrect folk song transcriptions he made close to two decades earlier. Johnson paraphrased Odum's explanation in an interview with folklorist Lynn Moss Sanders in 1985: "I think if we just went in for studying race relations, which is your main interest I know, nobody's going to pay much attention and we might get in a lot of trouble because things are so conservative. But practically everybody, no matter how narrowminded he is will say, 'Oh the Negro is a natural musician, he's a great singer,' and even conservative people can appreciate black music, so here we've got this chance, so let's do this."[58]

Odum and Johnson worked quickly, taking about five months to repackage songs, passages, and ideas from Odum's first two folk song publications. Although Johnson "rearranged and reclassified many of the songs" and scrubbed away the worst of Odum's racism and moralizing, there were no substantive changes to his ideas and images. Odum and Johnson minimized the book's sociological ambition and potential to offend black and white readers by emphasizing preservation over interpretation. This book, before it was too late, would provide yet another documentary record of a supposedly vanishing primitive culture rooted in the rural South. "If his music is primitive and if it has much of the sensuous in it, if his songs and verse are full of primitive art having many elemental qualities of great worth, this is all the more reason for the continuous presentation and evaluation of their merit," he and Johnson wrote in *The Negro and His Songs*.[59]

Ultimately, it was Odum's opportunism that rushed *The Negro and His Songs* into publication in early 1925. He was surely aware of recent novels, dialect stories, and song collections written by white southerners that had evoked the local color tradition of the late nineteenth century and received critical acclaim at the time. South Carolinian Ambrose Gonzales wrote *Black Border: Gullah Stories of the Carolina Coast* (1922) and *With Aesop along the Black Border* (1924), while Louisianan R. Emmett Kennedy also published in 1924 *Black Cameos*, a collection of stories about rural black life in his home state. In the same year, Julia Peterkin, another white South Carolinian, published her first collection of stories, *Green Thursday*, which portrayed a struggling rural black couple sympathetically. W. E. B. Du Bois described it as a "beautiful book" in a review he wrote for *The Crisis*. In his review of a rush of books published in 1925 on black folk music, including Kennedy's 1925 book, *Mellows: A Chronicle of Unknown Singers*, Dorothy Scarborough's *On the Trail of Negro Folk-Songs*, and Odum and Johnson's *The Negro and His Songs*, another sociologist, Robert Park, highlighted their documentary effect and value for white audiences: "What makes this racial literature interesting . . . is the degree to which it gives access to, and knowledge of, lives other than our own, lives that are strangely alien to us, considering their proximity to our own." In his 1935 overview of this new literature that "seemed to deal with an old subject in new terms," Donald Davidson—a poet who was a member of both the Fugitive and Agrarian groups at Vanderbilt University—argued that what effectively resembled blackface minstrelsy was made possible by the prominence of the Harlem Renaissance: "The vogues of Negro spirituals and blues, of Negro actors and singers, of exhibits of African art and the like, combined with the advent of Negro writers and with a fresh social interest in Negro welfare to make the moment propitious for these white southerners who entered so amazingly into black skins."[60]

Documenting or writing about black life in the rural South allowed whites to transgress racial boundaries and moral conventions, to become voyeurs in the name of literature, social science, or folklore. In the 1920s, to delve into the provocative, unseemly, and at times sexual aspects of life that made for rich literature, white southerners, as W. E. B. Du Bois noted in 1926, *had* to turn to black subjects. "White artists themselves suffer from this narrowing of their field. They cry for freedom in dealing with Negroes because they have so little freedom in dealing with whites," Du Bois noted. "DuBose Heywood [*sic*] writes 'Porgy' and writes beautifully of the black Charleston underworld. But why does he do this? Because he cannot do a similar thing for the white people of Charleston, or they would drum him out of town. The only chance he had to tell the truth of pitiful human degradation was to tell it of colored people."[61]

While Odum was repurposing his old collection of songs for publication during the fall of 1924 and winter of 1925, a new soundscape spread over the Chapel Hill campus. Crashing picks punctured old asphalt; creaking carts carried bricks to renovate old buildings or raise new ones. Rhythmic, doleful cries rose above the din. "Many a student and professor listened, spellbound, as a group of diggers sang a work song, with picks whirling in unison on the upstroke and a mighty 'hunh' of exhalation at the end of the downstroke. At twilight and dawn plaintive calls and 'hollers' could be heard in the barracks area where workmen lived, only a hundred yards across the Pittsboro highway." Odum and Johnson needed only to step outside the IRSS building during the day or sit on their porches at dusk to hear the haunting songs black men sang while constructing the South's premier public university. Soon the social scientists took up their pens and put to paper the "black songs" of these "builders of material progress." "They had these work songs that were made for digging . . . they'd get into a rhythm passing things along . . . quite a variety of work songs . . . you'd just sit there by the hour and pick these things up and put them in your notebook," Guy Johnson later recalled.[62]

Odum entered into the second phase of his career as a documentary fieldworker while collecting what he called "Negro workaday songs" in and around the UNC campus in 1924 and 1925. Rather than riding horseback into black neighborhoods in Mississippi and Georgia to find black songs, black laborers journeyed into his backyard in Chapel Hill, bringing their music with them. "In four years 8,504 laborers were employed and there was an average labor turnover of once each month, or forty-eight different sets of men working on the buildings and road under construction during that time," Odum and Johnson wrote in *Negro Workaday Songs*, also noting that the laborers came from all over the South. In Chapel Hill, Odum discovered a composite of the black South congregating, laboring, and singing on his doorstep. He no longer lugged around a graphophone, relying primarily on pen and paper to document the songs he heard. But as he did in 1906, he also experimented with the latest recording technology, this time while collaborating with a professor from the University of Iowa, Milton Metfessel;

Metfessel introduced Odum to phonophotography, which took pictures of sound waves to analyze the unique sonic characteristics of black folk singing. Odum, Johnson, and Metfessel also worked together to make some of the first films of black singers in the South for ethnographic purposes. The setting and technology might have changed, but their documentary work conjured familiar images and ideas that linked racial essence with the emotion, physical vitality, and primitivism of folk songs, in this case the work songs created by black laborers. As always, Odum faced resistance to his representational power as some of the black workers at Chapel Hill attempted to undermine his documentary work by refusing to sing, singing under protest, and creating songs on the spot that mocked the white academics' efforts to collect and possess their music and determine their identities.[63]

Combining his own description of work songs with a phrase borrowed from Du Bois, Odum saw the "workaday sorrow songs" as the basis of the blues, the folk foundation of a "formal" genre. Perhaps given the growing popularity of blues records, Odum again felt the need to distinguish his work as "scientific, descriptive, and objective studies." At a time when Odum said five to six million blues records sold annually, he made sure to emphasize the authenticity and noncommercial origins of his collection. The songs were "*sung or repeated by actual Negro workers or singers*, and much of their value lies in the exact transcription of natural lines, words, and mixtures," he wrote. "In this volume every type is represented except the 'dirty dozen' popular models and the more formal and sophisticated creations." Instead, as a fieldworker dedicated to documenting the raw materials of a folk culture for sociological purposes, Odum presented "spontaneous products of the Negro's workaday experiences and conflict. . . . Here are specimens of folk art and creative effort close to the soil." As he argued in *Negro Workaday Songs*, "Here are blues in the making."[64]

In *Negro Workaday Songs* Odum and Johnson present black folk culture as adaptive and generative, showing how it influences and is influenced by modern commercial culture in the form of the blues and jazz. And yet they continued to define black racial essence as rooted in the folk culture of the South's working class. In a prose poem Odum included at the beginning of the book, he used his portraiture style to document his images of black identity and folk culture. Portraiture, which according to Odum's biographer Wayne Brazil, resembled "a kind of subtle photography which exposed facts that were difficult for the unaided eye to see," provided Odum a way to combine his penchant for Whitmanesque verse, ethnographic description, and empirical facts to produce poetry masquerading as social science. He brought together an old romantic belief in the nobility and artistry of the folk with a modern social science methodology dedicated to accuracy and authenticity.[65]

> A vast throng of Negro workaday singers, mirrors of a race
> Workingmen in the Southern United States from highway, construction camp, from railroad and farm, from city and countryside, a million strong . . .
> A horde of Southern casual laborers and wanderers down that lonesome road
> A brown black army of "bad men"—creepers and ramblers and jamboree breakers, "travelin' men" de luxe . . .
> A swelling crescendo, a race vibrato inimitable, descriptive index of group character, folk urge, and race power[66]

Negro Workaday Songs created a new romantic image of the black South during the 1920s that imagined the wandering worker—the "bad man"—and his songs as the essence of a race. What Odum deemed a dangerous, potentially criminal class in his early community and folk song studies became the heroic standard bearers of folk expression in the modern world: "Today the laborer, the migrant, the black man offender constitute types as distinctive and inimitable as the old jubilee singers and those whom they represented." Odum replaced what he referred to as "the grand old 'saints,' white haired 'Uncles' and 'Aunties'"—the mythic images of post-Civil War plantation and local-color literature—with the "brown black army of 'bad men'" as the source of white romantic fascination and desire. The "shifting race background" brought about new iconic scenes of black folk in the South. "In the old days . . . there were characteristic and unforgettable scenes of groups of Negroes singing in the fields," Odum wrote. "Modern scenes, however different, are no less impressive." Summoning his portraiture style, Odum describes railroad section gangs, steel drivers, and pick-and-shovel men: "Four pickmen of the road sing, swinging pick up, whirling it now round and round and now down again, movement well punctuated with nasal grunt and swelling song. Another group unloading coal, another asphalt, another lime, or sand, sing unnumbered songs and improvisations."[67]

If white collectors of slave spirituals in the 1860s linked the true expressions of a race with the pain experienced in bondage, Odum and Johnson discovered the fount of folk authenticity in another oppressed people far removed from whites and modern influences. They found the true black folk and their songs, which the singers based on personal experience, not on plantations, but in prisons, on "wayside roads," and in work camps on college campuses. "Eloquent successors to the old spirituals with their sorrow-feeling, these songs of the lonesome road have gathered power and numbers and artistic interpretation until they defy description and record," Odum and Johnson argued. Despite the songs' seeming resistance to documentation, Odum, Johnson, and other white chroniclers of the blues and "workaday songs" not only associated "vagrancy with cultural authenticity," argues cultural historian Bryan Wagner, but also "made this association structural to the recording and documentation of the black vernacular tradition."[68]

Odum and Johnson never analyzed the social and economic forces that exploited black labor in the South or fueled the mass migrations of black people during the 1920s. Workaday songs were not political or social matters to explain, but aesthetic phenomena to extol—"superhuman evidence of the folk soul" still thriving in the modernizing South. The emotion and movement of the workaday songs mattered more to a romantic white sociologist like Odum than their origins in "struggle." The sudden and swift migrations of black laborers and the rhythmic, "swelling crescendo" of their songs as they swung picks and axes had a similar appeal for him as jazz and dance had for the white people who haunted Harlem nightclubs. The movement and energy of the black men Odum and Johnson saw and documented in Chapel Hill provided an enchanting contrast to the sedentary and emotionally repressed culture of professional academia. "In the war's aftermath," historian Davarian L. Baldwin writes about the broader white fascination for black culture during the 1920s, "the perceived black primitivism of emotional excess and bodily release became a life-affirming elixir where before it had been a dangerous element."[69]

Odum's attraction to the physical manifestations of movement in music and his romantic depiction of the wandering "Negro workingman" found full expression in the form of John Wesley "Left Wing" Gordon. In the chapter, "The Annals and Blues of Left Wing Gordon," Odum introduced him as a "picture of the workaday songster," a "sort of cumulative example of the whole story of this volume." Gordon was "representative of the Negro common man," but seemed to possess qualities that set him apart and fueled Odum's fascination. "He is very real," Odum insisted, "and one could scarcely imagine a better summary of the lonesome road, if made to order." A thirty-year-old itinerant laborer who had lost his left arm while serving in the military in Europe during World War I, Gordon worked for a time on construction projects in Chapel Hill where Odum first encountered him. "He had, at the last writing, given excellent tale of working, loafing, singing his way through thirty-eight states of the union, with such experience and adventure as would make a white man an epic hero." Gordon immediately captured Odum's imagination and served both as his creative muse and the focus of his documentary writing for more than five years. Between 1928 and 1931, Odum published three books based on stories, songs, and memories that Gordon told him while he worked in Chapel Hill. The books, *Rainbow Round My Shoulder* (1928), *Wings under My Feet* (1930), and *Cold Blue Moon* (1931), blend Odum's ethnographic description and prose poetry with transcriptions of Gordon's life stories and songs into a hybrid form of ethnography, memoir, fiction, and Homeric epic that transformed Gordon into a black folk hero, "Black Ulysses." In *Negro Workaday Songs*, however, Odum portrayed Gordon as "a very real person, 'traveling man' de luxe in the flesh and blood," lest anyone confuse his authenticity with a "mythical character" like John Henry.[70] One of Odum's colleagues at UNC, Gerald Johnson, captured the essence of Odum's fascination for Gordon in a letter he wrote to Odum after publishing *Rainbow Round My Shoulder* was published: "What sedentary white man can fail to feel a twinge of envy of the magnificent vitality of Left-Wing Gordon? In spite of his sufferings and wallowings, how the fellow lived!"[71]

Odum's encounter with Gordon forced him to consider new ways to document black folk culture amid the flux of the 1920s. The old, abiding fears of an imminent loss of black folk culture remained even while Odum seemed more willing to acknowledge its adaptability and dynamism. The threats posed by millions of phonograph records of the "formal blues" and jazz and, more generally, "what the white man calls culture" continued to make preservation a "chief objective" of the book. The more immediate and more confounding challenge, however, was how to capture the "working folk and wanderers moving suddenly and swiftly across the scene," to record and comprehend the seemingly limitless supply of songs with versions that seemed to change with each performance. Again, documentary work offered Odum a way to salvage and systematize. Social science and recording technologies produced what he called in the book's opening prose poem a "descriptive index of group character" that fixed on paper and film the qualities of racial difference that modernity unmoored. The breadth of Gordon's travels and the vastness of his song archive, which included blues songs based on his experience in nearly every place he worked, led Odum to declare "the recording of which would exhaust the time and endurance of the listener and call for an ever-recording instrument! For certainly the effort to transcribe everything Wing gave left the visitor amazingly exhausted,

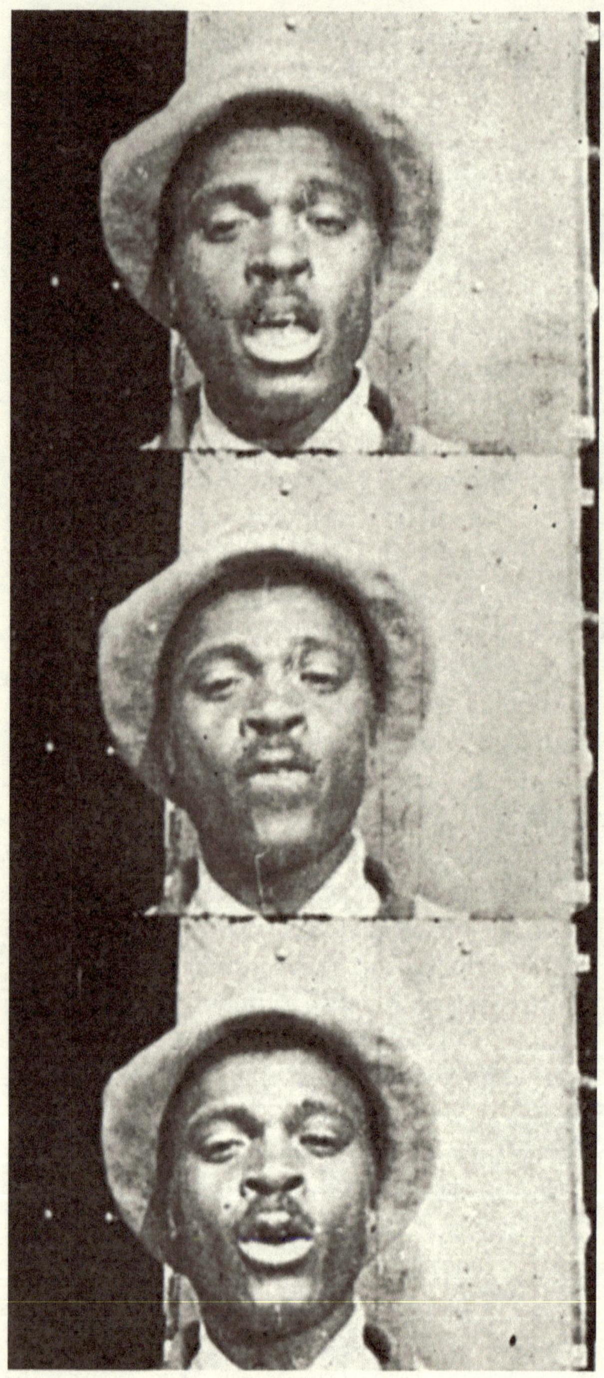

Folklorist Lynn Moss Sanders has suggested the man in the photograph is "very possibly John Wesley 'Left Wing' Gordon." Quoted in Sanders, *Howard W. Odum's Folklore Odyssey*, page 3 of illustrations. The same man who might be Gordon appears in another image in *Phonophotography in Folk Music* singing "Shot Ma Pistol," a song Odum ascribes to Gordon in the second volume of his "Black Ulysses" trilogy, *Wings on My Feet*. See Metfessel, *Phonophotography in Folk Music*, 114 and Odum, *Wings on My Feet*, 144.

marveling at the jumbled resourcefulness of the singer, wishing for some new type of photography which would register the voices, looks, experience, and inimitable temperament of this itinerant camp follower."[72]

Odum's invocations of an "ever-recording instrument" and a "new type of photography" were allusions to a new technique called phonophotography that he had used while doing collaborative fieldwork with two psychology professors, Carl E. Seashore and Milton Metfessel, of the University of Iowa while writing *Negro Workaday Songs* in the fall of 1925. Phonophotography represented music as a series of sound waves. The machine created photographs of sound waves by using diaphragms of three light points that responded to vibrations of sound. Mirrors then translated the vibrations into up and down light flashes represented as a series of sound wave lines on film that depicted pitch, timbre, tempo, and vibrato. "The sound waves may be intercepted, recorded, measured, and analyzed by instruments of precision so that we secure a detailed and faithful objective record of what the musician conveyed through this medium," Seashore wrote. "Thus we can isolate, describe, and classify all types of variants from the cold, non-emotional, and mechanical production of tones to the most highly artistic expression of aesthetic emotion." For Metfessel the goal was to "isolate certain constant tendencies in the expression of emotion in folk songs." Black folk song seemed primed for phonophotographic study: it was rich in emotion and resistant to traditional musical notation. "Much of the charm and distinctiveness of the singing of Negroes lies in queer pranks of their voices," Metfessel wrote, "but these twists and turns occur too quickly. One seeking to analyze them or find out anything about them is only bewildered. As a consequence, valuable detail and necessary accuracy have been lacking in studies of folk music."[73]

Analyzing phonograph records of black singers in an Iowa laboratory would not suffice, however. To ensure the accuracy of their phonophotographic method, the researchers needed to go to the source. Therefore, they needed to go to the South to find an "intact folk product." "It is, however, only those embellishments of Negro singing which were found among the Southern Negro folk that have been chosen as fitting examples," Metfessel believed. To ensure a complete picture of black folk singing in the South, they also wanted to combine an analysis of sound waves on graphs with moving pictures on film. "The future collector of the primitive music must carry not only the phonophotograph camera," he wrote, "but also a moving picture camera to record the social setting in which the singing is done." There was the need not only to record black folk music in situ but also to capture all facets of emotional expression, including aural and visual. If phonophotography could represent the distinctive features of vibrato and timbre, then film could document the body's physical expressions of emotion while singing. "It is the experience of simultaneously hearing and seeing exactly how the Negro sings which will give a more complete analytic comprehension," Metfessel believed.[74]

In the documentary work of social scientists, "Southern Negro folk" remained the object of fascination and description. Modern technological innovation—sounds waves scrawled across musical graphs, facial expressions fixed on celluloid film—became the newest evidence for an old conclusion: racial primitivism located in the South and rooted in emotion.

Metfessel and Seashore found evidence of an "intact folk product" by reading *The Negro and His Songs* and the other folk studies flowing out of the IRSS in Chapel Hill. Odum welcomed Seashore and Metfessel to Chapel Hill in the fall of 1925 to record the songs of black laborers like "Left Wing" Gordon and others. Metfessel credited Odum and Johnson with "selecting and supplying the Negro songs and singers" and contributing to the "field management of the project." While Seashore traveled to Hampton Institute in Virginia to do his recording work, Metfessel remained in North Carolina with Odum and Johnson, who introduced him to black men like Gordon and other workers on the UNC campus. They also recorded men and women from the North Carolina College for Negroes, as well as students from high schools and training schools in Raleigh and Chapel Hill. Given the diversity of people they recorded, the academics discovered a wide range of music, including work songs, yodels and hollers, the blues, hymns, spirituals, children's songs, and formal quartets. While Odum and Johnson featured some of the initial phonophotographic evidence in *Negro Workaday Songs*, a fuller account of their findings, including extensive sound-wave graphs and moving picture stills, came a couple of years later in 1928 with Metfessel's *Phonophotography in Folk Music: American Negro Songs in New Notation*, a book that was part of the folk background studies sponsored by the IRSS and published by UNC Press.[75]

For Odum, it had been almost twenty years since he first carried his graphophone into black neighborhoods in the South. As he completed some of his last direct documentary fieldwork he embraced what he saw as a new, revolutionary recording instrument. "I have the feeling that this particular little venture is going to be epoch making in that it is the first time in anthropological work that this highly refined method of substituting the camera for the phonograph has been used, and I feel certain that it will lead to great and rapid extension of the practice," Odum told UNC president Harry Woodburn Chase. While the technological means might have changed, Odum's ends remained the same—how to use documentary evidence to determine racial difference and, therefore, regional difference, because singing, and "the resultant emotional conditioning are perhaps the most powerful single force responsible for much of the culture pattern of the region," he declared. Once again, he relied on the seemingly scientific documentation of musical traits to define a race's social and mental traits and hoped the phonophotographic studies would one day determine if vibrato is a "native endowment," if it was "more frequent among Negroes than among whites," if "the Negro's capacity for harmony" was "greater than the white man's," and if his "sense of rhythm" was better. In the meantime, Odum simply marveled at the moving pictures Metfessel made of the singers that confirmed his long-standing images of the black singers he had recorded two decades before.[76]

In his review of *Phonophotography in Folk Music* in *Social Forces*, sociologist Read Bain echoed Odum's enthusiastic assessment of this innovative technology that promised new ways of preserving, experiencing, and analyzing folk music. It seemed to herald nothing less than a new documentary movement with scientific and popular appeal. In addition to the photography and phonophotography found in the book, Bain thought the films made by Metfessel, while viewable only in a "laboratory and lecture room," promised to make the subject "not only more scientific but immensely more interesting." Students and "the popular audience," he wrote, "will be able to get some of the thrills of the field worker and at the same time a vastly more accurate impression than the field worker can ever give by lecture or writing."[77]

The black folk singers whom Metfessel and Odum documented with their cameras did not seem to share Odum's and Bain's fervor for this apparent revolution in documentary fieldwork, however. Just as Odum's search for black racial essence through documentary work remained constant in the 1920s, so too did black resistance to being subjects of documentarians. One of Metfessel's main conclusions about phonophotography's importance was that it "lifts folk music out of the subjective and intangible into an objective, measurable physical reality." Some of the black men Metfessel and Odum documented challenged the researchers' right to "lift" their personal expressions of individuality, art, and emotion into a material possession and scientific specimen to be used by white men for their own sociological or psychological purposes. They did this by refusing to sing, singing under protest, or creating impromptu songs that ridiculed the whole matter of white men observing and documenting black men singing. They resisted because they did not want to relinquish their music to white men, because they did not want to perform at their behest, and because they wanted to maintain control of their art and identity during a time when white men wanted to possess and determine both.[78]

The documentation of a black man singing a song titled "I Got a Muly" captures every phase of the collaborative work between Metfessel, Odum, and Johnson in Chapel Hill in 1925, including phonophotography, film, and the resistance of black workers. Having recorded, photographed, and filmed two different performances of the song from different singers, Metfessel was eager for a third rendition. One man initially refused to sing again, but finally relented and sang the song "under protest." Metfessel wrote, "The frown seen in the moving picture and the queer sequence of notes and intonations in the song are expressive of the irritation he felt." In this instance, although Metfessel was hoping to document the telltale signs of black musical and emotional expression, he ended up photographing the sound and expression of black resistance. The phonophotographic graphs Metfessel published in *Phonophotography in Folk Music* appear to capture the singer "carelessly change key" on the song's final line. "There is the long irritated falling intonation on *-ly* [muly], graph 1, sec. 2; the steady climb in pitch on *mu-*, secs. 2, 3, for an octave; the snappy falling intonation on *-ry* [Jerry, the mule's name], sec. 5; together with the clipping effect before his short breathing periods, except in graph 2, sec. 2." Metfessel featured the stills from this performance "under protest" on the next page of the book. The caption describes the man as a "reluctant workman" while the images reveal the physical expression of his irritation. His brow becomes increasingly furrowed as he sings the "[o] sound in *wohn-uh* (want to)" while staring with anger into the camera. The man's resistance seemed to have an impact on Odum too. He recounted a similar situation in *Negro Workaday Songs*. After exclaiming, "How often the song collector wishes for some instrument which will record group singing in its native haunts!" he recognized the potential problems that such an instrument was powerless to resolve. "If he coaxes the singers to keep repeating their song, some of them become self-conscious and drop out. Perhaps the whole group will refuse to sing any more."[79]

Odum, of course, was very familiar with black resistance to his work, having faced it since the early 1900s, and in *Negro Workaday Songs* he not only alludes to some of the tensions that existed as a result of Metfessel's phonophotographic work but also offers an overview of his own difficulties as a white documentarian. While equating the search for black songs as akin to discovering "the Negro," he also acknowledged that "the task of finding and recording accurately the folk expression is a difficult one under most circum-

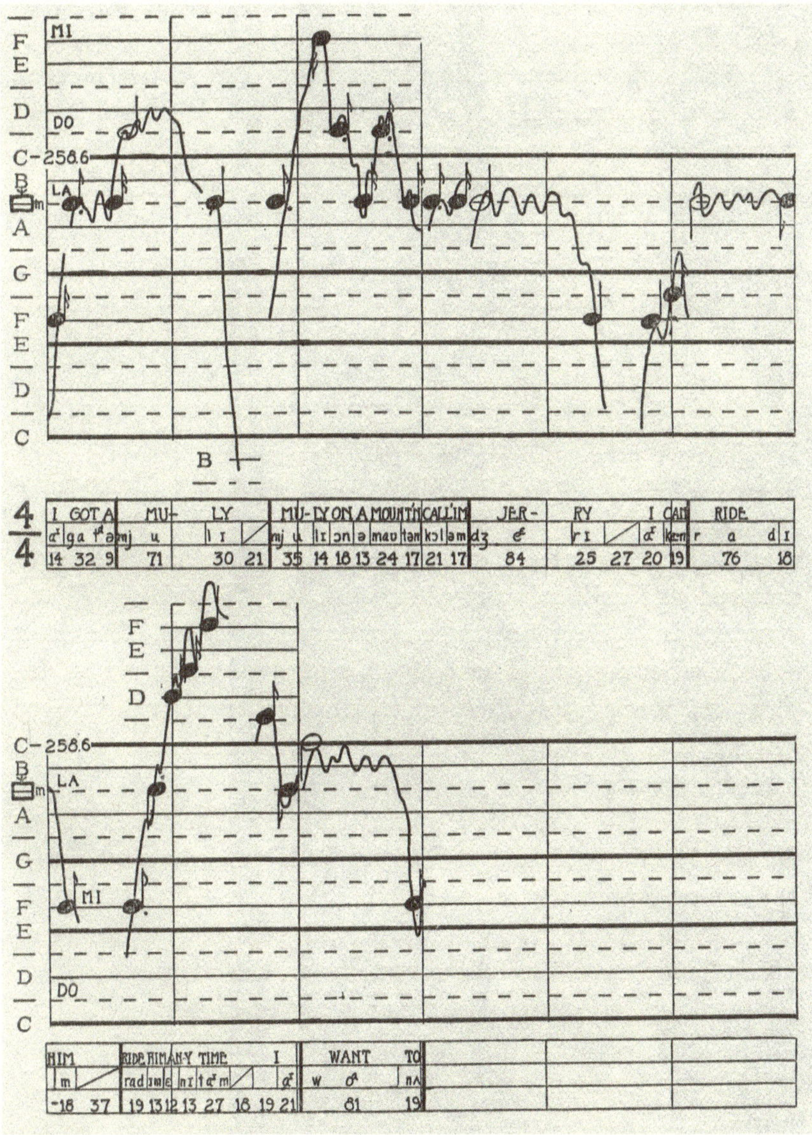

"The long irritated falling intonation." Metfessel, *Phonophotography in Folk Music*.

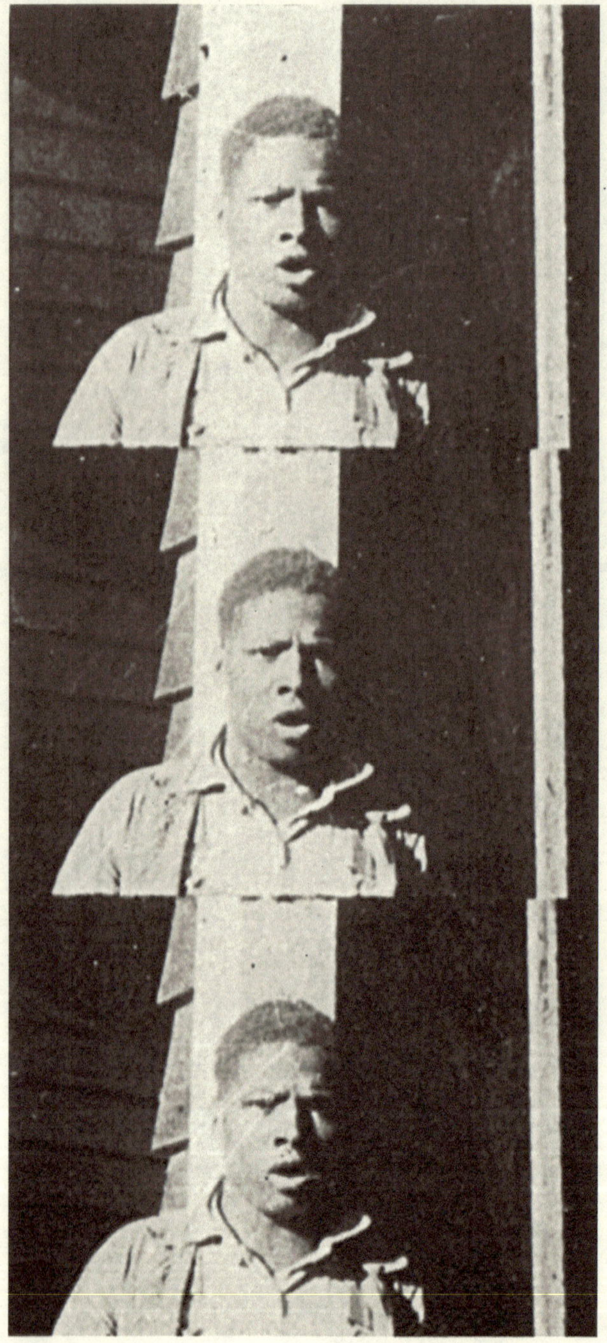

“Third Version of ‘I Got a Muly’ by a reluctant workman.” Metfessel, *Phonophotography in Folk Music*.

stances." In characteristic fashion, Odum provided contradictory evidence that at once confirmed near-constant resistance from black singers and complete cooperation. It seemed as if, after acknowledging his struggles to secure the treasured evidence of "folk expression," he needed to reaffirm his authority as the white social scientist with an easy rapport with his black informants. "If we keep a record of efforts, taken at random, as experimental endeavor, in a cross country visit through North Carolina, South Carolina, Tennessee and Georgia, about ten percent, at best, of the requests for songs will be successful," he noted. Though Odum's 90 percent failure rate could be attributed to individuals saying they simply did not know any songs, obfuscation and polite opposition appear more likely. "He protests vigorously that he does not sing well enough, that he cannot say the words of songs unless he can sing, that he cannot sing unless others are singing, that he has to be in the spirit of the song, or that he will get some songs together and bring them in, or that he will bring a quartet or a pal. Rarely ever does he 'produce' if let alone with only a first approach," Odum wrote in *Negro Workaday Songs*.[80]

The subtlety, and even politeness, of some of the opposition Odum faced while doing fieldwork made it no less an expression of personal power and autonomy than outright refusals or visible forms of anger. "The Negro offers a feather-bed resistance," Zora Neale Hurston famously wrote in her 1935 memoir, *Mules and Men*, which details her own fieldwork experiences collecting black folklore in Florida as an insider who grew up in the communities she documented and as an outsider, a graduate student and ethnographer from Barnard College and, later, Columbia University. Like most folklorists, Hurston found the most authentic folk expressions in places that seemed isolated and sealed off from the modern world. The apparent isolation of these folk also made them seem shy and suspicious, particularly of white interlopers. "They are most reluctant at times to reveal that which the soul lives by," she wrote. "And the Negro, in spite of his open-faced laughter, his seeming acquiescence, is particularly evasive. You see we are a polite people and we do not say to our questioner, 'Get out of here!' We smile and tell him or her something that satisfies the white person because, knowing so little about us, he doesn't know what he is missing."[81]

Odum actually offered a measure of admiration for such tactics even as he was easily taken in by them. He regarded the initial refusal to sing as an act of self-protection that was both "characteristic" and "commendable." Indeed, Odum presented these kinds of interactions as forms of good-natured haggling. Requests were met with refusals, offers returned with counteroffers, which were followed by more negotiation and then resolution. "He has his own fun, too, in the situation," he observed. He suggested that the "Negro is at his 'best' when being urged to cooperate in the rendering of his folk songs." By his "best," Odum said he "reveals a striking nature and strong personality, whether in affirming stoutly that he knows no songs now or that he has forgotten what he used to know." He indicated that he often heard a singer say, "'Naw, sir, cap'n, I don't know no songs much,'" only to then have him eventually tap into an inexhaustible "supply of songs." Guy Johnson remembers that Odum often had to ply "Left Wing" Gordon with food and whiskey in exchange for stories and songs. Gordon's view of Odum can be partly inferred from an unpublished paper in the Odum family archives: "Black Ulysses to Professor Who Asks Him Too Many Questions." In her *Mules and Men*, Hurston describes the "theory behind our tactics: 'The white man is always trying to know into somebody else's business. All right, I'll set something outside the door of my mind for him to play with and handle. He can read my writing but he sho' can't read my mind. I'll play this toy in his hand, and he will seize it and go away. Then I'll say my say and sing my song.'" Odum recorded Gordon expressing similar sentiments in *Rainbow Round My Shoulder* from 1928: "They don't know nothin' 'bout me," Odum wrote in Gordon's voice. "I don't keer nothin' 'bout them. White man ignorant 'bout colored folks. Don't know nothin'. We talk polite to his face, sometimes laugh behind his back. Ain't nothin' else to do."[82]

Black laborers often expressed their resistance to academic observers like Odum through impromptu songs that depicted white men as lazy, intrusive, and oppressive. In singing these songs, the black men flipped the power dynamic and became the documentarians describing the essential qualities of a white academic. The use of rhythmical song, while working, softened what otherwise would have been a dangerous proposition—mocking a white man's identity and authority while challenging his right to document their music. "To the uninitiated the laborer is merely a laborer, silent, reserved, certainly keeping back from the white man his innermost thoughts, wishes, and feelings," Odum wrote in *Negro Workaday Songs*. "But hear him sing—hear him repeat the formal songs, hear him make new ones." The "new ones" Odum referred to were songs about the "white man" or the "captain," and he found them in abundance; there were so many in fact that he planned to gather them in a separate chapter in a future book. These new songs, though folk in origin, were also "modern," reflecting what Odum once called "self-feeling" and now called "self-portraiture": "The modern singer, albeit not always in a joking mood, still thrusts 'at' his 'captain' or 'boss' or 'white man.'" These "white man" songs, while highlighting the clear class and racial divides that shaped Odum's interactions with and documentation of black singers, also express the desire of convicts and laborers to exert power and control in another kind of exploitive relationship shaping their lives. Singing these songs and portraying white men as immoral and inferior provided some black men a sense of exhilaration. In recounting the performance of "Mr. Epting" in *Negro Workaday Songs*, a song with lines that include "Good morning, Mr. Epting/Your hair just nappy as mine/Good morning, Mr. Epting/You belong to the K.K. kind," Odum and Johnson described how one of the four singers of the song started to dance a "jig" during the performance while exclaiming, "Lawd, Lawd, I feels funny when I sings this song. Lawd, Lawd, I can't keep still, it gives me such a funny feelin'. Whoopee! Singin' 'bout white man give me funny feelin'."[83]

Paul Green, a UNC dramatist and philosophy professor, described a particularly evocative example of the creation of these songs in his remembrance of a day he spent with Odum documenting the singing of black convict laborers in Chapel Hill in the 1920s. Odum and Green were close colleagues while at UNC and shared a deep interest in black folk culture. Some of the plays Green wrote during the 1920s and 1930s, such as *In Abraham's Bosom* (1927), which won a Pulitzer Prize for drama, and *Roll, Sweet Chariot* (1935), focused on black folk life and included language that Green had documented as an amateur folklorist in North Carolina. It is likely that the materials Green gathered during this time found their way into *Roll, Sweet Chariot,* which included depictions of the grueling life on a chain gang. Like Odum, Green enjoyed walking from his office to where the laborers worked and "on the sly try to write down any of their songs" when he had the chance. One day Odum joined Green on his stroll, and the two sat on a nearby wall, listening to the singing of convict laborers brought to town to build a new road. As Green remembers, "One huge black Negro convict would lead away with the call—'Going away from here!'—this being half-sung and half-shouted into air as the picks were lifted, and then as all the picks came down the whole group gave the 'sponse 'Dig on down!' The rhythm of the piece kept on, never changing, but presently I heard new words coming in. 'Listen, Dr. Odum,' I said, 'they're making up a song about us.' 'Is that a fact?' he said joyously. 'Yes, I hear it.' And we both out with our notebooks to take it down. It began—

White men sitting on the big rock wall,
        Dig on down!
White men sitting on the big rock wall,
        Going away!

White men sitting on the big rock wall,
Easy and cool, don't work a-tall,
Dig on — going away!
Eigh Lord![84]

Odum documented a similar instance and song in *The Negro and His Songs*. Though the lyrics are different, and Odum seems to portray himself as the lone documentarian, the example has many parallels with Green's later remembrance, including the setting of a road construction site and Odum sitting on a rock wall while taking down the songs. Before the men began their song, he thought how "oblivious the workers were to his presence and to all things save their work." Suddenly, they started singing. Odum struggled to get the words down, but, as he wrote, "He would be persistent, he would get them."

White man settin' on wall
White man settin' on wall
White man settin' on wall all day long
Wastin' his time, wastin' his time[85]

Odum "immediately moved on" after writing down the song and never reflected on the song's message to him. When the "white man" songs involved him, Odum ignored their "thrusts" at a white academic and focused on their aesthetic rather than political importance. "What skill and pride are found in the improvisation of the song leader whose song had been sought by a university dean who had listened with growing interest to the road gang singing as they worked in front of his house," Odum wrote. Such songs reminded him only of the difficulties of accurately documenting the improvisational songs of black laborers and the "vividness" of other examples of "Negro songs about the white man."[86]

The encounters here between the academics with their notebooks and pens and the laborers with their picks and voices highlight the tensions lurking just beneath the surface in documentary or ethnographic encounters, especially in cases such as these where the imbalance of power is seemingly so stark. Green's admission that he wrote down the songs "on the sly," and Odum's mistaken belief that the workers did not initially recognize him, indicates their desire to remain inconspicuous, which would, ideally, result in unselfconscious singing. As Odum and Green sat on the wall, the singers were captive, and their only recourse was to call out their onlookers with an ironic and cutting commentary that flipped the stereotypes Odum and whites in general used to describe young black men—lazy, loafing—onto the sedentary white documentarians.[87]

Odum and Johnson recognized their outsider status as white collectors of black culture even if they did not always reflect on the resistance they faced while doing fieldwork. In *Negro and His Songs*, they acknowledged, albeit implicitly, that their race limited their access to a larger cache of songs and skewed the ultimate truth of their work. Consequently, they called on black writers and fieldworkers to enter the fold to fill in "much that is incomplete. . . . It would be a fine thing if Negro writers of ability today would set themselves the task of collecting and presenting the great body of folk material, in abundance of which they would find rare opportunity. . . . This collection is suggestive of that larger body of material which can be gathered only through the devotion and ability of Negro writers and students."[88] Again, Odum seemed unaware of the pioneering efforts of his black predecessors such as the folklorists at Hampton Institute who collected and published songs, stories, sermons, and spirituals in the "Folk-lore and Ethnology" section of the *Southern Workman* going back to the 1890s.

In February 1927, two years after the publication of *The Negro and His Songs* and a year after *Negro Workaday Songs*, Zora Neale Hurston began her fieldwork in the South under the direction of Franz Boas while at Barnard College before becoming a graduate student in anthropology at Columbia University. Hurston, of course, hardly needed Odum's call for black "writers and students" to realize the value of documenting black folk culture. She did not read Odum's work before beginning her own fieldwork in Florida where she grew up, but when she did so in 1928 she found it an inaccurate and misleading mishmash of songs and conclusions about black people that only confirmed the myopia of white fieldworkers. In a letter to Alain Locke, who, like some other black writers such as folklorist and poet Sterling Brown, praised Odum's folk song books and "Black Ulysses" trilogy, Hurston argued that *The Negro and His Songs* "is not so stupendous as the critics make out. It is inaccurate in a number of places," she wrote, but also "misinformed." In letters to Boas, she wrote that she found Odum and Johnson "in error constantly." They mistook English ballads for black songs among other lapses. "They have distorted by tearing fragments from the whole and bloating the bit out of all proportion," she complained. "Let them but hit upon a well turned phrase and another volume slops off the press. Some of it would be funny if they were not serious scientists! Or are they?" In a 1928 letter to Langston Hughes, who had favorably reviewed *Rainbow Round My Shoulder* that year, Hurston expressed her anger: "It makes me sick to see how these cheap white folks are grabbing our stuff and ruining it. I am almost sick—my one consolation being they never do it right and so there is still a chance for us."[89]

Despite the fact that Hurston's criticism of Odum and Johnson resembled critiques leveled at her own work—and that she held them to a standard of ethnographic and folkloric positivism she herself disdained—her suspicion of their methods, conclusions, and images represented an attempt to take back the "spy-glass of Anthropology" from white fieldworkers. Hurston, particularly in *Mules and Men*, developed hybrid forms of documentary writing that constitute what cultural studies scholar María Eugenia Cotera calls an "intervention against a mode of ethnographic meaning making that had claimed the power to 'truthfully' and transparently describe cultural difference." Cotera argues that Hurston's writing in *Mules and Men* "dodges and feints, moves in and out of discursive guises and narrative genres"; it presents a "vision of native ethnographic practice that calls into question the truth-value of ethnographic representation itself." By placing herself at the center of the text—"Zora, the folklorist"—Hurston created a "gendered vision of resistant subjectivity to the 'man on the streets.'" The development of this dual identity for Hurston—both the folk and folklorist—was born from her own experiences with black resistance to her initial fieldwork in Florida in 1927. "The glamor of Barnard College was still upon me," she later wrote in her memoir, *Dust Tracks on a Road*. "I dwelt in the marble halls. I knew where the material was all right. But I went about asking, in carefully accented Barnardese, 'Pardon me, but do you know of any folk-tales or folk-songs?' The men and women who had whole treasuries of material just seeping through their pores, looked at me and shook their heads. No, they had never heard of anything like that around there." Hurston would later dispense with the "Barnardese"—the stance and language of white professional social scientists like Odum—and effectively blur the boundaries between observer and observed throughout her work.[90]

Odum's Documentary Legacy

The legacy of Odum's pioneering contributions to the documentary impulse in the South during the twentieth century can be seen in his diverse pursuits from the end of the 1920s and into the 1940s. As the 1920s came to a close, Odum focused his creative energy on two projects. The first was writing his "Black Ulysses" trilogy about one individual, a "primitive man in the modern world"—"Left Wing" Gordon—that completed his series of folk background studies begun in 1925. "Thus the chronicles of Black Ulysses Singing tell such a story of folk backgrounds and folk urge," he wrote in *Rainbow Round My Shoulder*, "of picaresque tension, of regional culture and contacts, and of a hidden cross-section of American civilization as has not hitherto been told in the loose-woven epic of any man." The book in his mind was "first and last an exact picture," he told his colleague Gerald Johnson. "It is a sort of untouched photograph, nevertheless presented with the idea that the Negro is a human being, with a sort of timeless, spaceless folk urge." Odum's description of his book brought together the early influence of Wundt's and Hall's conception of a "folk soul" and his perennial desire to make such an abstraction a material reality, one he could preserve, possess, and define in the form of a phonograph record, a book, a phonophotograph, or simply a photograph. Alan Lomax, whose folklore films, particularly from the 1960s to the 1980s, and his resultant theories of musical and choreographic expression, cantometrics and choreometrics, which recall Odum and Metfessel's phonophotographic and film work and theorizing from the 1920s, would later write that "Howard Odum's magnificent *Rainbow Round My Shoulder* . . . inspired me to begin to use the recording machine to create 'oral histories'" of white and black folk musicians he documented in the rural South.[91]

By 1931, Odum had turned his attention to another immense undertaking, the "Southern Regional Study" that would culminate five years later in the publication of his renowned book on regionalism, *Southern Regions*. Instead of fieldwork, Odum and his UNC colleagues and research assistants gathered together a decade's worth of the IRSS's community and folk background studies, along with reams of statistics, maps, charts, and tables, to describe, compare, and explain the South's human, environmental, economic, and cultural resources and demonstrate its differences and deficiencies relative to the rest of America. While Odum was no longer doing documentary work in the field, he nevertheless presented *Southern Regions* as a documentary book, one that contained "vivid" and "authentic" descriptions, "map pictures," and "a clear-cut cumulative picture of the southern regions which could not be attained in any other way." For too long, Odum argued in *Southern Regions*, a self-defeating sectionalism had infected the South that led to economic stagnation and "chronological lag." Taking statistical and descriptive stock of nearly every aspect of the region, Odum hoped to make a case for the South's critical place in the nation by identifying its human and natural resources and then planning how to harness them in an effort toward regional reconstruction. On page after page of this more than 600-page tome, Odum placed national maps that provided snapshots of almost every conceivable social, economic, cultural, and demographic category, ranging from the distribution of soil erosion to church membership percentages, Eighteenth Amendment voting patterns, hospital beds per 1,000 residents, suicide rates, and the number of stills and distilleries seized in a year. According to historian Daniel T. Rodgers, "Nothing could have made Odum's central point more dramatic than the parched white spaces and black smears that marked off the Southeast from the rest of the nation in everything from libraries and milk production per capita, to wealth, lynchings, and radios. Even Odum's turgid prose could not significantly reduce the visual impact."[92]

Three years after publishing *Southern Regions*, Odum turned to a new project, the Subregional Laboratory for Social Research, which borrowed ideas and documentary photographers from the New Deal state. The project provided a test case for regional planning and development in a particular subregion of the South: the old tobacco belt region of the North Carolina and Southside Virginia Piedmont. Odum and his colleagues chose this area because of its proximity to Chapel Hill and its diversity: comprising tobacco- and cotton-growing counties, large and small industrial centers, and cooperative organizations, it seemed like the South in miniature. Researchers associated with the project conducted "new and more realistic studies for implementing theories," which included ethnographic and photographic investigations into the region's people and culture. The IRSS researchers, including Odum and his colleagues, and the social scientists Margaret Jarmon Hagood and Harriet Herring soon discussed making documentary films with documentarians from New York and collaborated with Roy Stryker of the Farm Security Administration's photography division. Three of its photographers—Dorothea Lange, Marion Post-Wolcott, and Jack Delano—came to North Carolina in 1939 and 1940 to document life in the subregion. These photographers produced a remarkable body of work that documented in rich detail the social and economic textures of the Piedmont: tobacco farms in the countryside, tobacco warehouses in Durham, Saturdays in small towns, community gatherings at country stores and Primitive Baptist churches, and the faces and expressions of tenant farmers—black and white, male and female. For Jack Delano, the experience collaborating with Odum and the IRSS provided his most extensive experience photographing in the rural South before he embarked on what would become the most thorough photographic documentation of a single county in the South during the New Deal while working alongside Odum's former graduate student, Arthur Raper, in the Georgia Black Belt.[93]

The Subregional Laboratory provided Odum with the perfect venue for his new mode of regional study—folk sociology—which represented yet another attempt to make sense of disorienting social, economic, cultural, and technological changes transforming the South during the New Deal and then World War II. Odum feared the imminent loss of the South's folkways under the influence of alien forces that were spreading "in this hectic world of bigness, speed, technology, super-organization." Folk sociology constituted "research into the startling new phenomena of the technicways, which, in contemporary civilization, transcend the old folkways and supplant the mores, thus, so modifying human behavior and institutions as to outmode the earlier state of societal evolution." As always, Odum searched for order and balance. The South could not sacrifice "folk beauty" to "technological pathology," he wrote earlier in *Southern Regions*, sounding a note that his former nemeses, the Nashville Agrarians, would have found pleasing to the ear. "What shall it profit to gain a world of civilization and lose the folk-soul?" he wondered in 1939, returning once again to the ideas of his intellectual forebearers who set his folk background studies in motion three decades earlier. "Above all it was Odum's affection for the 'folk,'" argues Rodgers, "that echoed most widely beyond Chapel Hill. It was of a piece with a yearning, unmistakable by the end of the 1930s, for places outside the straightforward course of progress . . . those islands of earthy human strength toward which the Farm Security Administration photographers were ever more rapidly tending. James Agee's descent on Hale County, Alabama, as he worked that experience into words, partook of the mood." So too did Jack Delano, who, beginning in 1941, would collaborate for two years with Arthur Raper and create a remarkable documentary portrait of one of those "islands," Greene County, Georgia, that both men hoped would justify the New Deal reform programs transforming the area. Delano's photographs celebrated the "folk beauty" of the impoverished black and white tenants who tilled Greene's eroded red soil and evoked Odum's dream of a South that preserved its folkways despite the necessity of federal intervention and the inevitability of technological change.[94]

CHAPTER TWO

What a Place This South Is

Jack Delano's Farm Security Administration Photographs of Greene County, Georgia, during the New Deal

In 1942, the same year Howard Odum declared the South to be the most documented region, Greene County, Georgia, could claim to be the most documented county in the most documented region. From the 1920s to the beginning of World War II, Greene County, which is located in the state's old Black Belt seventy-five miles east of Atlanta, served as a kind of laboratory for social scientists, journalists, and documentary photographers who investigated the area's agricultural economy and rural communities. Its distinctive status had its roots in Chapel Hill when one of Howard Odum's most promising graduate students, Arthur Raper, began his doctoral dissertation in 1927. His research project grew out of Odum's and his collaboration with Will Alexander, head of the Commission on Interracial Cooperation (CIC) in Atlanta. Alexander initially wanted Raper to conduct an intensive study of lynching in the South, but they placed this project on hold for a few years and instead began studying population shifts occurring in rural Georgia. They hoped to uncover the fundamental causes of rural black migration into urban areas of the North and South. "Arthur and I began to study census reports," Alexander recalled, "and we discovered two counties in Georgia: one [Greene County] had lost 45 percent of its farm population in the last census period, and the other [Macon County] hadn't lost any, or practically none. I told Arthur to go down to those two counties and see if he could find out what happened in one that didn't happen in the other."[1]

Raper eventually published his findings in 1936 in an expanded version of his dissertation titled *Preface to Peasantry*. The book was a product of seven years of intensive studies of more than three hundred farms and numerous white and black communities in Macon and Greene Counties. Raper concluded that Greene's large population loss resulted from the breakup of the cotton plantation system caused by the ravages of the boll weevil and tumbling cotton prices during the early 1920s. When the soil eroded, cotton prices and land values plummeted, and farmers and their families became refugees, many of whom relocated to Atlanta. "They were *fleeing from* something rather than being *attracted to* something," Raper noted in *Preface to Peas-*

antry.[2] The exodus left behind a rural landscape dotted with deteriorating homes; by 1938, almost 50 percent of the houses in Greene County had been abandoned and were unfit for occupancy. The land also bore the scars of the county's devastated cotton economy. The soils that once sustained Greene's livelihood had been worn away by exploitive single-crop agriculture, leaving behind a landscape gashed with gullies.[3]

By the late 1930s, Greene County seemed like a microcosm of the rural South's social, economic, and environmental woes. If the South, in the words of the Roosevelt administration's controversial 1938 study, "Report on Economic Conditions of the South," was "the nation's number one economic problem," then Greene County became the symbol of the problem South. Raper's pioneering research and fieldwork in the county that resulted in *Preface to Peasantry*—a book that blends rigorous sociological analysis with poetic ethnographic description—opened the door for a long line of social scientists, journalists, and photographers who came to Greene County to document the sources and impacts of these problems. They in turn produced iconic images of the Depression-era South.

In 1937, Farm Security Administration (FSA) photographer Dorothea Lange took nearly fifty photographs of Greene County, some of which appeared in *An American Exodus: A Record of Human Erosion*. In 1938, *Collier's* magazine sent journalist Owen P. White and photographer Lawrence Monahan to the county to chronicle the plight of cotton farmers and assess the impact of New Deal agricultural programs. To the local white establishment, White and Monahan were sensationalist muckrakers hunting for scenes out of *Tobacco Road*, Erskine Caldwell's 1932 fictional depiction of Georgia sharecroppers, in an effort to sell magazines. Their resulting story, "Devil in de Cotton," set off a firestorm in the county that culminated with Greene County's congressman, Paul Brown, reading a condemnation of the *Collier's* piece and a defense of Greene's honor and image on the floor of the U.S. House of Representatives.[4] In 1939, Raper, along with Swedish social scientist Gunnar Myrdal and Howard University political scientist Ralph Bunche, came to Greene County to conduct interviews for *An American Dilemma*, the monumental study of race relations in the United States that was published in 1944.[5] Also in 1939, another FSA photographer, Marion Post-Wolcott, visited Greene County and took more than one hundred photographs of the area. Unlike White and Monahan, she traveled through the county with Arthur Raper's guidance. Around the same time, Fisk University sociologist Charles S. Johnson examined the county's black adolescent community for his 1941 book, *Growing up in the Black Belt: Negro Youth in the Rural South*.[6] Yet another FSA photographer, Russell Lee, also made a brief appearance in Greene County in 1941 as did FSA publicist George Stoney who took a series of portrait photographs of white Greene County residents that appeared in the *Atlanta Journal* in August of that year alongside FSA photographs by Post-Wolcott and Jack Delano.[7] Later in 1941, Raper guided Eliot Elisofon, a photographer from *Life* magazine, around Greene to photograph the county's black schools for a story on "Negro education" in the Deep South.[8]

In the early 1940s, the poet and folklorist Sterling Brown visited Raper in Greene County and wrote short essays based on his observations in an effort to deepen the picture of black southerners as presented in recent documentary books such as *A Southerner Discovers the South* by Jonathan Daniels.[9] Also in the early 1940s, renowned anthropologist Margaret Mead visited Raper in Greene County during her first trip to the South as part of her study of American food habits. According to Raper's wife, Martha Jarrell Raper, Mead analyzed "everything in sight, including us." Raper, who had taken numerous photographs of Greene County while conducting his sociological studies over the years, also recorded interviews with many of the documentarians who visited him in the county including Myrdal, Brown, Meade, and Delano.[10]

Of all the social scientists, writers, and photographers who explored and documented Greene County during the New Deal, no one created a deeper or more expansive record of the county's people and their landscapes or formed a stronger bond with Arthur Raper than FSA photographer Jack Delano. Raper's ideas about Greene County and his connections there shaped the work of almost all of these documentarians, but especially influenced Delano due to the depth and length of their collaboration. In September 1940, Raper returned to Greene County for the first time since the publication of *Preface to Peasantry*, and for the next two years he examined the effects of the New Deal's Unified Farm Program (UFP) on the community and its black and white farmers, 75 percent of whom were tenants. At the time, Greene County had a population of almost 14,000, down from a peak of nearly 19,000 in 1920.[11] Created in 1939, the UFP enlisted county, state, and federal cooperation in implementing New Deal initiatives, including those spearheaded by the FSA that addressed land-use planning, education, health, diet, and other matters in a "demonstration area" like Greene that continued to struggle with problems of tenancy and out-migration. From 1940–42, Raper conducted intensive community studies in Greene County that documented the effects of the UFP and justified the continuance of federal assistance in a county once synonymous with the problem South.[12]

Delano collaborated with Raper in 1941 not only to document the activities and beneficiaries of the UFP in Greene County but also to photograph nearly every phase of life in this rural community, which was attempting to retain the local rhythms and customs of a past that was swiftly succumbing to federal bureaucratization, agricultural mechanization, and cultural standardization. Raper provided Delano with unparalleled access to and information about the county's social, economic, and cultural life. As he had done during his work on *Preface to Peasantry*, Raper rooted himself in the community by establishing relationships with judges, doctors, and lawyers, as well as tenant farmers and mill workers. Delano photographed funerals and football games, barbecues and bridge clubs, convict laborers and county commissioners, ex-slaves and the sons of slave owners, street scenes in small towns and CIO pickets at cotton mills, mule-drawn plows and motorized tractors, a movie theater and a midwife. Ultimately, he produced one of the most comprehensive collections of photographs of the rural South in the twentieth century. Delano took well over 1,000 photographs during his time in Greene County. No other FSA photographer documented a place in such depth, and no other county in the South was as heavily photographed as Greene during the Depression and New Deal.[13] The collaboration between Raper and Delano culminated in *Tenants of the Almighty* (1943), a panoramic portrait of Greene County from its early history to the outbreak of World War II. It combined Delano's documentary photography and Raper's history of the county, particularly the transformations in its agricultural economy, and his fine-grained assessment of how New Deal initiatives revitalized the people and the land.[14]

Delano's photographs in *Tenants of the Almighty* reveal how Delano—"the ultimate FSA photographer" in the words of critic Sally Stein[15]—used documentary photography to expose the South's problems of racial oppression, erosion, and poverty *and* celebrate the beauty and dignity of the poor and the land on which they lived. Delano did not focus "on the very worst he could find" as a prominent Greene County citizen and local historian Dr. T. B. Rice believed the *Collier's* article had done. Raper once noted that Delano would take careful pictures of a tenant family's cabin "inside and out," but not of a "scar-disfigured" woman who lived there.[16] Nor did Delano simply follow Rice's preference for photographs of Doric-columned buildings and verdant pastures. His photographic vision blended the formal sophistication and aesthetic sensibilities of a trained artist with the liberal reformism of a dedicated New Dealer. Delano used the aesthetic tools he developed as an artist to vivify and expose the poverty, racism, and environmental exploitation he saw with Raper while in Greene County. The tension between art and reform resulted in photographs that aestheticized and ennobled the same conditions Delano and the FSA hoped to ameliorate. The rural South's landscape and the rural southerners themselves became the bucolic, preindustrial antidote to the forces of modernization, including urbanization and mechanized labor, that were transforming the region and the nation. His photographs imagined poor farmers, both black and white, as heroic, at times even prophetic, figures whose poverty marked them with a rough-hewn beauty and dignity missing from stolid elites beholden to the status quo. Delano's body of work from Greene County presents a pastoral vision of the South during a period of profound change and transition. As the South modernized and the nation found itself embroiled in a fight against fascism, Delano's photographs of rural southern farmers highlighted their individualism and rootedness in place just before agriculture became mechanized and another rural exodus occurred.

A history of local resistance to documentary work also influenced what Delano photographed in Greene County and how his work was later presented to the community and in *Tenants of the Almighty*. Raper's Greene County fieldwork between the 1920s and the early 1940s had aroused suspicion among some whites, who feared it was part of a progressive or even radical plot to bring about social equality. Suspicion of outsiders with cameras and notebooks only intensified in the wake of the 1938 *Collier's* magazine article that generated so much outrage. Raper, and later Delano, operated in this atmosphere of white suspicion and resistance during the early 1940s, which often forced them to make concessions and cooperate with local elites. A modest and affable person by nature, Raper went to great lengths to establish a rapport with locals who wondered about his intentions. He later worked out an arrangement with the local newspaper, the Greensboro *Herald-Journal*, to publish installments of his book, *Tenants of the Almighty*, so Greene Countians could read what he had been researching and offer comments and critiques if necessary. This kind of community involvement extended to Delano's photographic work. Delano was occasionally joined on his photographic trips by local whites, and he and Raper later created an exhibit of his photographs that traveled around the county so local people could see his work before publication. Their documentary collaboration with the white community, however, ultimately forced them to sanitize their message and images and reinforced the more idealized and bucolic image they presented of Greene County. In the case of Delano's photographs of black Greene County residents, the romantic patina obscured not only the reality of white supremacy in the rural South but also belied the often contentious encounters that occurred between a white government photographer who worked in the name of art and reform and black residents who at times saw such work as just another unwanted intrusion of whites into their private affairs. Subtle acts of resistance—silence, stares, and glares—often greeted Delano's requests to make photographs in the name of New Deal liberalism and, when taken into account, unsettle the image he created of a compliant, stoic, and heroic black folk still nobly rooted in the southern soil.

Jack Delano and the Farm Security Administration's Photography Unit

Before he became an FSA photographer, Jack Delano tapped into another New Deal program that launched his career as a documentary artist. The National Youth Administration, founded in 1935, provided tuition assistance that allowed him to attend college at the Pennsylvania Academy of Fine Arts (PAFA) in Philadelphia where he majored in illustration. Delano and his family were Russian immigrants who arrived in the United States in 1922 and struggled to get by on the meager wage Delano's father earned at a Philadelphia furniture factory. While at PAFA, Delano aspired to become the next Norman Rockwell, and like Rockwell, Delano hoped to use his talent as an artist to portray the experiences of the common, anonymous American. He felt a strong affinity for the "great artists [he] had studied in school who showed a concern for ordinary people." During his final year of college Delano received a scholarship to travel in Europe for four months and study the art he had learned about at the academy. While there he purchased a small camera to take some "tourist pictures," but soon realized that through photography he could "show the same concern and understanding of ordinary people" that he found so compelling in the work of the artists he admired.[17]

Delano's concern for the plight of the poor and common person and his desire to use art to ennoble them placed him squarely in the tradition of the documentary impulse and cultural politics of the Popular Front during the 1930s. His immigrant background and fragile middle-class existence in America allowed Delano to identify with the "ordinary" people or those whom others referred to as the "folk." And yet his ability to attend art school and travel through Europe increased his distance from these "ordinary" people and provided him with the ability to represent them in his art and photography.

Soon after graduating from PAFA, Delano went to work for another New Deal program, the Federal Arts Project in Philadelphia sponsored by the Works Progress Administration (WPA). His first assignment was to photograph Pennsylvania Dutch furniture and other examples of local folk art. He disliked the assignment since it offered little room for creativity and no outlet for his social concerns. He eventually got permission from the project's director to go into Pennsylvania's mine country and document the plight of the unemployed miners instead. Delano spend a month in the coal fields photographing the miners and their families, the coal mines, and the surrounding landscape. When he returned from his trip, he developed his film and exhibited the photographs at an art gallery in Philadelphia's Pennsylvania Railroad Station. The show was a success and received glowing reviews in the press. Most importantly, Delano heard words of praise from one of the early twentieth-century's foremost photographers, Paul Strand. Strand had learned to use the camera as an instrument for social reform under the guidance of Lewis Hine, the pioneering documentary photographer and social reformer. Later, along with Alfred Stieglitz, Edward Steichen, and Edward Weston, Strand helped transform photography into a fine art. Strand saw a kindred soul in Delano and promised to recommend him whenever he applied for work in the future. Strand in part passed on to Delano a tradition of documentary photography that tried to reconcile politics and aesthetics, objectivity and subjectivity. Strand's style, according to one critic, exhibits "a passion for the real, for exact, living detail." But as Strand himself said, "It is not the subject matter alone which is important but the significance the artist sees in it and heightens."[18]

Delano did not stay long at the Federal Arts Project. He chose instead to move to New York City to live with his future wife Irene Esser. He scraped by with a series of freelance jobs and borrowing money from Irene and his parents. Around 1938, Delano began noticing the work of FSA photographers in magazines such as *Look* and *Saturday Review* and in books by Walker Evans (*American Photographs*) and Dorothea Lange (*American Exodus*). That year he went to see an exhibit of Evans's work at the Boston Museum of Fine Arts and felt "stunned by the simplicity, sureness, power, and grace of the images." But elements of Evans's style left Delano unsatisfied: he found some of the photographs "too cool, precise, and emotionally aloof, like technically perfect, interesting specimens of humanity rather than human beings of flesh and blood and joys and sorrows." Yet Evans, Lange, and their fellow FSA photographers inspired Delano; they showed how art could function as the handmaiden of reform by illuminating the plight of the poor. "I was deeply moved by the pictures," he remembered, "and I thought that surely people everywhere and legislators in Congress would be equally affected and therefore impelled to do something to alleviate the misery of so many of our people."[19]

With his professional experience documenting unemployed Pennsylvania coal miners, Delano felt a connection with the FSA and its photographers and wanted to join its staff. He sent some of his work to Roy Stryker, director of the FSA's Information Division, in the fall of 1939. Though Stryker could not hire him at that time, he told Delano how impressed he was with his work and how he wanted him to try his "hand at some of our problems" in the future.[20] Paul Strand, along with other influential advocates, helped Delano secure a position with the FSA a few months later in March 1940. His official civil service classification was "Artist Photographer." Nearly thirty-six years later, Delano met Strand for the first time in person as the older photographer lay in bed near death. "I'm responsible for you, you know," he said while pointing his trembling finger at Delano. "I'm responsible for you, and don't ever forget it."[21]

By the time Delano started at the FSA in the spring of 1940, the agency had been engaged for five years in what historian Alan Trachtenberg has called "the greatest collective effort (though not the first) in the history of photography to mobilize resources to create a cumulative picture of a place and time." Though hired to document the circumstances of the nation's rural poor and, later, to highlight evidence of New Deal relief and reform, FSA photographers ultimately produced a peerless archive of more than 250,000 photographs that captured nearly every aspect of American life between 1935 and 1943 as it made the transition from enduring the Depression to preparing for war. The FSA's origins go back to the creation of the Resettlement Administration (RA) in 1935 during the Roosevelt administration's Second New Deal. The RA's purpose was to resettle rural refugees displaced by the Dust Bowl and the agricultural crisis in migrant labor camps, farm collectives, or cooperative communities. In 1937, the RA became known as the Farm Security Administration, which continued to support resettlement efforts while also providing loans to tenant farmers to help them purchase their own farms and equipment, rehabilitate deteriorating land and homes, and improve their diet and educational opportunities. RA/FSA administrators immediately created a documentary wing of their agency to lay bare before the public the scope and human face of rural poverty and to justify the existence of a program many conservative congressmen deemed "socialistic." The RA/FSA's Historical Section and Information Division, led by Roy

Styker, a former Columbia University economist, hired photographers like Walker Evans and Dorothea Lange to carry out that mission. The early FSA photographers, including Evans, Lange, Ben Shahn, and Arthur Rothstein, produced thousands of photographs, many of which transcended their public relations purpose and became heralded for their ethnographic, historical, and artistic significance. While Evans, Lange, and Rothstein no longer worked for the FSA when Delano was hired in 1940, he joined John Collier, Russell Lee, Marion Post-Wolcott, John Vachon, and later Gordon Parks, the FSA's only black photographer, among others, who carried on the photography unit's mission while increasingly emphasizing the beauty and resilience of a nation emerging from the depths of the Depression into a world endangered by totalitarianism and war.[22]

Delano's first duty as an FSA photographer was to read. Roy Stryker insisted that his photographers educate and attune themselves to the nuance and diversity, blight and beauty, lurking in all facets of American society. Part of the photographers' training under Stryker consisted of studying books on geography, sociology, and economics. Stryker directed Delano to Stuart Chase's *Rich Land, Poor Land*, a 1936 study of natural resource use, and J. Russell Smith's 1,008-page tome, *North America, Its People and the Resources*, published in 1940. Stryker would also "talk and talk and talk in great detail" about what the FSA photographers would discover while traveling. "Roy gave you the feeling that he knew more about everything than you did," Delano once recalled, "and, above all, he knew more about America than you did, by far." Rather than finding Stryker pompous or pedantic, Delano relished his boss's enthusiasm and his ability to impart a "feeling" about America. "This enthusiasm and love for the detail and the deeper meaning of everything American," Delano remembered of Stryker, "was something that he must have transmitted to everybody. He certainly did to me." Stryker wanted to stimulate, not dictate his photographers. He allowed them to pursue their own agenda despite the page-long "shooting scripts" he would send along when they went out into the field. As Delano remembered, "If you got up there and found that there was something else that interested you, and something else you felt was more important and more pertinent, you just went ahead and did it; and wrote to Roy and said, 'Look, Roy, it wasn't like you said.'"[23]

In the spring and summer of 1940, Delano made his first foray into the South to photograph migrant laborers and work as part of the FSA's collaboration with Howard Odum, the Institute for Research in Social Science (IRSS), and its Subregional Laboratory whose purpose was to document the social, economic, and cultural life of the old tobacco belt of North Carolina and Virginia. Odum and his IRSS staff members, including Margaret Jarman Hagood and Harriet Herring, hoped the photographs Delano produced, as well as those taken in the subregion by Dorothea Lange and Marion Post-Wolcott before him, would result in an exhibit on "photographic portraiture as exploration in the field of research through photography." Delano had never been south of the Mason-Dixon Line, and the region's infamous legacy of lynching, segregation, and "poverty and despair" swirled in his mind. "From my first assignment on," Delano recalled, "I was to learn what racism meant both to blacks and whites in all the Southern states I visited." The visible signs of a segregated society immediately struck him—signs marking white and black at water fountains, in waiting rooms, and movie theaters. Delano also had to learn how to navigate the South's racial "rules of behavior: Don't shake hands when introduced to a black person, don't address a black man as 'mister,' don't be surprised if you're not allowed into a restaurant with a black friend of yours, don't do this and don't do that." Stryker tried to advise and empathize with Delano's new predicament: "The observations in your letter of the 9th were most interesting: I guess you will have to develop some callousness if you are going to stay in the South. At least, that is what everyone else seems to do."[24]

The South's poverty and the "attitude of whites to the Negroes" jarred Delano, but the region's rural landscape and cultures also made it exotic and alluring to someone who grew up in the urban North. This tension between revulsion and fascination would shape how Delano photographed the region, particularly in Greene County. His photographs at once romanticized the rural landscape and the seemingly premodern small farmers who lived and labored on it while also exposing the exploitive systems of white supremacy and farm tenancy. "What a place this 'south' is—it's got us ga-ga but we like it," Delano wrote in the spring of 1941. Though Delano, and his wife Irene, who joined him on his photographic trips, could not imagine living in the region, he told Clara Wakeham, Roy Stryker's assistant, "What we have seen of the South so far fascinates us and I sure hope to be able to do some intensive work here." One Sunday before they made their way to Greene County, the Delanos "went hunting for churches" in Heard County, Georgia, which lies about sixty miles southwest of Atlanta along the Alabama border, and found one to their liking, a black church, unpainted and wooden framed and located along a dirt road. The beautiful simplicity of the vernacular architecture and the a capella singing they heard inside enraptured them and inspired Delano to immediately start photographing. At the same time,

Delano described the South as the "most tortured, primitive, poverty stricken (economically and socially) and wasted area I've ever seen." Nevertheless, he maintained hope, even implying a kind of looming redemption for the region. "Yet the potentialities are so great that one doesn't become disgruntled with it but feels rather that the South *must* come out of it even tho it has so many strikes against it," he concluded. Roy Stryker seized on Delano's fascination for the region, however conflicted, and hoped it would continue to inspire him as he made his way through Georgia in April. "You evidently like the South—all excited and on your toes which is the proper spirit for an FSA photographer and makes for good pictures."[25]

Jack Delano's Documentary Work in Greene County, Georgia

On April 25, 1941, Jack and Irene Delano packed up their Dodge Coupe, which they got as a wedding present the year before, and drove 125 miles east from Heard County to Greene County. Delano was eager to get to work with Arthur Raper, to tap into his knowledge of Greene County's landscape, people, places, and history. In advance of Delano's arrival, Stryker wrote to him and told him to soak up Raper's knowledge before getting to work, suggesting he dedicate two weeks to "looking around" Greene County and taking "preliminary photographs." Stryker's suggestions reflected his hope that his photographers would pay particular attention to the social, economic, and cultural forces that made a place unique and that gave its land and people an identifiable "feel."[26]

Delano later acknowledged that Arthur Raper provided him with his most important lessons about life in the South and unparalleled access to Greene County's people and places. Many FSA photographers relied on local officials associated with the agency to shepherd them to photographic projects, but these officials were mostly concerned with specific publicity shots. Raper, in contrast, opened Delano's eyes to the social, economic, environmental, and cultural forces that shaped Greene County's landscape and the people they visited on farms and in communities like Siloam, Mosquito Crossing, Scull Shoals, Union Point, White Plains, Woodville, Veazey, and Greensboro, the county seat. "I learned a tremendous amount about what the South means," Delano remembered, "the attitudes in the South, from our few months' stay in Greene County during this project. I think I remember that as one of the significant things of our project that we were involved in." Delano's wife Irene echoed her husband's assessment of Raper's importance to his work. Raper, she remembered, "knew practically every individual in [the county]."[27] Despite their vastly different backgrounds and experiences, Delano and Raper established an immediate rapport. Delano remembered Raper as a "very warm and sympathetic type of person" and someone who was "obviously a Southerner," traits that ingratiated Raper and Delano with the Greene County community. "Although he disagreed with most of the community on the question of race," Delano recalled, "he was not an activist and was never strident. . . . By his easy manner and nonconfrontational attitude, he managed to maintain good relations with the influential intellectuals who were in power—the lawyers, bankers, judges, and news media."[28]

Not everyone in Greene County was fond of Raper, however. Suspicion of his intentions and liberalism stalked him even though he had lived and worked in the county at various times since the 1920s. His use of titles when speaking to black residents, his hiring of black FSA employees, and a growing fear he was part of a subversive plot to overthrow the government or usher in social equality earned him a trip before the local grand jury in 1941, which admonished him for engaging in these practices. Raper responded by no longer using titles to address anyone. He was also relieved of his Sunday school teaching duties because of his progressive views, and his children faced harassment at school because of their father's reputation. Raper also told the Delanos the story of a man from the small community of Siloam who once announced, "Raper should be electrocuted *under* the electric chair. He's not good enough to sit in it." The resentment Raper faced clearly made an impression on Delano, who wrote about it in a journal he kept at the time: "Arthur's fears of his office burning up, and his family. . . . Ignorance of what Arthur's doing." As Delano suggested, the resistance Raper faced resulted from his research and writing on Greene County and not just his racial views and etiquette. "They also knew he was writing a book," Irene Delano later recalled. "And writing a book about a county in the South is always suspect because you don't quite know what they are going to say in that book." Raper's representation of Greene was a form of power that carried the potential to challenge local authority and the idyllic image of the county some local officials wanted to maintain in the face of increasing national scrutiny about the rural South's social and agricultural problems.[29]

Raper was hardly alone in generating local resistance to documentary work and the resulting images of the county made by outsiders. The photographers, social scientists, and journalists who visited Greene County during the 1930s left behind an atmosphere charged with suspicion of strangers with cameras and notebooks. One of the most notable acts of community resistance to documentary work in Greene County and, perhaps, the South during the Depression and New Deal occurred in the wake of the earlier mentioned 1938 *Collier's* magazine article titled "Devil in de Cotton," written by Owen P. White and with photographs by Lawrence Monahan. In the article, White described Greene as one of the South's former "garden spots" that "went to seed," a place in desperate need of New Deal intervention due its dissolute farmers, desolate land, and disinterested elites who seemed unable to manage local affairs. The article came during the height of the nation's fixation on the tenant farmer as the symbol of the South's problems, a time when, according to Alfred Kazin, "the sharecropper haunted the imagination." In 1937, Margaret Bourke-White and Erskine Caldwell published their dramatic depiction of the South's rural poor, *You Have Seen Their Faces*, while Roy Stryker exhorted his photographers to "make a big drive on tenancy pictures," which he circulated to national papers and magazines in order to sway Congress to support legislation that would eventually create the Farm Security Administration. These images of a problem South mixed with growing fears in old plantation communities like Greene that federal intervention in local affairs would undermine the status quo and elite white authority. Consequently, two of Greene County's leading white citizens, Judge James Park and Dr. T. B. Rice, launched a full-throated defense of Greene County to counter the aspersions cast by a "snooper" like White who never bothered to present a more balanced picture of the county, one that showed verdant green fields and the white-columned courthouse. The two men published letters and articles in local and regional newspapers and eventually got their congressman, Representative Paul Brown, to read Rice's defense on floor of the House of Representatives one month after the article appeared in print.[30]

This history of resistance to documentary work in Greene County loomed over Delano's collaboration with Raper in 1941 and shaped how they represented the county's people and places, particularly in *Tenants of the Almighty*. "Apparently it didn't help his standing in the community to be escorting a 'Yankee' photographer around town," Delano later recalled. Raper responded to local suspicion by purposefully involving the Greene County community in his documentary work, publishing early drafts of *Tenants of the Almighty* in the local paper, the *Herald-Journal*, and soliciting comments on it before he published it. He and Delano also brought along Dr. Rice on some of their photography trips through the county, made sure to photograph local elites and places of pride in the white community like the Doric-columned courthouse, and created an exhibit of Delano's photographs that traveled around the county for residents to see. Though not quite a collaborative ethnography in the sense that members of the local community under observation created their own images, texts, and interpretations, Raper and Delano's interaction with Greene County residents was unique for the time. It seemed to insulate them from the sorts of objections that Dr. Rice raised in his defense of Greene County against White and Monahan and that eventually resounded in the halls of Congress. And yet, the necessity of currying favor with Greene County residents, like Rice and Park, would also compromise the reformist agenda of Delano's photographs and Raper's writings.[31]

Delano's work, in particular, created a visual record of the county's people and their society conditioned by the demands of local acceptance and filtered through his romantic fascination for the rural South's apparently premodern landscape and people who seemed exotic in comparison to the urban world of Philadelphia. Delano's photographs created a pastoral image of Greene County, a place where Jefferson's agrarian dream still seemed possible, a place nurtured by the hearty black and white folk who labored on the county's red and white soils, and a beautiful place that seemed cut off from the modern world, rather than a place people were fleeing for the city. The peaceful and pastoral surface of Delano's photographs belies the legacy of white resistance to documentary work Delano had to adapt to while photographing in the county and the occasional resistance he faced from the black community who resented the intrusive nature of white men, even polite and progressive ones, who believed that they had unimpeded access to their homes and churches in the name of the New Deal and documentary photography.

On the Delanos' first day in Greene County, Saturday, April 26, 1941, they rendezvoused with George Stoney, a publicist for the FSA's southern regional office in Montgomery, Alabama, at the Greene County courthouse in Greensboro. Stoney's role, as he recalled, was "to bring a positive response to FSA's programs." He courted newspaper editors and radio stations to run favorable stories and wrote his own "model news story" that circulated in papers throughout the region, "based on [his] field observations." Before working in depth with Arthur Raper, the Delanos drove around Greene County with Stoney who had prearranged places for Jack Delano to photograph. It seemed clear from the start that Delano's work habits did not match Stoney's pace or aspirations. To begin with, Delano was "bafflingly silent most of the time," Stoney recalled. "My eager-beaver attitude and pace must have irritated him to no end, but he never let me know." Then, at the places Stoney wanted photographed, Delano would usually walk around, shrug his shoulders, and say, "There's no pictures here." In other places and circumstances, ones Stoney saw no point in photographing, Delano "would spend endless time . . . taking pictures." Only later, after spending an entire day at a white tenant family's house, did Stoney begin "to understand Delano's methods and objectives." For Delano, a photography shoot involved careful arrangements of people and objects and close attention to available light. As he explained later, "light, color, texture" were not ends in themselves, but the means to creating an "honest portrayal of what is in front of the camera." Delano believed a documentary photographer could not reveal unvarnished reality, only interpret it. Creating a photograph that captured the "*essence* of the truth" often required staging objects, arranging people in particular poses, and using both natural and artificial lighting techniques for dramatic effect. Consequently, many of Delano's FSA photographs appear rich with narrative resonance and metaphorical meaning that reveal how he imagined the "essence" and life, land, and labor in the rural South.[32]

While Delano received guidance from Stoney and Raper during his first days in Greene County, he remained committed to photographing the people and places that seemed to him to capture the "essence" of the rural South, and not simply taking the "required shots" for Raper's study of the FSA and the Unified Farm Program. He and Irene would often spend time together creating shooting scripts that contained the "most detailed and, for us, exciting things we could imagine." In addition to the appearance of people and the land, they "would get into things which were non-photographic but which were fascinating to use, such as the accent and inclination and the songs and everything having to do with it, which to me was a revelation and was fascinating." Delano said he was "documenting everything I possibly could at [the] time" both because he thought doing so fulfilled Stryker's bureaucratic mission and because he saw his photographs as important historical records of American "cultural values" that would be "valuable for the [FSA] file." The "cultural values" Delano found fascinating during his time in the Deep South, including in Greene County, were those associated with the rural poor, both black and white—including the land on which they lived, their faces and appearance, and their vernacular architecture—everything that seemed so different and distant in time from the urban North. He was an amateur folklorist, ethnographer, historian, and sociologist with a camera.[33]

During his time in Greene County, Delano drew from three different shooting scripts: one from Stryker that asked him to focus on specific FSA activities, one from Raper that provided a detailed outline of Greene County's people and places, and his own that distilled the essence of Raper's far more comprehensive plan. Delano's script focused on the landscape, architecture, and people of Greene County:

> (1) What the land looks like (general long shots) (2) the old plantations and what has become of them (old plantation's barns, abandoned buildings etc), (3) the people and how they live (exterior and interior of homes and shacks—Negro and white—family groups in the home and working in the field—portraits of individuals etc.) (4) community life (the "church," entertainment—going to the movie, the [dame ball?] etc) (5) the county seat (Greensboro)—what it looks like and something of the political set-up) (6) Contrast between red-land plantation area of the northern part of the county and the white land small independent owner of the South.

Delano admitted these were just "rough headings" and that in "filling them out most of the important things will be covered."[34] Part of Raper's script added a salvage mission to Delano's work in Greene County. It reflected both a desire to document Greene County history and a nostalgia for those things that seemed threatened by looming modernization and standardization: Indian relics and people with "Indian blood," ex-slaves, slave huts, members of slave-holding families, antebellum homes, plantation bells, gravestones, and early churches.[35]

Delano's most recognized and evocative photographs depict the Greene County landscape and the people, particularly the county's black and white farmers, who labored on it. His panoramic landscape photographs highlight the sublimity and beauty of the land while, at times, evoking the nobility of the Jeffersonian agrarian farmer even when the land was scarred by erosion and the farmer was debt-laden and dependent on New Deal assistance. Nevertheless, Delano's photographs were not simply products of a sentimental agrarianism. His images, partly because of his collaboration with Arthur Raper and other FSA officials, remained attuned to the folly of attempting to exploit nature for profit. Delano's Greene County landscapes reflect an abiding tension at the heart of his work and that of many other FSA photographers. Like images of tenant farmers, the bureaucratic and political demands of the FSA required photographs that depicted the land as tortured and in need of New Deal-funded reform. Yet that same land, like the farmers who lived and labored on it, appealed to the aesthetic and cultural sensibilities of photographers from northern and urban backgrounds like Delano. The rural South's landscape in the eyes of FSA photographers, argues historian

Stuart Kidd, "was a stimulating antidote to the predictable, anonymous and modernized cities with which they were associated professionally. Man's traces on the southern landscape, in contrast, were personalized, rooted in history, and culturally 'authentic.' A beleaguered status and tenuous presence reinforced the imaginative appeal." This tension between "romance and recrimination" in Kidd's phrasing, captures the dynamics at play in Delano's portrayal of the Greene County landscape, which represented a microcosm of the rural South during the Depression and New Deal.[36]

Just as Delano had to adjust to the South's culture of segregation and white supremacy, he had to acclimate to the region's agricultural landscapes and natural environment and develop an appreciation for the interaction between people and the land. Growing up in urban Philadelphia, Delano admitted to having no appreciation of rural life. "Land and the soil were, to me, just 'dirt.' I had always been a city boy," Delano said once in an interview, "and it was all great and new and wonderful to me." At the same time, and with Raper's help, he saw not only cultivated soil but also scarred, eroded, and gullied land worn out from years of cotton farming. Raper shared his perception of the gullies and erosion as physical manifestations of an exploitive cotton economy and tenant system in the South. Gullies in his mind were the "region's receipts for the 'bargains' the [tenant] system got out of virgin soil, slavery and farm tenancy combined."[37]

Stryker believed Delano possessed a unique knack for capturing a sense of place in his landscape photographs and directed him to an article written by the documentary filmmaker Pare Lorentz, in which Lorentz argued that the "continent made the people, not the people, the continent." Stryker lamented the fact that so few Americans living in the urban centers of the North knew what the rural American landscape looked like in other places.[38]

The differences in topography and "vegetation" between the rural North and the rural South likely spurred Delano's creativity, enabling him to evoke the Georgia Piedmont's unique landscape. After his first trip to Greene County in 1941, Delano journeyed to the Alabama Black Belt, including Hale County, which he described as the most "thrilling country" he had seen to date. His experience in a new part of the South gave him a "better perspective on Greene County," he said. In Alabama's "black prairie area" he was amazed to see "thousands and thousands of acres of what used to be cotton land" turned to pasture, where cattle now grazed on terraced land once the preserve of man and mule.[39] His experience in the rural North and in the Alabama Black Belt allowed Delano to approach Greene County more attuned to its natural and vernacular features that evoked a unique sense of place.

And in Greene County, the contrast between pastoral beauty and rural blight abounded, which fascinated Delano, Raper, and so many others who studied the area. With one eye, Delano looked on Greene County's landscapes and used photography to expose the "tortured" and "wasted land" ruined by the folly of the cotton tenant system, capturing images of soil erosion and gullies that the FSA needed to justify its programs and existence. With the other eye, he saw beauty within and beyond the blight and composed evocative photographs recalling the landscape paintings of Romantic-era artists.

Delano's landscape photographs from Greene County often transform the viewers' perception of the rural South from a "wasted land" into a pastoral retreat far removed from the noise and bustle of urban America. Delano's photograph, "Greene County landscape on the Jackson farm near White Plains, Georgia," from June 1941 shows three black farmers walking single file along a path away from a general store. The lead man, dressed in overalls and a long-sleeved shirt, does not look directly into Delano's lens, but rather slightly aslant toward the ground. He seems to walk languorously in the heat of early summer, as do the two men behind him. The path they walk links the men like an artery to the store in the distance, a place that provides the necessities of life on credit while also saddling them with debt. The black men are also subsumed by the broad expanse of parched white soil owned by the white Jackson family. They appear caught between material forces of the land—tenants in thrall to white landowners—and natural forces from the sky—the vagaries of the weather that determine the fate of their crops. Ultimately, these critiques of the rural South's agricultural economy evident in Delano's photograph are secondary to its focus on the beauty and sublimity of the landscape and the men's presence on it. As the photograph's caption attests, this is primarily a "Greene County landscape" image. The caption does not mention the men, and so they appear as natural appendages to the land. The white cumulus clouds stretching from the horizon to the foreground, like tufts of cotton in the sky, and the early afternoon summer sunlight bathing the land evoke an aura of pastoral tranquility. Delano's background as an artist and a painter provided him with the aesthetic awareness to compose and frame the image in such a way that it primarily functions as art rather than sociology, as a depiction of a culturally "authentic" and aesthetically beautiful place so different from the streets of Philadelphia, rather than the site of economic and racial exploitation.

Delano often obsessed over taking a photograph that would capture the unique look and feel of the place where he was working. Roy Stryker recalled sending Delano on assignment to Vermont. "Jack was the artist and being the

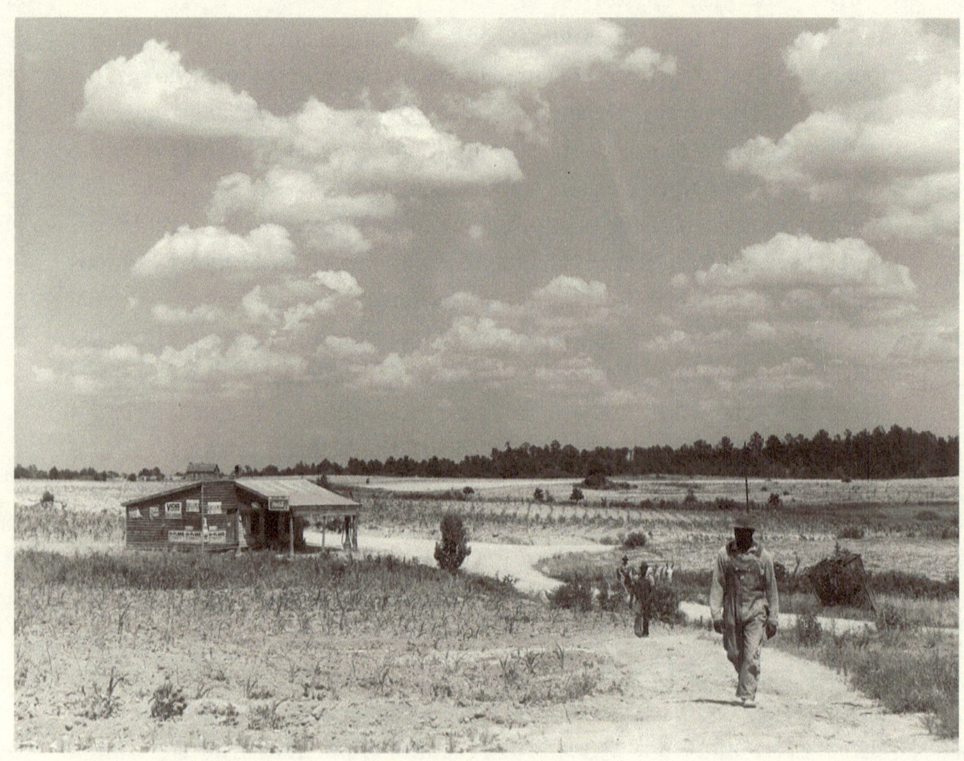

Jack Delano, *Greene County Landscape on the Jackson Farm near White Plains, Georgia,* June 1941. Arthur Raper Papers, Southern Historical Collection, Louis Round Wilson Special Collections Library, University of North Carolina at Chapel Hill.

artist," Stryker remembered, he would spend "hours asking himself, a bit self-consciously, 'What is the *one* picture I can take that will say Vermont?'" Stryker, as noted earlier, believed Delano possessed a unique talent for taking photographs that evoked a sense of place. Referring to some color photographs Delano took in Greene County with Kodachrome film, Stryker said, "I am very much pleased with Delano's style of photographing landscapes. The low foreground and the tremendous amount of sky seems [*sic*] to me to give quite a feeling for the land."[40] Stryker believed such photographs, which recalled nineteenth-century paintings and photographs of the West, aspired to art. "There's no question that photographers like these produced some great pictures," Stryker said, "pictures that will live the way great paintings live."[41]

Some Romantic artists, as Stephen Behrendt notes, portrayed nature as both "Destroyer and Preserver," an immense and almost omnipotent force that dwarfs the human figures in the painting. The focus on the premodern, pastoral, and rural scene and the ennobling of the seemingly independent farmer, thus links the Romantic landscape painting tradition with FSA photography. Two striking photographs Delano took in Greene County in May and June 1941 exemplify these Romantic themes. In the first, a black tenant named Lloyd Rhodes works his field with a mule-drawn plow. Great swaths of sky and land once again pit themselves against the noble farmer attempting to eke out a living against overwhelming odds. Similarly, in the photograph captioned "Plowing a field of cotton," a farmer and his mule are seen only as dark specks in a seemingly limitless sea of cotton rows and cirrus-streaked sky that blurs the horizon line, creating the sense of an infinite expanse. A couple of cumulus clouds hang overhead in symmetry with the man and his mule. Both photographs depict farmers with mules, rather than tractors, despite the increasing number of the latter in the county, while evoking feelings of awe at the immensity of nature and respect for a man's attempt to coax a living out of such unforgiving forces. Delano's landscape photographs also captivated Arthur Raper, who wanted to use them prominently in his work in progress, *Tenants of the Almighty*. "Arthur keeps talking of the one of the Man-plowing-in-the-cotton-field-with-lottsa-sky-and-white-clouds-in-a-row as the frontispiece," Delano wrote to Stryker from Greene County.[42]

In a series of photographs Delano took of a tenant named Leroy Dunn and his family chopping cotton, he presented other pastoral scenes free from any hint of industry that emphasized the beauty and gracefulness of the human form in motion while at work on the land. Delano's photographs direct the viewers' attention to the Dunn family's bodies that almost seem to sway in dance like motion as they each hold their hoes off to their left sides. On this particular day, Monday, June 2, 1941, Delano carried with him both color and black-and-white film. Delano was one of the few FSA photographers who had the opportunity to experiment with color film, which Roy Stryker hoped would result in eye-catching images for viewers of the new popular magazines that showcased photography. Though they never appeared in print, Delano had hoped to use his color photographs from Greene County as "symbol" shots that would "introduce chapters" in Raper's book. A similar photograph that Delano shot that day in black and white did appear in *Tenants of the Almighty* two years later: its caption reflects the image's bucolic message while only subtly acknowledging the injustices faced by such farmers. "We live and work in the country. We know the smell of fresh plowed earth. To break and plant and cultivate one acre of cotton, we walk 40 miles."

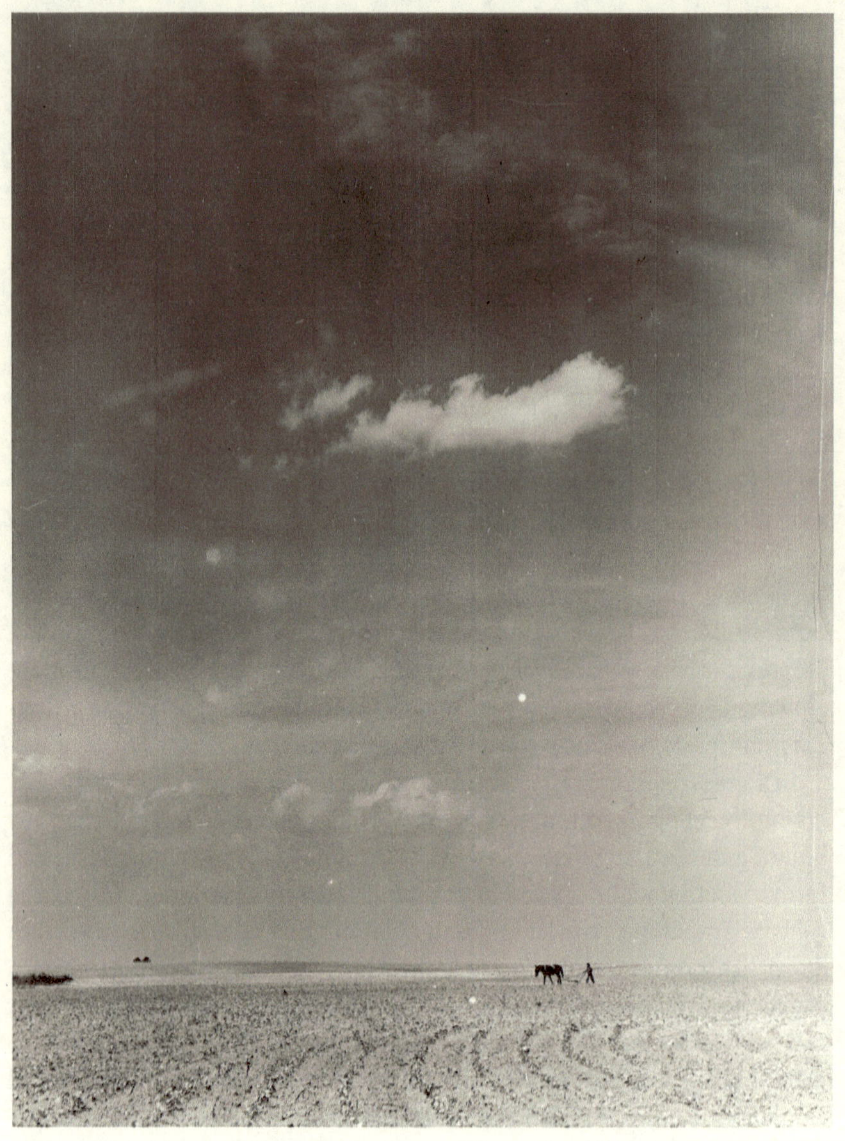

Jack Delano, *Plowing a Field of Cotton, Greene County, Georgia,* June 1941. Arthur Raper Papers, Southern Historical Collection, Louis Round Wilson Special Collections Library, University of North Carolina at Chapel Hill.

Delano's color photograph of the Dunn family not only focuses on the seemingly choreographed motion of their work but also on how the afternoon light emblazons their clothing, including their straw hats, Mr. Dunn's blue overalls, and the women's floral print dresses. A line of trees and vegetation bisects the image and marks the edge of the field. Like his photographs of lone farmers plowing expansive fields under wide skies, this color photograph captures the interplay of earth and sky on the Greene County landscape. The photograph's rich color brings out the blue sky streaked with white cirrus clouds, the verdant green vegetation, and the bronzed soil on which these black tenants labor. The photograph functions foremost as a work of art, one that captures elements of how many documentarians imagined the South in their work: a premodern place, rooted in the folk who worked the land by hand. Delano carefully composed the scene and, as he was wont to do, seems to have arranged the Dunn family so that the best angle of light bounced off their bodies. On the left edge of the frame of both the color and black-and-white photographs, there is a child standing in the field watching his family hoe. His presence suggests that no capable worker in the family could afford to supervise a child at home when all of their labor was needed to get by.[43]

The photographs do not provide additional insight into the particular labor arrangement the Dunns had with T. C. Moore, the white man who owned the land they worked. Raper could have provided more contextual details in order to highlight the exploitation of tenant labor as he did in *Preface to Peasantry* in 1936. The history of local resistance to documentary work, however, often prevented Raper and Delano from creating photographs and captions that communicated political messages or could be construed as protests against Greene County's social and economic order. Raper in particular needed as much local cooperation as possible to implement modest New Deal reforms in the county. Images and words that evoked the beauty of the land and the nobility of labor seemed designed to assuage local fears that Raper and Delano intended to defame the county, as did the article in *Collier's* magazine, in order to justify federal intervention.[44]

The need to curry local favor and even involve some elite white men in the photographic process, along with Jack Delano's own romantic fascination for the rural poor, also shaped who Delano photographed in Greene County and how he portrayed them in his portrait photographs. His photographs of local white elites, such as Judge Park and T. B. Rice, not only constituted the "required shots" needed to create a comprehensive portrait of the community but they also served to alleviate the fears that the documentarians

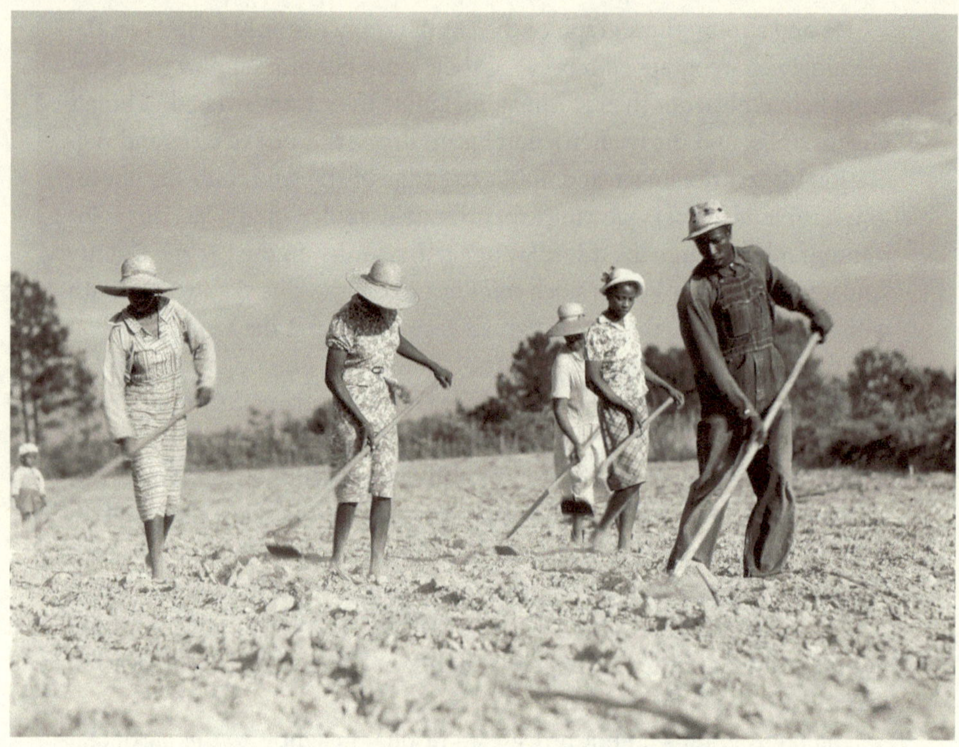

Jack Delano, *Chopping Cotton on Rented Land near White Plains, Greene County, Georgia*, June 1941. Courtesy of the Library of Congress, Prints and Photographs Division, FSA/OWI Collection. LC-USF35-599.

would only focus on the county's "worst" as did the article in *Collier's* magazine. Delano told Stryker that he "won't be especially proud of some of the shots" because some of what he had to photograph was "important and necessary because of its documentary rather than pictorial significance." Early in his time in Greene County, Delano lamented to Stryker that his photographs so far in his trip were "predominantly *factual and* very little *human*." He acknowledged that "Arthur realizes it but feels these factual things must be gathered first."[45] Delano felt uninspired photographing Greene County's white elite because they did not engage him politically or aesthetically. In contrast, documenting the county's black and white farmers provided him an opportunity to use photography as an instrument of political reform and creative expression. "We idolized President Roosevelt," Delano later recalled. "We thought that he was the savior of the country and the New Deal programs were doing a great deal of good . . . the New Deal programs were very much part of what I believed in."[46]

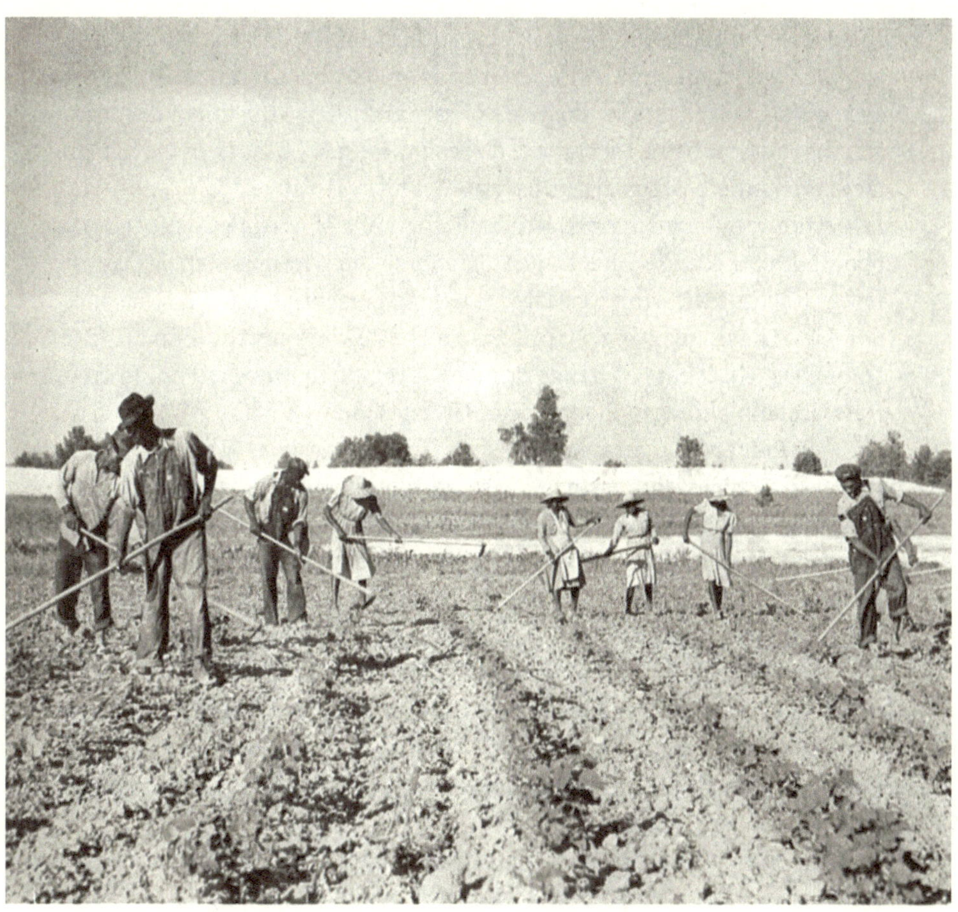

Jack Delano, *Chopping Cotton on a Large Farm near Greensboro, Greene County, Georgia,* June 1941. Courtesy of the Library of Congress, Prints and Photographs Division, FSA/OWI Collection. LC-USF34-044719-D.

Tied up with Delano's New Deal liberalism was a romanticism that ennobled and aestheticized the South's black and white rural poor. An unresolvable tension existed between the assumed power of photography to present incontrovertible truth, prick a nation's collective conscience, and inspire reform and its propensity to beautify, to turn potentially political subjects into artistic objects. The very things a New Dealer like Delano hoped to reform were often sources of romantic and artistic attraction—the unadorned tenant house, the sharecropper in overalls and a straw hat, the seemingly preindustrial, pastoral landscape. His photographs, like so many others from the FSA, endure not for their power to spark reform, but for their formal sophistication and ability to make poverty beautiful. "I think it is true," Delano recalled later about his experience as an FSA photographer, "that the struggle against adversity, the years of care and worry, the toil of drudgery and the constant battle for survival do bestow a kind of beauty on the human face and figure to which artists have always been sensitive."[47]

Delano created his most striking photographs of Greene County's rural poor, both black and white, by photographing them from low angles, an effect that grants the subjects a large, looming presence, ennobling the once ignoble. These images also emphasize the "beauty on the human face and figure" that years of struggle and toil seemed to leave behind. In contrast, Delano photographed none of Greene County's white elite, such as Dr. T. B. Rice and Judge James Park, from this perspective. While his photographs of Greene's elite seem less aesthetically and politically engaged, they constitute a subtle visual challenge to the entrenched social order. Rather than looking up at the elite, viewers look at them at eye level or even down on them. Delano's photographs of the white elite display an emotional and literal distance absent from his images of Greene's black and white small farmers. While he did not compose every portrait he took of Greene County's rural poor from low angles, he seems to have used this stylistic technique with more regularity in Greene County than in other places, perhaps because of the closer connections he developed with some of his subjects with Raper's assistance.

Two photographs, one of a black female tenant farmer and the other of a white male tenant farmer, both taken on Thursday, June 5, 1941, are representative of Delano's compositional techniques when photographing the rural poor. In his photographs of Mary Willis and Carl Lankford, Delano shot from a very low perspective that forces the viewer to gaze up into their faces. Willis and Lankford, however, look away into the distance. They appear absorbed in thought, oblivious to Delano's presence, and abstracted from any potential audience that might view his photographs of them. Such compositional techniques ennobled Willis and Lankford by imbuing them with a capacity for emotion, introspection, and heroic individualism that is virtually absent in his photographs of Greene County's middle-class and elite whites. Willis, a widow whose photograph appeared in *Tenants of the Almighty*, wears a rumpled, floral print dress and a brass wire bracelet on her right wrist to take away her rheumatism. She appears to tower over the line of trees in the background. Her arms and face glimmer in the mid-afternoon sunlight. Lankford, blind in one eye and a World War I veteran, "won't ask for a pension," according to Delano. He wears the iconic clothing of the

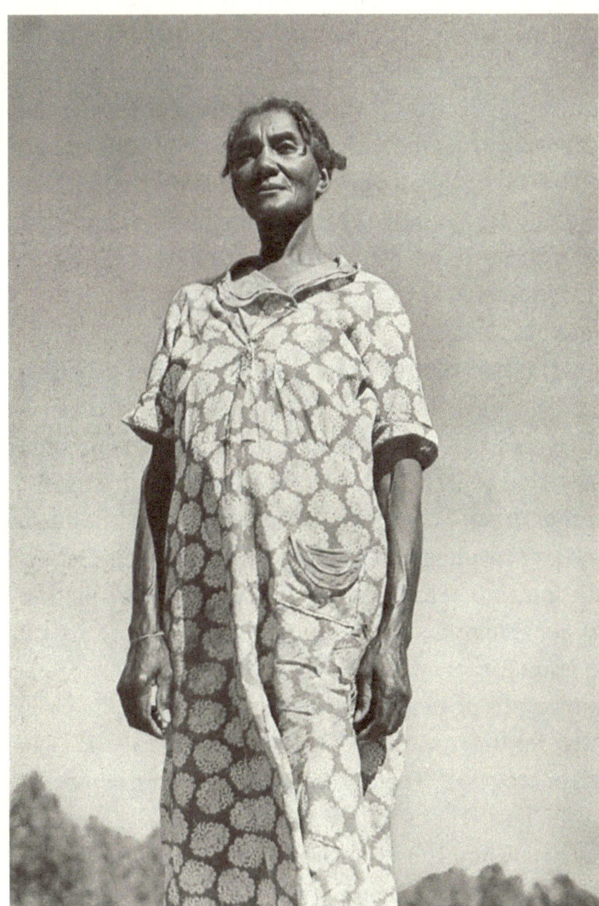

Jack Delano, *Mrs. Mary Willis, Widow, Who with Two Children Runs a Rented Farm near Woodville, Greene County, Georgia*, June 1941. Courtesy of the Library of Congress, Prints and Photographs Division, FSA/OWI Collection. LC-USF 34-044763-D.

South's farmers—overalls, a long-sleeved cotton shirt, and a straw hat. The viewer looks straight up toward his shadowed face, his eyes, like Willis's turned away from Delano's lens and staring off in the distance. His straight posture and crossed arms evoke stolidity and determination. Both Lankford and Willis appear statuesque, monuments to the beauty and nobility conferred on the human form after years of toil and struggle.[48]

Delano's photographs of former slaves living in Greene County humanized, dignified, and romanticized their subjects in a similar manner. Five years earlier, when Dorothea Lange worked in Greene County, she also photographed ex-slaves, though not in as much depth. Delano documented many more ex-slaves during his time in Greene, no doubt because of the connections Raper provided him. His photographs do not attempt to convey the irony of those by Lange, such as one that depicts the former slave couple now living in an old slave-owning family's plantation house. Rather, Delano's close-up images of ex-slaves reflect his romantic ideas about the poor southerners he encountered during the early 1940s. He specifically remembered being enthralled by the image and presence of an ex-slave in Greene County named Tony Thompson who, as Raper noted, also had "Indian blood," which added to his exotic background. "This ex-slave just looked like a black prophet . . . it's just his presence. You thought you were in the presence of a visionary," Delano later recalled.[49]

When Delano photographed him in May 1941, Thompson was living alone on a farm owned by a white family and had not had a haircut in six years. He had just started receiving local old-age assistance from the county welfare board, which was led by Dr. T. B. Rice. Rice and Raper joined Delano on the day he photographed Thompson. Raper noted that Thompson thanked Rice at the time for providing him with financial assistance. Delano's photographs create an image of Thompson that reveal little of his life's difficulties—or of his achievements, including having attended Atlanta University some forty years earlier, which was about the time W. E. B. Du Bois had compiled photographs of an aspiring black middle class, including the university's students, for the "American Negro" exhibit at the 1900 Paris Exhibition. In Delano's photograph, Thompson, seemingly deep in thought, looks wistfully beyond the lens. Though Delano does not peddle in the demeaning caricatures of happy and contented slaves, his conscious attempt to realistically portray and evoke the humanity and dignity of an ex-slave like Thompson creates a new romantic image in the place of the old plantation mythology developed in the late nineteenth century. Delano sees Thompson as someone almost saintly and superhuman, a "prophet," a "visionary." His portrayal undeniably stems from a genuine respect and admiration that almost all preceding portrayals of slaves and ex-slaves lacked. Nevertheless, Delano's photographs of Thompson reveal how New Deal documentarians working in the rural South could undermine the gauzy representations of African Americans and of the region as an Old South idyll, only to replace them with new mythic images that seemed tantalizingly real because they resulted from fieldwork carried out in the name of social science and federal reform.[50]

Just a few months after photographing Thompson, this 1941 photograph of him appeared in Richard Wright's groundbreaking book of documentary photography and African American history, *12 Million Black Voices: A Folk History of the Negro in the United States*. Wright's book, abundantly illustrated

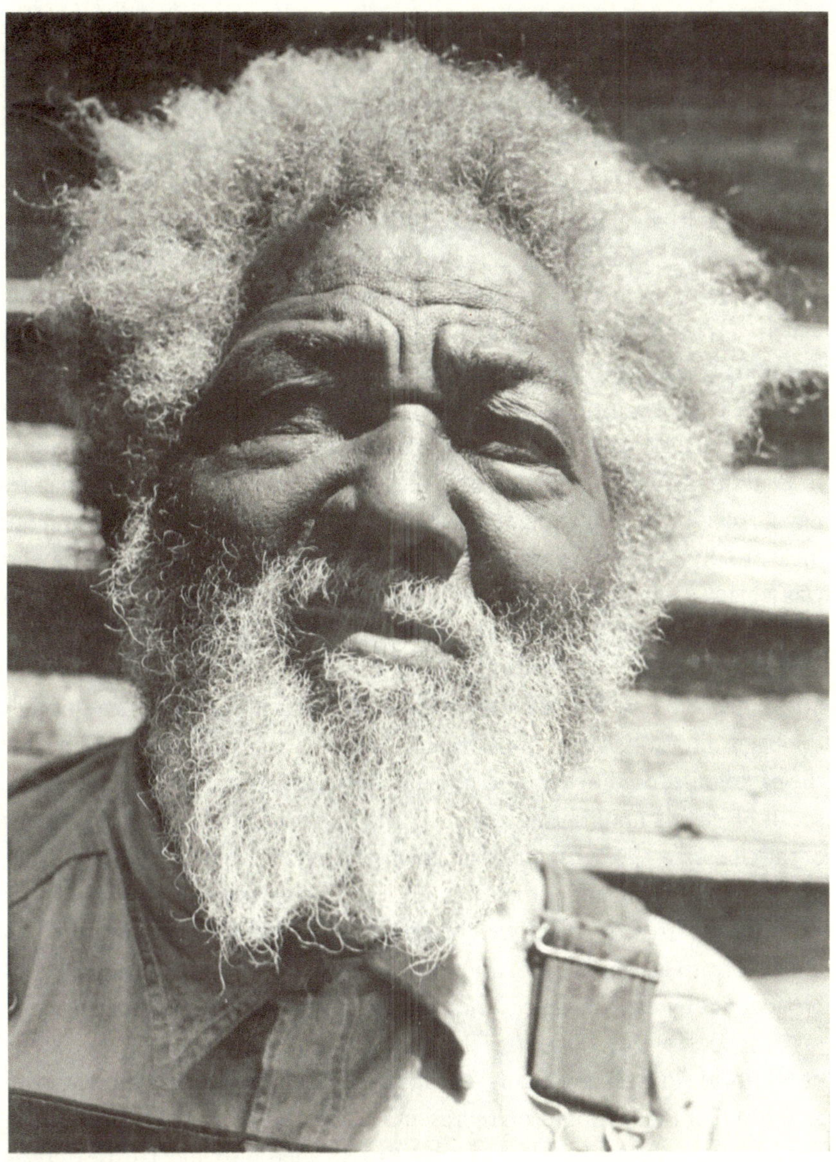

Jack Delano, *Tony Thompson, Born in Slavery. Greene County, Georgia,* June 1941. Courtesy of the Library of Congress, Prints and Photographs Division, FSA/OWI Collection. LC-USF34-044266-D.

with photographs by white FSA photographers selected by FSA photo editor Edwin Rosskam, intended "to render a broad picture of the processes of Negro life in the United States" and counter the demeaning images of black people that Margaret Bourke-White published four years earlier in *You Have Seen Their Faces*.[51] It focused not on the black middle class or elite, as W. E. B. Du Bois did in the photographic exhibition he presented at the 1900 Paris Exhibition, but instead depicted the "complex movement of a debased feudal folk toward a twentieth-century urbanization." Wright insisted that his words and the FSA photographs were to "seize upon that which is qualitative and abiding in the Negro experience, to place within full and constant view the collective humanity whose triumphs and defeats are shared by the majority, whose gains in security mark an advance in the level of consciousness attained by the broad masses in their costly and tortuous upstream journey." For his chronicle of the "feudal folk's" plight Wright relied in large measure on *Sharecroppers All* (1941) by Arthur Raper and Ira de Reid, who was a black sociology professor at the time at Atlanta University.[52]

Delano's photograph of Thompson, one of the rare close-ups featured in the book, appears on the second page of Part One, "Our Strange Birth," in *12 Million Black Voices*, which covers the period from capture in Africa through the beginnings of slavery in colonial America. It takes up three-quarters of the page while four lines of Wright's text fills out the rest: "Each day when you see us black folk upon the dusty land of the farms or upon the hard pavement of the city streets, you usually take us for granted and think you know us, but our history is far stranger than you suspect, and we are not what we seem." With these words, Wright—or Thompson—might as well have been speaking directly to Jack Delano, Arthur Raper, or T. B. Rice and not just the book's broader audience. For Raper, Thompson was a man to be photographed for his own book project, *Tenants of the Almighty*, since he represented two kinds of "survival" in Greene County—that of the legacy of slavery and of native America. For Rice, Thompson represented, perhaps, a memory of plantation life from his youth, a man for whom he performed his paternalistic duty as an elite white man. For Delano, an urbanite from the North, Thompson was the visionary "black prophet" whose unkempt appearance made him all the more exotic and picturesque. In *12 Million Black Voices*, Thompson's image represents black America's slave experience; his aging face and graying hair convey the toll exacted by this arduous journey from enslavement to feudalism. And yet, his past as a slave is only implied and not stated outright.[53]

The *New York Times*'s review of *12 Million Black Voices* featured two photographs from the book, one of which was Delano's photograph of Tony

Thompson bearing the subtitle, "Georgia Sharecropper"—the same one used in the captions found in the back of the book. According to reviewer William Shands Meacham, the FSA "has seen the faces of the folk." But when readers of the *Times* look at Thompson's face they see yet another anonymous "sharecropper" in a long line of others—both black and white—who had populated the books, newspapers, and magazines of America during the past decade, whose image was symbolic of the Depression and the American capacity for noble suffering and redemption.[54] His experience in slavery, his determination to attain a higher education, his life after college, his daily existence as an impoverished elderly black man living in Greene County, Georgia, all remain mysteries. Delano's elegant photograph of Thompson, his romantic admiration for this "visionary," along with the politically charged use of Thompson's image in Wright's book, represented a more humane and progressive vision of rural black southerners than images seen and read in popular culture, including recent documentary books like Margaret Bourke-White's and Erskine Caldwell's *You Have Seen Their Faces*. Still, Delano crafted a photograph that romanticized an impoverished elderly man as a "black prophet" and was used elsewhere as a representative image of a "sharecropper." In either case, the image was as mythic as other competing representations of black southerners found in photography, fiction, and film both past and present. Delano's photographs of the rural poor function primarily as documentary art that helped create a powerful regional and racial imaginary, rather than as political propaganda that brought about social reform.[55]

Delano's photographs of black Greene County residents created not only a romantic image of the black folk in the rural South but also an illusion of complete cooperation between photographer and subject. Just as local white resistance shadowed and shaped Delano's work in Greene County, so did acts of resistance from black residents. Though there is no evidence to suggest Thompson and Willis were unwilling participants, a situation that occurred between the Delanos and a black church's congregation one Sunday morning in 1941 highlights the unease and suspicion that hovered in the air when even sympathetic and progressive whites appeared with cameras. Delano was aware of the intrusive nature of his work and, along with his wife, often went to great lengths to assure the people he photographed of his intentions. George Stoney recalls that both Jack and Irene Delano were "so wonderfully shy" around the people they photographed, a trait that occasionally endeared them to their subjects.[56]

But Delano's diplomacy was not always on display, and his subjects, particularly those in a Greene County church one Sunday morning, could express visible if silent forms of resistance that challenged the power of a white photographer to enter into their social space and represent them. The encounter reveals how Delano's seemingly stable and even respectful images of rural black southerners often contain an undercurrent of questioning and resistance. On a Sunday morning in 1941, Jack and Irene Delano spied a "tiny white church on a little hillside." According to Irene, it "looked absolutely marvelous," the kind of place with its unadorned vernacular architecture that appealed so deeply to artists from the urban North. Jack Delano got out of the car and approached one of the church's deacons. He asked him if he could photograph inside his church. "There was a long pause," Delano remembered. "I think he would have been happy if a huge hole had opened up and we had just disappeared. He wanted us to go, but he probably felt he couldn't say no." Delano also asked the church's minister for permission to photograph. "I could see by the cold expression on his face that he wished we would disappear and leave him alone, but after a long, awkward pause he nodded and said we could go ahead." Despite the obvious displeasure expressed, if only silently, Delano and Irene grabbed their cameras and flashes and set up their equipment inside the church as the service began. Irene recalled that, almost immediately "We could see the look of resentment in all those people; I mean the attitude, 'You won't even leave us alone now.'" Irene pleaded with Jack to change his mind and leave, but he demurred and insisted she help him place the flashes in proper places throughout the church. "They didn't say we could come in, and of course they didn't say we could not come in. And I walked right up to the front of that church and shot the flash off and, you know, held it so that it would go off in one area of the church. I came out of that place just shaking, and so was Jack." The Delanos justified their actions that Sunday morning on the righteousness of their mission—they were part of a New Deal reform effort and hoped their photographs would find their way into print and transform how people thought about the rural South, poverty, and perhaps race.[57]

The resistance Delano encountered that morning at a church in Greene County was not an isolated event. "We ran into a kind of deference on the part of the blacks we approached," Delano later recounted. "We stood in front of the house and asked if we might come in—they said yes, but you felt that it was a 'no' because they were afraid to say no . . . it was an intrusion and we felt it was always an invasion." But penetrating his subjects' private spaces was a critical part of Delano's purpose as an FSA photographer. Unrestricted access to the poor and their private spaces seemed justified given the documentarian's reformist agenda. "Getting into a lot of homes could be very important . . . the only thing they had really was their homes [that were], strictly speaking, theirs."[58] FSA photographers, like Delano, argues Stuart Kidd, "were not above behaving like Gaugins with Leicas and fanciful notions of the rural South as an innocent, premodern culture seemed to make the restraint and reserve of metropolitan etiquette unnecessary." But for the black people Delano photographed, their homes and churches were places of autonomy and independence from whites, sacred places, and private spaces, not sources of evidence of poverty in need of reform or the persistence of folk cultures lingering in the rural South. Suspicion and tension coursed through these often-awkward encounters between photographers and subjects who occupied opposite sides of racial, class, and geographic divides.[59]

Stuart Kidd refers to these interactions between subject and photographer, between "the individual and the liberal state and its functionaries," as "dissonant encounters." FSA photographs did not empower the rural poor, but rather transformed them into icons, symbols of poverty or premodern simplicity and stoicism that photographers like Delano found so appealing in modernizing America. Some of Delano's subjects, like the members of the Baptist church he photographed, tried to become actors in the documentary encounter rather than just icons. The illusion of complicity and consonance that often exists on the surface of Delano's and other FSA photographers' photographs obscures the tensions and power dynamics that played out during these "dissonant encounters."[60]

Delano's photographs of black congregants at churches offer evidence of the tension and undercurrents of resistance that he occasionally encountered and generally concealed in most of his images. In two images taken outside a church in Greshamville, Greene County, Delano shows a family sitting in their car waiting for the service to begin. In the first photograph, Delano stood at the front of the car and photographed three members of the family sitting in the car's front seat and two in the back staring at him through the glass. The young boy and woman in the front seat seem to glare at Delano, while the man in the middle seems to have a more relaxed expression, if not a smile. In a related shot, Delano photographed the people in the front seat from the side with the driver's side door ajar. The woman has her head turned away from Delano and rests her chin on her hand. The man next to her again has an almost wry, quizzical smile as he looks into Delano's lens. The woman's facial expressions in both photographs charge the images with tension and demonstrate the suspicion and unease that existed when a strange white

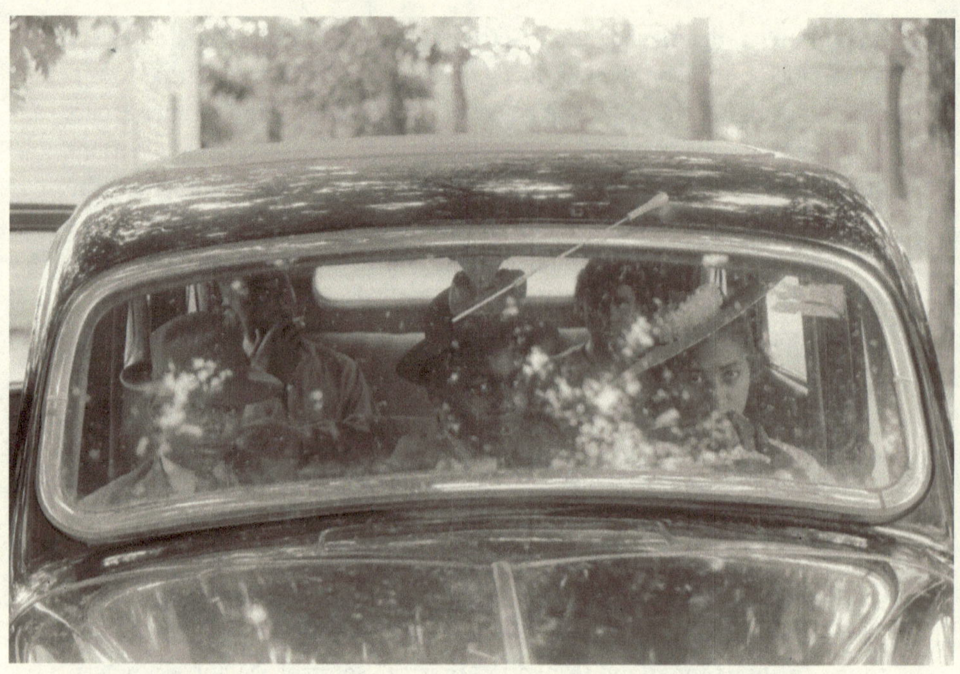

Jack Delano, *Waiting for Church to Begin, near Greshamville, Greene County, Georgia, No. 1*, June 1941. Courtesy of the Library of Congress, Prints and Photographs Division, FSA/OWI Collection. LC-USF33-020955-M5.

photographer suddenly appeared at a place once thought to be free from white interference. The aura of the "dissonant encounters" between FSA photographers like Delano and their subjects is also evoked in a photograph titled "Before the church meeting at a Negro church in Heard County, Georgia." In this photograph from April 1941, Delano photographed a group of four deacons standing outside the church house. The distance from which Delano took the photograph evokes the social and racial divide between the photographer and his subjects. Three of the men stare back at Delano, though the clarity of their expressions is obscured by the poor light on this gray, overcast morning and their distance from the photographer. These photographs not only evoke the tensions and suspicions of the "dissonant encounters" between FSA photographers and their subjects; they also reveal that the photographs of black churches Delano later published in *Tenants of the Almighty*, such as "Siloam, Greene County, Georgia (vicinity). The Mount Pleasant colored church," that appear to depict willing participants in Delano's documentary work often mask subtle acts of resistance that challenged the authority of white photographers to surveil and intrude. As

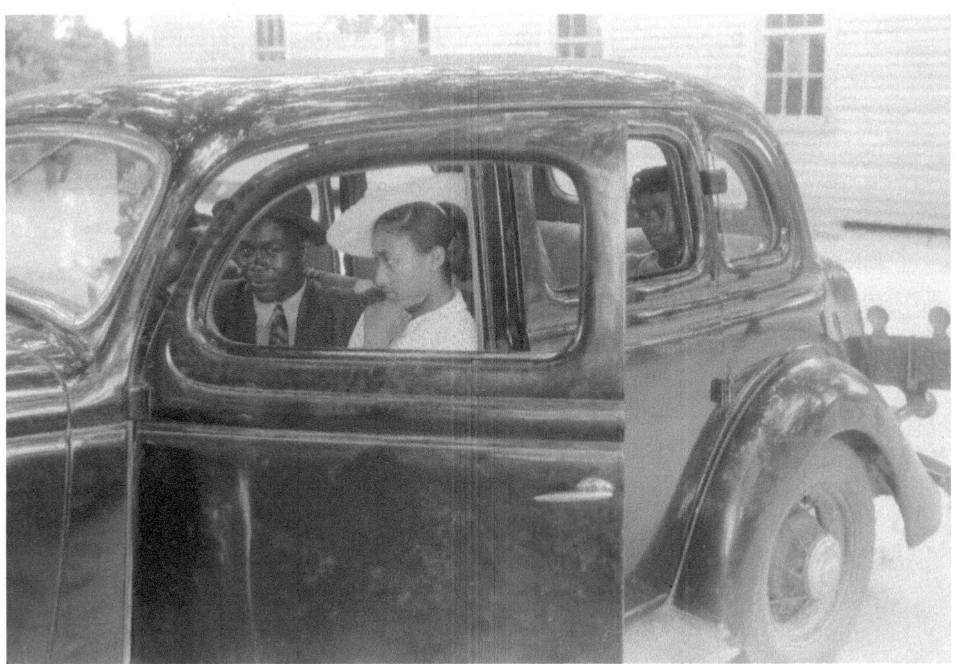

Jack Delano, *Waiting for Church to Begin, near Greshamville, Greene County, Georgia, No. 2*, June 1941. Courtesy of the Library of Congress, Prints and Photographs Division, FSA/OWI Collection. LC-USF33-020955-M4.

Arthur Raper notes in the caption to Delano's photograph of Mount Pleasant Church in *Tenants of the Almighty*, "The church is the Negro's most important institution. It is his own, and he supports it." Accordingly, even when a liberal, sympathetic photographer from the federal government appeared to photograph such an institution, black congregants demonstrated their desire to maintain control and independence, and not become icons or evidence for someone else's mission, by expressing palpable and visible displeasure toward the documentarian.[61]

Community Collaboration and the Making of *Tenants of the Almighty*

The history and persistence of resistance to doing documentary work in Greene County ultimately led Delano and Raper to make an unprecedented attempt to engage locals in the documentary process. They purposefully avoided the inflammatory tactics of *Collier's* journalists Owen P. White and Lawrence Monahan. Instead, Raper heeded a suggestion made by his wife

Martha and published installments of *Tenants of the Almighty* in the local newspaper, the Greensboro *Herald-Journal*, before it was released. He titled the series "Greene's Going Great" and included the following lines in the first installment: "We are presenting it because we believe you will be interested in the materials. [Raper] in turn is happy to have it appear and invites comment from the readers. Dr. Raper may be seen at his office in the Brown Building, or reached by letter through Box 267, Greensboro." Raper thanked the people of Greene County for the "cordial cooperation" they gave him, especially Dr. T. B. Rice who provided him with "voluminous historical files on early Greene County."[62] Raper also later distributed more than 100 copies of *Tenants of the Almighty* to Greene County residents, not only to elites like Rice but also to some of the farmers Delano photographed. According to the Greensboro *Herald-Journal*, Raper later told the paper, "This is the first time, in so far as he knows, that a government report has ever been submitted to the people of a county for them to check upon its accuracy and adequacy." Though Raper hoped *Tenants of the Almighty* would reach a broad national audience, the pressure to please Greene County's elite white population in particular led him to reassure readers of the *Herald-Journal* that he was "writing it primarily for Greene County people."[63]

Before Martha Raper came up with the concept of the "Greene's Going Great" series, Delano developed the idea of exhibiting his photographs in various locations across the county to allow as many people to see them as possible. Shortly after his second trip to the county in June 1941, Delano informed Roy Stryker that "we showed some of the Greene County pix to a group of the people down here and they were tickled." In October, Delano and Raper set up a photography exhibit in Raper's office and publicized it in the *Herald-Journal*. The article, "Delano Photographs Greene County," also gave readers an overview of Delano's background, the purpose of his photography, and a synopsis of the larger FSA photography project. "Mr. Delano has made photographs of FSA clients and what they are doing, general farm conditions, improvements that have been made here by the FSA and other agencies, conditions that need improvement, schools, churches, town pageants, objects of historical interest, and almost anything else that you can think of. The FSA is particularly interested in the people, of all kinds, who make up rural communities." The article also pointed out, "More pictures have been made in Greene County than in any other locality that Mr. Delano has worked in," and noted that his photographs belong to the Historical Section of the FSA and "will be placed in files along with over fifty thousand other pictures of rural America." Readers also learned that Delano's photographs would be available for use in government publications and books and that Arthur Raper "will make a selection from the pictures of Greene County to illustrate the report his is now writing on the county."[64]

The exhibit lasted about two months, and a number of residents of Greene County stopped by to see their homes on display. "We are continuously and pleasantly reminded of the Delanos," Raper wrote to Jack and Irene a few weeks after they left the county, "as people still come in to see the pictures. Practically every one comments on *how clear and natural they are*."[65] At about the same time Raper wrote to Delano about the community's reaction to his photographs, he told Roy Stryker that the "local people here are expressing a genuinely hopeful interest in our Study." Raper said he "remained convinced that we can say what needs to be said in such way that they will recognize it as dynamic truth; that is, the facts can be presented in such way to be helpful in the furtherance of the farm program here."[66] It appears that Delano and Raper's engagement with the Greene County community was unique among documentary projects carried out during the New Deal. The ties to Greene County and its residents that Raper had established for more than a decade, the frequent and prolonged trips Jack and Irene Delano made there, and the FSA's active role in the county all fostered more intimate interactions between documentarians and locals than existed anywhere else during the New Deal.

This sense of community collaboration and engagement, however, was also the necessary product of the history and persistence of resistance to documentary work in the county. Raper and Delano wanted to allay fears about potentially subversive government workers who pried into residents' private lives with the intent of bringing about social equality. "Now, our job," Raper said early during the creation of the book, "is to tell the whole truth in an acceptable manner." Both Raper and Delano hoped their work would lead to reform—of agricultural practices, of race relations, of impoverished living conditions—under the guiding hand of federal expertise and intervention. Anything redolent of radicalism or journalistic sensationalism could spark another firestorm, like the one White and Monahan left burning in their wake, and ruin prospects for change. The image of Greene County that Raper and Delano presented to its residents acknowledged the obvious problems of poverty and exploited land, but emphasized community cohesion and stability, racial cooperation, and the once and future ideal of the Jeffersonian farmer. *Tenants of the Almighty* functioned not only as a promotional piece for the benefits of New Deal agricultural programs but, like Delano's photographs of the county's landscape and people, also as a romantic, idealistic image of a down but redemptive South whose rural folk constituted the region's lifeblood and beauty, rather than its pathology and blight.[67]

The first two parts of the book present Delano's photographs and Raper's text to tell a story about the county's past and its present under the influence of the New Deal agricultural programs. Book I—"If You Like Your Story Short"—provides a photographic narrative of the county's history and includes images of the Oconee River that comprises the county's western border, Indian pottery, small shots of a historic church, and the Confederate monument in front of the courthouse. A larger photograph, and one that captures Delano's aesthetic sensibility, is a shot of a plantation bell on the Jackson farm near White Plains. The photograph, which represents the county's plantation past, combines Delano's fascination with the rural South's built environment and landscape. The plantation bell, used to call slaves and tenants to and from the fields, sits atop the slim trunk of an old tree that still has the small stubs of branches jutting from its sides. Just behind the bell, and to the left of the frame, sits a small wooden farm building, its open door providing a black rectangular form to the composition. In the background is an open field stretching to a forest of pines in the distance. Scattered white puffs of cumulus clouds dot the sky above, adding to the sense of pastoral beauty. Aesthetically, it is one of the most striking images among Delano's seventy-nine photographs chosen to illustrate the book. Nevertheless, it presents the county's former slave system as an institution that left behind quaint architectural relics rather than a legacy of racial inequality, which photographs of impoverished former slaves might have suggested. Similarly, in an effort not to immediately alienate white southern readers, Raper presents slavery as a fait accompli foisted on the region by Yankees and African chiefs: "The white settlers brought black men to work for them, black men sold into slavery by African Chiefs and carried to America in New England ships." Yet Raper does not play into stereotypes of a mythic moonlight-and-magnolias Old South, an image conjured just four years before in the cinematic depiction of Margaret Mitchell's *Gone with the Wind*. In Book III, where Raper writes in more depth about Greene County's history, he offers a richer and less sanitized version of slavery that includes descriptions of the brutality and follies of planters bent on domination and profit. This tension between compromise and critique, between catering to a white Greene County audience and making a case for reform, lurks on every page of *Tenants of the Almighty*, including in the photographs of Jack Delano.[68]

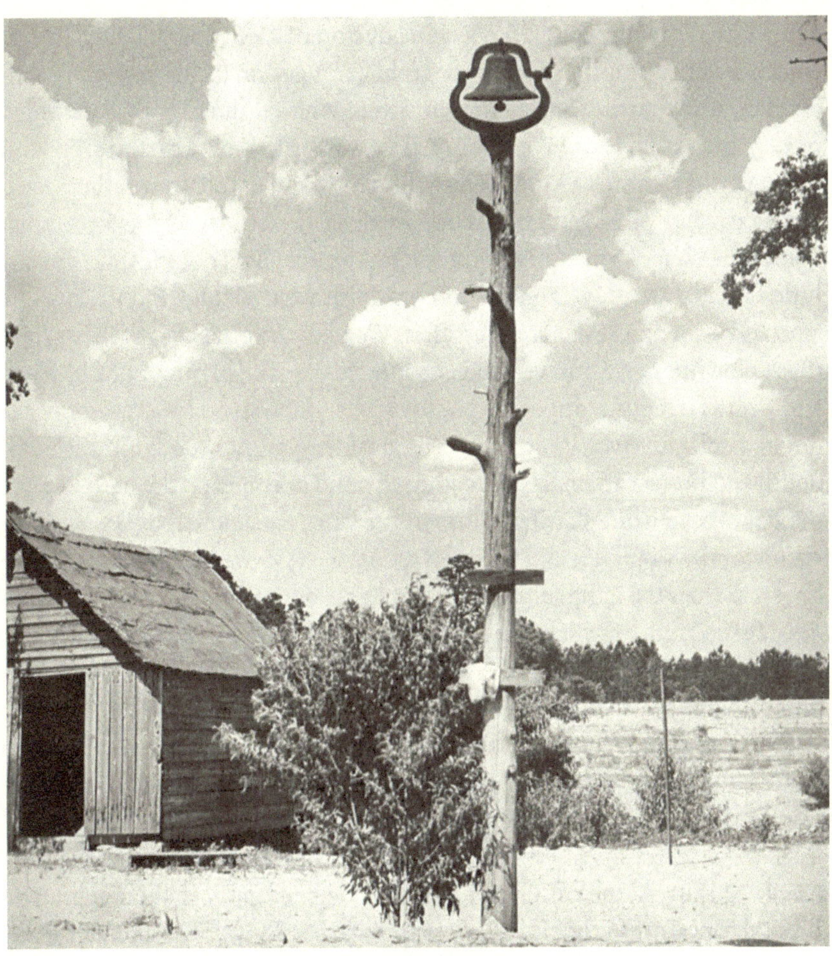

Jack Delano, *Old Plantation Bell on the Jackson Homestead. Near White Plains, Greene County, Georgia,* June 1941. Courtesy of the Library of Congress, Prints and Photographs Division, FSA/OWI Collection. LC-USF34-044743-D.

Book II—"And so we live . . ."—presents Delano's photographs of local people, agricultural labor, New Deal farm program activity, and scenes of small-town life. The FSA's photo editor Edwin Rosskam, who selected and arranged the photographs for Richard Wright's *12 Million Black Voices,* played a similar role in the production of *Tenants of the Almighty*. His arrangement of Delano's photographs, combined with Raper's captions, reveals the tension between romance and recrimination that characterized the book's depiction of Greene County. The "we" used by Raper in the title of Book II creates the illusion of community cohesion and conflates the voices of black and white, rich and poor, into a collective omniscient voice. For example, consider Raper's caption for photographs arranged on facing pages of an individual black farmer and of an individual white farmer, both handling a plow (Plates 19 and 20): "We borrow some money to grow a cotton crop, and we live by hard work. Mostly we use the same kind of tools our fathers used before us. But we have to buy more fertilizer, and the weevil is here now. Sometimes it looks like things are stacked against us. Looks like we get too little for what we grow, and pay too much for what we buy. But we love the land and want to rear our children on it. We know no other way of life. When these plowlines give out we will get some more." The photographs of black and white farmers in opposing photographs, but framed by a caption written in a collective voice, obscure the racial inequalities rooted in the rural South and project an image of a common bond in enduring the hardships of the boll weevil while sharing a "love of the land" and a Jeffersonian agrarian vision for their families and themselves. As one reviewer acknowledged, the book's "hero is the Jeffersonian farmer." The exodus from the farm to the city of Greene County farmers that Raper chronicled in *Preface to Peasantry* has been replaced by a heroic attachment to the land despite the obstacles, a condition shared by black and white alike.[69]

Some readers of the book, even those sympathetic to Raper and Delano's larger aims, found such photographs and captions more romantic than realistic. A friend of one of Raper's government coworkers in Greene County, U. T. Miller, wrote to Miller and said, "The pictures are beautiful. But a little more restraint in the comments would have been more convincing." The letter writer said that her husband "would have read the book and enjoyed it thoroughly if I could have cut out all the pictures before he started reading. The aggregate of the comments was too much sweetness and light for him—made him suspicious of political whitewash, I am afraid. 'They all lived happily ever after'. . . . [T]hat man who came down from Washington [Edwin Rosskam]—the high powered fellow—is the one who limited the effectiveness of your gorgeous book if you ask me. He overreached himself."[70] For example, Rosskam and Raper displayed photographs of controversial subjects—black convicts inside the county prison camp, white women protesting on the frontlines of a CIO union "lockout" near a mill in Greensboro—that had the potential to upset the image of community cohesion and consensus, but the photographs they chose and the captions they wrote blunted their political message. In one of the two photographs Delano took inside the Greene County prison camp with Raper's assistance, a prisoner plays a guitar and another dances while two other men clap along. "Colored convicts work on the

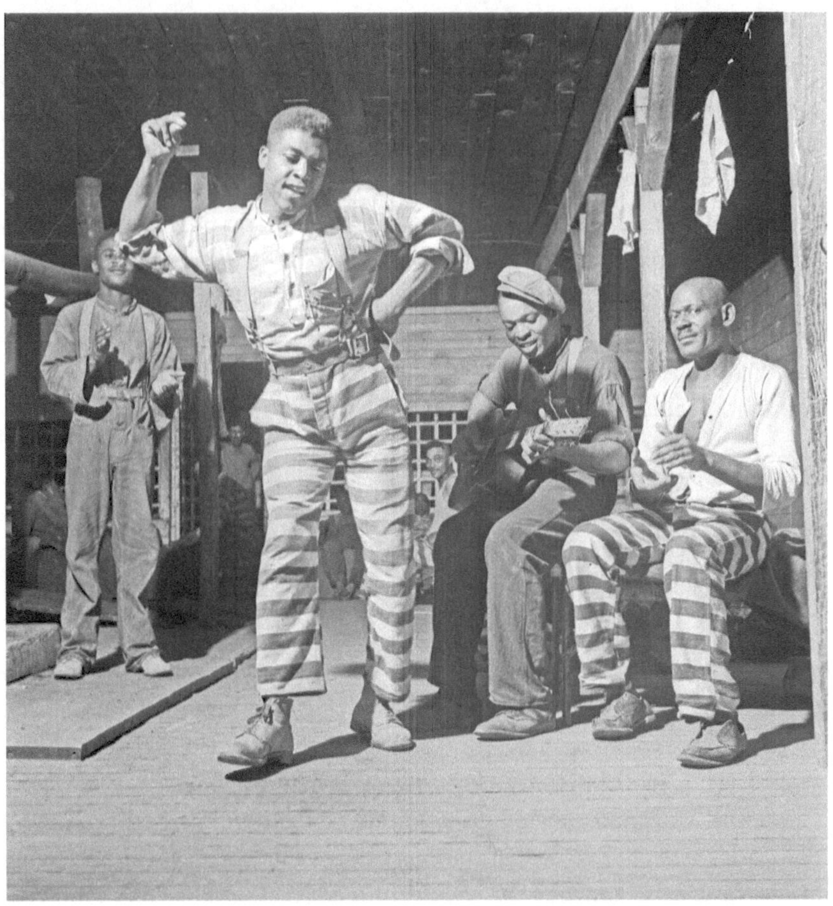

Jack Delano, *In the Convict Camp in Greene County, Georgia,* May 1941. Courtesy of the Library of Congress, Prints and Photographs Division, FSA/OWI Collection. LC-USF34-044770-E.

public roads," reads the caption. "They sleep and eat behind bars, and will dance like the dickens for your dime." And of the forty-five photographs Delano took of the CIO picket line in the mill town of Union Point, Raper and Rosskam chose the photograph in which the women are smiling, not jeering, grimacing, or gesticulating at the workers who broke what they called a "lockout." If Raper and Rosskam were not engaged in "political whitewash," they were responding to the demands of making *Tenants of the Almighty* palatable and acceptable to the Greene County community.[71]

Ultimately, Delano's small number of photographs of pickets, cotton mills, and spindles are subsumed by the peaceful, pastoral image of agrarian

Greene County. It is fitting that Book II of *Tenants of the Almighty* opens and closes with preindustrial scenes of nonmechanized labor in the fields and close-up portraits of two young farmers—a black woman and white man. These images create a neat narrative arc of past, present, and future linked to the land. Like Delano's photographs of poor black and white farmers that focused on their dignity and nobility, the heroes and protagonists of this book are the county's rural residents who retain their agrarian roots in the face of rapid change. Even the title of Raper's book, taken from a poem by a local black woman, Louisiana Thomas Dunn, reflects the book's agrarian focus and its message of redemption, stewardship, and community that transcends its academic origin and technocratic and bureaucratic purpose.

We are tenants of the Almighty
Entrusted with a portion of His earth
To dress and keep
And pass on to the next generation
When evening comes and we must fall asleep[72]

Reviewers from the pages of the *New York Times* to the local Greensboro paper, the *Herald-Tribune*, almost uniformly praised *Tenants of the Almighty* for its realistic portrayal of the rural South and the beauty of Delano's photographs. The Greene County paper ran a review by Wayland J. Hayes, a Vanderbilt University sociology professor, which highlighted the book's powerful sense of realism: "The book produces the feeling of actually living in the county and knowing the people intimately." Caroline Sherman, writing in the journal *The Land*, also noted the power and immediacy of the book and its ability to get "its story of Greene County well into the consciousness of even a superficial reader." Russell Lord, writing in the *New Republic*, declared that the "author and photographer are at one in a burning sense of compassion for the poverty-stricken subjects of King Cotton, and for the heart-breaking humility and courage of their efforts to improve." Like many reviewers, Lord reserved particular praise for Jack Delano's photography: "No other photographer, not even Dorothea Lange, can show shining through a body of land, or buildings, or hands or backs and faces, the living spirit of the people more clearly than Jack Delano."[73]

Almost all of the reviewers who praised Delano's photographs focused on his images of the black and white rural poor or of the landscape. The book's sense of realism and the respect and compassion Raper and Delano demonstrated for their subjects were common refrains. Some reviewers also noted, at times unwittingly, the aesthetic relationship between blight and beauty, between poverty and an emotional sense of redemption that was particularly evident in Delano's photographs. "But the volume itself is a large one with magnificent photographs by Jack Delano of the FSA," Caroline Sherman wrote. "The work-eroded hands and feet and faces of some of the Negroes and laboring whites he pictures are quite as shocking and appealing as the deeply gullied soil. Here and there youth and improvement and serene age adumbrate recompense for today and hope for tomorrow." Worn-out hands and soil, when presented within the borders of a carefully crafted photograph, elicit an initial sense of shock that gives way to a recognition of their aesthetic appeal. Here, again, a well-intentioned and "compassionate" documentary portrait with a reformist agenda transforms a sociopolitical issue of power and powerlessness in the cotton culture of the rural South into romantic art. The relationship between poverty and aesthetic beauty also resonated for Russell Lord in another review he wrote for the *Land Policy Review*: "Delano's pictures are marvelous. The grief and hope and courage of Southern poor blacks and whites shine through his photographs of fields, huts, churches, hands, backs, heads, people." Time and again, Delano's documentary photographs with their beautiful depiction of the rural poor and the South's landscape captured the imagination of reviewers, who tended to celebrate Delano's pastoral vision, rather than critique the underlying structures of exploitation they also suggest.[74]

While reviewers, who were all white and generally sympathetic to New Deal reform, praised Delano's photographs, his images did receive criticism from outside of the media. Marie Brown Frazier, the wife of prominent black sociologist E. Franklin Frazier, criticized his photographs for what she saw as their *lack* of realism. While working on *Tenants of the Almighty*, Raper visited the Fraziers at their Washington, D.C., home and showed them Delano's photographs that would appear in the book. Raper recalled this conversation, beginning with his question to the Fraziers: "'What do you think of a spread of pictures like these?' Mrs. E. Franklin Frazier, in her well-appointed living room, said, 'These folks don't look like that. These are not fair pictures.' Raper replied, 'That's the way they look when Jack Delano's taking the picture and I'm talking with them. That's the way they look.'" Raper did not indicate which photographs Mrs. Franklin objected to nor what she believed a more accurate portrayal would look like. Nor did he mention what E. Franklin Frazier, who later criticized the racism found in Howard Odum's early sociological writings, particularly *Social and Mental Traits of the Negro*, thought about the photographs. Raper's response to Mrs. Frazier indicates that he did not claim Delano's photographs presented unadulterated reality, but rather the particular interpretation of Jack Delano at a specific time and place.[75]

Most importantly, Franklin's criticism of Delano's photographs reveals how the FSA's photography file from the South and its public reception were, and have been, filtered through the eyes of an educated white class sympathetic to the liberal reformism of the New Deal. The FSA employed only one black photographer, Gordon Parks, during its existence. Parks was brought on the staff in 1942 as a Rosenwald Fund intern and photographed extensively at Bethune-Cookman College and the surrounding black neighborhoods in Daytona Beach, Florida; however, he did most of his work outside of the South, including his iconic series of images from Washington, D.C., of a government charwoman named Ella Watson. As a result, the dominant black image in the South constructed by FSA photographers during the Depression and New Deal must be understood through the background, ideas, and aesthetic sensibilities of individual white photographers like Jack Delano. What Raper and Delano considered realistic could be very easily, and correctly, seen by someone else like Mrs. E. Franklin Frazier as misleading.[76]

The conflicting reactions to Delano's photographs in *Tenants of the Almighty* reflect his own, often discordant, responses to a modernizing rural South still in the clutches of white supremacy, poverty, and peonage that many other documentarians who worked in the region during the Depression and New Deal shared. Delano abhorred the injustice and inequality he found, and he used his talents as a photographer to expose the plight of the dispossessed. The sense of realism and immediacy that documentary photography conveyed, he believed, would move members of Congress to act on behalf of the poor. But while the rural South may have been "tortured," "primitive," "wasted," and "poverty stricken" in his mind, these qualities also contributed to his aesthetic interest in the people who lived there. Delano's depiction of Greene County imagined the South as a place of premodern authenticity untouched by the corrosive forces of mass culture and industry, a place where, however precariously, heroic individualism still survived.

Tenants of the Almighty arrived right at the beginning of what photography critic John Tagg has referred to as "the Breakup of the Documentary Moment," a time he pinpoints in 1943. It was that year, he argues, that "the moment of social documentary—and, one might say, the moment of social democracy in the United States—was over. The convergence of conditions that had worked in the 1930s to rupture the conventions and constraints of consensual culture and open demands for new languages of reality, new guarantees of truth, and new securities of identity no longer held." While the demise of New Deal reform, the transition to a wartime economy, the fracturing of the Popular Front and its cultural movement, and, later, the fears and suspicions of the Cold War era did diminish the era's documentary impulse, a new generation associated with the folk revival of the 1950s would discover and repurpose the images made by FSA photographers like Delano and other fieldworkers. New Deal-era photographs and sound recordings would reappear like revenants from the archive, haunting the minds of young musicians and luring them into the rural South to do their own documentary fieldwork not in the name of liberal reform, but as a search for personal fulfillment, tradition, and authenticity.[77]

CHAPTER THREE

Field Trip—Kentucky

John Cohen, Roscoe Holcomb, and Documentary Expression during the Folk Revival

In May 1959, John Cohen, a photographer and member of the old-time music group, the New Lost City Ramblers, decided to leave New York City with its "grey dirt and second-hand folk music" to do documentary fieldwork in eastern Kentucky. As a high school and college student during the postwar folk music revival's formative years in the late 1940s and early 1950s, Cohen had heard haunting banjo tunes and ballads from southern Appalachia on commercial recordings made during the 1920s and 1930s that appeared on collections like *Mountain Frolic* and *Anthology of American Folk Music*. He also discovered the field recordings from the region that Alan Lomax and his father John Lomax made for the Library of Congress during the New Deal. The songs' tales of "feuding, moonshining, depressions, and striking miners" evoked a more vital, emotionally resonant, way of life in the mountains and provided a bracing antidote to what Cohen later referred to as the treacly "Frank Sinatra style sentiments" that saturated popular music in the 1950s. The aural impact of the recordings ultimately inspired Cohen to seek out their oral sources, to meet the torchbearers of Appalachian song traditions, to learn their songs and styles in order to fill out the Ramblers' repertoire, and to make his own field recordings.[1]

Around this time Cohen also discovered another legacy of New Deal-era documentary work, Farm Security Administration (FSA) photographs, including iconic images of the rural South made by Walker Evans, Ben Shahn, Dorothea Lange, Jack Delano, and others. These photographers' portrayals of the Great Depression appeared like the visual analogs of the era's sound recordings, so it only seemed fitting to display FSA photographs on the covers of New Lost City Ramblers records from the 1950s and 1960s that featured songs from and about the Great Depression. The visual impact of FSA photographs lured Cohen southward to see social and economic conditions redolent of the Depression that shaped the music he loved and motivated him to make his own documentary photographs and films about this fabled place and its musicians. Unlike many of his predecessors, Cohen was an independent documentarian, not a photographer, folklorist, or social scientist employed by the federal government or a university. Personal desire and fulfillment, rather than political advocacy or scholarly study, inspired his fieldwork in southern Appalachia. "I went to Kentucky in the disguise of photographer and song collector," Cohen wrote in 1960, a year after he completed his first fieldwork in Appalachia. "In truth I was a spy, trying to find out what it was in myself that had always sat up to the reports of sounds and a powerful atmosphere which emanated from that part of the country."[2]

From the late 1950s to the 1970s, John Cohen created his own remarkable body of documentary work that disseminated an influential image of southern Appalachia and of individual artists from the region, particularly Roscoe Holcomb of eastern Kentucky, who came to embody the folk revival's search for cultural and personal authenticity—tradition uncorrupted by commercialism, emotion uncompromised by sentimentalism. Cohen met Holcomb by chance one day in June 1959 while searching for fiddlers and banjo players in the coalfields of the Cumberland Mountains. Holcomb lived at the end of a hollow near an old timber camp called Daisy. He was forty-seven years old, a former miner and part-time manual laborer who suffered from asthma, emphysema, a bad back, and black lung and worried about supporting his wife and children. He occasionally played music at square dances and in Pentecostal churches near his home. He hardly stood out in his own community. He was just one of the "good old boys," recalls his cousin and celebrated folk revival singer Jean Ritchie. Yet by 1966, Holcomb was a "rural star," as Robert Shelton wrote in the *New York Times*, elevated by John Cohen, one of the "city field students who have collected people while collecting folk song."[3]

Holcomb's transformation into an icon of the revival and a muse for musicians like Bob Dylan, Eric Clapton, Jim Morrison, and so many others began that hot, muggy June day soon after Cohen heard him perform a song he composed called "Across the Rocky Mountain." The pulse-like rhythm, combined with Holcomb's reedy, yearning voice and the driving, droning notes of the guitar, which he tuned high to sound like a banjo, mesmerized Cohen; later, in 1962 Cohen would describe Holcomb's music as the "high lonesome sound," a descriptive phrase that later become synonymous with bluegrass music. The song sounded both ancient and modern, a medieval chant mixed with the abandon of the twentieth-century avant-garde.[4]

During the 1960s and 1970s, Cohen recorded, photographed, and filmed Holcomb in Kentucky, across the nation, and in Europe where they shared the stage as performers at folk music festivals. Cohen in turn produced a powerful body of documentary work, including recordings that appeared on

Folkways Records LPs such as *Mountain Music of Kentucky* (1960) and *The High Lonesome Sound* (1965); photographs that accompanied those records and appeared in magazines, newspapers, and gallery exhibits; and a groundbreaking documentary film, *The High Lonesome Sound: Kentucky Mountain Music* (1963). Holcomb became the personification not only of the folk revival's ideals—Cohen said that Holcomb had "come to represent tradition, pure and living"—but also of a mythic image of southern Appalachia itself. Cohen emphasized Holcomb's isolation from a young generation in the mountains that was then embracing popular culture that infiltrated Appalachia via radios and television. Holcomb, like his native region, appeared as a heroic holdout resisting the trends transforming the rest of the nation. According to Cohen, "he was part of a vanishing breed of people who have held onto their own traditions despite mass-culture. His attachment to work, and to the land is becoming a rarity."[5]

Mythologizing Appalachia's supposed premodern purity was not unique to the postwar folk revival, of course. Like some of the South's other subregions, Appalachia had been portrayed by generations of folklorists, songs collectors, and writers as an isolated idyll that in particular nurtured the last vestiges of pure Anglo-Saxon culture from corrosive forces of industrialization, urbanization, and immigration. Such chroniclers sought out a "Back of Beyond," in the words of Horace Kephart, who in 1913 published *Our Southern Highlanders*, an idealized documentary account of his early twentieth-century experiences in the western North Carolina mountains: "With an inborn taste for the wild and romantic, I yearned for a strange land a people that had the charm of originality . . . and, in Far Appalachia, it seemed that I might realize the past in the present, seeing with my own eyes what life must have been to my pioneer ancestors of a century or two ago." Cohen's descriptions and images of Holcomb at times evoked similar myths about Appalachia folk created by writers like Will Wallace Harney and William Goodell Frost in the late nineteenth century; song collectors like Cecil Sharp and writers like Kephart in the 1910s; photographers like Doris Ulmann in the 1930s and those associated with the FSA during the New Deal; and by members of the Popular Front in the 1930s like Charles and Pete Seeger, and Woody Guthrie, who championed and mythologized another Kentucky balladeer and mining strike organizer named Aunt Molly Jackson.[6]

Cohen broke from his predecessors by combining elements of old myths of southern Appalachia with new insights provided by the postwar folk revival, as well as modern art and thought, specifically abstract expressionism, existentialism, and the Beat movement. Holcomb's art seemed to display for

Cohen and some of his peers the same force, movement, and vitality of artists like Jackson Pollock or Robert Rauschenberg. Jon Pankake, editor of the folk revival magazine, *The Little Sandy Review*, described Holcomb and his music as "at once so archaic and so abstractly avant-garde" and as "the most moving, profound, and disturbing of any country singer in America." His admirers also romanticized his apparent isolation not only from urban America and popular culture but also from his own community in Perry County, Kentucky. "He was so much of the mountains and their culture," Mike Michaels, a participant in the folk revival from Chicago who knew and visited Holcomb in the 1960s, later wrote, "but the artist within him that had created such unique music ultimately set him apart from his family and neighbors." Maintaining his image as a torchbearer of Appalachian tradition relied in part on emphasizing his roots in the poor and, apparently, isolated hollows of eastern Kentucky, while his image as creative genius and avant-gardist required depicting him as separate from the people and places that comprised the region. What made him unique also made him isolated, and Holcomb became the image of the solitary existential hero who expressed life's dilemmas in anguished, uncompromising music.[7]

Unlike the previous generation of documentarians and folk musicians, Cohen shunned the political implications of his work. He dispensed with the radicalism of his predecessors of the 1930s who often viewed folk songs as proletarian protests against capitalism and fascism. The anticommunist crusades of the 1950s that persecuted politically engaged folk groups like the Weavers and blacklisted performers like Pete Seeger and folklorists like Alan Lomax, who fled to Europe during the 1950s, led Cohen to focus more on the aesthetics, style, and philosophy of folk music than on its politics. At the same time, Cohen avoided the liberal reformism of New Deal documentarians like Jack Delano who saw their work as instruments of social change orchestrated by the federal government. Writing about the ideals of the postwar folk revival, including those who engaged in "first-hand research," in response to critiques by Lomax, Cohen argued that the "emphasis is no longer on social reform or world-wide reform. The effort is focused more on a search for real and human values." This included a desire to understand, but not reform, the "way of life" of musicians like Holcomb and "to respect them as people who have something to offer in their way."[8]

For Cohen, doing documentary work therefore became a process of personal, human interaction, not of cultural salvage or appropriation. Rather than seeing someone like Holcomb as solely an "informant," Cohen emphasized his identity as an "artist." Meeting someone like Holcomb and documenting his music and life in the process, Cohen hoped, could also forge relationships and apprenticeships between city revivalists and southern artists and "find linkages between peoples who would otherwise be opposed to one another" in terms of political views and cultural backgrounds. "We were putting our stamp of approval on these white guys who until that time had been stereotyped as racists, lynchers, and all those nightmarish things about the South," Cohen later recalled. Free from the institutional, academic, and governmental demands and restrictions faced by a previous generation of fieldworkers in the South, Cohen believed he and others like him had established a new model of documentary work that emphasized cross-cultural exchange and personal fulfillment. "We set a model of activity," he wrote in 1992, "which encouraged many other young people to do similar work in the field: collecting, recording, meeting and getting to know traditional musicians as people and as friends—learning to play their music, as a form of personal enrichment."[9]

A sympathetic interpreter, Cohen still controlled the means of representation. He acknowledged that subjective desires and motives dominated the documentarian's objective conceits. Documentary workers revealed and described, but also framed, selected, and interpreted. "Although I had come to Kentucky to document what I heard," Cohen later reflected, "inevitably the undertaking required me to become an editor. I was put in the position of determining . . . how [Roscoe] was presented, and photographed. Like it or not, my task was to shape Roscoe's image. I was uneasy with this situation, but then again, there were few alternatives." Ultimately, Cohen's documentary work turned him into what historian Benjamin Filene has called a "cultural middleman," someone who, like other folklorists, musicians, and documentarians such as John and Alan Lomax, "'discovered' folk musicians, recorded them, arranged concert dates for them, and, usually, promoted them as the exemplars of America's musical roots." Cohen, in turn, created a "cult of authenticity" around Holcomb and the music and culture of southern Appalachia during the height of the American folk revival from the late 1950s and into the 1970s.[10]

Cohen occasionally faced criticism and resistance, even from Holcomb and his family, in his role as documentarian and "cultural middleman" that sometimes justified his feelings of unease. He recognized early on that many people in Appalachia deeply resented their portrayals in popular culture as pathologically poor hillbillies in an otherwise prosperous nation. These tensions exploded eight years later when Hobart Ison shot and killed visiting Canadian filmmaker Hugh O'Connor in Jeremiah, Kentucky. While Holcomb was a willing participant in Cohen's fieldwork and performed at folk festivals, he also challenged Cohen's broad access to his life by refusing to perform or be filmed for an extended period while Cohen was shooting his documentary *The High Lonesome Sound*. Holcomb's wife Ethel also expressed outrage about how Cohen portrayed her husband and their corner of Kentucky and questioned the legitimacy of images that many in the folk revival saw as beautiful documentary art and evocations of pure "tradition." If Cohen made Holcomb and southern Appalachia into sites of representation for a national and international audience during the 1960s and 1970s, some in Appalachia, including the Holcombs, occasionally countered and created their own sites of resistance.[11]

John Cohen: Folk Revivalist and Photographer

In 1948, at the age of sixteen, John Cohen first heard Woody Guthrie's *Dust Bowl Ballads* at summer camp at a site called Turkey Point between Saugerties and Kingston, New York, north of New York City. The music entranced him. Guthrie's ballads and other albums of old songs and fiddle tunes sparked Cohen's fascination with old-time music. This music also evoked a romantic life in rural America where a young man could discover more "visceral" experiences than his suburban "cocoon" on Long Island offered. "It reawakened memories of my imagined peasant mother and sent me looking for a large world outside the suburbs," Cohen recalled. At Turkey Point, he listened to a record compiled by Alan Lomax called *Mountain Frolic* that gave Cohen his first glimpse into the world of old-time music and string bands; there he also learned how to make and play a banjo. When Cohen returned to his suburban high school in the fall, familiar with sounds from Appalachia and interested in playing the guitar and banjo, he began to feel alienated from his peers.[12]

Cohen's sense of alienation persisted when he attended Williams College in 1950. Fraternities dominated the school's social scene, and he met no one with a fascination for folk music. He found solace playing the banjo in his room and listening repeatedly to the Library of Congress recordings in the school's library. At night, he tuned his radio to WWVA and listened to country music broadcasts that came from many miles south: "The songs spoke of Honky Tonk life and cheating wives and husbands on the one hand, and of the longing for home, farm and tradition, on the other." Enraptured, Cohen spent his first summer after college hitchhiking to Virginia and North Carolina to experience the music firsthand, perhaps from the renowned western North Carolina musician, Bascam Lamar Lunsford, known as the "minstrel of the Appalachians," whose songs Cohen had heard on various anthologies and on Lunsford's own Folkways record from 1953, *Smoky Mountain Ballads*. When one of his rides stopped for gas somewhere in Virginia late at night, Cohen noticed the bugs swarming around the station's lights as a radio outside blared Flatt and Scruggs. He had heard Flatt and Scruggs before, but never so close to the source. Their songs and the setting seduced him. Unfortunately, Lunsford refused to meet with Cohen when he learned that he was from New York and Jewish, and he would have to make another trip to southern Appalachia to record and learn from traditional musicians there.[13]

Fed up with the preppy culture of Williams, Cohen transferred to the art school at Yale in 1951 and fell in with a group of students and professors who played a profound role in shaping his career. Cohen found Tom Paley, a mathematics graduate student, who shared his passion for southern folk music. Cohen, Paley, and other enthusiasts started hosting and promoting "hootenannies" in 1952 and 1953. Early on, the "hoots" attracted only a few art and graduate students, but word spread, and the next thing Cohen knew "two or three hundred students were showing up to sing with us on Friday nights."[14]

In 1952, Cohen also sought out Reverend Gary Davis, a blind blues and gospel singer originally from South Carolina and then living in Harlem. He started hanging around with him, recorded his music, and documented his daily life. Cohen followed him as he begged in the streets and even accompanied him to a "testimonial show" in Harlem that honored him. He was unaware of the records "Blind Gary" had made in the 1930s when Davis lived in Durham, North Carolina. Members of the folk revival of the 1960s would later worship Gary Davis as an authentic black folk artist, and Cohen's interest in his music and his careful photographic documentation of his larger social and cultural life prefigured his later fascination with Roscoe Holcomb. For Cohen, Davis represented the marginalized, segregated, isolated "folk" whom he had to leave his middle-class surroundings to discover. The search in the city anticipated Cohen's travels to Appalachia where the white folk musicians lived supposedly isolated lives that nurtured indigenous, noncommercial music traditions. Davis's status as an urban dweller did not diminish the apparent authenticity of his music because he, like many black people living in New York City, had roots in the South. If you were an urban folk revivalist who could not afford to travel to the South, you could at least take the train to Harlem.[15]

Cohen spent time playing hoots and hanging out with musicians at the same time as he was pursuing his formal education. At Yale, he studied painting with Josef Albers and photography with the Swiss artist Herbert Matter, who introduced him to another Swiss photographer "in retreat from the Swiss bourgeois life," Robert Frank. While at Yale, Cohen also learned about archaeology, anthropology, and Peruvian textiles and combined these interests with his lessons in color studies from Albers to develop an abiding interest in weaving. As part of his Master of Fine Arts (MFA) project at Yale, Cohen traveled to Peru in 1956 to study weaving and used the opportunity to photograph extensively. He would return to Peru on numerous occasions during the coming years to photograph, film, and record indigenous music. He found there an isolated group of people, their mountainous surroundings providing a bulwark against outside influences that might change their indigenous culture. Eastern Kentucky would later remind him of Peru.[16]

After graduating from Yale, Cohen returned to New York City and began his life as an independent photographer. He did some of his early work at black Pentecostal churches in Harlem. While at Yale, Herbert Matter had made some short films documenting the dancing in black churches, and Cohen had tagged along. Later in 1957, he recalled, "I just went up to Harlem, Sunday morning, walked around and listened for that sound." He would walk up a dark staircase and follow the source of the sound until he came upon a room with about eight people inside, all darting about in a trance. "How they could tolerate me or how I made myself present with a camera in a small room [was] pretty nervy," he remembered. But the experience and the emotion were just as important to Cohen as the act of shooting photographs. "I loved the music, I loved the energy," he said. "In every sense they filled my needs with a great mix of spirit, music, dance, trance, and raw energy. There wasn't room for anything else." The black Pentecostal church service fulfilled Cohen's same aesthetic and emotional desires that the southern mountains did: those small Harlem rooms mirrored the isolation and spatial distance of a place like eastern Kentucky. To Cohen, they were veritable incubators of music, emotion, and energy, and he connected the frenetic energy encountered there with the abstract expressionist art scene on the other side of the city. On any Sunday morning, he might witness an ecstatic service at a black Pentecostal church in Harlem and then that night see Franz Kline, Philip Guston, or Willem de Kooning in Greenwich Village.[17]

In New York City, Cohen lived next door to Robert Frank, the Swiss photographer he met at Yale, in the Lower East Side. In 1957, before his book

The Americans was published, Frank showed Cohen a stack of photographs he shot during his travels across the country, and these photographs captivated Cohen, showing him another way of seeing his surroundings. Frank focused more on the interiority of American life—the "hollowness and corrosion" that lurked beneath the sheen of mainstream middle-class society—compared to FSA photographers. Cohen believed Frank's photographs evoked a visceral and subjective response that focused on emotion and feeling.[18]

During the late 1950s, Cohen also worked in New York as a photojournalist, but found the freelance life frustrating and uncertain. He and other photographers responded by creating an informal organization of independent photographers, including Lee Friedlander and Garry Winogrand, that held meetings at Cohen's loft. Cohen found his assignments mostly dull and unsatisfying, although he did get an eight-page spread in *Esquire* for a photo-essay on motorcyclists at a rally. *LIFE* also paid him for his photographs of the Beats, including Jack Kerouac, Allen Ginsberg, and Gregory Corso, that he took on the set of *Pull My Daisy*, a pioneering experimental film made by his neighbor Robert Frank. Cohen used that money to finance his first trip to Kentucky during the late spring and summer of 1959. Cohen hoped his trip would help him establish an independent means of making a living, one that fulfilled creative desires, rather than stifling them.[19]

Cohen's idea for a Kentucky trip emerged from his involvement with an old-time music group he formed in 1958 in New York City with Tom Paley, his friend from Yale, and Mike Seeger, Pete Seeger's younger half-brother. The three called themselves The New Lost City Ramblers. They bonded over a mutual obsession with Harry Smith's seminal *Anthology of American Folk Music*, which came out on Folkways Records in 1952. The collection's powerful combination of creative packaging, Smith's humorous annotations, and the occult sounds of distant folk cultures seduced all three. Southern music provided a vicarious connection to a distant place very different from Long Island or Greenwich Village. Writing in 1966, folklorist Ellen Stekert argued that for the "middle-class white (sub)urban youth" like Cohen and his peers "to 'suffer' with the downtrodden"—including the "Negro" and "Southern Mountaineer"—"has become the ideal; in a society where there is little left that is not synthetic, aping the 'natural man' has become an end in itself."[20]

When Cohen and his friends listened to the *Anthology*'s songs, they heard the "voices of people from the rural tradition" facing their own worries and singing about them in their own style. The revivalists projected concerns on the thoughts and emotions of folk singers from the rural South who, they believed, felt similar internal anxieties to their own. They used the language of existentialist philosophy prevalent in the literature and art of the 1950s' American underground and intelligentsia to construct their image of the folk performers on the *Anthology*, such as the Carter Family or Dock Boggs, who, they believed, shared their sense of alienation from postwar America. Alienated from the malaise of modern life that produced and surrounded them, Cohen and his peers had to look for personal and creative authenticity outside of themselves and their native cities and suburbs. They found this authenticity, and a reflection of their true selves, in their discovery of folk music on 78 RPM discs and musicians in remote corners of the southern mountains. In this regard, the postwar folk revival was less a revival than a personal quest "where one searches to encounter his own image in the world" and not simply remake the world in one's own image, as Cohen wrote in the liner notes to the New Lost City Ramblers' first record from 1958. "In this process one examines all kinds of elements which come in his path."[21]

By reproducing the old songs in their performances, the Ramblers hoped to convey the same power and authenticity they discovered when listening to old 78s and LPs. "There are certain qualities which we demand from the music," Cohen wrote in *Sing Out!* magazine in 1961, "a sense of immediacy, of personal involvement, a sense of tradition as well as appreciation for that which carries things to a point where they can go no further—a feeling of 'way out,' a rejection of compromise for commercial or artistic reasons, an obsession with the song material." Cohen's desire for immediacy, experience, *and* transcendence—a "feeling of 'way out'"—guided not only his relationship to traditional or old-time music but also shaped his documentary work and how he represented someone such as Roscoe Holcomb. Cohen drew from the same aesthetic and emotional well when playing old-time music or making photographs and films about musicians and their cultures.[22]

Two years earlier in the pages of *Sing Out!* Cohen responded to charges leveled by Alan Lomax who had accused "citybillies" and "folkniks" of not understanding the real emotion of rural singers in their efforts to play authentic folk music. Cohen countered that Lomax assumed an elitist position that characterized him as a "holy ghost" sent from on high to reveal the gospel of true folk music. Cohen portrayed Lomax as out of date and unaware of the new ideas that characterized the folk revival in the United States. While Lomax had been out of the country collecting folk music across Europe (and avoiding the House Un-American Activities Committee hearings), he missed folk music's shift in emphasis from what Cohen characterized as "social reform or world-wide reform" to a movement "focused more on a search for real and human values."[23]

Just as there was a shift in documentary photography during the mid-twentieth century from producing photographs designed to provoke public reform to a focus on personal experience, Cohen's acknowledgment of the folk revival's existential search signaled a similar transformation, one he believed Lomax did not appreciate. The Old Left and Popular Front politics that Lomax had adopted growing up during the New Deal, and that had informed his important work as a collector and concert organizer during the 1930s, no longer mattered. Cohen looked back to the New Deal era for aesthetic, not political inspiration. The New Deal and Depression, he believed, were a time when people *did* search for values, when people *did* have a cause to fight for, something that defined their place in society. Cohen's search for values used the past to give meaning to an uncertain and seemingly nihilistic present. His quest also pushed him to do more than learn and practice the music of old-time musicians. He felt he needed to go where they lived, to photograph and film their lives and to experience and embrace their culture.

As with the New Left's rejection of top-down leadership and authority during the 1960s, Cohen argued that he and his peers in the folk revival were not "looking for someone to lead us" because they were "looking within themselves." There was no particular "truth," no law or formula that defined folk expression. "The emotional content of folk songs is a different thing to different people," Cohen argued, "and it is hard to say that there is a single, correct way to emotional content." Echoing an old refrain in the romantic tradition, truth, according to Cohen, was "available to anyone who will seek it—and there will be eventually be as many ideas of truth as there are people pursuing it. . . . There is no truth except that which we make for ourselves."[24] Depression songs and eastern Kentucky itself, where an actual depression was ongoing, provided Cohen and others with a vital experience unavailable in the emotionally and aesthetically barren landscape of 1950s suburbia. In the liner notes to the Ramblers' 1959 LP, *Songs of the Depression*, whose cover was a 1935 photograph taken by Ben Shahn for the FSA of two guitarists playing along an east Tennessee roadside, Cohen argued, "There is an element in young people today which feels a yearning for the thirties as a desire to have a clear and humane cause to fight for." While early Ramblers records featured photographs from the rural South on their covers by FSA photographers such as Shahn and Russell Lee, the band used other forms

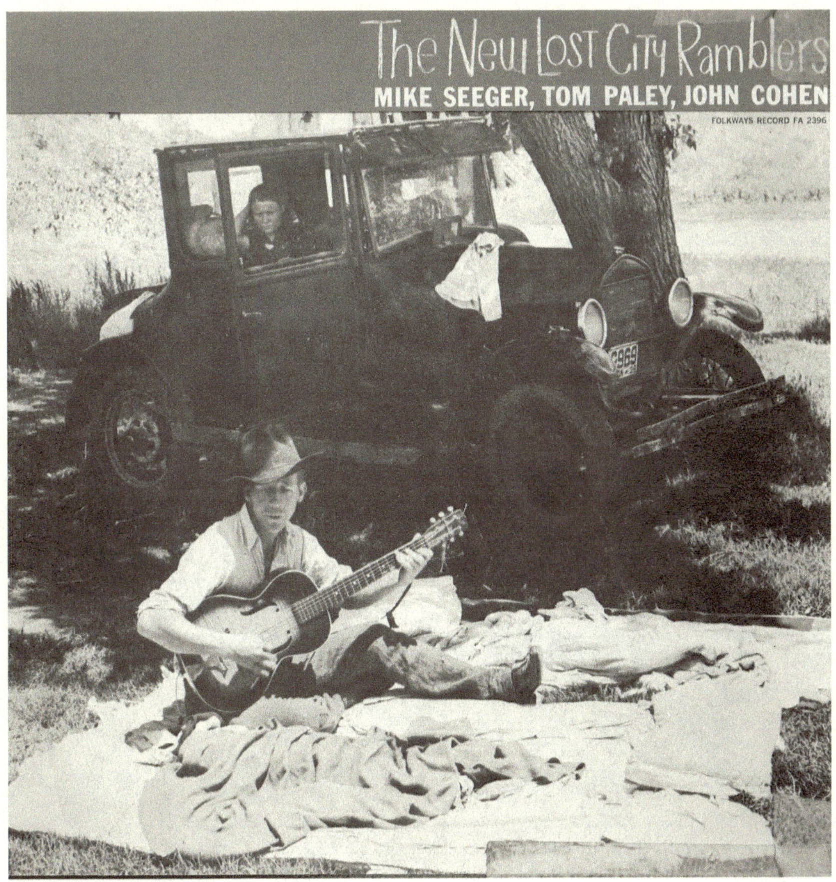

Cover photograph by Russell Lee, Farm Security Administration. *New Lost City Ramblers: The New Lost City Ramblers*, FW02396, courtesy of Smithsonian Folkways Recordings. © 1958. Used by permission.

of New Deal iconography to advertise their concerts, including the Blue Eagle of the National Industrial Recovery Act (NRA) and the slogan, "I am lost. Take me back to 1932."[25]

The 1930s were also when John and Alan Lomax made recordings of some of the songs and tunes from southern Appalachia that Cohen listened to while in college. The plaintive and powerful sounds of Luther Strong's fiddling and Justus Begley's banjo playing, recorded by Alan Lomax in eastern Kentucky in 1937, inspired "awe, just as a poet or artist might view their sources of inspiration," Cohen later acknowledged. For folk music fans, the Great Depression seemed like an incubator of authentic music. The urge to depart the 1950s for the 1930s sprung from the revivalists' appreciation of images of the

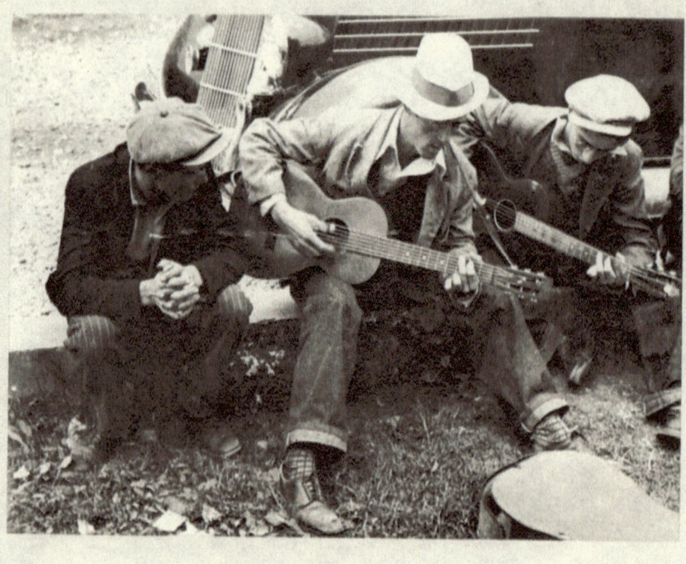

Cover photograph by Ben Shahn, Farm Security Administration. *Songs from the Depression: The New Lost City Ramblers*, FW05264, courtesy of Smithsonian Folkways Recordings. © 1959. Used by permission.

Depression and New Deal, as transmitted through FSA photographs, field recordings, and Harry Smith's *Anthology*, and not from nostalgia for the Old Left or New Deal liberalism. Cohen took the leftist idea of a political cause and aestheticized and psychologized it. To say one had *Gone to the Country*, as the Ramblers titled their 1963 Folkways LP, suggested a state of mind as much as a place in the southern mountains. Going to this imagined rural idyll was a quest for emotional and personal authenticity in a society compromised by commercialism and urbanization. They searched for something "more sincere, nearer nature," one of Cohen's contemporaries, a University of Michigan student, wrote in 1953 of the budding, youth-led folk revival. "The quest of the True Font of Authentic Folk Music by Americans today, and es-

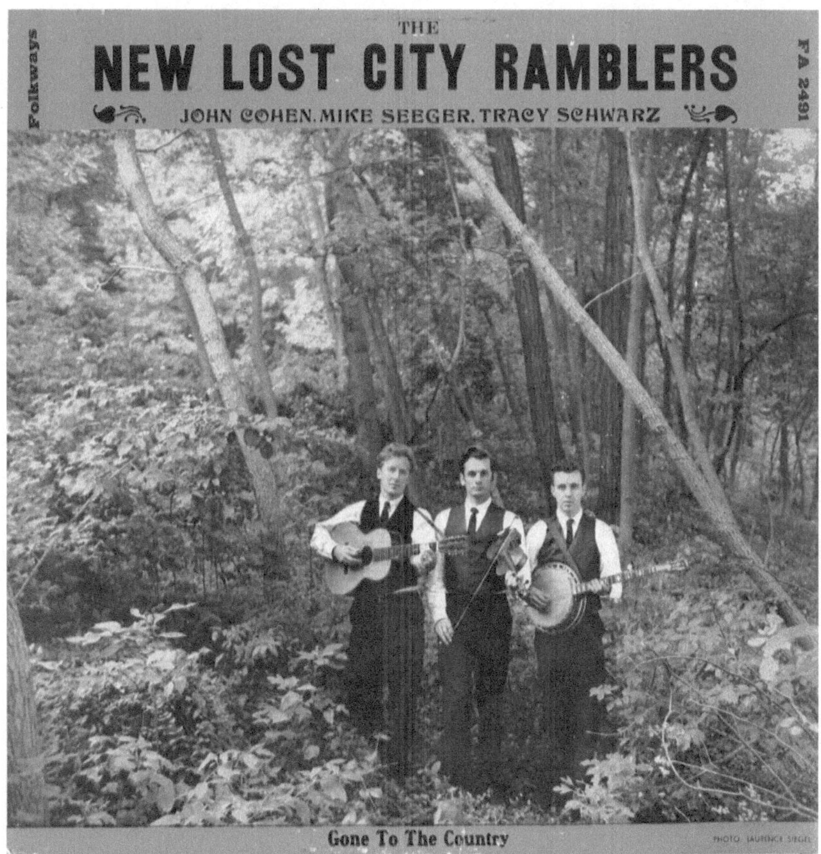

Cover photograph by Laurence Siegel. *The New Lost City Ramblers with Tracy Schwarz: Gone to the Country*, FW02491, courtesy of Smithsonian Folkways Recordings. © 1963. Used by permission.

pecially by college people, is part of the longing for an Authentic Arcadia." Looking back in 1972, Cohen echoed this pastoral vision of the revival: "The feel and the sound of the country experience was the fresh air we needed to avoid being smothered by our immediate urban surroundings. . . . Folk music wasn't a revival for us, it was a discovery of something from which we had been insulated."[26]

Writing for *Mademoiselle* magazine in 1960, Susan Montgomery wondered what lurked at heart of the folk revival, noting that young middle-class folk revivalists were "desperately hungry for a small, safe taste of an unslick underground world." In a "brutal and threatening" time, clouded by prospects of nuclear war and corrupted by materialism, the folk revival, according to Montgomery, functioned as a religious movement led by idealists like John

Cohen—"seekers, value hunters and extremists who are willing to go all the way for something they believe in." Some of the most intense revivalists, committed to embracing and understanding the roots, styles, and aesthetics of American folk music—those whose interest extended beyond participating in group folk sings, festivals, or hootenannies; those who diligently learned their instruments and the significance of the songs they sang—these young adults, as Cohen acknowledged, turned out to be the "best city folk musicians." These same people, Montgomery observed, often wished "*they'd* come from the Kentucky mountains or (depending on the music they play) that *they* had been born Negroes. . . . The sounds and emotions these students sing so furiously are eventually incorporated into their consciences. They are, in a sense, bedeviled people who, even though they are fine musicians, should be counted among the casualties of contemporary American life."[27]

Cohen was certainly not the only person to mythologize the Kentucky mountains as a bastion of authentic folk music, and he was not the only person making field recordings in the area in 1959. Despite jokes that young folk song collectors were overrunning the Appalachians with recording studios dragging behind them, there were actually only a few folk song collectors working during this time. The only other visible collector in Kentucky that year was Cohen's nominal nemesis, Alan Lomax, who visited the southeastern part of the state in early September with English folk singer Shirley Collins, well after Cohen had returned to New York City. Cohen recalled speaking to Lomax in February during the "Folk Song '59" festival that Lomax organized at Carnegie Hall. Cohen mentioned to Lomax his intention to travel to Kentucky to record and photograph musicians. Lomax sensed a competitor and tried to dissuade the naïve Cohen with the cautionary tales of a seasoned folk song collector. "Oh, well you're going to places where they don't have electricity," he warned, telling of carrying heavy batteries up steep hills.[28]

Lomax spoke from experience, having recorded in the region for more than two decades. He and his father John first made a recording expedition into eastern Kentucky in 1933. Alan returned in 1937 with his wife Elizabeth for a two-and-half-month trip while he was employed by the Archive of American Folk Song at the Library of Congress. He came back to the area alone in 1938 and 1942 to make more recordings. In all, the Lomaxes made nearly 1,400 recordings of fiddle and banjo tunes, ballads and hymns, protest songs and religious testimonies.[29] They were hardly the first song collectors in eastern Kentucky, however. Most notable was the Englishman

Cecil Sharp, hoping to find the Elizabethan ballads preserved by years of isolation from modern industrial society.[30] The romanticism expressed by an early collector like Sharp differed from Cohen's. Where Sharp kept his ears attuned for Child ballads, supposed vestiges of old English lineage, Cohen went to Kentucky in part because of its mining culture, which he believed produced the closest thing he would ever get to a setting reminiscent of the 1930s. In 1959, "while the rest of America was busy and prosperous," Cohen wrote, "Kentucky was experiencing a depression caused by troubles in the coal mines." He hoped to find songs sung by miners that would tap into the pathos of a recent past when rural Americans struggled nobly in the face of deprivation and hardship and produced emotionally resonant music. Unlike Sharp and even the Lomaxes, Cohen also saw fieldwork as a personal quest for meaning, not a folkloric, literary, or anthropological mission. "The opportunity to visit traditional artists in their homes was seen as a privilege," Cohen recalled, "an activity of reaching out, a dynamic process that might bring meaning and music to one's own life."[31]

Cohen arrived in eastern Kentucky in May 1959 with a list of contacts provided by Jean Ritchie, an eastern Kentucky native, cousin of Roscoe Holcomb, and heralded figure in the folk revival. He also carried with him another reference that had guided some FSA photographers as they did fieldwork in the South during the New Deal—W. J. Cash's *The Mind of the South*, a book that had nothing to say about life in Appalachia. Harry Caudill's influential and controversial book on eastern Kentucky, *Night Comes to the Cumberlands*, did not come out until 1963. Cohen's limited reading of southern history had taught him how plantation owners tried to establish a Herrenvolk democracy that reinforced racial divisions and mitigated class conflict between white planters and yeoman farmers. Cohen looked out at the economic depression ongoing in the mountains, searching for things that reinforced and added to Cash's analysis.[32]

Nevertheless, Cohen later said he did not want his documentary work reduced to mere political propaganda about poverty and exploitation, which reflected a documentary approach different from his New Deal and Progressive predecessors and in tune with the views of the postwar folk revival and other cultural currents of mid-century America. "I always knew that I didn't want to *use* the culture in the South or in any rural or traditional places that I'd been," he recalled. "I didn't want to use them as examples. I didn't want to point out, 'Look at the poverty here' or 'Look what the capitalist system has done' or 'Look at what the mining system has done.'" Instead, Cohen said, "I am interested in music, culture, and people who I find beautiful, exciting and moving, who I find traditional and wonderful. And that is why I show the whole setting where the music comes from. I don't do it to point out some poverty issue. Really, I'm not interested. That is not my purpose." But, as he would later recognize, it was impossible to push aside the political and economic implications of what he photographed, filmed, and recorded in southern Appalachia. They were part and parcel of the entire documentary process.[33]

Before he started photographing, Cohen spent a few days walking the streets of Hazard, Kentucky, the largest town in Perry County. He observed and thought about how he wanted to represent the region. He considered the "depressions" that drew him to Appalachia, "mining people vs. farming people, religious music vs. dance music." And despite the growing influence of Robert Frank, the photographs from the FSA file still haunted his mind while in Kentucky, shaping the way he saw the landscape. A year before, based on a suggestion by photographer Lee Friedlander, Cohen visited the Library of Congress and spent hours "looking through thousands of images of rural America during the Great Depression. This shaped the way I looked at Kentucky . . . while the impoverished life in the mountains had the look of the 1930s." At the same time, he knew he wanted to avoid the "obvious," what he had seen in photographs and what he knew people like the editors at *Life* expected to see: hillbillies amid squalor. He avoided stereotypical pictures, but chided himself later, knowing that by rejecting these "good" images, he also "kicked out the possibility of sale" for his photographs. Nevertheless, as Cohen wrote his friend Ross Grosman in a letter from Kentucky in 1959, "this leaves me with a strange sense of freedom in relation to what I finally do produce—for it can come from a more personal or profound part of myself."[34]

Cohen ultimately produced an image of eastern Kentucky that was humane, yet still mythic. During his 1959 trip, before meeting Holcomb, he wrote again to his friend Grosman about the impressions and ideas that shaped this documentary vision, revealing the tension between his desire to depict reality and a tendency toward romanticism. "It has been a hard time here in Kentucky and I just don't know how much I have accomplished." He wondered about the ideas and impressions "communicated on film." On the one hand, he felt a "certain spirit of this region is akin to Shakespeare's England, with motivations coming from a sense of gallantry + duty primarily. People here are rugged individuals." On the other, he witnessed a less idealized reality: "But still, there is something which isn't yet clear—which

I can't get with. Although there is real + warm love within families—there is something extremely opposite that—which manifests itself in feuds, shootings, cuttings, etc."[35] Domestic violence and murder occurred everywhere, but in Appalachia such acts became stereotypical "feuds" or signs of a deviant and primitive culture in the minds of many Americans who knew little about the region. Cohen never associated eastern Kentucky with deviance or attributed violence to social pathologies. Instead, the cognitive dissonance caused by seeing "Merry England" in Kentucky alongside explicit talk of familial violence only deepened the region's allure and mystery, just as Roscoe Holcomb's apparent combination of the traditional and the avant-garde heightened the power and artistry of his music.

These regional contradictions played out one day when Cohen drove with two brothers, both banjo players (aged sixty-eight and seventy-one), some seventy miles "out over wild mountain country," he wrote at the time, "to a section of these mountains . . . which is generally feared by people in Hazard—(who also have a fearful enough reputation themselves.)." Their destination was the home of James Crase, an old fiddler whom Cohen wanted to photograph and record. "The music we made (I taped) was just exactly the greatest type which I've only heard before in the Library of Congress." And, yet, while he was among the fiddler's children, grandchildren, and great-grandchildren, he also overheard talk "about local murders, brothers killing brothers, wives killed by husbands, violent automobile accidents, snipings at coal operators, dirty dealing in coal contracting, moonshining, illegal hunting, etc." He also sensed that the home held an "arsenal of guns"—and "all the while we were making all that nice old music." The dissonance produced by the pleasant old-time music and the talk of murder, by the scene of a mother nursing her baby daughter and the whispers of fratricide, intoxicated and bewildered Cohen. Here he was in remote Leslie County, Kentucky, recording seemingly ancient fiddle tunes while a television flickered in the corner of the house. When Cohen wanted to capture these visual impressions of Appalachia, however, his request to make photographs, unlike his request to record music, "was vehemently denied." Someone there had "something particular to fear," and the passionate refusal to allow photography filled Cohen with fear. Nothing else happened that day, he wrote, "but this is the atmosphere in which things operate once you leave your warm bed." The air of violence and resistance wafted among more seemingly quaint and traditional scenes and sounds. The mixture created a place that seemed like no other in America, susceptible to romanticizing.[36]

Imagining Roscoe Holcomb

Cohen finally met the man who embodied all of the ideas and images that he associated with southern Appalachia late in his Kentucky field trip. After spending weeks in the area, he had exhausted the list of musicians Jean Ritchie had provided him and had followed all the leads he gathered at gas stations from mechanics and locals who knew of area banjo players. On a muggy Sunday afternoon in June, he drove along eastern Kentucky's winding mountain roads without a destination in mind. Neon, Bulan, Vicco, Viper, Defiance, Daisy—tiny coal and timber towns with sonorous names popped up around each bend. At Daisy, Cohen turned onto a dirt road on a whim to see what or who might turn up. He approached a couple of small houses and, at the first one, asked some children standing out front, "Any banjo players around here?"

"Over there in that house," they replied.

Cohen pulled up and recognized a young man named Odabe Halcomb he had recorded the night before at a nearby roadhouse.

"What are you doing here?" Halcomb asked, surprised to see this outsider on his doorstep.

"Well, I'm looking for music," Cohen said.

Halcomb turned to his adopted aunt, and Cohen asked her to play a banjo tune. Mary Jane Halcomb played a couple of songs including "Charles Guiteau," about the assassination of President James A. Garfield. Suddenly she announced, "Here comes Rossie!"[37]

When Cohen met Holcomb, he saw "a little, wiry person, stooped from hard physical work, coughing from asthma, black lung, and too much smoking." He was quiet, unassuming, melancholic. But after hearing him play "Across the Rocky Mountain," Cohen said Holcomb "seemed gigantic and full of inner strength." In Holcomb, Cohen found what he had been searching for. Cohen acknowledged his "Appalachian posture," his "hard life," and his "broken health," but these features, along with his conflicted relationship with old and new ways in the mountains, "all gave an edge to his music." Something "heroic and transcendent" emanated from his voice. His singing "had a power that went straight to the listener's core." In fact, "his spiritual concern was beautiful," Cohen recalled, "and always present, revealed with a sharp, cutting expression of pain." The poverty Holcomb faced each day shaped the man and his music, but he never dwelled on it. Cohen nevertheless emphasized the poverty in Holcomb's life, not as a personal burden that took a toll on his physical and mental well-being, though Cohen certainly

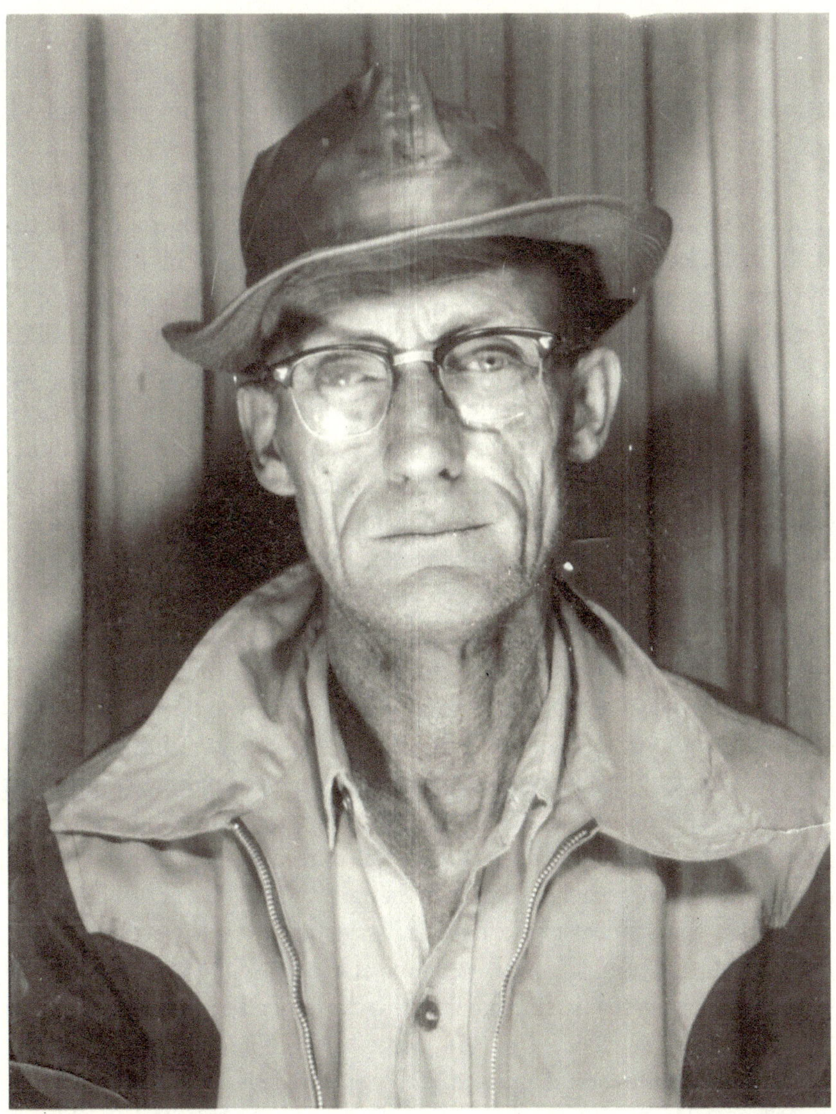

Roscoe Holcomb, undated photograph from a photo booth. Author's collection, courtesy of Odabe Halcomb.

recognized this, but as an abstract force that gave the older musician's music its power, its "edge."[38] Hard labor in coal mines, sawmills, and automobile factories and a long smoking habit left behind a haunting, sui generis sound, "high and lonesome."[39]

In 1959, poverty was only one of Holcomb's many worries. Cohen sensed tension in his home. "His old ways were in conflict with the rest of the household. He was tolerated, but there was little feeling for his music, which was met with indifference or scorn." Earlier in his life he had played with a small country band, but in 1959 if Holcomb played music, he played it alone or occasionally with the older members of his family, such as Mary Jane Halcomb and his adopted nephew Odabe, or with his old friend Lee Sexton. The children in his home (his wife Ethel's from a previous marriage to a miner who died in an accident) preferred to listen to rock 'n' roll music on the radio rather than the old ballads and blues Holcomb played on guitar or banjo.[40]

The tensions and conflicts that defined Holcomb also had roots in the social and economic changes affecting eastern Kentucky during the mid-twentieth century. "Roscoe was right in the center of conflicting Appalachian values," Cohen observed. He was born in 1912, and when Cohen met him, the agrarian world of Holcomb's youth had given way to one dominated by the mining and timber industries. "I was raised up when there were very few coal mines," Holcomb told Cohen, and "we made our living mostly in farming." He was also raised in the Old Regular Baptist church singing slow, solemn, lined-out hymns. But as the Pentecostal-Holiness sect spread throughout the Appalachian region in the early twentieth century, he turned away from the Baptists who believed musical instruments were sinful and, instead, started playing guitar and banjo at a local Holiness church. Nevertheless, Cohen noted that Holcomb still sang the Old Regular Baptist hymns at concert performances and alone at home, "rekindling feelings, reliving lost pleasures, and immersing self and sentiments in days gone by."[41]

When Cohen first met Holcomb, he admitted he "had no idea what he was about. . . . I only knew that he usually worked at construction jobs and that the way he sang his songs had a great effect on me. Now, after almost forty years, I have come to realize I was hearing a man confronting the dilemma of his own existence." Cohen's trip to Kentucky also allowed him to confront his own existential dilemma. Going to Appalachia was for Cohen a pilgrimage, a search for meaning, values, and traditions missing from his own life in New York City. The region's apparent isolation and poverty, Cohen believed, nurtured music that combined tradition with powerful expressions of sorrow. For Cohen and others in the folk revival, Holcomb soon became the personification not only of the region but also of the old songs he sang, like "Wayfaring Stranger" and "I Am a Man of Constant Sorrow," even though he learned them from 78 RPM discs by Burl Ives and Ralph Stanley, respectively. Holcomb often resisted singing "Man of Constant Sorrow" not only because he felt it almost belonged to Stanley but also because he said it was "too true" and revealing of his own feelings and pain.[42]

A year after Cohen met Holcomb and did fieldwork in the region, Folkways released *Mountain Music of Kentucky* on LP with an accompanying booklet of Cohen's notes and photographs. He initially tried to donate his tapes to the Library of Congress, but given his anonymity as a folk song collector the Library refused his offer. Crushed, Cohen went back to New York and contacted Moe Asch, head of Folkways, and asked if he would release his recordings and reprint his photographs. Asch gave him a $200 budget for music editing, notes, photographs, cover design, and typesetting, along with instructions to "pay the artists." Cohen searched for a vivid typeface for the cover, choosing one resembling the type featured on Walker Evans's 1938 book, *American Photographs*. Like Evans's and James Agee's collaborative book, *Let Us Now Praise Famous Men*, which was reissued the same year, Cohen's booklet paired sections of photography and text. His visual and written record captured eastern Kentucky's rugged and verdant landscapes and the mining and agrarian economies that molded the lives of its people in the late 1950s.[43]

Holcomb appears as the visual and emotional representative of the region and its musical traditions on the record, despite Cohen's inclusion of a wide array of singers, musicians, and styles. A photograph Cohen took of Holcomb graces the record's cover. In it, Holcomb is holding his banjo as if playing it while standing in front of a small wooden storehouse with the dark woods of Leatherwood Mountain looming in the background. Dressed in wrinkled clothes and wearing a crumbled broad-brimmed straw hat and horn-rimmed glasses, he stares somberly back at Cohen's camera—the visual manifestation of his version of "Wayfaring Stranger" featured on the record. The photograph, which Cohen later called a "talisman image" because of its cultural impact, evokes the signifiers of authenticity that revivalists like Cohen sought out in music and documentary work: deep, unmediated emotional expression and links to the land and tradition that were missing in the suburbs and cities.[44] "That part of Kentucky may be out of phase with the rest of country," Cohen wrote in 1960 after his recording trip, "but it can work well for itself right there. Those people have ways of doing things and attitudes which we in the city feel missing in ourselves—which is probably one of the big

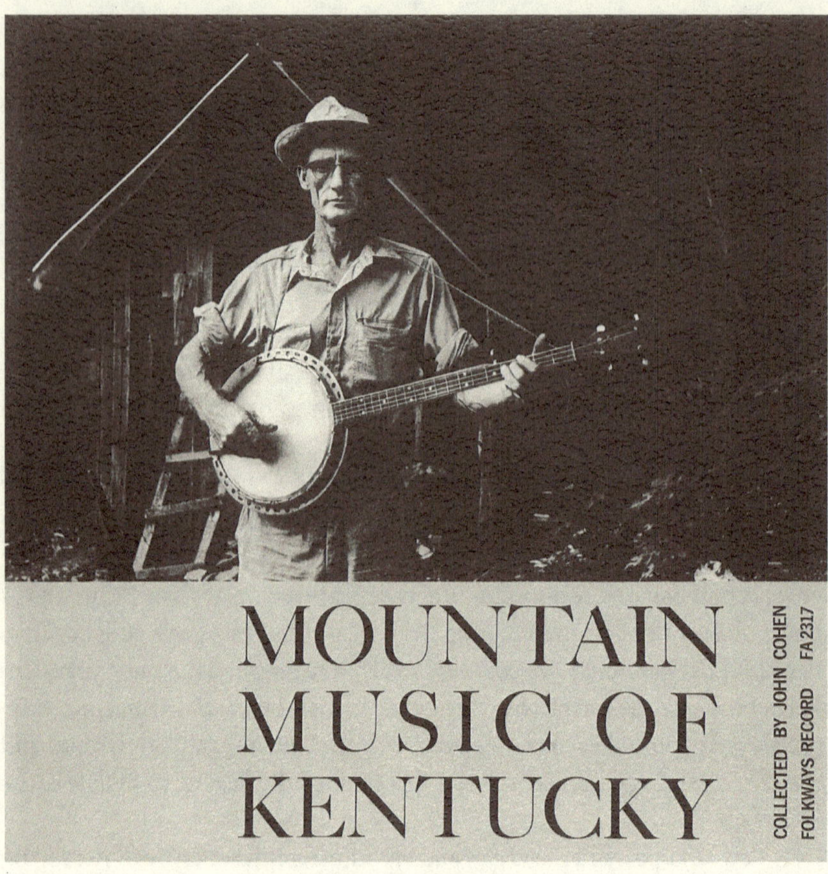

Cover photograph by John Cohen. *Mountain Music of Kentucky*, FA2317, courtesy of Smithsonian Folkways Recordings. © 1960. Used by permission.

reasons we get so much from their songs." With the release of *Mountain Music of Kentucky*, one of those people, Roscoe Holcomb, soon became the embodiment of Cohen's description of the region and a rising "rural star."[45]

Cohen introduced the recordings and photographs on *Mountain Music of Kentucky* with liner notes about the singers and the variety of music that existed in eastern Kentucky in 1959. He took some pride in presenting singers from all walks of life—farmers, coal miners, construction workers, a disc jockey, a housewife, a politician, a banker, and a horse trainer—and music from a range of styles and backgrounds. Listeners heard Child ballads and more recent banjo and guitar tunes, some influenced by the blues. Cohen also provided selections from the main religious traditions in the Kentucky mountains—the Old Regular Baptists who sang unaccompanied lined-out hymns and the Holiness church singers who displayed "a style similar to popular Hillbilly music" that combined "guitars, banjos, cymbals, hand clapping, shouting" with "wild harmony." Along with the diversity of styles, Cohen noted a diversity of motives. For Willie Chapman, a retired miner and a banjoist who played "Little Birdie" and "Jaw Bone," music was an important way "to keep active" in his old age. For Lee Sexton, a coal miner and a five-string banjo player who performed "Fox Chase" and "St. Louis Blues," playing at square dances was a "social role he maintains." But for Roscoe Holcomb, Cohen wrote in his liner notes, "Music has become a deeper means towards a lonely and passionate artistic expression." Holcomb, represented with recordings of "Wayfaring Stranger" on five-string, and "East Virginia Blues" and "Across the Rocky Mountain," stands as the obvious star of the record.[46] Robert Shelton, writing for the *New York Times*, believed Holcomb particularly deserved "to be heard in person at some of the big Eastern folk festivals"— as he eventually would. A *San Francisco Chronicle* reviewer declared *Mountain Music of Kentucky* "one of the greatest records in the entire literature of American folk song" and Holcomb "a true genius of the white blues and Anglo-American ballad."[47]

As the sound and image of Holcomb began to circulate, he came to "symbolize an ideal of the folk song revival," according to Cohen, "a bed-rock 'roots' musician free from adulteration by the commercial recording and academic worlds. He had a backwoods 'purity' sustained by isolation, and if I hadn't found him and recorded him, he would never have looked outside his home community for listeners."[48] Cohen's "discovery" certainly granted Holcomb notoriety he would not have otherwise received, but the exposure created an image that reinforced the romantic myths many folk revivalists held about folk music and folk musicians. Holcomb shared the experience of poverty and "backwoods purity" with some of the other singers on the record. But what gave his music its power, emotional force, and credibility was his ability to express the psychological toll of poor mountain living not through the lyrics themselves, but through a quavering high-pitched voice that channeled the pathos and emotion of old traditional ballads and blues, revitalizing them with his own feelings of anguish. Stylistically, his voice drew from Old Regular Baptist hymn singing, old-time "country," and the blues, particularly Blind Lemon Jefferson, the first black blues musician he had ever heard on record. "Up til then, the blues were only inside me; Blind Lemon was the first to 'let out' the blues." As he told Cohen, "I sing the blues when I feel blue." Even if Holcomb did not mention the sources of his pain, his emotion seemed a personal response to his condition, certified by his image on the record's cover. For consumers who equated apparent isolation and poverty with powerful music, the photograph of Holcomb standing with his banjo in front of a deteriorating wooden storehouse near his house only heightened the authenticity. Producing *Mountain Music of Kentucky* gave Cohen an independent creative control he relished and would never relinquish. Yet, by appearing on the record, Holcomb relinquished creative control of his music and image, something he would never regain.[49]

At times, however, Holcomb and his wife Ethel would attempt to reclaim control over how Cohen and others portrayed them and their home. Lacking access to cameras and recorders, they still found ways to resist or challenge Cohen's representational power while also continuing to cooperate with him. In 1962, Holcomb refused to perform on film for five weeks while Cohen was shooting footage for what would become the documentary, *The High Lonesome Sound*. More immediately, in the aftermath of the release of *Mountain Music of Kentucky*, Ethel Holcomb objected to Cohen's depiction of her husband's and her home. She resented the photograph of her husband that appeared on the record's cover because Cohen showed the unpainted wood-framed storehouse, rather than her nice white home. And it seemed she was not the only one around Daisy who resented that image. "Why do the people around here object to the photograph of your shed on the record cover?" Cohen asked Holcomb two years after the record was released. "The people, when you take these old things," Holcomb replied. "You see, we live in these old mountains here and we've been raised up pretty rough and a lot of them does the best they can do and they take it as if you take the worst you can find to make a picture to take back to New York to show the people. That's the way a lot of them feel about it. Course it don't matter with me."[50]

Although Holcomb said the image did not matter to him, he was not in a position to protest. In general, he wanted Cohen's cooperation, and to call into question Cohen's work would upset their amicable relationship. For his part, Cohen tried to understand where the apprehension from the Holcombs and others in the region came from and why it existed. Something more elemental than music, rooted in the long history of exploitation of the region, fueled their doubts and fears. "Suspicion starts with a feeling of being different from the mainstream culture," Cohen later said, "and comes down to a power struggle over who controls the means of representation." Yet what first attracted Cohen to Kentucky was its seeming difference. Instead of exploiting stereotypes, Cohen used difference to heighten his aesthetic experience of the musicians, their music, and their region. Kentucky mountain people, he wrote, "have been made to feel as if their own way is inadequate in the face of the sophisticated luxuries which bombard them from the national advertisements—and they know the stereotype which the national press has given of them, as ignorant, primitive and barefoot, and they resent it."[51]

The release of *Mountain Music of Kentucky* coincided with the spread of new stereotypes of the "hillbilly" through American culture. In the late 1950s and 1960s, an unprecedented migration of poor Appalachian people from the mountains to the mid-Atlantic and Midwest coincided with a federal War on Poverty that used the region as a symbol of America's failings. Fears of a hillbilly invasion combined with the discovery of Appalachia as an aberrant "pocket of poverty" to produce a mix of anxiety and wonder toward southern highlanders. A 1958 article in *Harper's*, "The Hillbillies Invade Chicago," argued that "the city's toughest integration problem has nothing to do with Negroes," but rather "involves a small army of white Protestant, Early American migrants from the South—who are usually proud, poor, primitive, and fast with a knife." About the same time, television shows such as *The Real McCoys*, *The Andy Griffith Show*, and *The Beverly Hillbillies* played a significant role in shaping public perceptions and stereotypes about southern mountain people. Since Cohen and his peers questioned and challenged the supposed benefits of modern civilization, Appalachia, to them, did not seem deviant or a land of hillbillies, but instead a bastion of authenticity, a retreat from the commercialism of contemporary mass culture. And yet, while folk song collectors like Cohen longed to leave the city for the mountains, many in the mountains yearned for middle-class comfort and a steady city job.[52]

If Holcomb's wife and others in eastern Kentucky resented Cohen's depiction of Holcomb and their home, others praised his humane and evocative images, particularly when compared to more pernicious stereotypes. Folklorist D. K. Wilgus recognized the effort as one of the first to respectfully represent Kentucky folk music and life. "John Cohen's collection of *Mountain Music of Kentucky* is another raid on our resources by a 'furriner,'" Wilgus wrote before adding in the same breath, "but put away your long rifles, boys. We couldn't have asked for a more sympathetic interpreter than Cohen." Cohen, wrote Wilgus, "presents the core without the peeling." An Appalachian journal, *Mountain Life and Work*, expressed similar sentiments by quickly assuring readers that Cohen's record was not another stereotyping of the region's people and culture. "Anyone who is touchy about the subject of mountain people and music, as talked about or misconstrued by outsiders, will thank Mr. Cohen for a sympathetic, 'whole,' treatment of the music and people he met at Hazard and nearby," the reviewer wrote.[53]

Soon after the record's release, Holcomb's image began to circulate widely, appearing not only on the cover of the album but also in the *New York Times* review of *Mountain Music of Kentucky*, in which critic Robert Shelton described the singers as being "rooted in the earth" with the "lusty propulsion of their music reflect[ing] it."[54] What Holcomb's wife and others in the Kentucky mountains found offensive or exploitive, the New York art world to which Cohen belonged during the late 1950s and 1960s found beautiful and poetic. In the fall of 1959, the Image Gallery exhibited Cohen's Kentucky photographs, many of which appeared in the booklet that accompanied *Mountain Music of Kentucky*, and Jacob Deshin reviewed the exhibition for the *Times*. "The dreary world of a Harlan County [Perry County], Kentucky community down its luck is the major theme of John Cohen's one-man exhibition," Deshin wrote. "Suggesting the documentary approach of the early Thirties, when photographers were faced with similar material, the pictures are reminiscent of work in that period, but with a difference. Mr. Cohen adds the poetic touch and the vision of the artist that have become associated with his photography."[55]

The distinction from 1930s documentary photography that Deshin alluded to suggested the influence of photographers such as Robert Frank and Helen Levitt on Cohen's vision and his seemingly more apolitical motives compared to FSA photographers working for the Roosevelt administration. Cohen's search was for beauty and not propaganda, but the unintended consequences of his photographs were no less persuasive. Perhaps in response to Ethel Holcomb's resentment, Cohen shot another photograph of Holcomb in 1964, again holding his banjo, but this time he is dressed in a suit and tie and wearing a fedora. The shot is close up and presents the musician as the larger-than-life figure whom many in the folk revival imagined. Cohen would feature the photograph on the cover of Holcomb's first solo LP for Folkways records in 1965, *The High Lonesome Sound*. Having established Holcomb's rural Kentucky roots, Cohen perhaps felt compelled to temper the image of a poor, aging musician with a photograph that represented eastern Kentuckians' desire to seem less like caricatures to the eyes of outsiders. Yet the image of Holcomb as a premodern rustic "rooted in the earth" could not be overturned so easily, which only confirmed Ethel Halcomb's fears and resentment. A few years after the release of *Mountain Music of Kentucky*, some German filmmakers found their way to eastern Kentucky to make a documentary about the musicians Cohen featured on the record. The film showed Holcomb singing on his porch, dressed in a white shirt and wearing a tie and his fedora hat, while the narrator described him as a

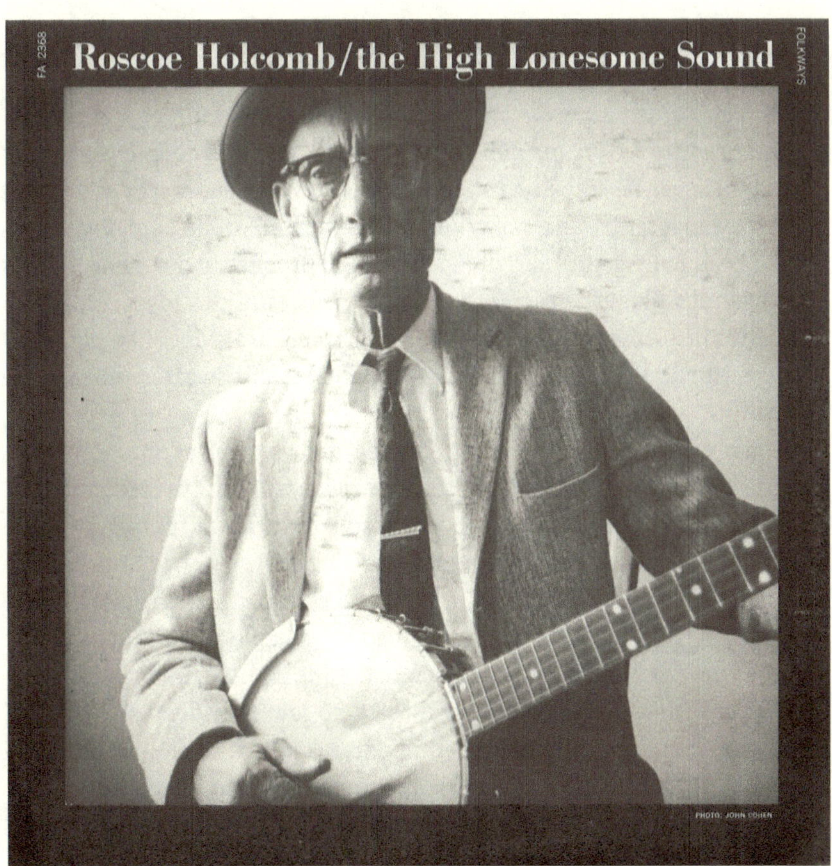

Cover photograph by John Cohen. *Roscoe Holcomb: The High Lonesome Sound*, FW02368, courtesy of Smithsonian Folkways Recordings. © 1965. Used by permission.

strange person "living far back in the woods on nuts and mushrooms which he gathered from the forest floor."[56]

By 1961, *Mountain Music of Kentucky* had sold only 362 copies nationwide, despite enthusiastic reviews from national publications. This meant paltry compensation for the singers, which Cohen regretted. "I'm glad the money we sent you came in handy," Cohen wrote to Holcomb after the record had sold some copies. "I only wish I could've sent more." While sales were slow, Cohen told Holcomb that the "record is serving as a calling card and people are hearing it. The *New York Times* published your photograph and said you were a singer who should be heard at folk festivals." As a way to capitalize on the folk revival's fascination for Holcomb and possibly to generate more income for him, Cohen acted on his role as a "middleman" and brought Holcomb to a festival at the University of Chicago in February 1961. The festival's "key words," according to the *Times*' Robert Shelton, "were tap-roots, tradition, authenticity, and non-commercial." Those who bought Holcomb's records believed he embodied all these attributes. Cohen, however, avoided the demeaning contrivances of other "middlemen" like John Lomax who presented Lead Belly in prison stripes and Big Bill Broonzy in denim overalls as signifiers of folk authenticity to urban audiences in the 1930s. Holcomb dressed as he pleased and often appeared on stage "in a fedora hat, blue suit, white shirt and tie, with a red, white and blue tennis sweater beneath the jacket."[57]

In many ways, Cohen and his peers projected themselves onto Holcomb. Cohen's portrayal of Holcomb as a solitary, romantic, creative artist mirrored in many ways his own existence and resonated with participants in the revival. When he first heard Holcomb sing, he believed he had found someone in the mountains who shared a need for personal expression. "At the first song he sang for me, with his guitar tuned like a banjo and his intense, fine voice, I knew this was what I had been searching for—something that went right to my inner being, speaking directly to me. It bridged any cultural differences between us . . . his sentiment was profound and not at all detached."[58] Holcomb could erase the "cultural differences" because he powerfully expressed the loneliness and alienation that Cohen sometimes experienced as a young man. But what made Holcomb's music authentic and powerful for Cohen were not only its emotional force but also its origin in a world far away from New York. If Holcomb's musical emotion could erase cultural difference, the particular Appalachian poverty that seemed to fuel his emotion reinforced this difference and contributed to the mythic image that Cohen's work spread.

Other revivalists who heard Holcomb's music in the coming years also created a romantic image of him. John Pankake and Paul Nelson, who attended Holcomb's first public concert at the University of Chicago in 1961, mythologized him because of his difference from them in terms of geography, class, and culture. As they described him in 1961 for the *Little Sandy Review*,

> Roscoe is a man's man who returns your handshake firmly and looks you straight in the eye when he speaks to you. He is slender and soft-spoken—yet tough enough to have endured a hard life in the Kentucky coal mines. . . . His feeling for people and his complete immersion in life give his conversation a sensitive, almost visionary

quality. There is really only one topic of conversation with him and that is the meaning of human experience. His every word is a reflection of his thoughtfulness and deep insight—he wouldn't know the meaning of "small talk." He speaks of the people of his region with the poeticism of a good writer, and he knows and understands their poverty, their violence and their loneliness. . . . We watched him walk away wondering if we had talked to a great man—or to a man who only seemed so because he had miraculously come to us from a time and place before the race of Americans had fallen.[59]

Poverty, violence, and semi-isolation in eastern Kentucky certified Holcomb as the real thing. His poeticism and focus on "the meaning of human experience" seemed to represent qualities and ideals that Pankake, Nelson, and Cohen's generation desired. And, yet, they recognized their place among the "fallen" race of Americans—those who participated in and benefited from modernity no matter how much they tried to shun or shed it. If earlier folklorists like Cecil Sharp romanticized Appalachian folk singers as Elizabethan relics, members of the folk revival romanticized Holcomb for his seeming imperviousness to popular culture; he was a man who resembled the existential hero of literature in his lonely quest to maintain a meaningful life in a meaningless society. By the early 1960s, the view of Holcomb held by revivalists like Pankake and others became a kind of bellwether of the revival itself, signaling its core values, motivations, and desires. He became the embodiment of their existential quandaries, their quests to find evidence of a prelapsarian world uncorrupted by the cheap imitations that American commerce churned out. "For me," John Cohen wrote about Holcomb in 1970, "the reception that Roscoe has received in the city has always provided an indicator of the state of affairs of folk music, and of America toward its own traditions."[60]

In 1961, Holcomb made his first trip to New York City to record for Cohen a follow-up to his appearance on *Mountain Music of Kentucky*. The new record, *The Music of Roscoe Holcomb and Wade Ward*, a split release with the Virginia fiddler Wade Ward, "was made . . . when he was here in person to present his music to the city people," Cohen wrote in the liner notes. "On one hand, Roscoe had been wrenched out of his own ordinary background and thrown into the nervousness which seems to particularize the city," he said, "and which brought out this same quality in him." Of course, Holcomb was a worried man back in Kentucky. His physical decline from long years of manual labor had left him unemployed, poor, and unsure as to how he would provide for his family. Cohen emphasized the centrality of work and manual labor in his life, and indeed, for Holcomb, work was more important than music. Few, if any, of Cohen's compatriots in the folk revival could claim a blue-collar background, but Cohen still believed he and his peers felt "something of ourselves . . . in his music . . . qualities and ideas inherent in this music, seldom stated but strongly evident, which give direction and meaning to this."[61]

Cohen also portrayed Holcomb for the first time in terms of the primitive. He emphasized his art's "simplicity," "directness," and its "care" and "honesty which are found in the works of true primitive painters," but in the same breath, he argued that Holcomb transcended primitive and folk art in general. Holcomb's music was a sophisticated and dynamic example of creativity with a parallel "in classical western art, and deserves similar critical consideration." Cohen, a modernist, represented Holcomb as both primitive and avant-garde, folk and high artist, a simple man who worked with his hands and "close to the land," someone whose music's "lack of refinements" and "errors" produced an "artistic statement" full of "brutal reality."[62] Robert Shelton argued that "young collectors" like Cohen continued to find in the "Southern Highlands a bottomless reservoir for music and for the whole ambiance of romanticized rural life that so often embellishes the interest of the music."[63]

Holcomb on Film: The Making and Reception of *The High Lonesome Sound: Kentucky Mountain Music*

Despite exposing Holcomb to a larger audience through recordings and folk festival appearances, Cohen still thought those modes fell short of conveying the complexity and depth of Holcomb's life and the social and economic forces that helped shape his music. In 1961, he traveled again to Kentucky, picking up Holcomb to take him to the Chicago Folk Festival. While driving through the landscape of eastern Kentucky, he thought he needed a more evocative way to present Holcomb's home and music to an audience fascinated by both. On this trip, he wondered about the "tensions, contradictions and beliefs" that made the man. By themselves, listening to Holcomb's music and seeing Cohen's photographs of Kentucky musicians and the mining and agriculture worlds of Perry County, could not communicate "the feeling of having these things happen at the same time." So Cohen decided to "make a movie to bring sound and image together, to try to capture some of the music, culture and countryside."[64]

Once Cohen decided he wanted to make a film, he needed an assistant. Cohen asked Helen Levitt if she knew anyone who might be interested. She sent Cohen a young man about his age named Joel Agee, the son of her friend James Agee; Joel had grown up in Germany, but was then living in the United States and looking for direction. Agee, like his father, was interested in filmmaking, but had never ventured into the interior of America. Neither he nor Cohen knew the first thing about operating a movie camera, but they borrowed one from Albert Maysles who, along with his brother David, had pioneered direct cinema in the United States. Cohen had worked on the set of Robert Frank's experimental *Pull My Daisy,* but only as a set photographer. Before Cohen and Agee left for their six-week filming expedition in Perry County, Kentucky, they decided to practice operating the camera, a 16 mm Arriflex. They went on top of a neighbor's roof with the intention of filming the roofs of Greenwich Village, birds, and whatever else caught their eyes. But before they began, a friend of Cohen's dropped by and wanted them to hear some new songs he had written, so they ended up making a three-minute film of Bob Dylan.[65]

In August 1962, Cohen and Agee left New York City for Perry County. Though Agee "grew up with" *Let Us Now Praise Famous Men,* and Cohen had read it when it was reissued in 1960, neither of them thought much about the parallels between their trip and the one Walker Evans and James Agee made in the summer of 1936 to Hale County, Alabama. Joel Agee said that he never focused on the analogy "very strenuously" and that "there was no project" to do something similar to his father.[66] For the most part, Cohen and Agee lived peacefully together in a rented little house in the timber village of Daisy, a place, Agee remembered, as consisting of "some twenty wooden houses scattered in a valley among rugged hills." Roscoe Holcomb lived at the very end of the hollow. Agee's first impressions of Holcomb were of a man with a "long, haggard face . . . looking old in his early sixties, with thin sad lips and creased cheeks, deep-set puzzled pale blue eyes shaded by a wide-brimmed hat." They spent their days shooting footage, ultimately some nine thousand feet of film, at coal mines, churches, roadhouses, and train yards and in the homes of local residents including Holcomb's. Cohen shot most of the film except for some scenes at the Shepherd family's house, at the train yards, and in the streets of Hazard. "I was unaware of film grammar," Cohen recalled, "which was very fortunate because I didn't shoot cutaways, I didn't think of close-ups versus this and that. None of that training, none of that vocabulary, therefore none of that framework to work against. I was just trying to get the sound and picture together in a strange way."[67]

Cohen's inexperience as a filmmaker, when combined with his unique approach that drew from elements of folklore and ethnography, resulted in a documentary film that he later said possessed "an unusual quality that may never be duplicated." Cohen's camera did not allow for synchronized sound so he had to film and record separately, which occasionally created a feeling of artificiality for him and, especially, for Roscoe Holcomb. When Cohen first arrived at Holcomb's house, he recorded "Across the Rocky Mountains" and then played it back for Holcomb to sing with while he filmed. Cohen stood on top of a long table with the camera set on a tripod as Holcomb sat playing on the porch. The scene was contrived and unnatural. For Holcomb, playing music was a personal, emotional experience, and the awkward recording process felt like manipulation. "I don't feel like singing anymore," he told Cohen after recording "Across the Rocky Mountains." "And he didn't feel like singing for the next five weeks," Cohen recalled.[68]

Ultimately, Holcomb faced more pressing problems in the summer of 1962 than whether or not to accommodate two young men from New York hoping to make a documentary film about him. He was depressed. He was unable to work, and more so than music, work gave meaning to his life. His body had suffered the consequences of years spent working in coal mines and lumber mills, on construction jobs in eastern Kentucky, and briefly at an automobile plant in Indiana. He loved to work, but that summer and fall he was not able to do so. Sometimes the depression that would fall over Holcomb during periods of idleness prevented him from playing music: "I like it [music] and I don't like it; I love to hear it and I love to play sometimes but after so long a time I get burnt out with it. Long as I'm able to work and do, it ain't so bad—been used to it all my life. When I can't do nothing it worries me and you don't feel like playing anymore."[69]

Depression and the artificiality of performing on film certainly played a role in Holcomb's refusal to sing or play for Cohen for more than a month, but so did an urge to claim control of a documentary process that had transformed his life and image. Although Holcomb's warm personality made him wary of causing offense, much like the black singers who refused Howard Odum or the black Georgians resisting Jack Delano's photography, Holcomb's refusal to sing or perform on film challenged the authority of outsiders, even ones he genuinely liked and considered friends, to represent him on their own terms alone.

Cohen would later reflect on why Holcomb ever agreed to such demands and invasions of privacy in the first place: "If it was strange for me to be making recordings in [Holcomb's] house in the hills of Kentucky, I wonder how odd it was for Roscoe to have me as a stranger in his house. I probably would not have been so accommodating to someone arriving this way in my own house." Cohen's recognition that he would not have consented to such a documentary highlights how class shapes assumptions about whose privacy can be compromised in the name of documentary work. These issues of economic and representational power and of resistance made *The High Lonesome Sound,* like any other ethnographic encounter and document, a political matter, though not in the activist or reformist manner Cohen said he disavowed in his work. "Any film dealing with traditional music in its contextual setting must inevitably have political implications," Cohen later wrote in 1990. "The cultures where this music flourishes most strongly are usually the most economically impoverished. The music functions as a rally point for social identity or as a cultural affirmation. Most often, there is an inherent social inequality present, with implicit economic and class distinctions." For Cohen, only a documentary film, it seemed, could capture the true sensory experience of Holcomb's music, which many in the folk revival cherished for its emotional power and historical importance. By resisting the demands of documentary work in the summer of 1962, Holcomb hoped to reclaim his music as a personal and private form of expression that he played on his own terms all the while realizing that contrived public performances, whether on film or on stage at a festival, increasingly seemed like the only way to support himself and his family.[70]

Despite his limiting himself being filmed, Holcomb's brief presence in *The High Lonesome Sound* provides it with its human face and emotional resonance. He appears as both an individual representative of eastern Kentucky's social and cultural milieu, including its musical communities and economic struggles, and an exceptional figure alienated from his community and even his family, because he continues to sing in his inimitable manner the songs and hymns of his past while others embrace the modern pleasures of the present like the radio and even Bill Monroe's bluegrass band. Cohen crafted the film to reveal Holcomb not simply as a singer of ballads, blues, and hymns but also as a person who lived in a particular part of Kentucky, who deeply felt and was largely shaped by the region's social, economic, and emotional pressures, and, yet, whose music was an intensely personal expression of pain and alienation. In *The High Lonesome Sound,* Cohen portrayed

Holcomb as an existential hero, an introspective and solitary creative genius maintaining his uncompromising and "untamed" (to quote Bob Dylan) musical style in the face of the homogenizing and fracturing forces of modernity. The film is both a paean and an elegy to Holcomb.[71]

In the film, Cohen balanced his voice-over narration with Holcomb's voice that described in his own words his life and the role music plays in it. Following some opening scenes of a baptism at a nearby river, the focus turns to Holcomb sitting on his front porch swing. "This is Roscoe Holcomb," Cohen narrates, "an unemployed construction worker who's no one different from his neighbors. He is faced with the same problems that they are—no work and no desire to move out of the mountains."[72] Cohen broke new ground with *The High Lonesome Sound* by establishing the social and economic context in which Holcomb and others lived before documenting the music. Earlier films that documented folk music or folk musicians focused exclusively on the performance of a particular song by a particular musician such as those made by Milton Metfessel and Howard Odum. Folklorist Sharon Sherman traces the rise of the "folkloric film" back to the "March of Time" film series made in 1935 that shows John Lomax interviewing and recording Huddie Ledbetter (Lead Belly) for the Library of Congress. That film focused only on Lead Belly's performance and not the social and economic background of the man and his music.[73]

The High Lonesome Sound, in contrast, provided a new model of folkloric filmmaking when it was released in 1963 by situating the unique musical styles of eastern Kentucky in their social, cultural, and economic context. It showed the distinct religious experiences of Kentucky mountain people by depicting Old Regular Baptist and Holiness services. And it revealed the influx of modernity into the mountains with scenes of mechanized coal mines, pop music playing on a radio at Holcomb's house that his children listened to, and Bill Monroe's band playing bluegrass in downtown Hazard. Cohen presents Holcomb as both deeply embedded in that society and yet also alienated from it. He immediately portrays Holcomb as being similar to his neighbors in terms of class, but soon distinguishes him by allowing him to express deeply felt personal insights into his music and life. Holcomb's class standing, as well as his poverty, almost disappears because the film emphasizes his uniqueness as a musician.

In 1977, Keith Cunningham assessed *The High Lonesome Sound* and its cultural impact throughout the preceding decade for the *Journal of American Folklore*. "Such a great variety of folklore related films is being produced now," he wrote, "that it is difficult even to remember, much less explain, the excitement generated by the film. It became a combination eucharist and shibboleth, and *Rolling Stone* loved it. It is still widely praised and fondly remembered by many folklorists who can agree on little else." While Cunningham thought *The High Lonesome Sound*'s realism and its "comprehensiveness" make it "a good and useful film," he believed what makes it a "great film is its great theme." The film endured and remained vital because it shared a kinship with "Sandburg's poetry, Steinbeck's fiction, Agee's reporting, Evans'[s] photography, Benton's murals, and Dorson's loving description of J. D. Suggs. Through its images, the music it records, and its narration ('Music is the celebration of life.') the film speaks subliminally, as do all the works mentioned above, of the awe-inspiring dignity, beauty, and art of the common man in the face of adversity and hardship." Hardship in the film becomes a mere obstacle—something to fight nobly against, much as Cohen and his peers imagined life during the Great Depression. Replacing the caricatures of the "hillbilly" that festered in popular culture during 1950s and 1960s, and the old associations of Appalachian folk singers as pure Anglo-Saxon relics, was a new romantic focus on the interior life and existential struggles of a singular male hero whose passionate but sad music sprang not solely from isolation but also from a search for the meaning of life.[74]

Very early in the film Cohen reveals the interior emotions and private spaces of Holcomb's life for the viewer. Cohen's camera enters Holcomb's home, highlighting its order and simplicity. Dresses hang against a wall adorned with a picture of Jesus. Two neatly made beds are separated by a table supporting an electric lamp beside a window covered with lace curtains—"the particular look and lifestyle of a rural home," Cohen later wrote. These are not the images of squalor and of sunken and rotting homes Harry Caudill described in *Night Comes to the Cumberlands* and the national media depicted in popular magazines and television documentaries. The Holcombs may be poor, but they maintain an understated dignity. When the camera returns to Holcomb's face, he reflects on the spirituality of music in a voice-over while appearing silent and introspective on his porch: "You know music—it's spiritual. . . . It draws the attention of the whole human race."[75]

The technological limitations of Cohen's equipment meant that he could not get Holcomb's recorded monologue in sync with the filming. Consequently, the scene focuses on Holcomb's face, which wears a pensive expression as he stares out from his porch into the hollow below. The lack of synchronization allows for a deeper probing into Holcomb's interior life, revealing more of his personality. Viewers see him seemingly at ease and indifferent to Cohen's camera. The scene lacks any sense of being staged. This early image, combined with Holcomb's monologue, produced an emotional effect Cohen never intended. "I was pleased it worked so well," he later recalled, "and when I showed my film to other people they said, 'Look. That can work. You can do it that way.'" Cohen's technical naivety and restrictions ultimately made the scene more powerful than if Holcomb's voice and image had been synchronized.[76]

Holcomb's image and voice close *The High Lonesome Sound*, providing a somber parting shot of a "worried" man caught between a fading past and a bewildering present that left him unemployed and alienated. Holcomb sits alone with thoughts and memories and his old Baptist songbook. He sings "The Wandering Boy" in the lined-out, Old Regular Baptist manner in which he was raised. The scene begins in silence as the camera pans across the exterior of Holcomb's house and then toward a dark mountain in the distance. It shifts to the interior of the house where Holcomb sits alone. He begins reading and singing lines from the song and then, toward the end of the scene, slouches on the couch, his face bisected by shadows as he stares off absorbed in thought. His singing of "The Wandering Boy" continues in the background, adding poignancy to the scene. The song's themes of longing for a lost mother and yearning for home make it particularly personal both for Holcomb, who lived at home with his mother until he was in his mid-forties, and for Cohen whose mother's death in his early twenties prompted his own search in the wider world for meaning:

As I've traveled this wide world over
Friends I've found wherever I roam
But to me there's none like mother
None like mother dear at home

They may treat me very kindly
And bid me welcome everywhere
But it just only reminds me
Of a loving mother's care.

Although Holcomb's singing of "The Wandering Boy" was the film's finale, it was not among the last scenes Cohen and Agee shot in Kentucky. On a muggy overcast Sunday morning in September, Cohen returned to Daisy from the Little Zion Old Regular Baptist church in Jeff where, after five Sundays of refusing to be filmed, the congregation (to which Jean Ritchie's mother belonged) finally allowed him to document their church service. The

Baptist church had not been alone in denying Cohen access. The Holiness church in Daisy threw out Cohen and Agee one night when it seemed the presence of their camera prevented the spirit from descending. "I feel the devil moving in this room," Cohen recalled the preacher say. "I'm gonna ask that cameraman to take his camera out of here!"[77]

After the church service, Cohen and Agee returned to Daisy, packed their Volkswagen, and prepared to head back to New York after six weeks in eastern Kentucky. Roscoe, Odabe, and Mary Jane Halcomb sat on their porch watching these two young men stow their equipment and bags. And then, without being asked, Roscoe picked up his banjo and started "playing up a storm" while Odabe and his aunt Mary Jane danced along together on the porch. "And I just dived into the car and grabbed the camera," Cohen recalled, "and no sound."[78]

Cohen thought their impromptu performance conveyed multiple messages: "This is what you missed, or this is what you came for." Or, perhaps, "This is what we wanted you to get, but we couldn't find a way for you to get it," or "This is what we really do. Bye." It happened so quickly that Cohen did not think about the reasons as he filmed. But the scene and the Halcombs' motivation to perform as a parting shot highlight the conflicted relationship between documentarian and documented. Were the Halcombs giving the reality of their lives, or were they performing what they knew Cohen and Agee were after? While Cohen and Agee may have spent the past five weeks walking around with cameras and recorders, the Halcombs still wanted to demonstrate some control over their image.[79]

Cohen also thought that the Halcombs' performance signaled a sigh of relief that he and Agee were leaving "because we were chasing around with [Roscoe] so much," while also suggesting a way to assuage any guilt Holcomb felt for refusing to play music for almost the entirety of their visit. "I'm not sure if guilt is the word," Cohen recalled, "as much as the fact that he agreed that we were making a film and that he hadn't come through."[80] Well after Cohen completed *The High Lonesome Sound,* he reflected on these tacit understandings of obligation that had occurred. Cohen says he always informed the subjects of his films in advance about what he wanted to do and then asked about their wishes. "The concerns for the people who are in the film are very important. . . . If you're really open, then I think people will edit themselves."[81] For weeks, Roscoe Holcomb effectively edited himself by refusing to perform music while being filmed. On that Sunday morning, as Cohen and Agee prepared to leave, perhaps he felt like he got the final word.[82]

Holcomb's Last Years and Legacy in Folk Revival

That fall, while Cohen wondered what kind of reception the newly released film would have, *New York Times* journalist Homer Bigart traveled to eastern Kentucky to report on "the poverty, squalor and idleness." "In the Cumberland Mountains," he wrote in a front-page story, "tens of thousands of unemployed coal miners and subsistence farmers face another winter of idleness and grinding poverty." Those who ventured into the area, he observed, "seldom see the pinched faces of hungry children, the filth and squalor of cabins, the unpainted shacks that serve as schoolhouses. These dramatic manifestations of want and governmental neglect are usually tucked away in narrow valleys, the 'hollows,' off the main road."[83]

Earlier in that summer of 1963, Holcomb had written a letter to Cohen that provided glimpses of the desperation he and others faced:

> Hi John. How are you fine I hope . . . this leaves me OK. I have been working in the garden as I haven't got no other work to do. I lost my job an I don't know where I will find a nothern' at. Well John, I got a letter from Peat Seeger. He said he really like the way I played and sang. John I have been getting letters from just about everywhere. . . . I sure glad to hear that I hope to get more pretty soon if I don't I will have to leave here to find work. . . . So try to get some more work for us—very far I have to go somewhere to find some work. . . . from your old friend, little Rascal Halcomb.[84]

Letters from Pete Seeger and other fans meant nothing materially unless there was a prospect for employment, a way to provide for his family. Holcomb traveled and performed nationally and, later, internationally, for the money, not the fame.

The year after *The High Lonesome Sound* was released, Roscoe Holcomb remained in Daisy, his health declining along with his prospects for steady employment. "Well John I am Having it Pritry tuff," Holcomb wrote to Cohen in December 1964. "I only git 7 Days work a month[.] You know that isn't much[.] I Had Been very Sick[.] I only Way 116 lbs[.]" Still, Holcomb said, "I can sing like a Bird ho ho." Sometime earlier during that same year, Holcomb wrote to Cohen about his predicament and his hope that performing at a folk festival might bring some relief: "This finds me OK. Ethel is some better. John, g[e]t all the work you can for me. . . . Came home, things were looking very bad around here so when you send my ticket send a little extra money for food and I will make it up to you. John, do you want me to bring my guitar? Answer real soon. From your friend, Roscoe." No matter how ill Holcomb got, he wanted to play and sing so that he could support himself and his family.[85]

By 1965, Holcomb's music had appeared on three Folkways records: *Mountain Music of Kentucky* (1960), *The Music of Roscoe Holcomb and Wade Ward* (1962), and *The High Lonesome Sound* (1965). Since meeting John Cohen in 1959, Holcomb had made occasional appearances at folk festivals in California: the Berkeley festival, Ash Grove, and Monterey Jazz Festival. He had performed at festivals across the country, including the Newport Folk Festival in Rhode Island, at concerts put on by the Friends of Old Time Music in New York, and in venues such as Club 47 in Cambridge, Massachusetts and the Ash Grove in Los Angeles. He had also played for adorning students at Brandeis, UC–Berkeley, UCLA, the University of Chicago, the City College of New York, and Cornell. Two students who missed Holcomb's performance at Berkeley's folk festival in June 1962 drove 2,500 miles to Daisy later that summer and appeared unannounced at the musician's door requesting a private concert. "During all of these trips," Cohen wrote in 1964, "no attempt has been made to give him any idea that he could make a living as a folksinger, although the large audiences have greeted him most receptively. It is my feeling that we in the city are given a rare privilege to hear and meet and know this man, but there is no call for him to change his life or his relationship to his home community on our account, and to do so would be misleading and wrong."[86]

Cohen's reflections on Holcomb's folk festival performances seem at once respectful and painfully realistic. The dim prospect of earning a living as a folk festival performer seemed a moot issue to Cohen; for Holcomb it meant much more. He did not leave Kentucky for Berkeley and Cornell just to receive a warm reception. The fact that his recent LP, *The High Lonesome Sound*, was nominated for a Grammy Award in 1965 for the "Best Folk Recording" category "scarcely impressed him," Cohen remembered, and Moe Asch, the founder of Folkways Records, attended the award ceremony in Holcomb's absence.[87] The next year Holcomb appeared on Pete Seeger's short-lived television show, *Rainbow Quest*, which ran for about a year on a few stations in the Northeast and featured folk musicians performing on stage. He seemed nervous and uneasy throughout. Coughing repeatedly, he told Seeger about his personal trials: "Older I gets the worser I get and can't do no work hardly."[88] There is no record of what fee Holcomb received for his performance. Gestures and offers like Seeger's presented a glimmer of hope during a bleak time. He no doubt felt honored, but exposure, praise, or mountain/city cross-cultural dialogue never seemed to matter.

In fact, the class and cultural cleavages between Holcomb and his middle-class admirers in the folk revival often generated conflicts that deepened the divide between his desire to use music to make a living and their urge to harness his image as the embodiment of folk authenticity for their own ends and fantasies. "In the past few years, folk music festivals have seen less and less of Roscoe," Cohen wrote in 1970. "Perhaps his unwillingness to venture out has been caused by home circumstances, but I also suspect that his traditional upbringing was shaken by letters from Peace Movement 'angry artists' which advised him to join their anti-war protests through the cities, and told him how to help young men burn draft cards. Visits to his home community of Daisy, Ky. by hip girls travelling alone in VW buses and offering up wine has [*sic*] not helped the situation either." The cultural divides between Holcomb and his fans, and between Holcomb's desire to profit from his music and the desire of others outside of Kentucky to use it for their own personal, aesthetic, and political ends, culminated in 1970 when Michelangelo Antonioni featured a 1959 recording of Holcomb singing "I Wish I Was a Single Girl Again" in his film, *Zabriskie Point*, along with music by Pink Floyd, the Grateful Dead, and John Fahey, among others. "Roscoe has never heard of Antonioni," Cohen wrote soon after the film came out, "and I doubt whether 'Zabriskie Point' will show at the drive-in in Hazard, Ky., and I can't even send Roscoe a copy of the sound track album from the film, for its psychedelic nudity on the cover and 90% rock music content would only produce more confusion at home. . . . One can't blame these mountain people for having the impression that they are being taken advantage of."[89] Cohen always remained a close, respectful friend of Holcomb, never possessing the slightest inclination toward exploiting or using Holcomb and his music for other than good intentions. But the process of doing documentary work, of spreading sounds and images through popular culture as a way to break through the sterility of that culture, can leave the documented, the Roscoe Holcombs, wondering why they remain as poor as they were before their "discovery."

On a few occasions Holcomb faced such dire circumstances at home that he wrote to Cohen and Moe Asch, the founder of Folkways Records, requesting copies of the records that had turned him into a "rural star" elsewhere in order to survive. Holcomb hoped to sell the records back home to generate income he otherwise could not earn because of his physical condition and the lack of jobs. In 1965, after the release of his third Folkways record, Holcomb wrote to Asch: "Hello Moses. . . . This leaves me not feeling too good; have a very bad cold. Moses I would like to have about 20 records 'the hi an lonesome sound' if you'd care to send them to me I hope this isn't asking you too much, Moses. I haven't got the money now but will settle with you when I come up for the concert." Two years later Holcomb wrote to Cohen with even more urgency: "I need some more records — send me 6 of me and Ward [Wade Ward], 2 of the first one and send 6 of the hi lonesome sound — send them as soon as you can and that will help me get money to go to the Doctor."[90]

Despite his physical infirmities, Holcomb also relied on folk festival performances to make a living, but the income he earned often created new, unintended problems. In March 1966, he left the United States for the first time to perform in Europe for three weeks with Ralph and Carter Stanley. On tour Holcomb occasionally shared the stage with Ralph Stanley, and the two would sing together from a Baptist songbook. After Holcomb returned home, the Department of Economic Security in Hazard cut his public assistance money, which was his only reliable source of income. Out of work and out of money, Holcomb found himself facing complete deprivation. Cohen knew this, and he left New York for Kentucky to plead with the department staff to restore Holcomb's income, "but they didn't listen," he recalled. "In fact, someone in that office tried to convince me that Roscoe's wasn't a good singer, and offered to take me to someone who was a 'better musician.'" Cohen left more certain than ever that "Roscoe's music wasn't much appreciated in this locale."[91]

More than a decade later, on May 7, 1978, Holcomb summoned the energy to travel to New York by bus and perform for the final time in public at an event sponsored by the famous flutist Paula Prentiss at the Brooklyn Academy of Music. His final song was an Old Regular Baptist hymn. These old hymns often made him choke up on stage, leaving the audience sitting in stunned silence before breaking into applause. On this night, Holcomb once again could not finish the hymn. In Cohen's words, "a spasm of coughing" forced him from the stage, leaving behind another stunned and silent audience. "Everybody felt deep into the song," Cohen recalled, "and that was his last performance. He had the songbook in his hand."[92]

After Holcomb's death in 1981, John Cohen wrote an obituary for *Sing Out!*, the folk revival magazine that had spread some of the first word about Holcomb in 1960:

> He confirmed our belief that such a profoundly moving musician could grow and exist in America apart from the commercial art and music which surrounds us. His homemade music conveyed a precise clarity which reached people far beyond his home in eastern Kentucky. Roscoe's very closeness to his local tradition was the recognizable feature which permitted so many to understand the value and expressiveness of his, or any, regional sound. . . . He expressed for us our love of traditional art, the painfulness of life and the glory of music that comes from such a source. He enriched our lives and we will miss him.

In this obituary Cohen listed the characteristics he and others had found in Holcomb during the 1960s: profound emotional depth, separation from popular culture, being grounded in regional tradition, and personal pain as a precondition for powerful music. Holcomb and his music enriched many lives during his time and after his death. Yet how much was his life enriched by being documented and mythologized? He received praise from the vanguard of American culture and earned international acclaim, but died destitute. He traveled widely, not for self-promotion or to enrich young, middle-class lives, but to try to earn a living. He often returned home from these trips financially poorer than he left.[93]

Cohen started to grapple with the ethical dilemmas of doing documentary work after he returned from his first eastern Kentucky trip. He acknowledged he was a spy, a characterization that James Agee also copped to in *Let Us Now Praise Famous Men* some twenty years earlier. "Spying, intruding, poking my camera into the lives of people," Cohen admitted in the pages of *Sing Out!* in 1960, "getting farmers and miners to give their music into my tape recorder—and I couldn't promise them anything in return except my interest which they had done pretty well without until then. (If it wasn't for the fact that something worthwhile might come out of this, something that will cause people to look with open eyes—and open their hearts to sounds other than those they already know—then I would never want to put myself in such a situation.)"[94]

Decades later, Cohen delved deeper into the ethical quandaries and said he had "always wondered about the implicit arrogance of any collector's stance, for in this role you have no choice but to be part confidence man, part academic, part spy. . . . In the most self-critical light, collecting music from innocent informants is an exploitative act—taking from them to serve a function such as a term paper, or credits toward a degree, writing a book, or producing a record"—or in Cohen's case, filling out an old-time music group's repertoire and satisfying personal, emotional, and aesthetic desires.[95] Cohen attempted to resolve the tension between the documentarian as exploiter and appreciator, and perhaps placate his conscience, by understanding songs, people, and places not as things or objects to be collected, cataloged, and torn from their human sources, but rather as more ethereal and "spiritual" traces. This interpretation allowed him to see his documentary work not as cultural theft but as a cultural gift to audiences who might be similarly moved by the people and the music. In turn these audiences would develop an appreciation and respect for people and places they previously knew little about. One of Cohen's teachers told him, "To distribute material goods is to divide them, while to distribute spiritual goods is to multiply them." He applied this guiding notion while documenting music and society in Kentucky. "Since my first drive through eastern Kentucky," he wrote years later, "I have viewed traditional culture as a hidden spiritual resource, and my only aim throughout has been to share it with others, an enterprise which is its own reward." For Roscoe Holcomb, the reward remained in question.[96]

Looking back on his work, Cohen finds a mixture of pride—pride for the body of photographs, films, and recordings that revealed a wealth of artistic and musical vitality in the hollows and hills of southern Appalachia—and confusion, because his documentary work occasionally generated bitterness in the communities he portrayed. His work still resonates and provokes, from the classroom to the mountains. "And in the South in recent years," he said, "there's been a very confusing—to me confusing—*resentment that I was down there* before some of them were born. 'What right do you have to make *The High Lonesome Sound*? You're an outsider.'" Cohen replies, "Nobody was interested in documenting that music back then. So I did it. If I hadn't found [Roscoe Holcomb] where I had found him, he would have never been recorded. No one was interested in him, and he wasn't interested in coming out. No one was interested in coming to listen. He didn't want to go make records or anything."[97]

CHAPTER FOUR

Documenting SNCC and the Rural South

Danny Lyon and the Cultural Politics of Civil Rights Movement Photography

Between 1962 and 1964, Danny Lyon, an undergraduate at the University of Chicago from Forest Hills, Queens, worked as the first official photographer for the Student Nonviolent Coordinating Committee (SNCC), documenting the civil rights organization's activities and activists in the South's most defiant outposts: southwest Mississippi and southwest Georgia, the Alabama Black Belt, and the Mississippi Delta. Formed in 1960 to coordinate the student sit-in movement spreading across the South, and to provide young activists with their own self-directed organization independent of groups like Martin Luther King's Southern Christian Leadership Conference (SCLC), SNCC quickly established itself as the vanguard of the civil rights movement. It harnessed the currents of idealism and activism animating black and white college campuses across the country and channeled that energy into organizing grassroots voter registration and direct action campaigns in places once deemed too dangerous. SNCC also introduced radical new conceptions of decentralized, community-based leadership. In the process of conducting long-lived grassroots campaigns in southern communities, SNCC's fieldworkers developed deep ties with "local people"—black farmers, high school students, and business owners—many of whom became SNCC fieldworkers and leaders themselves.

Danny Lyon photographed these defining aspects of SNCC's work in the South. SNCC, in turn, displayed his images in its pamphlets, posters, newsletters, and filmstrips. Lyon and SNCC also featured his photography prominently in innovative documentary books such as *The Movement: Documentary of a Struggle for Equality*, published by Simon & Schuster in 1964, and photography exhibitions, including *NOW*, which opened in New York City in 1965 and featured Richard Avedon as honorary chairman. SNCC sent out his photographs to wire services, newspapers, and magazines across the nation and the world to highlight its work in places most major media outlets ignored. Equally important, SNCC used Lyon's photographs to craft a compelling public image for itself, one designed to counter the misrepresentations of the white-controlled press and to help the organization raise funds and recruit support. "SNCC's idea of photography was functional: it was to provide pictures for SNCC's propaganda and for press releases to those papers that would print them, and it was used to illustrate fund-raising brochures and document the movement," writes Julian Bond, who worked as SNCC's first communications director from 1960–65. "Danny Lyon took this function and made art."[1]

Danny Lyon's documentary art during the civil rights movement also created a powerful, persuasive, and what he would later call a "mythological" image of SNCC, its activists, the "local people," and the landscape they encountered in the rural South during the critical early phase of the group's existence. It represents a pivotal contribution to the visual history of the civil rights movement and the long history of documentary work in the South by once again revealing why mostly white and well-educated documentarians found the rural South a compelling place to do documentary work, how they represented people quite different from themselves in terms of race and class—often identified as the "folk"—and created powerful and dominant images of the region in the process. It is not coincidental that Lyon used the same phrase Howard Odum once did in 1930 to describe his own documentary style: "romantic realism." Both tangled together realist representational methods (sociological empiricism, in Odum's case, the camera in Lyon's) designed to expose the South's social problems with an explicit desire to romanticize and mythologize their mostly black subjects whose lives and cultures seemed to offer an alluring antidote to the social and cultural malaise brought on by modernity.[2]

New social and cultural influences swirling in the minds of middle-class white youth in the early 1960s, such as the Beat movement, the folk revival, and the New Left, distinguished Lyon's "romantic realism" from his predecessor's and shaped the production and reception of his photographs for SNCC. Consequently, this chapter focuses on the broader cultural work of Lyon's SNCC photographs, rather than on their efficacy as "documents of social change," in the words of historian Leigh Raiford, who has characterized the political purposes of SNCC photography as "performances of liberatory possibility and as documents of democracy in action."[3] Lyon's documentary style, influenced in part by the documentary work produced during the Depression and New Deal, including *Let Us Now Praise Famous Men* and Farm Security Administration (FSA) photography, created a powerful mythology about the Student Nonviolent Coordinating Committee, its black activists, and the rural South. His photographs for SNCC combine Jack Delano's political engagement and sense of place with the psychological depth of Robert Frank's pioneering photographic style. By documenting the South's rural poor and the relatively unknown civil rights workers associated with SNCC, Lyon recalled the FSA photographers' celebration of anonymous but noble Americans confronting the Depression. But his motivation to take photographs reflected the influence of the Beat movement and the politics of the New Left, not the New Deal. Unlike the New Deal's strong government-focused ethos, Lyon's New Left liberalism reflected a distrust of American institutions, including the federal government, and sought change from within oneself and the local community. Lyon's documentary expression, like that of John Cohen's during the folk revival, also revealed a more overwhelming personal desire for self-discovery and new life-affirming experiences among America's marginalized, a solipsism that at times seemed contrary to the movement's broader aim of public rather than private transformation. Like the Beats he admired, Lyon also embraced Frank's desire to see himself reflected in his photography. In Frank's words, it is the "instantaneous reaction to oneself that produces a photograph."[4]

But during the early 1960s, Lyon tried to balance these social and subjective concerns. He made photographs that helped create a powerful romantic aura about SNCC, which the group then used to garner financial support and recruits in the North and to spread an important message of black political empowerment in the Deep South. At the same time, these photographs of the rural South's black residents and black SNCC workers highlighted the political limits of white liberal romanticism. They reflected and appealed to the cultural concerns and desires of white liberals just as much or more than they functioned as instruments of political change for the black people they portrayed. Later, during the middle and late 1960s, as SNCC shifted its focus from interracial coalitions and voter registration and direct action campaigns toward Black Power and black nationalism, black SNCC photographers like Julius Lester would reorient SNCC's documentary purpose accordingly: they moved from mythologizing leaders and providing images for the media and white progressive audiences to making photographs of the black poor for the black poor, particularly those in the rural South. Rather than producing more posters and books for mainly white audiences, Lester would create new forms of visual culture such as calendars, engagement books, and postcards that often featured the faces of the rural South's black population. He envisioned these materials adorning the walls of black homes, countering the dominant media's depiction of beauty as white, recording important dates in black history, and instilling self-confidence and racial pride. In making the rural South yet again a critical site of documentary representation, Lester and other black SNCC photographers also made it into site of resistance against not only white segregationists in the region but also white liberal representations of black southerners.

Mythologizing SNCC Activists in the South

In the fall of 1959, Danny Lyon left home in Queens and enrolled as an undergraduate at the University of Chicago. His family expected him to pursue a "respectable" career, perhaps as a lawyer, an accountant, or a doctor like his brother. But, as curator Julian Cox writes, "conformity of any kind did not accord with him. Lyon was a dreamer and a romantic and ill-suited to a life in academia." Nevertheless, he relished his literature and history classes at Chicago and developed his passion for photography there. He joined the student newspaper, the *Chicago Maroon*, and began photographing campus activities and life in nearby neighborhoods. In his sophomore year, he purchased a Nikon F 35mm camera and processed his film in the *Maroon's* darkroom. "By the spring of 1961 he had progressed such that a selection of his earliest photographs was published in the student magazine the *Phoenix*, with the promising title 'The Camera of Danny Lyon,'" writes Cox.[5]

While at Chicago in the early 1960s, Lyon discovered Walker Evans's photographs in *American Photographs*, released in 1938, and in *Let Us Now Praise Famous Men*, first published in 1941 and reissued in 1960. The civil rights movement felt reminiscent of the Great Depression because it appeared to involve a heroic fight on the part of a marginalized people against seemingly insurmountable forces, with white supremacy replacing capitalism as the enemy. Most importantly, those dramatic fights were occurring in the rural South where the lines between right and wrong, good and evil, seemed clearer than they did in the streets of urban or suburban New York. If James Agee and Walker Evans could convey beauty and pathos in the worn-out fields of Hale County, Alabama, in 1936, certainly the rural South of the 1960s could provide Lyon with a similar opportunity to for aesthetic inspiration. He acknowledged that "after *Let Us Now Praise Famous Men* no one could go back to the old way," meaning photographic reporting for news magazines that reflected middle-class values. By the early 1960s Lyon "had become convinced that *Life* was a reactionary publication. That made my mission as a young photographer simple," he said. "I would create photographs that would be stronger, more truthful, and more powerful than *Life* Magazine, and *Life* Magazine would be destroyed."[6]

Lyon discovered another example of a more honest and penetrating style of documentary expression in Robert Frank's groundbreaking book of photography, *The Americans*, published in 1958. Young aspiring photographers like Lyon, who also imbibed the countercultural oeuvre of the Beat movement, admired the Swiss émigré's ability to visualize deeply felt emotion, to expose the alienation and despair lurking in American life that magazine editors, advertisers, and television executives glossed over in the 1950s. Lyon also admired Frank's independence from the institutional demands of a magazine or any other organization. The essence of his documentary vision in many ways mirrored that of John Cohen. "In the context of the new subjectivity" of the 1960s, photographer, curator, and critic Ute Eskildsen argues, "where authorship became more important than subject," Lyon's photography was "based neither on societal criticism, nor on gathering evidence, but rather on the desire to experience things outside one's education and upbringing." In Lyon's case this meant leaving behind the rarefied air of the University of Chicago and the relative comfort of Queens.[7]

In the early fall of 1961, Danny Lyon saw a photograph that sparked his desire to leave behind the expectations of college and seek out places and experiences that might serve a nobler purpose. The photograph showed Tom Hayden, a member of the Students for a Democratic Society (SDS), being beaten in McComb, Mississippi, by a man named Carl Hayes. Hayden sits on the ground trying to shield himself from Hayes's blow. Hayden, then a University of Michigan college student, wears a black suit, while Hayes, an air-conditioning repairman, wears a sleeveless shirt exposing his large biceps. The photograph projects an image of class and physical difference between the two men and symbolizes the era's division between North and South. Hayden, along with Paul Potter of the National Student Association, traveled to the South in October 1961 because they had heard of McComb's particularly violent resistance to SNCC's presence in the community. They wanted to make a report documenting white supremacist violence and present it to the Justice Department and national media with the hope of getting federal protection for local activists. A month earlier, Hayden had written to SDS president Al Haber about a revolution brewing in the region. "In the rural South, in the 'token integration' areas, in the cities, they will be shouting from the bottom of their guts for justice or else." He added, "We'd better be there." For Hayden, "there" referred both to actual places where civil rights activity was occurring in the South and to an "imaginative place, 'the South,' a place far away from the white midwestern suburb where Hayden had grown up," argues historian Grace Elizabeth Hale. "It meant a space outside modern America, full of authentic and yet marginal people. It meant black southerners."[8]

Immediately after Hayes beat up Hayden, the photographer who documented the assault came up to Hayden and told him to leave the motel he was staying in since local whites planned to blow it up later that night. While warning Hayden, the photographer placed the roll of film he had just shot in his socks as the police approached to confiscate his camera. The next day the photograph went out on the national wire, ending up in student newspapers like the *Chicago Maroon*. "That picture made me famous," Hayden later said. It also moved Lyon. He was a photographer, a history major, and an admirer of Mathew Brady, as well as of Agee, Evans, and Frank. Here, it seemed, was his chance to document history in the making. And it was taking place in the remote recesses of the Deep South where the past—rural cultures, vernacular architecture, and a racial caste system only a few generations removed from slavery—was still accessible; it was still photographable. At the end of the school year in 1962, he packed an army bag holding two cameras and told his sister-in-law to drive him to old Route 66 in Chicago in honor of Jack Kerouac's Beat novel, *On the Road*, a book both he and Hayden revered. "Then I stuck out my thumb and headed south."[9]

Lyon hitchhiked 390 miles to Cairo, Illinois, a town located at the confluence of the Ohio and Mississippi Rivers—the state's southernmost tip. Cairo (pronounced Cay-ro) was little known to most Americans, except as Huck and Jim's destination in *Huckleberry Finn*. It was to be the gateway to freedom for Jim, but their raft drifted by during a foggy night. After an unintended diversion to East St. Louis, Illinois, Lyon arrived in Cairo at night by bus. A fellow University of Chicago student, Linda Pearlstein, had participated in a demonstration there and provided Lyon with key contacts: Chico Neblett of SNCC and Selyn McCollum, who participated in the Freedom Rides the year before. Cairo may have been part of a Midwestern state, but its history and culture were decidedly Southern. It was a short trip through Kentucky to Tennessee and the Delta region of Arkansas and Mississippi.[10]

Early that same summer another young college student named John Lewis, who participated with other SNCC members in the Freedom Rides, traveled to Cairo to help organize the movement there. "The first time I saw John Lewis," Lyon remembered, "he was sitting quietly, bored or dreaming, in the back of a church in Cairo. . . . Then [he] came to the podium. I had seldom been in a church before and never heard a black preacher. The speech, delivered in a heavy, rural Alabama accent, seemed to come up out of him, out of centuries of abuse, and explode from this unassuming young man. His voice was high pitched and trembling with emotion. John's speech would have converted anyone, and it converted me."[11]

As would happen time and again in the early and middle 1960s, SNCC's work in the South thrust together individuals like Lewis and Lyon, young people from opposite sides of America's racial, cultural, economic, and geographic divides. Lewis was black and Baptist; Lyon was white and Jewish. Lewis was from Pike County, Alabama, the descendant of slaves, and was raised on a farm by parents who were sharecroppers. Lyon grew up in a middle-class neighborhood in Queens with parents who had escaped persecution in Germany and Russia in the 1920s and 1930s. While bringing together people from such dissimilar backgrounds reflected SNCC's early attempt to create what Martin Luther King called the "beloved community," resentment and romanticism, among other factors, often strained or limited these alliances. For Lewis and Lyon, however, their chance meeting in Cairo began a lifelong friendship. A year later they became roommates in an apartment in Atlanta, where SNCC was headquartered. "Slim, with dark curly hair, he was a wonderful human being, very gentle, very quiet, very intense about his work," Lewis writes of Lyon during the early 1960s. "He loved taking pictures. He *lived* to do that."[12]

Along with Lewis's speech, presence, and aura, the bravery of local activists in Cairo enthralled Lyon as he photographed the civil rights movement for the first time. He was especially moved by the thirteen-year-old girl who, after praying and singing in the street, refused to move while a blue pickup truck drove toward her and eventually knocked her down. "Everyone who had demonstrated lined up in the parking lot nearby," Lyon recalled in the early 1960s. "A pickup truck came tearing down the street and drove straight into the crowd. We all scattered except this girl, who wouldn't move. The truck slammed on its breaks [*sic*], then hit her. She got up after that. She wasn't hurt too badly." While in Cairo, he also photographed the faces of black residents standing on the streets as both bystanders and participants in the protests. In a striking photograph, Lyon exposed the moral divide between black protesters and white segregationists standing behind a handmade sign declaring "Private Pool Members Only" at the entrance to the town's only swimming pool, which had recently been declared "public" by the Illinois state attorney general. The photograph, which later appeared in *The Movement*, the photo-documentary book produced by Lyon and

SNCC, appears to invite viewers into the movement, to participate by seeing themselves on one side of the divide or the other.[13]

In Lyon's memory the Cairo protest lacked the dramatis personae often associated with iconic civil rights protests, and so his photographs generated the emotion and narrative for an event that might have otherwise been forgotten: "There was no press, no video cameras (of course), no film cameras, no police, and no reporters. I had my camera, and I ran along as this brave little group marched through the sunlit and mostly empty streets of a very small American town." When a group of protesters, including John Lewis, first arrived at the pool they stopped to pray. Lyon photographed Lewis praying next to a teenage girl and boy. All three kneel in front of a brick wall with their heads bowed and arms resting on their knees. All three wear white shirts, and with the white window frame behind them, the trio seems to blend together as one. Their bowed heads suggest a deep spiritual commitment and a moral righteousness more powerful than the whites' grimaces, stares, and homemade blockades. Significantly, the teenage girl kneels at the center of the photograph between Lewis and the young man. The viewer does not see her face, but senses a passion that belies her youth. Kneeling at the center, she represents the future and hope for SNCC as its movement spreads throughout the South: cultivating indigenous leaders, regardless of age, gender, education, or prominence, whose courage and moral commitment will inspire the local and national community to its cause.

The photograph Lyon took of John Lewis kneeling and praying in Cairo in 1962 eventually became a poster bearing the caption, "COME LET US BUILD A NONVIOLENT WORLD TOGETHER." The poster's caption reflected the Judeo-Christian grounding and idealism of SNCC's early years. For SNCC, Lyon's photograph contained the essence of the message the organization wanted to spread throughout America. It also portrayed the South as a place where a clear moral cause was being waged with the potential to transform America into a more just society. A year after Lyon shot this photograph, SNCC's communication department printed 10,000 copies of the image as a poster and sold them for a dollar each, mostly in the North. They soon sold out of them. Two years later the photograph appeared in *The Movement*. Lorraine Hansberry, the playwright and SNCC supporter who wrote the text that accompanied the documentary book's photographs, captured the moral message communicated by the image: "The movement toward freedom has varied faces. It draws on the devotions of our culture—traditional Christianity." Forty-one years later, a *New York Times* art critic highlighted Lyon's Cairo photograph as one of the best in an exhibit of documentary photographs of America from 1945–75 at an art museum in Newark, New Jersey. The exhibit also featured the work of photographers such as Walker Evans, Robert Frank, Lee Friedlander, Gary Winogrand, and Bruce Davidson. "The serene countenance of the praying figures is humbling," this critic noted, "a reminder to the righteousness of their cause. The vision of a happy, prosperous America has started to crumble."[14]

While in Cairo, Lyon got the names of other SNCC people working farther south in places like Nashville, Atlanta, and Albany, Georgia. In August 1962, he headed for the first time into the Deep South and eventually found his way to SNCC's headquarters in Atlanta. The office was empty when he arrived: everyone was down in Albany, 150 miles to the southwest. When he finally got to Albany, a "plainclothesman," who must have sensed Lyon's disorientation, asked him, "Where are you going?" He pointed in one direction and said, "That's the white part of town" and then pointing the opposite way, said, "And that's the nigger part of town." The next morning Lyon went into black Albany to find the SNCC workers. Jim Forman happened to be there and welcomed Lyon with politeness and urgency. "You got a camera?" Forman asked him. He then gave Lyon a shooting script and an official role in SNCC. "James Forman would direct me, protect me, and at times fight for a place for me in the movement," Lyon recalled. "He is directly responsible for my pictures existing at all."[15]

Forman hired Lyon as SNCC's first full-time photographer in 1962 after recognizing the power and potential of the images that Lyon had made in Cairo and Albany. Before Lyon arrived, SNCC had relied on occasional photographs taken by Forman, white SNCC activist Bob Zellner, or supportive but unaffiliated photographers like George Ballis to illustrate the group's newspaper, *The Student Voice*. By the fall of 1962, SNCC's reach and influence had rapidly expanded as it established beachheads in southwest Georgia, southwest Mississippi, the Mississippi Delta, and in Atlanta. As SNCC's activities and profile grew, Forman recognized the need not only to document the group's voter registration and desegregation campaigns but also to create a powerful image and narrative about the group before others—white segregationists in the South and major media outlets—did it for them. Forman had already worked as a publicist for another civil rights organization, the Congress of Racial Equality (CORE), before joining SNCC in 1961 and was keenly aware of the need for effective communication strategies and self-definition. Soon after he joined SNCC, Forman highlighted the first order of business for SNCC's public relations push: "The first was simply to establish in the minds of the public that we existed, who we were and what we were all about." Forman, according to Lyon, "was singularly aware that SNCC needed an 'image' because to the watching world, SNCC was faceless." Beginning in Cairo in the summer of 1962, Lyon began making photographs that broke "the blockade erected between the South and the nation," SNCC's Julian Bond later noted. Lyon's images raised money, recruited workers, and personified the movement: they "put courage in the fearful, shone light on darkness," Bond said.[16]

Lyon provided SNCC with photographs filtered through his personal vision that played a significant role in generating a mythological aura around SNCC that was critical to recruiting and fundraising, particularly among sympathetic whites in the North. A white college student from the North, Lyon candidly acknowledged his romantic sensibilities and never made any pretense toward objectivity in his depiction of black SNCC activists, particularly men, putting their bodies on the line in the rural South. "There was a legend of SNCC," Lyon recalled. "These are legendary people. I'm a very romantic person. I'm an artist." Lyon's photographs helped generate this legend of SNCC and an attendant image of the rural South as an exotic and dangerous place where heroic people outside the media limelight fought for a moral cause that could transform the country. Lyon's photographs for SNCC presented mainly black civil rights activists who worked in rural Georgia and Mississippi as saintlike mythological heroes, thereby reflecting white desires for a more authentic existence and more vital experiences. On the one hand, these photographs by Lyon present black people working in the rural South as political actors risking their lives to overthrow white supremacy and not merely as passive victims of it. Photographs such as these helped promote a powerful image for SNCC that distinguished it from other competing civil rights groups like SCLC and created a heroic aura that helped garner financial support and recruits in the North and West. On the other hand, these same photographs highlighted the political limits of white liberal romanticism. Their creation by Lyon and their reception in photo-books and art exhibits more often reflected the social and cultural preconceptions of liberal whites, who often romanticized black activists, rural black southerners, and the region itself for their alluring distance and difference from their homogeneous and emotionally barren bourgeois existence back home. Ironically, for a civil rights organization that sought to empower rural black southerners as agents of social and political change, the documentary representation of the organization, the people it worked with, and the places they lived remained in white hands during SNCC's early years and reflected white preconceptions, however sympathetic they may have been.[17]

In Albany, Lyon picked up where he left off in Cairo and made close-up photographs of unknown movement activists, both black and white, as they participated in mass meetings at the Shiloh and Mount Zion Baptist churches. When he was in Cairo, he had photographed John Lewis speaking from a pulpit and captured the passion and emotion that could suddenly well up out of Lewis, a man who struck most people as quiet and unassuming. Lyon returned to black churches in Albany and, again, used photography to create a feeling of deep emotion and spirit among common folk in the South's small towns. His Albany photographs function in the same way as his Cairo images, revealing previously unknown black people in distant settings in the Deep South charged with drama. In Lyon's photographs, an elderly woman or a teenage boy becomes the image of selfless commitment and heroism that SNCC wanted to harness and spread. Such images, set in the South, "helped define SNCC—and the Southern movement—for a non-Southern audience," writes Julian Bond.[18]

Inside sanctuaries or on the streets, Lyon's photographs also countered the image of the civil rights movement leadership as exclusively middle class and ministerial and thus reflected the New Left's focus on youth activism. For example, in Albany he photographed a local high school student and ex-gang leader named Eddie Brown, as police carried him away following a sit-in. Brown wore in the words of Lyon "a look of beatific serenity on his face." Indeed, Brown almost seems to be asleep in the arms of two Albany policemen. One of the officers, who is older and overweight—the stereotypical, southern potbellied lawman—dangles a cigarette in his mouth as he carries the serene Brown to jail. Brown's visible hand rests limp, while the hands of the white police officers appear tense under the strain of the ex-gang member's weight. In the background, directly behind Brown's tilted head, stands the apparent proprietor of the restaurant where the sit-in occurred. He wears a white button-down shirt with a bow tie and has his hands on his hips as he watches the police carry Brown away. Despite his peripheral placement in the photograph, his stance seems defiant and creates a sense of complicity between the police and him. In the full photograph, there are a total of six white men struggling to subdue and arrest a single black teenager. Brown's countenance and body language, his serenity, and youth give him a saintly aura that contrasts with the stern expressions of the older policemen. His isolation and difference from the officers are heightened because he does not look at any of them or even acknowledge what is happening to him. Neither do the officers look at Brown, which also increases their moral distance from him. To look at him asks them to acknowledge their role in an unjust system

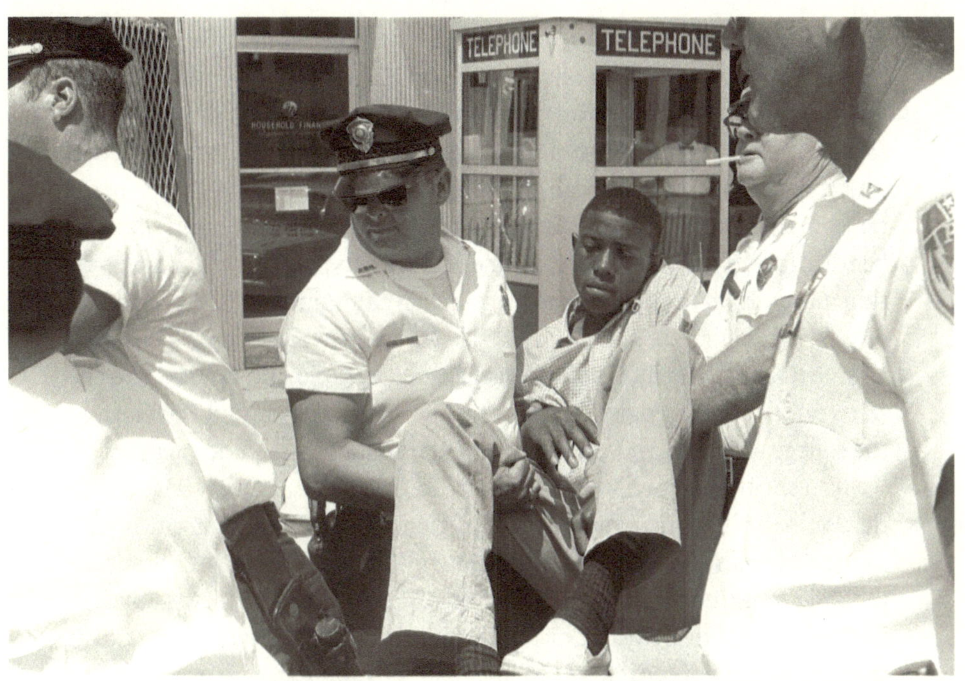

Danny Lyon, *Eddie Brown, Albany, Georgia,* 1962. © Danny Lyon/Magnum Photos.

of segregation. The photograph, like the image of Tom Hayden's beating, was reprinted widely in college newspapers and, like the image of Lewis praying in Cairo, used in SNCC fundraising flyers. A former gang leader becomes in an instant the movement's moral symbol to those sympathetic to it, who perhaps had not seen the movement portrayed with seemingly anonymous young people like Eddie Brown at its center.[19]

In Lyon's eyes, the courage and conviction of SNCC workers like Brown, their willingness to march downtown and face jail at the hands of Albany police chief Laurie Pritchett, or even walk up the steps to the courthouse to register to vote meant that "every person in the ranks of the movement had already achieved a revolution." Tom Hayden also emphasized the transformative effects social activism could have on the individual, which educated, middle-class whites who felt estranged from their true selves amid the materialism of modern America found appealing. "On a theoretical level, you can say that we believed in wanting to make history and achieve civil rights," Hayden later remembered. "But there was something else: the middle-class emptiness of alienation that people talk about, and then suddenly confronting commitment. The whole emotion of defining not only yourself, but also your life by risking your life, and testing whether you're willing to die for your beliefs, was *the* powerful motive, I believe." When viewed in this context, Lyon's photograph of Brown communicated an image of a personal, as much as a political, revolution that many young idealists like Lyon and Hayden found appealing. It was appealing not only for its setting in the Deep South, far from the "emptiness" one felt back home in the cities or suburbs, but also because it involved an outsider in American society, a young black man putting "his body on the line," whose race, social commitment, and geographic origins made him the antithesis of the sources of white middle-class malaise. SNCC activists like Brown thus became mythological figures, and the Deep South a mythological place, for whites such as Lyon and Hayden and the college students who viewed Lyon's photograph in their newspapers.[20]

Lyon spent the remainder of 1962 attending college and traveling back to the South to photograph for SNCC. The Friends of SNCC (FOS) group in Chicago had begun using his photographs from Cairo and Albany for fundraising and recruitment. Lyon also exhibited his photographs from the South in the lobby of a University of Chicago dorm. It was his first exhibit. "I think it made me a kind of local hero, so I got a lot of support in the environment I came out of," he later recalled. About this time, a SNCC worker and friend of Lyon's named Paul Brooks contacted Harry Belafonte, a key financial supporter of SNCC, and asked him to fund another field trip for Lyon so he could photograph the work of Bob Moses in Mississippi. Belafonte donated $300, which Lyon used to buy a plane ticket to Jackson. He then got on a bus and traveled 120 miles north to Cleveland, the middle of the Mississippi Delta.[21]

During his time in Mississippi, Lyon continued to create a romantic mythology around SNCC activists like Bob Moses who worked, organized, and lived there. "I've run around after them, driven cars for them, taking their pictures, trying to make them more famous and more mythological," Lyon remembered. "I was in love with all of them: they're great, great people, really absolutely remarkable."[22] Lyon especially used his photography to cultivate and reinforce the mythic image of Bob Moses that spread within and outside SNCC. Moses was a former high school teacher from Harlem who had received a master's degree in philosophy from Harvard University, whose organizing and voter registration work in some of the most intransigent parts of the most intransigent state had earned him a mythological reputation that he resisted and resented. His quiet, self-effacing personality aligned with SNCC's suspicion of strong figurehead leadership, while his philosophical cast of mind, including his ability to quote Albert Camus and the Bible to frame the moral imperative of the group's work, reflected the youthful idealism and Judeo-Christian persuasion of SNCC's early years. Consequently, Lyon's photographs of Moses—often shot in dramatic lighting and showing him deep in thought—not only reinforced the "Bob Moses mystique" but also added to SNCC's allure among young activists and journalists, who admired the courage and commitment of activists like Moses, identified with his existential philosophies, and romanticized the distant Deep South. Lyon's desire to make Moses and other SNCC workers in Mississippi "more mythological" was not the only end, however. His photographs of Moses, which would circulate in documentary books like *The Movement*, once again "helped define SNCC—and the Southern movement—for a non-Southern audience" in the words of Julian Bond. Ideally, the mythological image Lyon produced of Moses and, by extension, of SNCC would help garner support among this "non-Southern audience," often, but not exclusively, white liberals from the North or Far West, whose financial donations, political influence, or direct participation Moses knew were critical to the movement's survival.[23]

As with Lyon, a photograph of civil rights activism in the South drew Moses into the movement in the early 1960s. If the photograph of a white activist, Tom Hayden, being beaten in McComb, captured Lyon's imagination, Moses responded to the image of young black men like himself actively resisting segregation. Moses's response to the photograph, which showed four black North Carolina A&T students sitting in at a Woolworth's lunch counter in Greensboro, North Carolina, in February 1960, reveals how one's race can shape one's reception of a civil rights photograph. "I saw a picture in the *New York Times*," Moses said in 1962, "of Negro college students 'sitting-in' at a lunch counter. . . . [They] had a certain look on their faces—sort of sullen, angry, determined. Before the Negro in the South had always looked on the defensive, cringing. This time they were taking initiative. They were kids my age, and I knew this had something to do with my own life." The photograph also moved Moses because he could empathize and identify with these young black men. "The pictures attracted me because I could feel myself in the faces of the people that they had there on the front pages. I could feel how they felt. . . . I was mesmerized by the pictures I saw."[24]

In the spring of 1960, Moses, who was a high school math teacher at the time, went to Newport News, Virginia, to participate in a sit-in and visit his uncle. While in Virginia, he met Wyatt T. Walker of SCLC and soon decided to go to work for SCLC in Atlanta. While disappointed by the hierarchical leadership style and lack of direction he found at SCLC, Moses did meet

Ella Baker and Jane Stembridge in Atlanta that summer. Baker, a former SCLC staffer who helped found SNCC in the spring of 1960, would exert a profound influence on Moses's philosophy of organizing and leadership, while Stembridge, a white Virginian and seminary student who worked in SNCC's new headquarters in Atlanta, encouraged Moses to make a trip through Mississippi to recruit potential allies for a group conference in the fall. During his trip he met important black activists in the state like Aaron Henry in Clarksdale and Amzie Moore in Cleveland, who would play central roles in later SNCC-led voter registration campaigns and political parties. Moses returned to Mississippi in the summer of 1961 and began organizing in earnest in McComb with C. C. Bryant, a businessman and NAACP member, and in Amite County with E. W. Steptoe, a local farmer and NAACP leader.[25]

Moses's attempt to launch direct action and voter registration campaigns in southwest Mississippi, an area infamous for its particularly violent resistance to civil rights activism, soon earned him a permanent place in SNCC and laid a foundation for what his biographer, Laura Visser-Maessen calls the "Bob Moses mystique." In the late summer of 1961, Moses was beaten in Liberty, the seat of Amite County, by Billy Jack Caston while en route to the courthouse to help a group of black men register to vote. Though bloodied from repeated blows to his head with a knife handle, Moses, and his recruits, continued on to the courthouse where they rattled the registrar with their presence. Moses would later file charges against Caston, the first time a black man had ever done so against a white man in the county's history. A mythic image of Moses's work in southwest Mississippi in 1961 continued to persist for years afterward. "It was probably the most creative and heroic single act anyone in the New Left has attempted," wrote Jack Newfield, a white journalist who covered the New Left and civil rights movement. "Certainly much of the subsequent history of the New Left has flowed from that existential act of [Moses] disappearing into the most violent and desolate section of Mississippi."[26]

In the fall of 1961, Moses resumed his work in McComb and Pike Counties and was sentenced to jail in the Pike County seat of Magnolia along with other local SNCC activists such as Hollis Watkins and Curtis Hayes. While in jail, Moses wrote a letter that deepened and spread the growing mythology around him and SNCC workers in the South. He managed to slip the letter out of his cell, and it eventually arrived at SNCC headquarters in Atlanta. Tom Hayden soon reprinted it in *Revolution in Mississippi*, a Students for a Democratic Society (SDS) report he compiled that collected documents, reports, and newspaper accounts of civil rights activism and resistance in the state. Moses wrote, "This is Mississippi, the middle of the iceberg. Hollis is leading off with his tenor, 'Michael row the boat ashore, Alleluia; Christian brothers don't be slow, Alleluia; Mississippi's next to go, Alleluia.' This is a tremor in the middle of the iceberg—from a stone that the builders rejected." Moses's eloquent description of a particular moment inside the jail, including the close camaraderie that developed between activists, and his allusion to a verse from the Book of Psalms in the final line seemed to encapsulate the idealism, bravery, and moral suasion that characterized SNCC's early years for many in the movement.[27]

By the time Lyon arrived in Mississippi during the fall of 1962, Moses had moved up from McComb and the southwest part of the state and into the Delta. With the help of World War II veteran and local NAACP activist Amzie Moore, Moses began organizing voter registration projects there. Moses later looked back on the period from the fall of 1962 through the fall of 1963 as a time when he and his cohorts "were consciously trying to build a group of young people in Mississippi who would work and view themselves as having the right to work" on voter registration. People like Sam Block, Charles McLaurin, Dorie Ladner, Lawrence Guyot, Frank Smith, Willie Peacock, and Charlie Cobb worked alongside Moses in places such as Ruleville and Greenwood. Local people, Moses believed, were more responsive to black activists who displayed their commitment by living among them and participating in community life.[28]

By the late winter and early spring of 1963, the violent intimidation of SNCC workers had reached a fever pitch. The increased activity and national notoriety (including the presence of comedian Dick Gregory and folk musicians Pete Seeger and Bob Dylan) of the Greenwood movement had also heightened white fears in the city. Local police worked twelve- hour shifts. The White Citizens Council met nightly. The local newspaper expressed fear of federal intervention given the handful of Justice Department officials in town assessing the violence. And then on March 24, the Klan firebombed the SNCC office in Greenwood, destroying an $800 mimeograph machine, two typewriters, and important records. The day before, Danny Lyon had stood just outside the entrance to the office and photographed Frank Smith, Bob Moses, and Willie Peacock standing next to the open door. Moses leans forward against the door, supporting his body and head with his left arm, and stares outside into the light in thought. To his right, Frank Smith also stares outside, his left hand gently touching his chin, contemplating or just standing in silence. At the entrance, facing Moses and Smith, stands

Willie Peacock, a dark silhouette with the sun just touching the back of his head. The weathered wooden door has six windowpanes decorated with lace curtains and an SNCC sticker that reads, "COME . . . TOGETHER Let Us Build a Non-Violent World"—a rewording of the phrase from the Cairo poster.[29]

The photograph, which appeared in *The Movement* in 1964, evokes the interior struggle of individual civil rights activists who faced death every day by depicting them in poses that suggest introspection and reflection. Moses's gaze while resting his head on his arms and Frank Smith's stroking of his chin create the contemplative, philosophical aura often reserved for male activists in the movement. Lyon's photograph reflected the image of Moses created by white liberal chroniclers of SNCC and the movement in the South like Jack Newfield of the *Village Voice* who imagined Moses "as an existential hero, resembling figures like Albert Camus, who had cult status among white liberals," argues Visser-Maessen. Moses's education at Hamilton College and Harvard and his ability to quote Camus and other French existentialists made him a black civil rights leader whom many white liberal students could, perhaps, more easily identify with than southern-born and bred activists who framed moral issues in the language of evangelical Christianity. By evoking the philosophical aura of Moses and of other male civil rights activists, Lyon's photograph contributed to this "interface" between the movement in the Deep South and a mostly white and young audience in the North who found such images of black activists in the distant region so compelling.[30]

Another photograph Lyon took of Moses, a portrait, also appeared in *The Movement* and similarly evoked the philosophical, almost mystical, qualities that many inside and outside the movement attached to him and romanticized. Hansberry's text presents him as "The man in Mississippi" and mentions his Hamilton and Harvard education, his role in orchestrating the Mississippi Summer Project, and the violence he had personally endured in the state. The photograph was taken in Ruleville, Mississippi, sometime in 1963. Moses appears seated before a window draped with a translucent curtain. Sunlight spreads across his forehead, nose, and mouth, highlighting his checkered button-down shirt. Moses, wearing horn-rimmed glasses, looks down, avoiding Lyon's lens. His downward gaze reflects his self-effacing nature and his desire to avoid the limelight and, instead, to let others, particularly local people in the movement, assume center stage. And yet, as the existence of Lyon's photograph attests, such characteristics only heightened his allure inside and outside the movement. He appears pensive in Lyon's photograph, evincing the preternatural calm many admired about

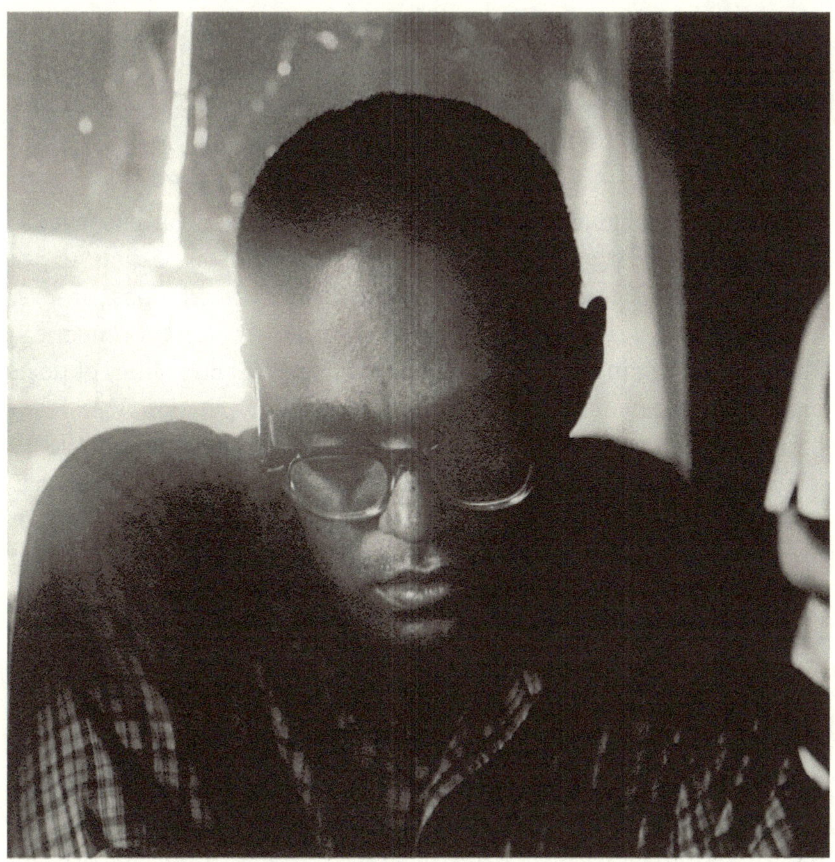

Danny Lyon, *Robert Moses, Mississippi,* 1963. © Danny Lyon/Magnum Photos.

him. "In the same way that one listens more attentively to a whisper, people were drawn to Bob," SNCC's Mary King remembers. "He was so unobtrusive that in his quiet self-possessed stillness, he fixed additional attention on himself. He seemed entirely nourished from within." Howard Zinn, in his chronicle of SNCC's early years, described Moses as someone "who talks slowly, quietly, whose calm as he stands looking down a street in Mississippi is that of a mountain studying the sea." Once again, Lyon crafted a compelling photograph that carried the potential to captivate a liberal northern audience with its focus on the contemplative, philosophical aura of Bob Moses risking his life in what Zinn called the "hinterland of the Deep South."[31]

Moses later discussed the power of documentary expression to mythologize, and turn individuals into abstractions, with psychiatrist Robert Coles, who worked with SNCC in 1963 and 1964 in the planning of the Mississippi

Summer Project. Coles, who conducted his own documentary work in the South by recording meetings and interviews with activists and local people involved in the movement, faced scrutiny from SNCC members, who wondered if, as a social scientist, he was simply searching for "traits" among SNCC workers, some "personality type" that captured their essence. Probing questions, including ones from Moses, forced Coles to consider whether he was "interested in getting to know individuals, as fully as possible" or perhaps was "on the lookout for general statements or descriptions" or, even worse, as one SNCC member said with "derision"—"data." "In America," Moses told Coles in a conversation about the power and politics of documentary representation, "a guy like you makes your reputation when you're here, studying us, if you come up with a bunch of psychological and sociological *ideas* about us: who we are, in our heads, and what our background is, and what 'ideology' we're pushing—and then you write your stuff up, and pretty soon it's news, and you write a book, and it's used in classrooms, and those poor students, they don't end up knowing *me*, and *Jim* [James Forman] . . . instead, they know about 'types' and 'problems' and 'beliefs.'" Moses could have directed his words at any number of photographers, like Lyon, or writers like Newfield, because the problem of representation remained the same—a photograph or a paragraph portrays someone else's idea of a person, not the person him- or herself. For Moses, this problem, inherent to any form of representation, carried very real individual consequences for black people living in a racist society. "Don't you see," he told Coles, "that's been our story—the black story: everyone calls us something! It's so hard for any single one of us to be seen by you folks [white people], even the kindest of you, even our friends [among you] as a person, nothing more."[32]

The Romance of the Rural South in SNCC Photography

Creating a compelling public identity and mythology for SNCC and its activists represented only one facet of Lyon's photography for the group during the early and middle 1960s. He also photographed the Deep South—its landscape and people, particularly its rural black residents. "My camera was an entrance into another world," Lyon recalled. "The South rolled out in front of me—highways and cotton fields, shotgun houses with screened porches, and nineteenth-century towns built around small squares. I loved it almost as much as I loved the movement." Lyon's photographs of the rural Mississippi landscape and its black residents link his work with the long history of documentary work in the South, particularly during the twentieth century. Like so many others, he envisioned the region as a pastoral place still rooted in the soil and vernacular tradition where the remnants of a nineteenth-century past provided aesthetic inspiration and demanded preservation before succumbing to the forces of modernization, agricultural mechanization, and even a potential social revolution wrought by the civil rights movement.[33]

While Lyon's representation of the region linked him with his documentary predecessors, his work reflected the influences of a new and unique historical context. Lyon was a white youth from the North who came of age during the Beat movement and folk music revival of the 1950s and 1960s and the political ferment of the civil rights movement and New Left. These youth-driven movements, which shaped the production and reception of Lyon's photographs during the 1960s, often romanticized people and places that seemed so different from their urban or suburban middle-class upbringings. Remote places like the rural South appeared more authentic because they seemed to nurture values and interpersonal relationships uncorrupted by commercialism and materialism and so might foster a new, more humane world. Thus, Lyon's photographs simultaneously exposed the oppression of rural black residents of places like the Mississippi Delta and aestheticized their impoverished and, thus, seemingly more authentic existence. They lived in a far country, both geographically and temporally. It was a place distanced and disconnected from the standardizing forces of mass culture originating outside of the region that many of Lyon's class and generation hoped to escape. It was also a place, however, that many of the relatives and descendants of these black Mississippians had fled for decades in order to establish better lives in northern cities like Chicago. These social and cultural dynamics resulted in photographs of people excluded from the post-war American dream that were created and often viewed by people eager to escape the middle-class comforts and expectations of that dream.

Like many others who got involved in the movement in the South, Lyon felt a mixture of fear and wonderment when he entered Mississippi for the first time. "When the DC-8 landed in Jackson, I might as well have been stepping off in Johannesburg," he recalled. "Everything frightened me." A year later, the author of a *Harper's* magazine article on SNCC also equated Mississippi with South Africa, reflecting how exotic the state seemed to people unfamiliar with the Deep South: "No one who has not seen Mississippi with his own eyes can really comprehend how different it is from the rest of the United States, including its Southern neighbors. In many ways it is almost as remote as South Africa, which it somewhat resembles."[34] "Passing the

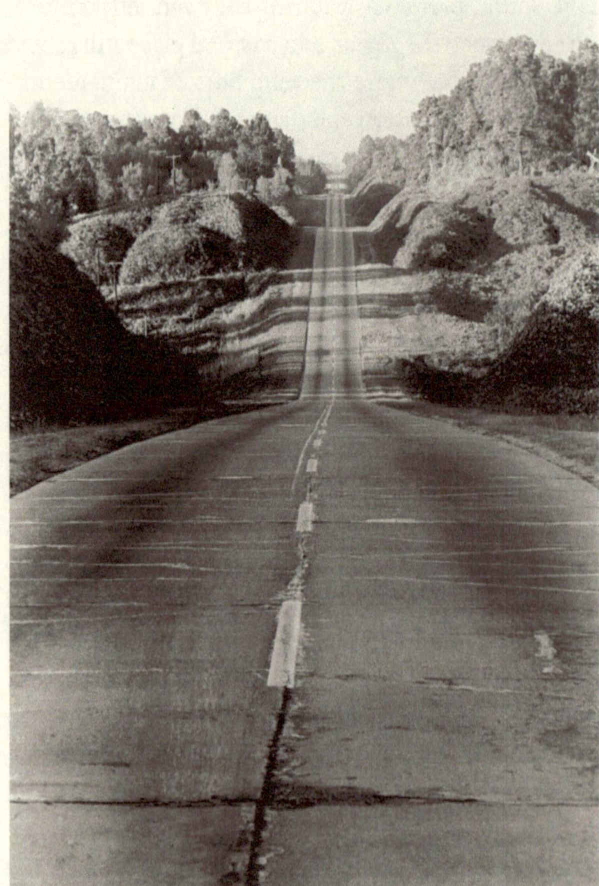

Danny Lyon, *The Road to Yazoo City, Mississippi*, 1963. © Danny Lyon/ Magnum Photos.

segregation signs that, though illegal, were still standing in front of the bus terminal," Lyon remembered of his first trip en route to Amzie Moore's house in Cleveland, "I rode up the highways to the rich, flat land created by the wanderings of the Mississippi . . . where single-lane highways run on raised roadbeds through miles of unfenced fields. It was September, and tufts of cotton that had fallen from wagons lay along the highway."[35]

A photograph that captures Lyon's fascination for the rural South's landscape, and speaks to the romantic ideas he and other, especially white, activists had about coming to the South during the early 1960s, appears as the first full-page image in *The Movement*. It is of an undulating rural Mississippi highway. Sunlight and shadows bisect the cracked two-lane road that runs alongside forests and kudzu-covered hills. "This is the road from Jackson to

Yazoo City, leading into the Mississippi Delta country, the heart of the Deep South," Lorraine Hansberry writes in the book's opening lines.[36] The highway rises and falls through ridges and swales to the horizon—an artery to the heart. Many young SNCC activists, black and white, native Mississippians and outsiders, traveled a road like this that delivered them to now- legendary places in the movement's history—Cleveland, Greenwood, Itta Bena, Indianola, Ruleville—where they risked their lives for racial justice. The highway image, according to a reviewer of *The Movement*, "set a rhythm of intense emotion" in the book. Ironically, for a documentary book about the civil rights movement, the photograph contains no activists, no segregationists.[37] It is, instead, a landscape photograph with only the faint trace of a car heading toward Lyon in the distance. Its focus on the aesthetics of the landscape lures the viewer in and presents an image of a pastoral South. By conveying mystery and emotion amid a lush kudzu-filled landscape, the photograph makes Mississippi a seductive place because of its jarring contradictions. There a young person, particularly a white one from Chicago by way of New York like Danny Lyon, can find aesthetic beauty *and* an opportunity to fight for justice in a place where the line between good and evil seems starker than in the suburbs or the city. In her 1965 book *Freedom Summer*, Sally Belfrage, a white woman from the North who volunteered for the SNCC-led Summer Project in 1964, addressed the personal and political desires that drew some white liberal youths like herself and Lyon to the South: "I go where they are changing things. Not to Harlem, a subway ride away, where on my own I might do penance for my city's sins. I go where the view is a different one. . . . It is a pilgrimage to a foreign country; traveling there, I can leave my guilt behind and atone for someone else's."[38]

The absence of people or any sign of a civil rights movement in the photograph also creates a feeling of isolation that breeds introspection. As Belfrage suggested, white college students like Lyon often lit out for the Deep South in a quest for deliverance from guilt or in a search for authenticity in life and culture. A desire for personal, interior transformation motivated many as much as working for a public, political revolution. For a young man like Lyon, under the sway of Jack Kerouac's novel *On the Road* and Beat culture in general, the open highway represented a retreat or escape route from the stolidity of college and the conformity of suburbia in the North. During one of Lyon's times in rural Mississippi, he drove a black 1957 Oldsmobile through the Delta at "100 miles an hour" and feeling joy "because I had fallen in the midst of this thing. I was twenty-one years old, I had a black Oldsmobile, it was incredible!" For other young white activists, particularly the many who participated in the era's folk music revival or in New Left political activism, the open road into the Deep South led to a place many believed to be more authentic because its rural, agrarian societies sustained premodern folk cultures that nurtured values and ways of living uncorrupted by consumer capitalism. Expressing the view of many in the movement and the New Left like himself, Tom Hayden, in his 1965 review of Howard Zinn's book, *SNCC: The New Abolitionists*, argued that rural black Mississippians lived in "a place remote enough from urban industrial society to make possible the beginning of a counter way of life. In these rural areas, contact among Negroes is veined thickly with direct human issues—the worth of men is likely to be measured by what they do, not as much by the labels and organizational imagery they project. Since the society is largely pre-industrial, men tend to have a direct and coherent relation to their work which contributes also to integrity of their personality and social relations."[39]

The romance of rural black southerners in SNCC was dominantly, but not exclusively, the domain of liberal whites from the North. Bob Moses, for example, who endured his own romantic mythology in the movement, spoke to Jack Newfield in an interview for the *Village Voice* of rural Mississippi's "pure and uncorrupted sharecroppers" who were "the greatest source of strength for the movement." He also spoke of "people who come off the land . . . and simply voice . . . the simple truths you can't ignore because they speak from their own lives." According to sociologist Randolph Hohle, the "rural black farmer was the initial representation of black authenticity within SNCC." When Moses and other black SNCC workers adopted overalls as a kind of uniform for voter registration work in rural areas, they wanted not only to erase the class divisions dress might create but also identify with a regional culture they found redeeming. While Moses and others tapped into the values and sense of community of rural black southerners to create a radical and cohesive social movement, Lyon provided a visual depiction of these same ideas. These visuals attracted others in the New Left into the movement, some of whom romanticized black folk culture because of its seeming opposition to their own middle-class upbringings. The tension for people like Moses and Lyon was how to expose and fight against a social system that kept people isolated and poor and, yet, admire the beneficial byproducts of rural life. Moses, and other black movement organizers like Ella Baker and Septima Clark, tried to harness the redeeming qualities of the rural South's folk culture into creative political activism. Lyon's photographs not only could inspire such activism among their viewers but also evoke a romantic myth that precluded political change.[40]

The byproducts of the rural South's oppressive, preindustrial economy—vast cotton fields, sharecroppers, and shotgun shacks—became sites of beauty and creative inspiration for young photographers traveling in the region for the first time. The same exploitive cotton culture that spawned the conditions SNCC sought to destroy also created a landscape that evoked an alluring agricultural past worthy of historic preservation and documentary art. Tamio Wakayama, a Canadian of Japanese descent who drove south to join the movement in 1963 and became a photographer for SNCC in 1964 under Lyon's direction, expressed a romantic fascination for the region that resembled his mentor's. "I loved the Delta. It was beautiful to me," he recalled. "There was a kind of visual integrity to it all—the soil, the sharecropper's shack, which didn't seem, like, man built, but as kind of extensions of the ecological framework. And the people themselves, they seem to have grown from the soil." He also said that when he looked out on the Delta landscape he did not see poverty: "I saw harmony between the sharecropper's shack, the outhouse, the black soil. It began my long love affair with that land and its people." Matt Herron, a white photographer and activist from Philadelphia who in 1964 started the Southern Documentary Project to assist SNCC with photographing the historical and social significance of the group's work, also acknowledged the aesthetic inspiration provided by the rural South's people and places, which he later described as a "visual feast." Herron modeled the SDP on the FSA and linked his work and that of other movement photographers to the documentary examples set by Walker Evans and Robert Frank whose photographs of the South from the thirties and fifties so influenced a new generation in the sixties. "There is a job to be done and that is to continue the work of Evans and Frank in a changing and beautiful country that more than ever lends itself to that record," Herron wrote in a letter from Mississippi in July 1964.[41]

Lyon took a number of photographs of black farmers in Mississippi that suggest the appeal they had as subjects for the young photographer. Near Ruleville, Mississippi, Lyon photographed a black field hand holding his cotton sack and standing on the edge of a gravel road. Behind him flat Delta fields of cotton spread out to the horizon. He stands between a bright white plantation house and a church situated in the background. Lyon's image creates an idea of the man's triangulated life—beholden to a white planter, he picks cotton for a living while perhaps finding his only salvation in the church. The cotton field dominates the photograph and thus holds ultimate power in the man's life. He wears a tattered long-sleeved shirt with holes dark pants, and a straw hat and stares directly into Lyon's lens. The photograph reflects Lyon's fascination with the rural South and, especially, the people he saw there who evoked a preindustrial past. The image of a black man preparing to pick cotton in a Mississippi Delta field was a scene Lyon previously knew only from history books or FSA photographs, which also, at times, evoked a rural nostalgia.[42]

Lyon published another photograph of this same man in *The Movement*. This photograph homes in on the sharecropper, revealing more of the holes puncturing his shirt and the weary expression on his face. This close-up shot suggests a man in his late thirties or early forties. He stands with his hands on his hips, with an expansive cotton field looming over his shoulder. In this photograph, the plantation home and church are absent, leaving the man alone in a cotton field bordered by forest. The accompanying text, written by Lorraine Hansberry, reads, "There's a great deal to endure. This man earns about $2.50 a day." Lyon's photograph, however, is less concerned with conveying a critique of the Delta's oppressive cotton economy. Instead, this photograph, and the others he took of rural farmers, evokes a premodern past by ignoring any indication of the modern, mechanized Delta agricultural economy that existed in the early 1960s. The field hand's clothing and placement amid cotton fields evoke not the 1960s but the nineteenth century, which is how Lyon often imagined the rural South.[43]

Lyon reinforces the image of the isolated, heroic male sharecropper in two other photographs in *The Movement*. Again, near Ruleville in the fall of 1962, Lyon photographed another black field hand alone in a cotton field. The photograph, taken from just above the waist, focuses on this man's face, which wears a worn expression, his eyes glassy, seemingly on the brink of tears. A cigarette dangles from his mouth as he looks directly into Lyon's lens. A straw hat rests on his head, and a cotton sack is slung over his shoulder and long-sleeved shirt. Behind him is a field of cotton with a blurred stand of trees looming on the horizon. The photograph draws the viewer's attention straight to the face and, specifically, the eyes of this man. Hansberry's text heightens the effect: "Who can look upon the turbulence in men's eyes and pretend he has witnessed contentment—or even resignation?" Lyon's photograph is full of pathos. Again, the image offers no explicit social or economic critique, even when connected to Hansberry's text, but conveys the psychological depth and emotion of the field hand. The presumed absence of resignation, according to Hansberry, reinforces the idea of this man as heroic, despite or because of his poverty. Further, the idea of "contentment" signaled capitulation to the middle-class values and expectations many whites of Lyon's generation who embraced the Beat movement, the folk revival, the New Left, and the civil rights movement.[44]

Lyon's photograph of the man creates the image of a person cut off from his community, enduring on the land alone. He becomes the existential and romantic hero, someone many whites involved in the movement romanticized for the sense of personal authenticity that suffering and marginalization seemed to confer on the rural South's black poor—the ultimate outsiders in postwar America. Jack Newfield, who romanticized Bob Moses's work in Amite County, created a similar romantic image of the "rural Mississippi Negroes" who lived there, one that he recognized could, occasionally, slip into sentimentalism. "There is a special quality to the Negroes of Amite County that is missing elsewhere," he wrote after visiting the area. "The routinized middle-class doesn't have it, the cynical Northern-ghetto Negro doesn't have it, and the violent, poor Southern white doesn't have it. In part this distinctive quality comes from living in a totally rural environment removed from the criminality, corruption, and violence in the cities. . . . And in part it comes from a people that has achieved an authentic nobility in one hundred years of stoic suffering." Such visions of rural black people in the South were common enough during the movement to prompt a black minister from Greenwood, Mississippi, to ask Robert Coles about the motivations and visions of documentarians in the region in a way that resembled the issues Coles discussed earlier with Moses. "I worry about who's doing the 'documenting,'" the minister said, "and what a person has in mind to see—before they get here to take a look or take a listen! I say to myself: will they 'document' our tears, but not our smiles? Will they 'document' our rough times, but not show us having a good time, now and then—no matter how poor we be, and how down-and-out it gets for us, and how bad the treatment we receive from Mr. White Man?"[45]

The image of the rural South and its black residents created by Lyon as a SNCC photographer, and by Newfield as a journalist, comprises what historian Grace Elizabeth Hale calls the "romance of the outsider." Lyon, a white, college-educated photographer from the urban North, was part of a group who wanted to become outsiders from the American mainstream, to "express their alienation" from middle-class culture and expectations through art and activism while the documented—black people in the rural South, the true outsiders in American life and culture—"wanted to get in, to the good jobs . . . and the possibility of upward mobility." A white student expressed the essence of this romance in his application to join SNCC: "I have chosen to be outside of society after having been very much inside. I intend to fight that society which lied to and smothered me for so long, and continues to do so to vast numbers of people." Another white student volunteer during the Freedom Summer project of 1964 wrote a letter expressing ambivalence about his work in the Mississippi Delta, since it threatened to undermine the folk authenticity of the black people he encountered there and integrate them into a world he wanted to escape: "I sometimes fear that I am only helping to integrate some beautiful people into modern white society with all of its depersonalization (I suppose that has something to do with its industrial nature). It isn't 19th century pastoral romanticism which I feel, but a genuine respect and admiration for a culture which, for all the trouble, still isn't as commercialized and depersonalized as is our Northern mass culture."[46]

Lyon expressed similar ideas about the corrupting forces of modern American culture, but emphasized his romantic desire to use photography to document the lingering vestiges of true "humanity" lurking on the margins before they vanished. "Over time I came to believe that as the modern world developed around me in America, humanity itself and reality itself were threatened," Lyon wrote later in his life. "Not necessarily with a physical extinction, but with a spiritual extinction. Humanity itself became an endangered species in my mind, and thus I was drawn to picture people and places that exuded their humanity. My negatives and my contact sheets became my memory. I wanted to experience forever the people and places before me, because I knew they were about vanish. I wanted to change history and preserve humanity, but in the process, I changed myself and preserved my own."[47]

As Lyon acknowledged, his photographs, particularly those he took of rural Mississippi and the black farmers who lived and worked there, functioned less as propaganda for political and economic change and more as evidence of the cultural values of white youth in America during the 1960s. If his photographs exposed the sources of black oppression, they also aestheticized the beauty and seeming authenticity of rural black life in the South. At the same time, the irony of photographs made by and circulated among insiders wanting to be outsiders of outsiders fighting to be insiders, also limited their potential to bring about change. A poster that SNCC made from one of Lyon's photographs of a black Mississippi farmer to promote its voter registration work in the area provides a relevant example. The poster, which bears the slogan "One Man One Vote," a phrase used in the anticolonial fights in Africa, shows a poor man wearing overalls and a straw hat and sitting on a small stool in front of his weathered home. The man smiles while he rests his arms on his thighs and clasps his hands to-

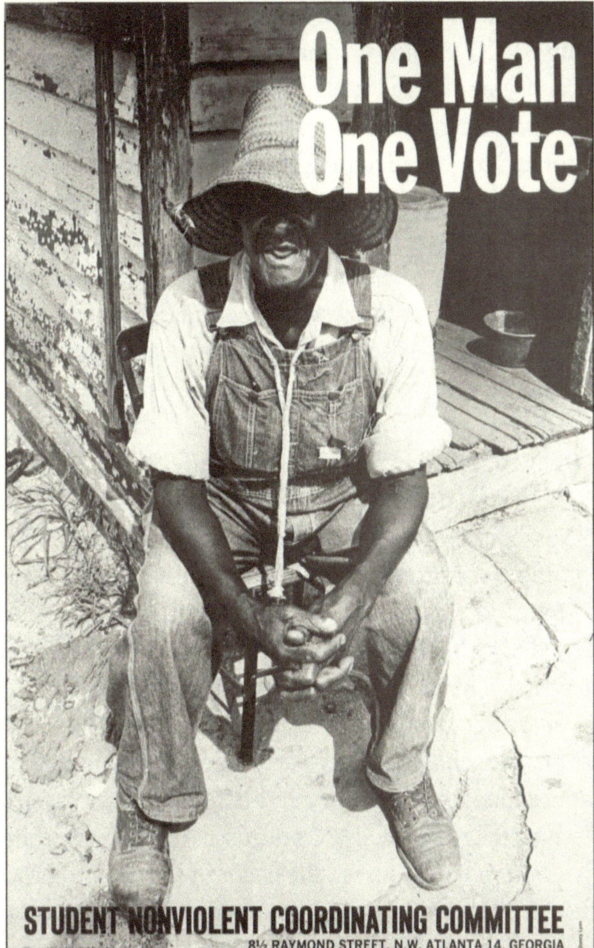

Danny Lyon, "One Man, One Vote" poster. © Danny Lyon/Magnum Photos.

gether. Lyon took the photograph from above the man, rather than straight on. The odd angle of the image, which forces the viewer to look down on the man, creates a dramatic air reminiscent of Margaret Bourke-White's Depression-era photographs of poor rural southerners in *You Have Seen Their Faces*. According to William Stott, Bourke-White's dramatically posed photographs along with Erskine Caldwell's accompanying captions caused the viewer to feel an "imagination twisting the facts to squeeze the easiest and most maudlin emotions from them; a spirit that regards craft, its effect, rather than its subject." Historian Leigh Raiford reads the poster in a similar light, arguing that the photograph's "somewhat patronizing and demeaning angle . . . vexes the facile employment of photography as a method of embodying SNCC ideology." The image creates a mirage of the individual agency and empowerment that organizers tried to create among local people. Instead it communicates the cultural desires and preconceptions of its creator and its intended middle-class audience.[48]

Reviews of *The Movement* also provide evidence of the political limitations of documentary photographs that white audiences often viewed as art. In his review, Hans Koningsberger, a Dutch-born novelist and journalist, not only emphasized the beauty of the book's photographs of places like the Mississippi Delta but also linked the discovery of that beauty to the personal pleasure volunteers expressed when they returned north after a summer spent in the South. *The Movement's* "cumulative effect," he wrote, "is to make one, suddenly, see beauty where one had expected to find suffering and bitterness only; to make one understand the statement, mysterious-sounding to newspaper readers up North, of civil-rights workers who came back last fall from Mississippi proclaiming the project there 'the happiest-making work they had ever done.'"[49] John Howard Griffin, a white journalist from Mansfield, Texas, who published *Black like Me* in 1961, his account of darkening his skin and going undercover as a black man in the segregated South, also focused on the book's power as art and how it aestheticized suffering. The transformation of suffering into documentary art, particularly in the minds of white reviewers, raises questions about photography's political efficacy. Lyon's photographs certainly served the needs of SNCC's outreach to northern white audiences, but one can question if they served the needs of the people SNCC fought for in the South. The common refrain in the reviews of *The Movement* was not how the book's photography inspired social change, but how it created a new, unexpected definition of beauty now immortalized in print.

The irony and tensions of these documentary dynamics could also be detected in SNCC's broader work in the region. Writing in 1963, former SNCC worker Bruce Payne noted that the cultural critique of middle-class values expressed by some SNCC members conflicted with the social and economic aspirations of the poor black people they worked with in the South. "In the long run, however, SNCC and the rest of the 'new left' faces problems that the values which they denounce are likely to be those that will be pursued by anyone liberated from poverty, indeed, they may *already* be the values which the poor aspire to," Payne wrote. "The greatest beneficiaries [of the romance of the outsider], in the end, were those middle-class young people who used their attraction to blacks as the folk to transform themselves," Hale argues. Newfield called this the "ultimate irony of the New Left's assault on the Closed Society." It was, he wrote, "an enduring paradox that all through Mississippi the lives of the white volunteers have been more enriched, and more fundamentally changed, than the lives of the maids and tenant farmers whom they came to help."[50]

By early 1964, Danny Lyon had begun to reflect on his role in SNCC, to wonder whether he might be better suited for something else. Many things weighed on his mind in February 1964. He felt a keen sense of responsibility to SNCC and the movement, but the stress and day-to-day drudgery were beginning to take a toll on him. "I'd rather be making a movie or money or generally enjoying myself," he told his parents in a letter, "which is the main thing I don't get to do in the South." If it is easy to romanticize the movement in retrospect, especially by looking at photographs made to mythologize, it is hard to deny the fatalism many felt in the movement even during its halcyon days. He wanted to go to New York City and Chicago, to relax and photograph motorcycle gangs rather than mass meetings. A few days before writing his parents, Lyon ate dinner with John Lewis who, according to Lyon said "what a waste of time this all was. He ment [*sic*] all the work all of us are doing. None of us want to be here." Lyon said he felt like leaving the movement and occasionally did after he became SNCC's staff photographer. "The trouble is I always come back, because I want to and because I feel I have to." He believed the movement was good for him because it gave him and his photography a social purpose. He also had an obligation to SNCC and felt "forced to face the responsibility." In February 1964, Lyon observed, "the system remains, segregation has not yet fallen, only victories keep everyone here." Lyon's own "little victories" amounted to a stirring pamphlet documenting the violent Danville, Virginia, desegregation campaign and a poster that made money for SNCC; displaying photographs in various Friends of SNCC offices in the North; and even selling some photographs and passing on the money to SNCC. "These things have for a brief moment given me satisfaction previously unknown to me."[51]

In early 1964, Lyon played a central role in helping produce *The Movement*, which was conceived by James Forman and Elizabeth Sutherland Martinez sometime in 1963. In 1964, Martinez was both an editor at Simon & Schuster and the head of SNCC's New York office, which provided the civil rights group with critical publicity and fundraising support. In conceptualizing the purpose of the book, she also drew on her experience as a UN analyst of anticolonial movements around the world and as an assistant to Edward Steichen, the director of photography at the Museum of Modern Art. Another editor at Simon & Schuster, Alan Rinzler, also helped produce the book; early on he noticed that "the best pictures were from this one guy, Danny Lyon." Lyon later admitted that after getting involved in the project he "began to photograph specifically for the book." He and Rinzler worked together to select the photographs that would appear in *The Movement*, and Lyon's role, Rinzler recalls, "gradually leaked into collaborator and fellow editor." In fact, it seemed that Lyon wanted to make the book into a collection of his photographs for SNCC. "He wanted to do it all, writing and photographs. He wanted to be both Walker Evans and James Agee, like in *Let Us Now Praise Famous Men* [1941]." Lyon ultimately wrote all of the captions for the photographs in the back of the book and came up with its full title.[52]

But Rinzler and Martinez realized that the book needed to appeal to a broad public audience and not simply SNCC members. A Simon & Schuster sales representative told Rinzler, "We want to sell this book to white people, too." They needed a celebrity who would pass muster with SNCC and appeal to the "general market." Rinzler, through personal contacts, convinced Lorraine Hansberry, a SNCC supporter whose 1959 play, *A Raisin in the Sun*, was the first by a black woman to appear on Broadway, to write the book's accompanying text. At the same time, Rinzler and Martinez acquired photographs from photojournalists like Bob Adelman and Tony Rollo, as well as images by Marion Palfi, of the radical photography cooperative known as the Photo League; Roy DeCarava, the black painter and photographer; and Robert Frank to go alongside those made by Lyon and the small number of other photographers associated with SNCC like Norris McNamara and James Forman. Ultimately, Lyon took 72 of the book's 123 photographs. According to Betty Garman, a northern SNCC coordinator, *The Movement* was "selling like crazy" in November 1964.[53]

Black Power and SNCC Photography in the Rural South

By the end of 1964, Lyon was no longer a SNCC staff member. "The world of SNCC was no longer mine," he said, "and I had been inalterably changed by the experience." Earlier in the year, Norris McNamara and Tamio Wakayama had helped conceive and develop a formal SNCC photography department, SNCC Photo, which also included Lyon and three black photographers: Bob Fletcher, Cliff Vaughs, and Doug Harris. During the summer of 1964, Lyon also ceded his dominant role as SNCC photographer to Matt Herron and his Southern Documentary Project. Herron believed the SDP would serve as the objective eye of the movement in Mississippi and provide a critical distance that SNCC photographers like Danny Lyon could not offer. Nevertheless,

SNCC photographers, including Lyon, contributed photographs to Herron's SDP, and SNCC retained the right to use them for its own publicity and propaganda purposes. For Lyon, the SDP did not represent a potentially history-making venture, but an unwanted intrusion and a resented attempt at organization. "I hated being organized," he said, "and even argued that what was now happening in the movement [Freedom Summer] did not lend itself to photography." The "politics of the movement," he argued, "were complicated. Photography dealt with surfaces." The surface appearance of Freedom Summer and its activities, which included voter registration and education projects and citizenship schools, seemed less primed to generate the drama and emotion of other movement work. Nevertheless, Herron said, Lyon produced the "most successful" photographs of anyone working for the SDP and SNCC that summer.[54]

Lyon's last contact with SNCC was at the Waveland conference in 1964, and he knew to document the moment. "I knew I would probably never see them again, and so I carefully made a picture of every person inside the room." His last photograph of Bob Moses reflected the mythological image Lyon had of many of these SNCC workers, especially Moses. In Lyon's photograph, Moses characteristically sits on the floor in the back of the room, writing notes in a journal. He appears disconnected from the meeting and out of the limelight. Yet he is illuminated by sunlight flowing in from a window behind him, which leaves him radiant while everyone else remains darkened by comparison. Lyon's parting shot of Moses evokes the romantic mythology he wanted to attach to SNCC workers as they risked their lives fighting for black civil rights in the South.[55]

After Lyon's departure, changes in both SNCC's photography department and in the organization brought in new photographers and ideas about the purpose of documentary work. The department's growth in late 1964 and 1965 was tumultuous, with SNCC Photo expanding to a staff of twelve photographers, nine of whom were black. Changes in departmental leadership, communication breakdowns, and conflicts between photographers making personal art and those creating more utilitarian records of SNCC activities led to confusion about the purpose of SNCC Photo and its relationship to SNCC as a whole. The tension and flux reflected the debates about SNCC's larger role in the movement in 1965, when the interracial coalition of the past and focus on direct action and voter registration campaigns began to give way to calls for Black Power and black nationalism. By 1966, SNCC members had voted for Stokely Carmichael to replace John Lewis as SNCC chairman. SNCC leaders like Carmichael framed their calls for black empowerment and self-determination in a global context, linking the struggles of black people in America with anticolonial and liberation movements occurring in Africa and Southeast Asia.[56]

SNCC's embrace of Black Power and black nationalism transformed the vision and purpose of SNCC Photo. Anticolonial struggles against Western domination generated debates about the authority and privilege of white ethnographers and photographers to represent African people. Black SNCC photographers like Lester linked black political and social empowerment to black representational empowerment. No longer would well-meaning white liberals like Danny Lyon represent SNCC and the rural black people it sought to revolutionize: black SNCC photographers would make photographs of black people for black people. While Lester and other black SNCC photographers would share Lyon's interest in the rural South and rural black southerners, and also continue to emphasize the beauty of the rural folk, their photographs performed very different functions than did Lyon's. Their images of the rural South and rural black people not only challenged white representations of black life but also constituted a kind of counter-archive. Rather than mythologizing SNCC leaders and generating white liberal support in the North, Lester and others in SNCC Photo celebrated the identity and beauty of black people, particularly in the South, in the name of racial pride and empowerment. While SNCC's first photography exhibit, *NOW*, opened in 1965 at the Visual Arts Gallery in Chelsea, Manhattan, Lester organized another exhibit, *US*, that opened two years later in Harlem at the Countee Cullen Library. Richard Avedon chaired the first exhibit; Gordon Parks chaired *US*, which proclaimed black unity and black representational power. Instead of books and posters designed with white audiences in mind, Lester and SNCC Photo created calendars adorned with documentary photographs of black people for the walls of black homes. As Julius Lester would later say, "Power is not only political, power is also self-confidence. And so you can't have self-confidence if the images you see reflect somebody else's world." Lester and other black SNCC photographers thus became "participatory documentarians" in the words of art historian, Iris Schmeisser, who "were motivated by a strong impulse for personal and political empowerment in representing the struggle of their own people."[57]

Until 1965, documentary work for and about SNCC had mostly been produced by whites. In addition to Lyon's work, a white filmmaker named Harvey Richards made two documentary films for SNCC, *We'll Never Turn Back* (1963) and *A Dream Deferred* (1964), and a white film crew made the film *The Streets of Greenwood* in 1963 that depicted "the effort of Negroes and white to achieve the right to vote in Mississippi, despite prejudice, illegal pressure, and actual violence," according to the film's brochure.[58] White folklorist Guy Carawan of the Highland Folk School in Tennessee made a series of audio documentaries of the movement in the South beginning in 1960 and released many of them as LP records on labels such as Folkways and Vanguard Records. These albums, which featured recordings of individual testimonies, mass meetings, hymns, and freedom songs, included *The Nashville Sit-In Story* (1960); *We Shall Overcome: Songs of the Freedom Riders and the Sit-Ins* (1961); *Freedom in the Air: A Documentary on Albany, Georgia* (1962), released on SNCC's own short-lived record label; and *The Story of Greenwood* (1965). Alan Ribback, a Chicago folk music club owner who later became known as Moses Moon, produced another LP of field recordings, *Movement Soul*, which he made in the Deep South in 1963 and 1964 with SNCC photographer and member, Norris McNamara. He released the record in 1967 on ESP-Disk, a label known for putting out experimental rock records by The Fugs and avant-garde jazz records by artists such as Albert Ayler and Sun Ra. It too featured photography by Danny Lyon, McNamara, and Wakayama and of black SNCC photographers such as Lester, Cliff Vaughs, Joffre Clark, Bob Fletcher, and Rufus Hinton. Once again, the intended audiences of these documentary LPs remained largely, but not exclusively, middle-class whites associated with the folk revival or avant-garde scenes in northern cities.[59]

Julius Lester would ultimately express a new documentary ethos for SNCC that shifted the control of cameras and recorders into black hands and made black people the main beneficiaries of SNCC documentary work. This shift would require Lester to call out the enduring, and unconscious, racism of sympathetic white liberals he met in SNCC and the folk revival. Before he joined SNCC Photo, Julius Lester had been a folksinger and performed at SNCC benefits in New York City in the early 1960s and later volunteered for the 1964 Mississippi Summer Project. Lester also wrote for folk revival publications such as *Sing Out!* and *Broadside* and had once been a friend of Guy Carawan and his wife Candie, helping them collect and transcribe civil rights songs during the mid-1960s. By 1966, Lester argued that the romanticization of SNCC and rural black southerners by white liberals had run its course. That year he published an article in *Sing Out!* titled "The Angry Children of Malcolm X" that expressed ire at what he saw as the self-serving and solipsistic nature of the embrace of SNCC by white liberals. "SNCC had been their romantic darling, a kind of teddy bear that they could cuddle," he wrote. "The time had come, however, when blacks could no longer be therapy for white society." White liberals had found "something that would put meaning into their lives, something that their country and society had not given them." White folklorists and their documentary work among rural black southerners during the folk revival represented the opposite side of the same romantic coin. Soon after critiquing white liberal involvement in SNCC, he challenged white documentary representations of black life and the presumption that whites, however well meaning, could document lives of people they found fascinating, but ultimately could not comprehend. In his 1967 review in *Sing Out!* he criticized a documentary book published by the Carawans on black life and culture on Johns Island, South Carolina, *Ain't You Got a Right to the Tree of Life?*, for failing to see the black community in all of its complexity and diversity, something he implied whites were incapable of doing. The time had arrived when black people must take control of their own organizations and their own representations from whites.[60]

Writing in January 1967 as director of SNCC Photo, Lester laid out the radical purpose of SNCC work, framing it as an important front in the broader Black Power movement. "The black American is constantly bombarded with images that are not his own—the Pepsi generation ads, Clairol, etc.," he wrote. "When *LOOK* magazine does an issue on American Youth, it shows white teen-agers at beach parties, playing tennis, etc., and includes a token black youth or two, but the reality projected there is not the reality of the black teenager of Watts, Harlem, Bedford-Stuyvesant and Alabama. They are presented with images that they are asked to emulate. We in SNCC say they should be allowed the opportunity to know their own images, their own values, their own lives, which are, essentially different from those of most Americans." In the previous two years, Lester had traveled through the Deep South—Alabama, Mississippi, and Louisiana—first looking for "indigenous musicians" for the purpose of organizing a folk music festival to benefit SNCC and then photographing black communities in the region. When he visited black homes he noticed walls adorned with calendars and advertisements created by and for whites. "The calendars pictured white women, of course, but what occurred to me was that the people wanted something 'beautiful' to look at, that perhaps there is within all of us a need for, an instinct for, beauty." These experiences inspired Lester to imagine new ways of empowering black people through documentary expression. SNCC Photo would use photographs taken by black SNCC photographers and place them on calendars and postcards that would replace the white images found on the walls of black homes. The idea of a calendar particularly appealed to Lester: he wanted to "create a calendar that would have images of blacks and other non-whites and to give the calendars to poor blacks in Mississippi so they could look at people more like themselves." As Lester wrote in January 1967, "Black power to us is exemplified by these calendars. . . . We are going to look at ourselves with our own eyes and define ourselves (if we must) after we've taken a good long look and found out that we're a beautiful people."[61]

Unlike Danny Lyon in his early work, Julius Lester and other black SNCC photographers such as Bob Fletcher, Doug Harris, Joffre Clark, and Rufus Hinton, did not focus on making photographs of SNCC leaders, mythologizing people like Carmichael or H. Rap Brown in order to recruit white liberal support in the North and West. Instead of SNCC leaders, the calendars featured the faces of anonymous black people, mostly but not exclusively those who lived in the rural South. If rural black southerners and the rural South's landscape constituted areas of interest for Lyon, they became a preoccupation for SNCC Photo's black photographers.[62] "The concern of SNCC photography was to make a visual record of the lives of ordinary black people in the rural south, especially," Lester later recalled. "Those were the people who were the most invisible, so it was very important to create images that showed their resilience, their dignity, their strength, their joys. Art was used in the service of documenting these lives."[63]

Like Danny Lyon, Lester found beauty among the rural South's poor black population. Like Lyon, Lester said he "set out to document the South as it entered a period of profound change." Lester's vision of the South was, in part, influenced by Walker Evans and the FSA archive, much as had Lyon's own views of the region. "Walker Evans was a big influence for me," Lester said. "But I knew nobody could see the way I saw."[64]

What distinguished Lester's documentary vision was his race—it allowed him to establish an easier rapport with the black people he met in the region so that they saw him "as being one of them rather than an outsider, a spectator." Yet Lyon, in a 1993 interview, said that he perceived his whiteness as a benefit to his doing documentary work in the Deep South of the 1960s. "I was white, I mean, which, in effect, was a disguise," he recalled. "I mean, if you were in the civil rights movement because, you know, a white person can do anything they want in the south. That's what the whole system was about, really. So, I had a kind of freedom that most of the people in SNCC didn't have." While this may have been true in regard to photographing segregation signs inside courthouses for instance, Lyon's whiteness still made him an "outsider" when photographing in black communities and could provoke resistance from some black people in the South during particularly contentious times. Lester, in contrast, found that a shared blackness broke down barriers that often faced white photographers. His family's background in rural Arkansas and Mississippi also made him more familiar with the complexity of people who lived in poverty. "Because my grandmother lived in a house in Pine Bluff, Arkansas, much like the ones I saw in Mississippi, when I was photographing in the south I did not see the poverty. What I saw was the dignity and beauty of the people."[65]

If both Lyon and Lester aestheticized the rural South's black poor, they did so for different ends. Lyon, like other whites in SNCC and the New Left, romanticized the black rural poor as quintessential outsiders who possessed an authenticity, purity, and beauty because they seemed so removed from the corrupting forces of industrialism and consumerism rooted in cities and suburbs. In contrast, Lester and other black SNCC photographers saw an emphasis on beauty as a way to resist and counter white images in American popular culture in the name of black self-empowerment.

By 1966 and 1967, when Lester took over as director of SNCC Photo and reimagined the purpose of SNCC documentary work, Danny Lyon no longer had any contact with the group or the civil rights movement. By that time Lyon had turned his photographic attention to the destruction of Lower Manhattan. In 1966 and 1967, he documented the razing of nineteenth- and twentieth-century architecture in the name of urban renewal. His photographs of vacant and silent buildings on the brink of collapse carry an elegiac air and suggest the larger upheavals and transformations sweeping urban America during this time. Having photographed the South's de jure system of segregation and white supremacy in its death throes, he turned his attention to the collapse of another old America. "I came to see the buildings as fossils of a time past," he wrote in his book, *The Destruction of Lower Manhattan*.[66]

Lyon also sought out new subjects on the margins of society after leaving the civil rights movement. "I've never liked to photograph my contemporaries," Lyon said in 1972. Some of the civil rights workers may have been university students, but their difference—their race, their economic and regional background, their willingness to face death for justice—made them seem not like "contemporaries," but instead larger-than-life figures and unlike anyone he encountered in the comfortable world of the University of Chicago. Without a noble fight to document in an exotic part of the country, Lyon searched for other outsiders to photograph as a way to experience a more vital life in the middle and late 1960s. So, he followed and photographed bike rider gangs, chasing their "spirit" on the open road.[67]

In 1967, Lyon again journeyed to the South, this time to visit Knoxville, Tennessee, where one of his heroes, James Agee, was born and lived during his childhood. He photographed the city's poor white neighborhoods, particularly young people who appeared far removed from middle-class comfort. In a photograph he titled "For Walker Evans and James Agee, Knoxville," he portrayed two boys, one sitting shirtless in a car, the other holding a black puppy in his arms and staring away from the camera with a morose expression. Twenty-two years later, Lyon wrote a eulogy to Agee and Evans around the photograph's borders linking his image of the white poor to the influence and legacy of *Let Us Now Praise Famous Men*: "For Walker Evans and James Agee, two gallent [*sic*] men, together in life, now united immortal in death. . . . Now they are both gone and we are left thoroughly alone. One would have thought that the world itself would end with [Agee's] death, so great was his vision, so powerful his art." With *Famous Men* as their sacred text, other documentarians made pilgrimages to the South, like Lyon, from the 1970s into the early twenty-first century in search of the people and places Agee and Evans immortalized. Hale County, Alabama, rather than Knoxville, was their mecca.[68]

CHAPTER FIVE

Protesting the Privilege of Perception

Resistance to Documentary Work in Hale County, Alabama, 1900–2010

Hale County, Alabama. For many, the words conjure images of Allie Mae Burroughs's face.[1] Appearing older than her twenty-seven years, she stands before an unpainted clapboard house staring straight into Walker Evans's lens, her lips pursed and brow furrowed. Others may see a kudzu-covered country store embalmed by William Christenberry's lush Kodachrome film. Some might hear in their heads James Agee's often-quoted archaeological list of materials he wanted to present to readers instead of words in *Let Us Now Praise Famous Men*: "If I could do it, I'd do no writing at all here. It would be photographs; the rest would be fragments of cloth, bits of cotton, lumps of earth, records of speech." For others, Hale County summons images of the Rural Studio, an innovative architectural project Samuel Mockbee started there in the early 1990s. The photographs by the Rural Studio's photographer, Timothy Hursley, vividly depict the striking designs of houses, chapels, and community centers made of salvaged tires, hay bales, license plates, and innumerable reusable materials. A writer who visited Hale County in 2005 for a story on the Rural Studio described its landscape as if it were a gallery displaying the work of these documentary artists: "Drive through Hale County today, and Agee and Evans' world will come to life. Broken-down pickup trucks and dusty storefronts are evidence of residents' hardscrabble lives, eking out a living on catfish ponds and in cotton fields, in endless battles against the kudzu."[2] A journalist for the *Washington Post* saw a similar scene when he visited the county the year before—an impoverished, isolated place fixed in the past and all the more beautiful for it. Documentary art and architecture made it a destination. "Hale County is a backwater characteristic of what used to be called the 'other America'—passed by, depopulated and poor," he wrote. "Its rich social and aesthetic landscape, however, has been put on the world's cultural map through the work of four creative individuals"—namely, Agee and Evans, Christenberry and Mockbee.[3]

Photography curator and critic Thomas Southall argues that, for these artists, Hale County—"or more accurately, the small part of it encompassing some farming families and roadside buildings in a few small towns"—functioned as a place of creative inspiration akin to William Faulkner's fictional "cosmos" of Yoknapatawpha County. Yet, as much as Hale County served as their "cosmos," these documentarians also created this cosmos, granting the county, in the words of historian Alan Trachtenberg, "the status of place in American art and imagination." Hale County has indeed become indelibly linked with the work of Agee, Evans, and Christenberry, but they were not the first—or last—to document the area. There, for more than a century, travel writers, folklorists, journalists, photographers, and filmmakers attempted to reveal the realities of life in rural Alabama and, by extension, the South through documentary forms of expression. Their portrayal of the county and its people, however, contributed to a broader twentieth-century romance of the rural South that transformed the faces, landscapes, and architecture of the poor into art that resonated with educated, middle-class audiences. As their work circulated in books, magazines, films, and galleries, Hale County became a renowned site of representation, a place defined by documentarians rather than local residents.[4]

A very different image of Hale County comes into focus, however, if we look at the history of documentary work there from the perspective of those who have been photographed, filmed, and described. Instead of a place defined by documentarians, Hale County becomes a battleground, a central site of resistance in the "interactional history" of documentary work, where struggles over who gets to represent a people and place, and why, have flared for more than a century. The resistance of the documented rather than the revelation of the documentarians becomes the dominant theme. Refusing to be photographed or interviewed, sabotaging a photograph by closing one's eyes, taking legal action against invasions of privacy or for recompense—all are forms of resistance to representation that demand we see the documented as actors, rather than just icons of poverty or the rural South. "Surprisingly," notes anthropologist Renato Rosaldo, who has studied how "natives" can "talk back" to ethnographers, "discussions of the 'native point of view' tend not to consider that so-called natives are more than reference points for cultural conceptions. They often disagree, talk back, assert themselves politically, and generally say things that 'we' might rather not hear."[5]

In Hale County, the history of resistance to documentary work highlights the role race and class play in determining who gets to represent a people and place and how the documented often challenge the legitimacy of that power. This history begins with the books of dialect poetry by Hale County native, Martha Young, a white woman from an elite family whose publications combined photography with verse that occasionally addressed the tensions and conflicts between white photographers and black subjects. Three decades before James Agee and Walker Evans arrived, Young and photographer J. W. Otts documented scenes, songs, and stories from the Hale County countryside that evoked an idealized plantation past—one that Young nevertheless challenged herself by writing poems from the perspective of black women who refused to pose for white photographers. James Agee's and Walker Evans's *Let Us Now Praise Famous Men* shifted the focus from black to white residents and transformed the popular image of the county from one associated with the Old South—black minstrels, white-pillared plantation homes—to one synonymous with rural white poverty and the beauty of tenant architecture. While the subjects and images changed, the theme of resistance persisted as Agee and Evans immediately encountered challenges to their project of documenting white tenant families struggling in the South's depressed cotton economy. Agee anguished over the ethical and moral pitfalls of his and Evans's work, but excoriating himself and his readers for voyeurism could not protect the families featured in the book or their descendants. Agee's recognition of a "privilege of perception"—the "economic advantages" that allow one not only to document the poor but also to see beauty in their circumstances and surroundings—could not temper the resentment and even rage some family members felt at becoming icons of poverty or "famous folk," in the words of Howell Raines of the *New York Times*. Raines and a legion of other writers, photographers, and filmmakers would flock to Hale County from the 1970s up to the present day to rephotograph people and places Agee and Evans documented, to lay bare the private lives of the poor for public consumption in the name of journalism, documentary art, or progressive politics.[6]

Hale County residents have pushed back at every stage of this long history, called this "privilege of perception" into question, and interjected their own interpretations of images that made them famous and their home a hallowed place in the history of documentary art and reportage. Resistance never took the form of violence there as it did in eastern Kentucky in 1967 when Hobart Ison murdered a Canadian documentarian filming on his property. Nor is there a comparable community organization like Appalshop that is dedicated to empowering local people to document their own lives. Still, Hale County provides a microcosm of the documentary impulse in the South, including the desires that motivate documentarians and the acts of resistance their work can inspire. "The mystery of this landscape is magnified by those who contest each other's remembering of it—as the site of triumphs and tribulations, achievement or injury," writes John Forney, a Rural Studio advisor and Hale County native. "Pride and resentment twine over this ground."[7]

"No, I Don't Want My Picter Took"

Hale County is located in west central Alabama about twenty miles due south of Tuscaloosa and ninety miles southwest of Birmingham. The Black Warrior River forms the county's western border and weaves a serpentine path southwestward as it descends beyond the Fall Line and the final hills of Appalachia and into the flat prairie lands of the Black Belt. About 1050 A.D., a Mississippian community developed on the terraced hills above the river, safe from frequent floods. The inhabitants eventually built a palisaded town, replete with a central plaza surrounded by a series of steep-sided, flat-topped, and platform mounds ranging from three to fifty-seven feet high and oriented in cardinal directions.[8] The rise and fall of Moundville, today a town in the northern part of the county, began a centuries-long process in the Black Warrior River Valley and, later, Hale County in which the landscape became a palimpsest. Repeating stories of environmental manipulation, labor exploitation, and resulting disparities of wealth and power have been inscribed on the land in the form of mounds and then later Greek revival mansions, slave cabins, tenant houses, and new forms of architectural experimentation. All of these structures and the people who lived in them formed an important part of Hale County's documentary image, even though the type of architecture and people documentarians focused on changed over time under the influence of broader social, economic, and cultural forces.

Created in 1867, Hale County was carved out from neighboring Greene, Perry, Marengo, and Tuscaloosa Counties. In 1860, Greene was one of Alabama's wealthiest counties. Slaves grew the cotton that thrived in the area's rich alluvial soils, generating immense wealth for planters and making the area renowned for the social distinction of its white population by the eve of the Civil War. In 1854, a writer for a publication called *A News and Complete Gazetteer of the United States* declared that Greene County was "probably not surpassed by any in wealth or refinement." The regal and pretentious homes of planters, as well as the presence of an imposing Gothic Revival building that was home to Southern University, heralded the dominance of the Black Belt's small but powerful aristocracy.[9]

Despite the *Gazetteer's* description, the romantic plantation image associated with the area would be a product of post-Reconstruction writers and photographers. The myth of "Old South" grandeur that they emphasized in their work obscured the messy and contradictory realities of antebellum life. A young girl who moved from Connecticut to Greensboro, Alabama, in the 1830s leveled complaints about the area that many southerners often associated with the North during the antebellum era. "It is all business and bustle, and men and 'niggars,'" she wrote soon after arriving. Another early settler near Greensboro confessed that many in the area "thought of little else but making money [and] came to this new country for that particular purpose." As historian G. Ward Hubbs notes in his study of community development in Greensboro, "Unscrupulous men on the make seemed to overrun this unsettled region."[10]

Life in the Black Belt of Alabama in the 1830s struck some settlers like William Beverly as the reverse of the dignified culture he left back home in Virginia. The area had "little or no society," he wrote his father. It was "beset with scoundrels," he lamented, "no confidence in one another, all is suspicion & distrust."[11] During his travels across the Deep South, Frederick Law Olmsted met a fellow traveler who told him a story about a man he knew who was turned away from every plantation house he stopped at while traveling the twenty miles from Eutaw to Greensboro in Greene County. To highlight the broader picture of inhospitality he and other travelers had received, Olmsted concluded the story by writing, "This is the richest county of Alabama, and the road is lined with valuable plantations!"[12] The popular romance of the Alabama Black Belt as a southern Arcadia would come later, largely from the pens and cameras of a generation of writers, such as Martha Young and Herdman Cleland, and of photographers such as James Washington Otts, born during or shortly after the Civil War.

More than thirty years before James Agee and Walker Evans arrived in Hale County to document the lives of three white tenant families, Martha Strudwick Young, a writer and amateur folklorist, and James Washington (J. W.) Otts, a local photographer, documented the county's rural black residents. Agee's and Evans's collaborative work, *Let Us Now Praise Famous Men*, would eventually immortalize Hale County as a place synonymous with white rural poverty. Yet Young's and Otts's collaborative work from 1901, *Plantation Songs for My Lady's Banjo*, which combined photography and dialect poetry, presented Hale County as an antebellum idyll where rural blacks lived carefree lives as preternatural singers and storytellers. Both Young and Otts came from prominent white families in Hale County. For many years, Young had collected the stories and songs she heard from the black people who lived on her family's land in northwest Hale County near the town of Akron. She later based her poetry on these folkloric materials that she had gathered firsthand in the field. Her poems and Otts's photographs represented an attempt to salvage vestiges of a nostalgic plantation past. The critical praise for *Plantation Songs* turned Young into Alabama's most heralded writer and folklorist by the early twentieth century.[13]

Young's writing mimics the tropes of the popular plantation romance genre of the late nineteenth and early twentieth centuries, including dialect poetry, situating it in a long line of white appropriation of black expression as a means of racial representation, including what Eric Lott refers to as the "love and theft" of blackface minstrelsy. Her use of photographs to illustrate a book of dialect poetry also links her with other black and white writers who embraced pictorialist photography to heighten the realism of the text during the late nineteenth and early twentieth centuries. Black poet Paul Laurence Dunbar published a number of books of dialect poetry between 1896 and 1906 illustrated with photographs of black people, albeit ones mostly made by white photographers associated with the Hampton Institute Camera Club. Anne Virginia Culberton's book of dialect poetry from 1905, *Banjo Talks*, features photographs by Heustis Pratt Cook of Richmond, Virginia, and Mary Morgan Keipp, a native of Selma, Alabama, who exhibited her work on black life in rural Alabama internationally and nationally, including in the famed 1902 Photo-Secession exhibit organized by Alfred Stieglitz.[14]

While black writers like Dunbar and Charles Chestnutt, as well as black folklorists associated with the Hampton Institute's Hampton Folklore Society, used a variety of methodologies and styles to question and challenge white representations of black life in the South during this time, Young's work stands out among white writers and folklorists. She not only did collaborative fieldwork with a photographer in rural black communities but also reflected on the ethical and racial dilemmas that characterized encounters between white photographers and black subjects in the region. These experiences led her to a critique of photography as an invasive, potentially exploitive medium. Young's poems on black resistance to photography emphasize the power of a photograph to surveil and control one's identity and fate. It was a curious and ironic critique, involving a prominent white woman writing dialect poetry from the perspective of black people who bristled at being photographed by whites. On one hand, Young's poems fit into a long tradition identified by literary scholar Katherine Henninger, who argues that since the mid-nineteenth century "southern women authors have employed fictional photographs as powerful figures of the markers and strictures of southern identity." Young ultimately possessed the power to write and publish poems that neutralized instances of black resistance and resentment by making them apparently comedic elements in a genre of writing that reinforced the South's culture of white supremacy and segregation. Nevertheless, these poems also provide hints that the black Hale Countians whom Young and Otts documented attempted to resist the power of a white photographer and writer to shape their image and define their identity—to portray them as stock characters happily beholden to the culture and customs of slavery. In Young's poems, black people appear to understand that photographs can "bear false witness." That "is an understanding born of cultures like the South's, an arena of tangible, even violent, representational politics," writes Henninger. "Where a visible characteristic (be it skin color, body type, or the condition of one's clothing) is the central marker of social 'place,' visual representations take on special weight and so become the site of weighty struggle."[15]

These poems by Young also introduce what will become a persistent theme in the storied tradition of documentary work in Hale County: the iconic images and words that made the county first into an Old South preserve before it later earned "the status of place in American art and imagination" have always been questioned and challenged, if not outright resisted, by those whose private lives were made into public spectacles or objects of art. While Young's work fits squarely into the plantation romance tradition, it also presages postcolonial analyses of representation, power, and resistance. Young unwittingly reveals that resisting white cultural representation provided a covert way of also challenging white social control during a time of lynching epidemics, black voter disfranchisement, segregation laws, and pervasive and demeaning visual depictions of black people in advertisements, postcards, cartoons, and books.

Martha Young began her literary career in 1880 shortly after graduating from the Livingston Female Academy in Livingston, Alabama. She entered the fold of folklore collectors and writers at a time when authors like Joel Chandler Harris began receiving acclaim for their stories that fed a national fascination for "local-color" literature. Local-color writing flourished after the Civil War, particularly by the 1870s, as regional newspapers and national magazines such as the *Atlantic Monthly, Lippincott's Magazine,* and *Scribner's* published comedic or romantic tales from far-flung places, like the Appalachian Mountains or southern plantations, that focused on the peculiarities of the rural folk and their native regions. The genre created an exotic sense of difference between increasingly urban and middle-class consumers and the quaint premodern people they read about who evoked nostalgic reminders of a simpler preindustrial America. Its appeal also rested on its aura of documentary realism. The "hallmarks of local color," explain literary scholars Barbara Ewell and Glenn Menke, "were manifestly realistic: an accurate attention to detail, an emphasis on landscape, carefully created characters, provincial customs, and the peculiarities of local speech (dialect)." Southern local-color writers in particular, they argue, "pursued an essentially ethnographic task of accurately recording the differing speech patterns and customs of the souths they knew."[16] For Young and others of her generation, the New South threatened to undermine old social structures, racial codes, and economic arrangements. The tumults brought on by modernity required the preservation of an imagined idyllic past through poetry that produced a "picture whose exquisite polychromatic beauties will not fade," according to Young. "While we cling close to the real let us sanctify our realism with the halo of idealism."[17]

Young's *Plantation Songs for My Lady's Banjo,* published in 1901 under the pseudonym Eli Shepperd, combines the rural and exotic settings found in local-color fiction with dialect poetry and photography. The book combines thirty-one descriptive and dialect poems with twenty-three photographs by J. W. Otts. His images depict men and women working in plantation fields and playing fiddles and banjos, and they show the architecture of homes and a church set back in the woods. The book created an aura of realism that enraptured readers and reviewers across the country because it presented an idealized past alive in the present. Time and again, reviewers focused on the book's ability to present "true" pictures of "real life" and praised Young's mission to preserve the songs, sayings, and traditions that harkened back to slavery. "A striking book, thoroughly true to the real life of the plantation negro," a writer for the *New Orleans Times-Democrat* declared. Reviewers found the photographs of J. W. Otts particularly evocative and revelatory, simultaneously presenting a true picture of black life in the present day and conjuring the reality of antebellum plantation life. A reviewer for the magazine, *The Era,* noted that Otts's photographs were the first things to "attract

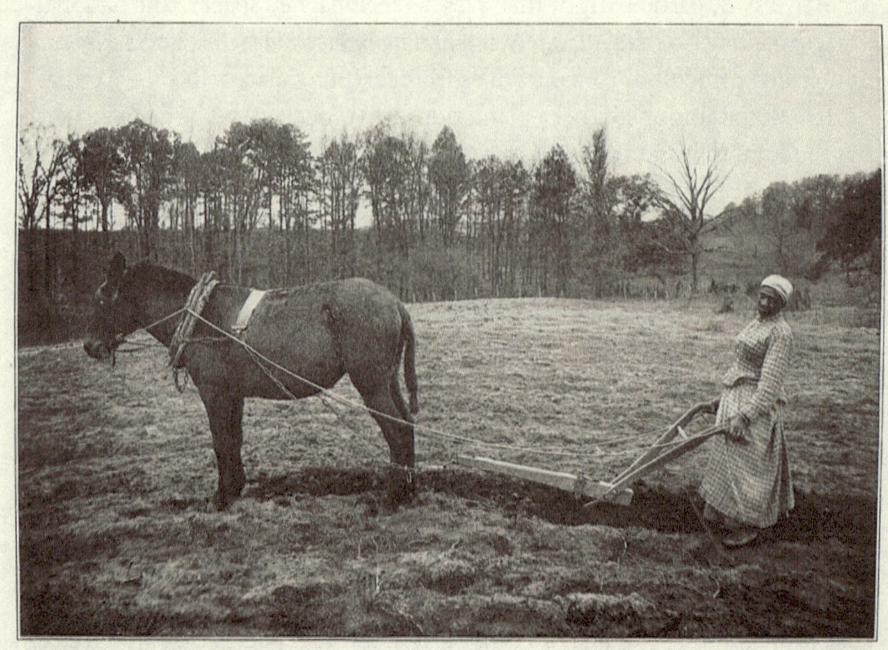

OH, mammy, dat drag at de plow handle,
And mammy dat drap at de hoe,
When you walk up de ladder to Glory
You won't hatter work no mo'.

J. W. Otts, "Oh, mammy, dat drag at de plow handle . . ." *Plantation Songs for My Lady's Banjo* (1901). Courtesy of the Rare Book Collection, Louis Round Wilson Special Collections Library, University of North Carolina at Chapel Hill.

the eye" of the reader and that they "are absolutely true to negro type, and to plantation life in the South."[18]

A handful of poems Young wrote after the publication of *Plantation Songs* suggest that the black Hale County residents depicted in the photographs would have not only challenged the critical praise the images received but also questioned the right of Otts to make them in the first place. Two of Young's poems seem to have never been published, while two others appear in her 1921 book, *The Minute Dramas: The Kodak at the Quarter*, which compiled poems previously published in places like *Century Magazine*, *Pictorial Review*, and the *New York Times*. In "Mammy's Photograph," an unpublished poem from 1920, Young writes from the perspective of a black woman who directly challenges the right of a white photographer to take her picture and even suggests that it is photography, and the viewing of photographs, that creates racial difference: in the dark and out of the light, we are all alike.[19]

MAMMY'S PHOTOGRAPH

I done spoken my mind to my Young Miss,
A-comin' and takin' niggers like dis!
Des 'cause she's white as a lily in June
And lively she as a corn-hollo-tune
Dat ain't no why to come takin' of we
As black as Old Man Appersarie! #

Well, I'll tell her dis: When it's pitch black night,
Every thing dark and dar ain't no light -
I done told her so — I know dat she
In dat plum dark is as black as me!
I don't care what sorter pic'ter she done —
  Us all de same — when dar ain't no sun.

#
Man's old adversary.[20]

Though a form of blackface minstrelsy, Young's poem, despite her comedic intentions, challenges common images of black people as happy and willing subjects for white photographers. The thoughts of a geographer named J. Sullivan Gibson seem more representative of the era. In 1940, Gibson traveled throughout the Alabama Black Belt photographing and writing about its geographic features, its people, and their cultural landscapes. In an article he published the following year, he included a photograph he took of a poor black family standing in front of their cabin with the following caption: "Black Belt negroes are a light-hearted happy folk, finding contentment in their lot, whatever it may be. They enjoy very much being photographed."[21] Young's poems offer another way of seeing the relationship between white documentarians and black subjects in the rural South during the twentieth century. Many whites, like Gibson, may have fallen victim to the "mask" black people wore while under white observation. As Dunbar writes in his poem, "We Wear the Mask," "We wear the mask that grins and lies/It hides our cheeks and shades our eyes . . . Nay let them only see us, while/We wear the mask." Gibson, like so many others, also might have simply misinterpreted politeness or obligation for willingness.[22]

Other white documentarians, such as Howard Odum and Jack Delano, often faced similar instances of resistance that echo Young's evidence from her poems. One of Odum's contemporaries, folklorist and Columbia University English professor Dorothy Scarborough, faced outright hostility from black southerners when her "Kodak" or even her "pencil" appeared while doing fieldwork, particularly in emotionally charged sacred settings. A white woman from Texas, Scarborough maintained a deep interest in black folklore and music and hoped to preserve the old songs she thought were endangered by modernity. Her experience documenting a baptism at a pond near Natchez, Mississippi, in the 1920s while doing fieldwork for her 1925 book, *On the Trail of Negro Folk-Songs*, provides an apparently real example of resistance to documentary work that relates to similar themes and interaction Young described in her poems. As the baptism candidate came out of the water, the congregation "surged back and forth" in an effort to greet the candidate. All the while, church members shouted with joy and joined in "vehement song." Scarborough said she "tried repeatedly to get a picture of the scene, but each time I adjusted the Kodak, some shouter would start up beside me and all but push me into the pond. The little black box seemed to have an unfortunate effect on the crowd. One time I thought I would persist, but in the melee I was all but crushed. . . . Even my pencil taking down songs upset them." While Scarborough chalked up their reactions to "emotional excitement" rather than the desire to inflict harm, resistance to the intrusion and power of a white woman with a camera and notebook seemed tied together with the fervor brought on by the baptism.[23]

Similarly, black people in Young's poems attempt to defy photography's capacity to surveil. They resist becoming objects of someone else's art. For instance, in "The Kodak at the Quarter" and "Aunt Dinah's Picture," both printed in *Minute Dramas*, Young addressed with uncommon candor the resentment black Hale County residents often expressed at being the camera's target and how they reacted to being photographed. "The Kodak at the Quarter" suggests the power of photography to create and define the meaning of blackness. Young writes about photographs taken of black people planting, picking, and ginning cotton, as well as photos of a man "on de jump or de run." These photographs, as suggested by her poem, associate "black" with hard labor and criminality even as they continue to imagine the Alabama Black Belt as a bastion of the Old South. The photograph's ability to arrest and punish is "wo'se" than that of the "Sheriff." Young recognizes that fulfilling the aesthetic desires of the documentarian comes at a cost for the identity and security of their subjects.

The Kodak at the Quarter

Somethin' 'nother done got loose on de Place,
Jumpin' right up in ever'body's face;
Des tetch off de trigger of one li'l box—
And it snatch up the niggers in droves and flocks!

It's wo'se 'n de Sheriff gwine 'round in de fall,
'Potin on de darkeys one and all;
Ever' thing dat a nigger hand do
Dat devil marks it down fer true

It got us dar hoein' and dancin' and prayin'
It got us plantin' cotton, pickin', ginnin', and weighin';
You stand 'round arguin' you won't be took—
But—tetch!—and dar! You's print in de book! . . .
It's enough to make a 'spectable man
Stay all day in de dark—if he can;
It make me b'lieve dese Las' Days sho'—
'Caze atter all dis de devil can't do no mo'.

Done 'range to take a nigger on de jump or de run,
Done press into service de Lord's own sun!
But de reason I 's'pize dat devil - Kodak
        Is des 'caze it love to paint a nigger—black![24]

In "Aunt Dinah's Picture," Young addresses the tension between a photograph's ability to represent reality and beauty and, at the same time, rob the subject of her identity and individuality and transform her into a commodity. Young's decision to write again in the voice of a black woman, as she did in "Mammy's Photograph," and reference photographs of black women ("Jiney," "Sis' Jane"), also suggests how one's gender could determine the nature, or even possibility, of resistance and why Young never wrote one of her poems about photography explicitly from the perspective of a black man, though she did so in many of her other dialect poems. Given the potentially explosive sexual tensions and fears that charged interactions between black men and white women in the region, black women would have certainly felt freer to challenge the authority of a white woman working alongside a white male photographer. In "Aunt Dinah's

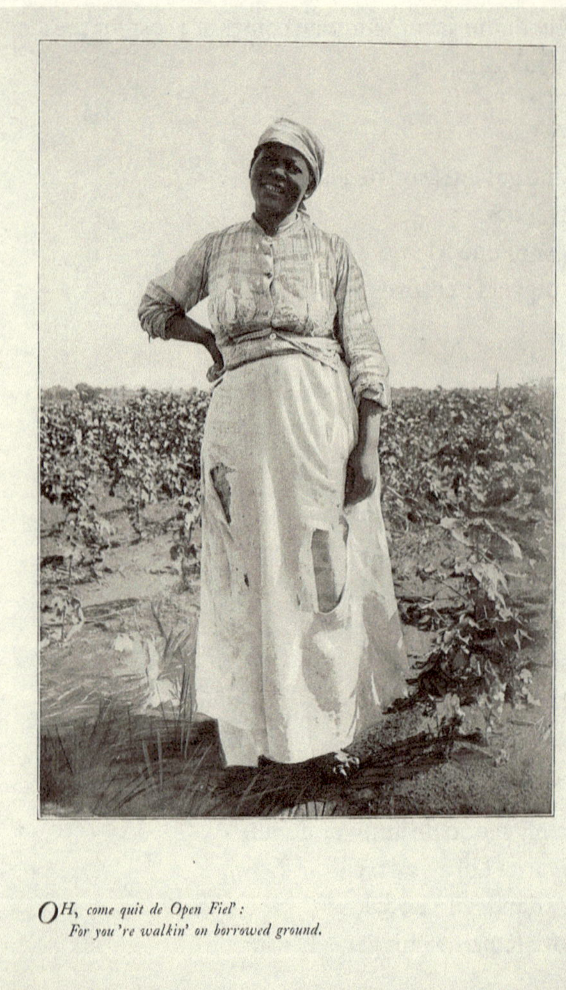

J. W. Otts, "No, I don't want my picter took." *Plantation Songs for My Lady's Banjo* (1901). Courtesy of the Rare Book Collection, Louis Round Wilson Special Collections Library, University of North Carolina at Chapel Hill.

Picture," Young again, unwittingly, shows how black women could try to control their identity, and their own conception of beauty, by refusing to become an object of documentary art that adorns the pages of a book intended for white audiences.

Aunt Dinah's Picture

Aunt Dinah:

No, I don't want my picter took.
Gwine all round in de paper and de book—
Ever-body knowin' des how I look.

You paint 'em good! I know you do,
Make ole folks look as good as new—
You tuck Jiney dressed for de Barbecue!

And dey say Sis' Jane's her ve'y spit,
Dey say folks can't tell her fum hit—
But dat don't change my mind a bit.

I'm gwine ter stay—des me—like I be,
If de Lord had-a wanted two er me
He'd-a made me twins at fust, you see![25]

Young's reliance on demeaning dialect writing gives her poem a comedic cast, but "Aunt Dinah's" refusal to have her picture taken, even if conjured in the mind of an aristocratic white writer, again suggests that Young might have encountered an undercurrent of resistance while observing Hale County's black communities. Even if Young ultimately neutralizes black resistance by poeticizing it in "Mammy's Photograph," "The Kodak at the Quarter," and "Aunt Dinah's Picture," her poems still suggest that black women in particular saw refusing to pose for white photographers as a way to control their identity and challenge whites' "privilege of perception" that promoted Hale County's idealized plantation image during the early twentieth century.[26]

In Young's undated essay, "Observations of Work among the Negroes of Hale County," she writes of the important task ahead for a local black educator who will continue the work of collecting folklore and, in particular, the spiritual songs "of the ancient church." "Who knows but that some day some Anton Dvorak may come to Hale County to find impetus and inspiration for some newer 'New World Symphony,'" she wrote. But Young concluded her essay on a dour note. While working on behalf of racial uplift and education among the county's black population was important, she lamented the neglect of the county's poor white population:

> But my heart bleeds for the illiterate white people of our county. . . . Here nothing is done to alleviate their lonely unlettered. . . . These have perhaps no great inheritance of unique song to give to the world, but they have a great heritage of pure Anglo-Saxon blood, brain and brawn; even the utter illiterates most likely hark back to ancestry of heroes of the Revolution. White people have not the blessed meekness, the contented fatalism, the usually joyous nature of the negro—of the Black Belt. The more do we need to help our own out of their unlettered condition.

Her essay's final paragraph unintentionally foreshadowed how the collapse of the southern cotton economy would unleash a new wave of documentary work in Hale County during the 1930s that would shift its image from one associated with plantation scenes redolent of the Old South to a place emblematic of the region's problems of white poverty and tenant farming. While documentarians would seek out new subjects, the theme of resistance to the camera, to voyeurism, and to documentary work itself would continue.[27]

"The Cold Absorption of the Camera"

In late July 1936, Hale County farmers learned that paid work was available for those who had suffered from the persistent drought. Some heard the news by word of mouth; others found out by reading the *Hale County News*. Titled "Subsistence Work Here," the brief piece in the paper read: "Greensboro, Ala., July 30, —Hale County farmers who have been made destitute by the drought may apply for work relief from the resettlement supervisors at the county resettlement office, according to the county supervisor, Hurtis Parr. This relief is not an effort by the Government to repay farmers for losses sustained in the drought but to give subsistence to destitute farm families suffering as a result of the drought."[28] Soon after hearing the news, three farmers from a tract of land in northeastern Hale County called Mills Hill decided to make the nearly nineteen-mile journey south to the county seat of Greensboro to apply for relief. Locals referred to their section of the county as "up in the valley"—a place of rolling hills, pine forests, and small farms. There "the last hills of the Appalachians provide soils too lean and terrain too rough for large-scale cropping," writes architect and Hale County native John Forney. "Farming on this fringe was most vulnerable to the vagaries of commodity price and crop failures. Many families lost their properties and frequently became tenants, caught in a cycle of debt working the parcels of others."[29]

The gradient dropped as the three men journeyed down Highway 69 and into the Black Belt. As they made their way to the courthouse in Greensboro, they passed by imposing white-pillared mansions, monuments to fortunes made from slave labor that bore names like Magnolia Hall, home of photographer J. W. Otts. Martha Young lived near the center of town, in a home described in 1927 as "what one would expect from a reading of her poems . . . tall white columns, stately and proud. . . . The very approaches to the house seem to exude the essence of Southern atmosphere and tradition." Accord-

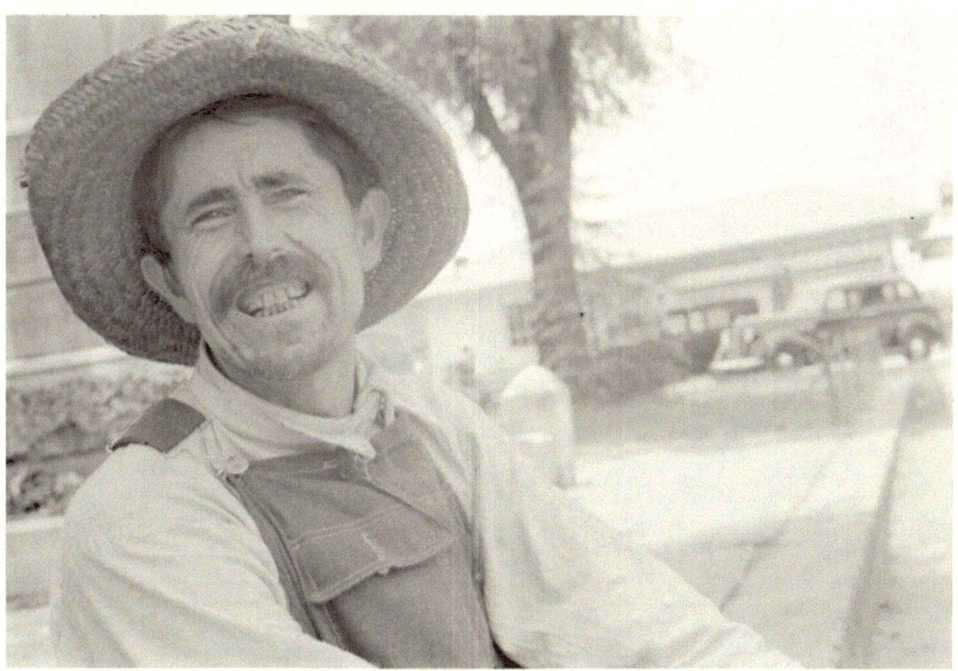

Walker Evans, *Frank Tingle, Greensboro, Hale County, Alabama*, Summer 1936. Courtesy of the Library of Congress, Prints and Photographs Division, FSA/OWI Collection. LC-USF33-031292-M2.

ing to Herdman Cleland, a northern professor who wrote a 1920 travel essay about his visit to Greensboro the year before, "A more perfect setting for the most romantic stories of Thomas Nelson Page would be hard to find." In Greensboro, these three tenants entered the seat of political, cultural, and economic power as outsiders in their own county—a marginalized poor white class from "up in the valley."[30]

At the foot of the Confederate memorial in front of the courthouse, one of the men, Frank Tingle, struck up a conversation with a man whose accent suggested distant origins. Soon another man emerged from the courthouse and joined their conversation. His voice too struck Tingle and, eventually, the other farmers as peculiar. Tingle talked the most and laughed the loudest. His volubility betrayed his fear of mockery from these seemingly sophisticated strangers. One of them, Walker Evans, eventually withdrew from the conversation and began taking photographs of Tingle using an angle viewfinder to prevent detection. Evans's partner, James Agee, later recalled that Tingle "never caught on." The scene made Agee reflect on how differently

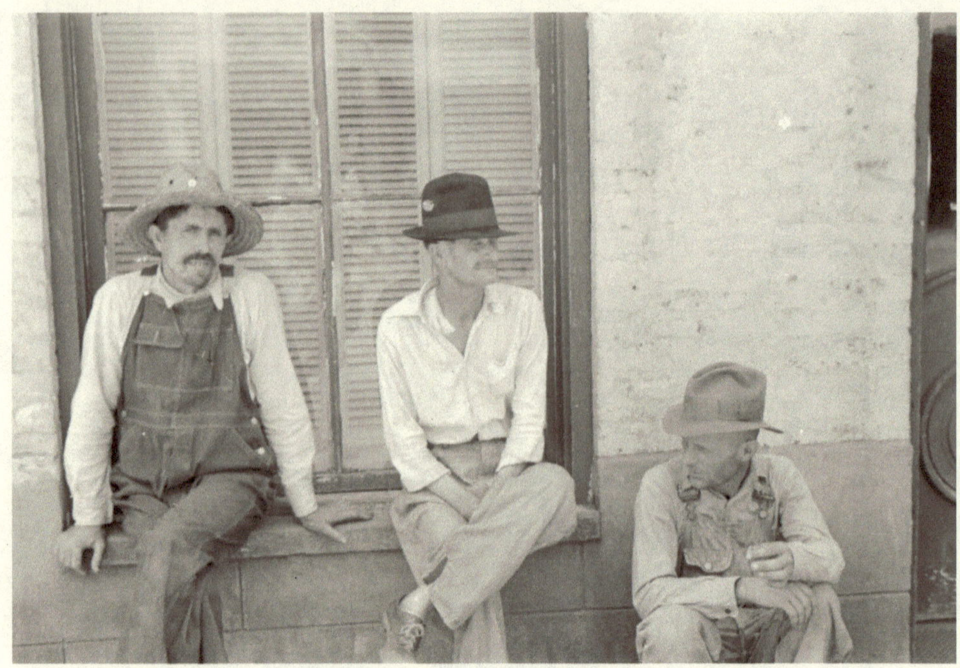

Walker Evans, *Frank Tingle, Bud Fields, and Floyd Burroughs, Greensboro, Hale County, Alabama*, Summer 1936. Courtesy of the Library of Congress, Prints and Photographs Division, FSA/OWI Collection. LC-USF33-031313-M2.

white and black people reacted to a stranger with camera: "I notice how much slower white people are to catch on than negroes, who understand the meaning of a camera, a weapon, a stealer of images and souls, a gun, an evil eye."[31] Agee had heard about how blacks in the South responded to cameras just a day or two earlier from an agricultural agent who was to help him find farmers who would be good candidates for his *Fortune* piece on white cotton tenants. He had asked the agent if Evans could take pictures. "Sure," he said, "take all the snaps you're a mind to; that is, if you can keep the niggers from running off when they see a camera." Eventually, however, even the agricultural agent felt manipulated when he saw the scope of Evans's photographic equipment in the car. According to Agee, "they showed that they felt they had been taken advantage of, but said nothing of it."[32]

Agee's assessment of the racialized response captures how the rural black Hale County residents equated the camera with white power and control. He did not need the agricultural agent to tell him how black people thought about whites wielding cameras. Agee's own pained confrontation with a black couple walking down a road near a church that Evans had broken into to photograph, and a performance by a group of young black men who were forced to sing for Agee and Evans at the agricultural agent's behest, captured the deep level of mistrust blacks felt toward whites, especially those armed with pens and cameras. "We might say that black people in *Let Us Now Praise Famous Men* are essentially invisible," argues cultural theorist Walter Benn Michaels, "almost literally unphotographable."[33] The white Hale Countians whom Agee and Evans would meet and eventually document for their putative article for *Fortune* would also quickly "catch on" and inject a current of resistance into the photographs and descriptions that would transform them into "famous men." Some of them passed this resistance onto their children, who would continue to bear the burden of their family's fame and their status as historical figures and icons of American art, as relentless waves of journalists and documentarians wrote follow-up stories, made films, or produced rephotography projects that once again opened their private lives to public view.

While the three farmers did not qualify for relief work since they were technically employed as tenants, they did meet the demands of Agee's and Evans's article for *Fortune*. The men rode with Agee and Evans in their car back north to Mills Hill to continue the introductions and for Agee and Evans to take preliminary notes and photographs. Some of them, Frank Tingle, in particular, still thought Agee and Evans were "Government men" who could provide help and assistance. The idea of a documentary exposé to introduce middle-class America to the plight of the white rural poor in the South did not register or matter. Sensing the possibility of assistance, Tingle was obliging and allowed Evans to immediately set up his tripod and begin taking pictures of the men and their families. In contrast, his wife, Katie Tingle, saw the men as intruders and seemed to barely contain her anger at having to stand before a stranger's camera. Describing Mrs. Tingle's response, Agee wrote,

> You realized what the poor foolishness of your husband had let you all in for . . . all to stand there on the porch as you were in the average sorrow of your working dirt and get your pictures made; and to you it was as if you and your children and your husband and these others were stood there naked in front of the cold absorption of the camera in all your shame and pitiableness to be pried into and laughed at; and your eyes were wild with fury and shame and fear, and the tendons of your little neck were tight, the whole time, and one hand continually twitched and tore in the rotted folds of your skirt like the hand of a

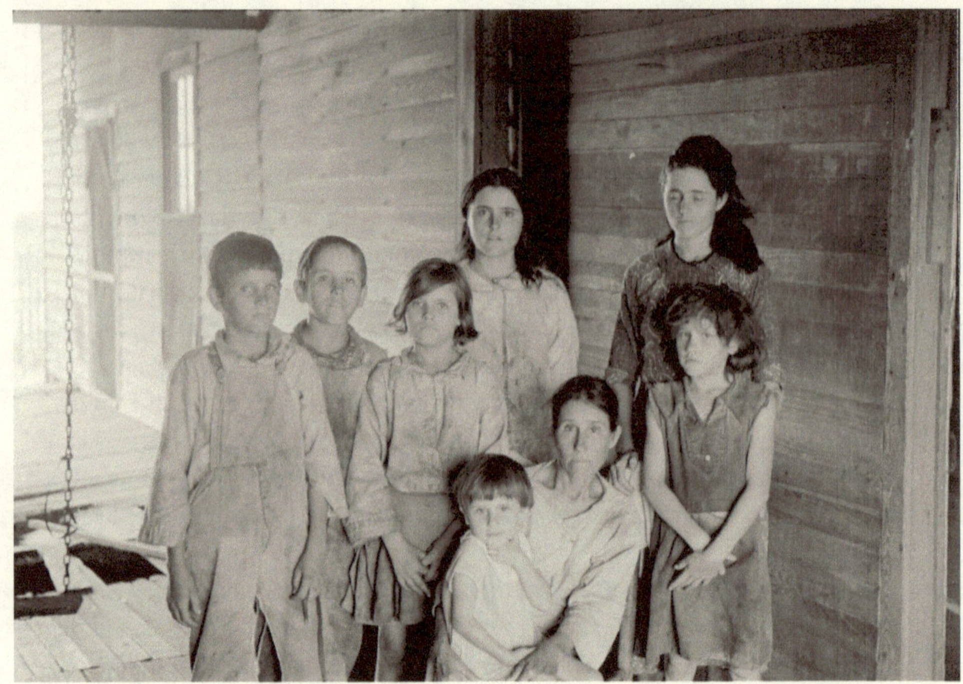

Walker Evans, *The Tingle Family, Hale County, Alabama*, Summer 1936. Courtesy of the Library of Congress, Prints and Photographs Division, FSA/OWI Collection. LC-USF33- 031322-M5.

> little girl who must recite before adults, and there was not a thing you could do, nothing, not a word of remonstrance you could make . . . for your husband was running this show, and a wife does as she is told and keeps quiet about it.[34]

Katie Tingle felt controlled by the camera, disciplined because of her gender. In this double bind, her only means of resistance was silent, demonstrable rage that deeply unnerved Agee, although not Evans, who later said he felt no qualms about photographing poor people in the rural South. In this instance, Agee saw Evans's tripod as "the terrible structure" that was "crested by the black square heavy head, dangerous as that of a hunchback, of the camera; stooping beneath cloak and cloud of wicked cloth, and twisting buttons, a witchcraft preparing, colder than keenest ice, and incalculably cruel."[35]

One of Katie Tingle's daughters, Elizabeth, later said that her nineteen-year-old sister Flora also demonstrated her defiance of posing before a strange man's camera by closing her eyes when Evans took their picture: this was an act of sabotage and rebellion, rather than a response to the flash. Flora stands in the second row of siblings and slightly apart from Elizabeth, as if she had been hoping to slowly slide out of the frame. Elizabeth later recalled that Flora "didn't want to cooperate with all this, in spite of her father's demands to please [Evans]," writes journalist Dale Maharidge in *And Their Children after Them*, his follow-up study on the families featured in *Famous Men*, which won the Pulitzer Prize in 1990. "She was forced to, but rebelled by keeping her eyes closed while the picture of their family was being made." All six of Flora's siblings, except one boy who musters a faint smile, seem uncomfortable or confused. Katie Tingle looks at Evans's lens with resignation and resentment. As Agee noted, she appeared like a "mother as before a firing squad." He imagined her pleading with him to end this indignity: "'if you are our friend, lift this weight and piercing from us, from my children.'" Flora Tingle, however, could not escape Evans's camera. On another August day, Evans took a series of nine photographs of her as she stood before a barn that sheltered cows and pigs. After each photograph it seems Evans moved his camera closer to Tingle until his spectral shadow spread to the tips of her toes. Tingle's stare and stance suggest a woman captured against her will, confined like the animals behind her.[36]

Flora Tingle's expression and Agee's interpretation of her mother's reaction recall Susan Sontag's provocative suggestion that the camera has the capacity to commit a species of violence against its subject: "To photograph people is to violate them, by seeing them as they never see themselves, by having knowledge of them they can never have. . . . Just as the camera is a sublimation of the gun, to photograph someone is a sublimated murder—a soft murder, appropriate to a sad, frightened time." Sontag's point hardly applies in all instances of photographic representation of people, but at Mills Hill on this day in August 1936, Evans's camera and Agee's pen drew distinctions of power and privilege with consequences that other markers of difference—speech or dress—did not carry. To photograph (or write) "means putting oneself into a certain relation to the world that feels like knowledge—and, therefore, like power," Sontag argues. Elizabeth Tingle's recollections of those first interactions between her family and Agee and Evans capture the divide between those creating the knowledge—those holding the instruments of power—and those under observation. "I can just see them in my mind," Tingle recalled decades later. "One of them making pictures and the other just writing things down. We didn't understand what he was doing; he was just writing things down. I just thought it was his business,

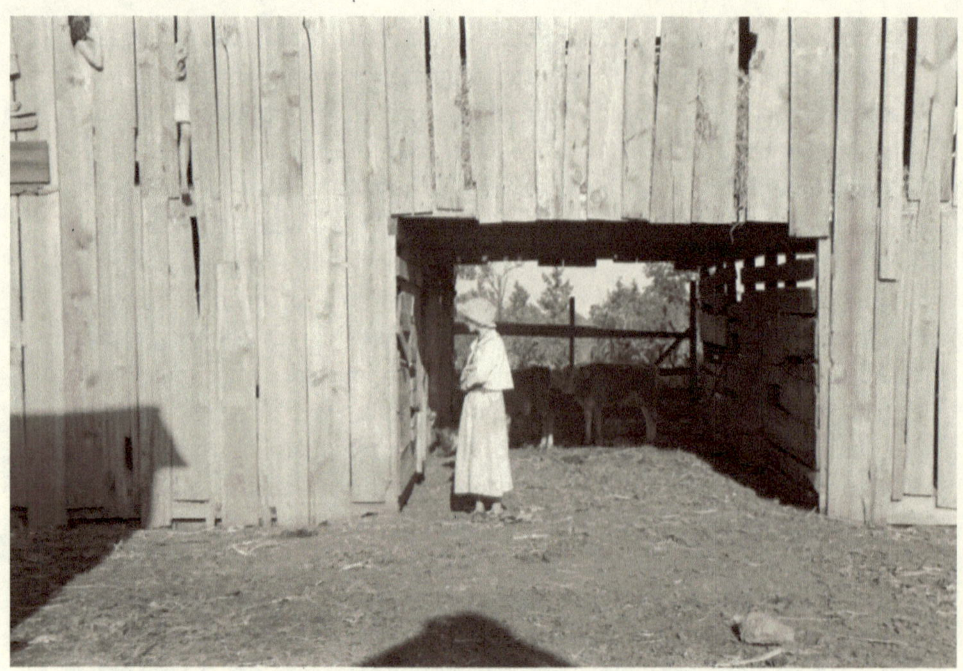

Walker Evans, *Flora Tingle, Hale County, Alabama,* No. 1, Summer 1936. Courtesy of the Library of Congress, Prints and Photographs Division, FSA/OWI Collection. LC-USF3301-031301-M2.

and it wasn't nothing for me to wonder about. He was going to put them in a magazine."[37]

As he and Evans prepared to leave the Tingles' home after their initial visit and documentation, Agee could not ignore Katie Tingle's bodily expression of resistance to their presence, pens, and cameras: "the unforgiving face, the eyes of Mrs. [Tingle] at her door: which has since stayed as a torn wound and sickness at the center of my chest, and perhaps more than any other thing has insured what I not yet know: that we shall have to return, even in the face of causing further pain, until that mutual wounding shall have been won and healed, until she shall fear us no further, yet not in forgetfulness but through ultimate trust, through love."[38] Agee's sentiments here, while undoubtedly sincere, were ultimately "irrelevant," as Walter Benn Michaels argues. The tensions and differences between Agee, Evans, and the Tingles were not products of "enmity" and could not "be overcome by friendship." Just as Martha Young's poems suggested that photographs created ideas of racial difference and, thus, power for those who control the cameras, so, too, did this documentary encounter produce an imbalance of power that Katie

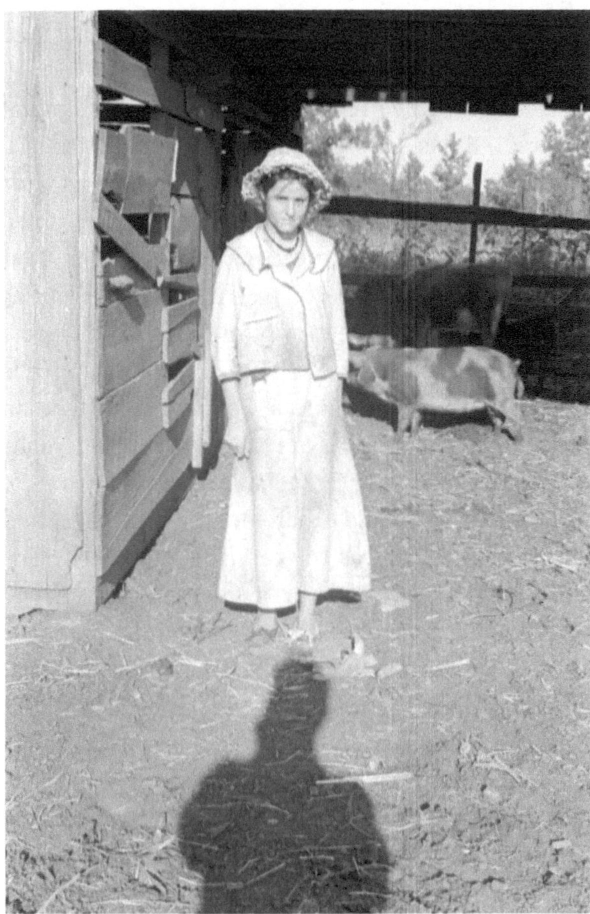

Walker Evans, *Flora Tingle, Hale County, Alabama,* No. 2, Summer 1936. Courtesy of the Library of Congress, Prints and Photographs Division, FSA/OWI Collection. LC-USF3301-031320-M2.

Tingle tries to right through her facial expressions and her daughter resists by closing her eyes.[39]

While Agee and Evans would not return again to Hale County together, another generation of journalists and documentarians would make their own journeys to follow up on the fate of the tenant families and their descendants. The initial run of *Let Us Now Praise Famous Men* in 1941 sold barely six hundred copies, and the book met with bewilderment or indifference as the country shifted its focus from the Depression to war. However, it resonated with a new generation when it was reissued in 1960. Idealistic and artistic youth, those in the folk revival and the civil rights movement who looked to the South for aesthetic inspiration and political purpose, helped turn the book into a kind of sacred text. Its influence continued to spread in the 1970s as new interpretations of documentary work during the 1930s highlighted how *Famous Men* embraced and exploded the genre's conventions.[40]

These changes in the book's fortune had a direct impact on the families Agee and Evans documented. "By the 1980s," writes Paula Rabinowitz, "*Let Us Now Praise Famous Men* had spawned an eerie industry of re-photographic projects, as journalists, film-makers, and photographers tracked down the Tingles, Fields and Burroughs to rephotograph them and elicit their impressions of the 'famous' book." Rabinowitz finds these investigations "eerie" because they once again turned middle-class journalists and readers into voyeurs riveted by the poverty and pain of others' private lives.[41] While an early twentieth-century essayist portrayed Hale County as a destination for tourists eager to see remnants of the Old South, these rephotography and follow-up projects also presented Hale County as a kind of museum of the Depression South where a person could experience the world Agee and Evans saw in the summer of 1936. As was the case that summer, resistance attended almost every effort to access and document the private lives of individuals who had become regarded historical figures or famous people. The irony of so much of this follow-up work in Hale County is that the documentarians often castigated Agee and Evans for the very voyeurism they engaged in while never reflecting on their right to do so, as Agee had done with self-lacerating contempt in *Famous Men*. According to Martha Rosler, these critiques take "the form of a new documentary, a 'rephotographic project,' a reconsignment of the marginal and pathetic to marginality and pathos, accompanied by a stripping away of the false names given them by Agee and Evans . . . to reveal their real names and 'life stories.' This new work manages to institute a new genre of victimhood—the victimization by someone else's camera of helpless persons, who then hold still long enough for the indignation of the new writer to capture them, in words and images both, in their current state of decrepitude." The irony was not lost on some family members and their descendants, who would have nevertheless taken exception to Rosler's characterization of them as "helpless."[42]

"I Never Did Like That Old Picture"

In November 1975, an English art student in his early twenties named Peter Cannon saw Walker Evans's photographs in *Let Us Now Praise Famous Men* for the first time. They mesmerized him. So he resolved to track down the people Evans photographed to "see what they looked like 40 years later." He was not interested in whether or not Evans's photographs changed ideas of rural poverty or promoted social reform. "It was the images," he said. "They just bowled me over." Cannon spent the next three and a half years tracking down the families who still lived in Hale County. He wrote a letter to the editor of the *Greensboro Watchman* that explained to local residents his desire to do a follow-up on *Famous Men*. Two people responded.[43] He took three trips from London to Hale County and eventually brought over a BBC television crew to produce a documentary about the book, the families, and their descendants. During his time in the county a local doctor introduced him to Allie Mae Burroughs's daughter, who eventually introduced him to Mrs. Burroughs. When he and the BBC crew met her and showed her Evans's famous photograph of her, she told them, "I never did like that old picture." She also made it known to her English visitors that she did not want to be photographed again. She was nearing seventy years old. Her hair was unkempt, and according to an article about Cannon's visit and photographs, "her face seamed and lined." It's unknown if Cannon knew just how much Burroughs disliked having her photograph taken by strangers. When Evans photographed inside her home in 1936 she was said to duck under tables or leave the room. But Evans's persistence wore down Burroughs's resistance. His photograph of her standing before her unpainted clapboard home is now regarded as the acme of his art, an image that serves as a symbol of the Great Depression for people around the world, much like Dorothea Lange's "Migrant Mother" photograph that immortalized a woman named Florence Thompson.[44] Cannon eventually won Burroughs over with his charm—something Evans decidedly did not do—and he photographed her and other family members featured in the book standing by a door or against a wall. "I didn't try to compete with Evans in making pictures," Cannon said. "I had a formula—just get them standing by their front door or wall. I didn't want them to pose too much."[45]

The interaction and negotiation between Cannon and Burroughs initiated a scenario that would play itself out again and again in these rephotography or follow-up projects in Hale County into the twenty-first century: individuals at first refuse to have their picture taken or participate in an interview only to have their will, or patience, broken by the persistence of the visitor. In time, their image or language appears in a reputable newspaper, magazine, or art exhibition. Even in these instances when resistance seems to collapse, it still constitutes their attempt to become an actor and not an object in the documentary process. Simply saying "no" or leaving the room can create a new identity as someone who possesses power, rather than always submitting to it.[46]

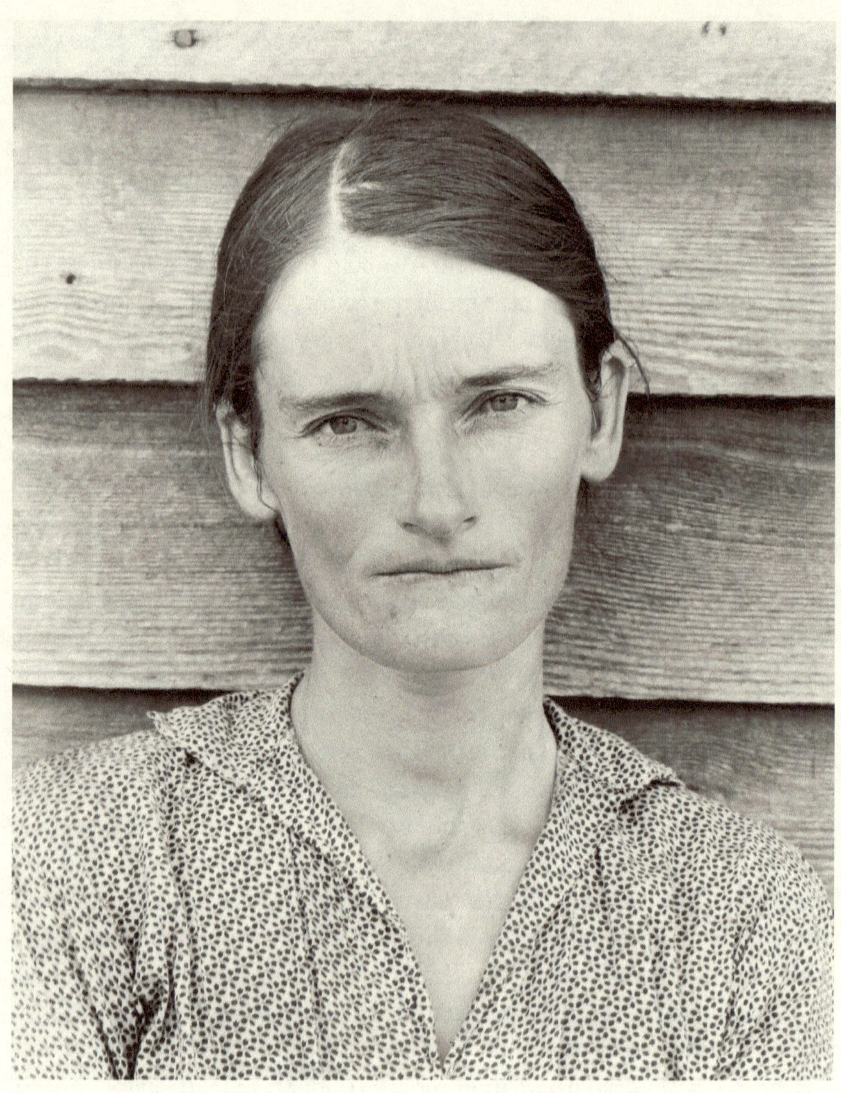

Walker Evans, *Allie Mae Burroughs, Hale County, Alabama*, Summer 1936. Digital image courtesy of the Getty's Open Content Program.

Cannon's trips to Hale County alone and with the BBC crew eventually resulted in an art exhibition at the Institute of Contemporary Arts (ICA) in London in March 1979 and a television documentary called *Let Us Now Praise Famous Men: Revisited* that was shown nine years later in the United States in 1988 as part of PBS's *American Experience* series. According to the ICA, the exhibition was about the people whose pictures "have become icons, symbols of America's rural poor in the Depression years." The show paired

Evans's photographs from 1936 with Cannon's from the 1970s in a manner the exhibitors described as a "potent document which spans the gap of nearly 40 years."[47] Alongside the contemporary photographs, Cannon included statements by the featured family members that reflected on their experiences in rural Alabama during those four decades. For one reviewer of this exhibit, placing these statements alongside the photographs performed a welcome function: it erased the "anonymity of the faces," which seemed to undermine the ICA's view of the tenant families as icons, symbols of a particular time in American history. "Suddenly we are not presented with icons but are reminded that beautiful aesthetic photographs of interesting faces are abstractions which cannot be separated from the lives and suffering they represent."[48] Yet the individuality or humanity that the reviewer highlights is not the product of the family members' own actions, but the effect produced by the exhibit's curators. The people seem knowable, placeable, accessible, but only in the imagination of the reviewer.

For the family members, exhibitions like these represented another intrusion into their private lives and an exercise of power in determining their public identities. First, Cannon and the curators provided the actual last names of the three family members that Agee had disguised in *Famous Men:* the Gudgers were now known as the Burroughs, the Woods now the Fields, the Ricketts the Tingles. The families were also now linked to real places in Hale County, Alabama. Whether they liked it or not, an English admirer of Walker Evans's photographs had removed the anonymity they—and Hale County—had maintained for forty years. Documentary art made them into historical figures and their home county into a historic place in "American art and imagination." Their traceable names and relative poverty made them accessible once again to legions of reporters and photographers. By 1988, it was possible for David McCullough, who introduced the PBS version of *Let Us Now Praise Famous Men: Revisited,* to declare "and because of this great book, which neither Agee nor Evans saw as a work of history, people like Floyd and Allie Mae Burroughs, Frank and Elizabeth Tingle, and their children, people who knew little of books or the world, who knew mostly deprivation and toil, are now part of our history—their lives, the look in their eyes, forever fixed in the national memory." Throughout the 1970s and 1980s, many of the family members would continue to contest and resist becoming spectacles for public audiences in galleries or for readers of newspapers, books, and magazines and to assert their "subjecthood" on their own terms. It was a fight they never truly won, but it ensured that a crosscurrent of dissent always disrupted the seemingly authoritative vision of those with the means to represent and define the identity of a people and a place—of those, as Agee wrote in *Famous Men*, who possessed the "privilege of perception."[49]

Resistance typically took the following forms: a refusal to be photographed (as Allie Mae Burroughs attempted on Cannon's arrival), a refusal to be interviewed again, or lawsuits. While some family members agreed to be photographed and did not support the lawsuits, others challenged the new incursions into their lives and highlighted the parallels between their past exploitation as tenant farmers and their current exploitation as icons of documentary art or as historic American figures. A flurry of retrospective stories about the families featured in *Famous Men* intensified some of the resentment. In 1979 alone, there was the ICA exhibit in London, magazines pieces featuring contemporary photographs in *American Photographer* and *Southern Exposure*, and the BBC documentary film version of *Let Us Now Praise Famous Men: Revisited*. In the film, Allie Mae Burroughs, who was described by Scott Osborne in his story for *American Photographer* as the "symbol of the Great Depression," is shown in a close-up, in a weary state, almost fully reclined and motionless in her bed at home during the last days of her life while looking at the photograph that made her, according to Osborne, a "Walker Evans Heroine." Soon thereafter, a Harvard senior showed up in Burroughs's hospital room in Tuscaloosa as she lay dying from cancer to ask her what it was like being poor when Agee and Evans visited her. She demurred. Allie Mae Burroughs died on January 26, 1979, before the magazines appeared in print and the film aired.

A year later, in 1980, another documentary film, *Agee*, was released that examines the life and career of the writer. It spends ten minutes on his time in Alabama and also features close-up shots of Allie Mae Burroughs and Elizabeth Tingle, along with recordings of their voices. According to a critic, "we hear fragments of their recorded comments as they stand stiffly, eyes darting, before the camera, their true identities disclosed in subtitles. Backed against the side of a house, in imitation of Evans's photo of her in the book, Allie Mae Burroughs, for example, appears trapped as the camera zooms in on her face. . . . Allie Mae offers little or no resistance to this ongoing saga of Agee's life."[50]

When Howell Raines arrived in Hale County in 1980 with his wife Susan Woodley Raines to do a story on the legacy of the *Famous Men* families for the *New York Times Magazine*, they traveled on roads trodden down by the documentarians who preceded them. His article, "Let Us Now Revisit Famous Folk," which included photographs his wife took of surviving members of the Tingle, Fields, and Burroughs families and their descendants, alongside Evans's photographs of them from 1936, continued the themes of return and rephotography, publishing before-and-after images in the magazine's spread. Raines also quickly discovered the persistent theme of resistance. Old and new wounds of public exposure and shame had yet to heal "through ultimate trust, through love," as Agee had hoped. Ruby Fields Darley, the daughter of Bud Fields who, along with Frank Tingle and Floyd Burroughs, was one of the three farmers Agee and Evans met that day at the Hale County courthouse, told Raines that Evans's photographs "were a scandal on the family." She could not imagine how they got her father to pose without his shirt and shoes on. "If you write something that's a scandal on the family," she told Raines, "you better give your heart to God because the rest of you belongs to me." Ruth Tingle, the younger sister of Elizabeth and Flora Tingle, expressed resentment to Raines not stemming from the fear of family shame—the Tingles, whom many regarded as outsiders in an already marginalized class, already experienced local scorn and responded with intense family loyalty and pride—but out of anger that the book had turned them into icons of southern poverty for a national audience. "I like to live a simple life, and I don't appreciate anybody going into my background," she told Raines. "I am not ashamed of being raised poor. . . . I just don't like everybody in the country reading that book and saying, 'Well, look what they are down South.'"[51]

For some family members, legal action offered the most effective form of resistance. Instead of being a stereotypical example of hotheaded rural southerners out for revenge, the decision to seek legal redress was a rational attempt to exert a measure of control over their own public identities, to become agents rather than icons. Filing a case constituted an assertion of power in a relationship that seemed stacked against them from the moment the first camera clicked and the first pen touched the page. Rumors of legal action first circulated among the family members before World War II when someone discovered a magazine that featured photographs that Evans had taken of them. Bud Fields, Frank Tingle, and Floyd Burroughs, it seems, thought they had secured promises from Agee and Evans that the photographs would not see the light of day in the South. According to the story, they consulted a lawyer in Moundville who told them they had no case.[52]

The scenario would repeat itself in ensuing years among descendants of the three men: feelings of betrayal or fears of financial exploitation mixed with the desire for power and control, prompting consultations with attorneys who told them they had no legal standing or leading to rulings that dismissed their cases. In the 1970s, after discovering the book, Floyd Burroughs's son Charles consulted lawyers in Tuscaloosa who told him that the statute of limitations had run out and that, anyway, he should think twice before fighting back against New York publishers who want to see the book in print.[53] In 1980, Ruth Tingle filed charges against several news reporters, including Howell Raines of the *New York Times*, and organizations that had sent writers and photographers to do follow-up stories on her family. Her suit sought $125,000 in punitive damages from each of the defendants. She accused one of them, a journalist for the *Montgomery Advertiser*, of invasion of privacy for publishing an article, without her consent, about her thoughts on *Famous Men* and what had happened to her since the 1930s. In the article she expressed anger at how Evans portrayed her family and questioned his and Agee's power to include a photograph of her in the book. "What right did that man have to put my picture in his book?" An Alabama circuit judge dismissed some of the defendants from Tingle's case while Tingle dismissed others herself.[54]

Filing charges against photographers, writers, and news groups allowed Tingle to use a public forum to challenge the right of journalists to expose her private life. It also provided an opportunity for financial recompense. Growing up in a tenant farm family in Hale County would have made her intimately familiar with how the powerful manipulated the poor for their own profit. As Charles Burroughs told a BBC film crew in the 1970s, "We were took advantage of by everyone—not only [Agee and Evans]—but by the landlords and people that owned the land and we had to work for. We've been took advantage of period."[55] After all of her cases had been dropped, Ruth Tingle told journalist Dale Maharidge the sources of her anger and the reasons why some family members decided to sue: "I don't want to be splashed all over the newspapers. We tried to sue when some stories came out. The judge said we're historical figures and have no right to sue. I don't have no rights, because I'm famous. If I'm famous, why ain't I rich? We never got anything out of it. They never gave us money, never sent us anything. You can take my picture the day when that tea set [a gift Agee gave her after she was injured while playing with him] sets over my grave." It is not known how Tingle reacted when Maharidge's own follow-up study on Tingle's family and the others featured in *Famous Men* won a Pulitzer Prize in 1990. Acutely aware of the enmity many family members felt at their public exposure, Maharidge and Michael Williamson, the photographer who collaborated with him on their book, *And Their Children after Them*, set up a trust fund that ensured that any profits resulting from the sale of their book would pay for the education of the descendants' children.[56]

Ruth Tingle's anger was amplified in the 1980s when she learned of an exhibition at a Birmingham, Alabama, museum that featured Walker Evans's photographs of her family and her. One day she decided to see the exhibit for herself. "There was her face, bigger than life, the tight shot of her as a wide-eyed, beautiful child," writes Maharidge. "She told no one she was the child in that photograph. She just wanted to see what it was all about. She left after she believed that the head of the gallery began staring at her, that he recognized her from the picture on the wall." Tingle and any of the other family members only needed to read Howell Raines's *New York Times Magazine* article to see evidence of financial profit from their likenesses in the art world. If financial gain from articles or books was nonexistent or negligible, profits from the sale of original Walker Evans prints from *Famous Men* were not. Raines recounted his interaction with the renowned international art dealer and gallery owner Harry Lunn at a party in Atlanta where Lunn let him in on the high prices that Evans's photographs of the Hale County families commanded at auction. According to his *Times* obituary, Lunn pioneered the marketing of photographs on an "unprecedented giant scale—with big inventories, slick catalogues and sales on several continents." Lunn told Raines that a "really good Allie Mae [Burroughs]" could bring $4,000 while a "Floyd" [Burroughs's husband] would go for about $3,800."[57]

The daughter of Allie Mae and Floyd Burroughs, Mary McCray, told Raines how much her mother loathed Evans's photograph of her. "Mother hated that picture," she told him. "She couldn't stand it. I hate that picture. It looks so hard. Mother didn't look like that." For W. J. T. Mitchell, writing in the late 1980s, the formal and compositional aesthetics of Evans's photograph of Burroughs—"the lines of her face, the weathered grains of the boards, the faded dress, the taut strands of her hair, the gravity of her expression"—combined to create an image "that is hauntingly beautiful and enigmatic." Evans's lauded "lyric documentary" style, the display of his photograph in *Famous Men* and museum walls, and the sale of reproductions that reaped $4,000 in 1980 made her into an "icon" rather than the woman Mary McCray called "Mother." This "icon" was "arguably the most famous of all the anonymous men and women captured by Evans's camera, a pure aesthetic object, liberated from contingency and circumstance into a space of pure contemplation, the Mona Lisa of the Depression." Mitchell, like Agee, noted the ethical quandaries and class dynamics involved in finding beauty amid "desperately impoverished circumstances." For Agee, of course, discerning and appreciating beauty, whether found in the architecture, land, or bodies of the tenant families, constituted a "class privilege"—the "privilege of perception"—that the drudgery of life destroyed in the families themselves. The presumption that the poor cannot discern someone else's definition of beauty can distort the matter, however. Burroughs and McCray disliked Evans's photograph, it seemed, not because they could not appreciate its formal beauty, but because it appropriated Burroughs's individuality and gave others the power to define her identity. She became an object, one with market value once unthinkable to the Burroughs, one "symbolically possessed" by others—a public icon, a "Walker Evans heroine," the "Mona Lisa of the Depression." It was that photograph that continued to bring the prying world to their doorsteps. Their contempt for it undermined that world's representational power and made a claim for the authority of their own knowledge of themselves.[58]

For Howell Raines, a descendant of Alabama "mule-plow cotton farmers," Lunn's financial assessments of Evans's photographs of the Burroughs also highlighted the cruel ironies of life in the South that motivated people such as Ruth Tingle and others to seek some semblance of justice. "In Alabama, I have observed, people who are not victims of injustice are often victims of irony," he wrote. "So it happens that, thanks to the soaring value of 'a Floyd,' this man who spent his 56 years looking at a mule's rump from between two plow handles and never owned so much as a postage stamp of his own land came to be worth more dead than alive."[59] When Floyd Burroughs Jr. refused to speak with Dale Maharidge in 1985, his anger and fears did not seem entirely misplaced, given the amount of money people made selling photographs of his parents. "Everyone gits rich offn us," he told them in Maharidge's account. "I ain't talking."[60]

"The Beauty and Menace of a Place"

In 2010, thirty-five years after Peter Cannon arrived in Hale County from England and seventy-four years after James Agee and Walker Evans arrived from New York, *Atlantic* writer Christina Davidson walked the streets of Moundville, the closest town to where the three tenant families lived in 1936. While the journalist took photographs of the "empty storefronts lining" the main drag much as Evans did in July 1936, an SUV pulled up next to her and pulled out a copy of *Let Us Now Praise Famous Men*. The woman in the passenger seat asked Davidson if she knew where to find any "information or historical markers commemorating the town's role in the literary classic."[61]

On this day no one in town seemed to know anything about the book except for these visitors, but back in the 1980s Dale Maharidge and Michael Williamson had no trouble finding people with intense feelings about Agee, Evans, and *Famous Men*. On seeing a copy, an older woman they met at Moundville's city hall exclaimed, "That book! We knew what he was up to! Come down here to low-rate the South. I just resent it to death, him picking those people. People up North are still eating that garbage up." Other people who lived near Moundville expressed similar feelings of rage and resentment, but not because poor tenant farmers had their privacy invaded or because profits were made from the sale of their photographs. Instead, *Famous Men* and the relentless follow-up stories on the families had infuriated some Hale County residents because they presented a skewed image of their home and region. "You have to remember those were very special people, and it would not be fair to use them to represent what people in the South are like in general," one man told Maharidge. The man's wife told Maharidge that the "New Yorkers" chose unrepresentative people and laments the fact that the "outside world retains an image of their county based on the [Tingles]."[62]

Hostility toward the book persists today. Hale County is now the site of numerous activist organizations and causes, some inspired by Samuel Mockbee's socially conscious architectural project known as the Rural Studio and all led by people who are not from the area. On arriving in Hale County, one of these young activists, an Ohio native, immediately went to the library in Greensboro to check out *Famous Men*. "Everyone who comes down here wants to read that book," the librarian told her. "You know this doesn't paint the whole picture. There are other perspectives." John T. Edge, who wrote about the activism of outsiders in Hale County, which includes an establishment that sells pies in order to generate conversation among diverse groups, notes that if "outsiders see Evans's photos and Agee's text as a candid examination of an ailing region, insiders often see the book as the product of crusading interlopers, the sort of people who parachute into the region today with little understanding of local concerns." Local resentment of "that book" is now of a piece with the anger some Hale Countians feel at becoming a place that activists see as in need of help and want to remake in their own idealistic image. Once again, the question of who holds the power to determine Hale County's image, and why, is at stake. "What does some guy in Maine know about my life in Alabama," asks Ann Langford, chief clerk of the Hale County Probate Court and a former Rural Studio administrator. "Who gave him the right to speak for me?"[63]

In 2010 Davidson did not talk with ordinary Hale County residents about the book, but she did eventually track down some of the descendants of Floyd and Allie Mae Burroughs, the county's famous forbearers. The tradition of resistance remained steadfast in the face of yet another exposé in the name of documentary reportage. The first person she spoke to was the grandson of the Burroughs, and he immediately expressed anger over how "that book" had caused "a lot of bad blood in his family." Davidson persisted until "his rigid stance against answering prying questions from another writer" became clear. When she found Dottie, the youngest child of the Burroughs, she encountered someone who had long refused to cooperate with reporters, photographers, or anyone else hoping to hear stories about her family's past. She refused to grant Dale Maharidge an interview in the 1980s for his Pulitzer Prize-winning book and has continued to turn away strangers seeking personal profit from her life. Davidson heard all of this while sitting in Dottie's living room after failing to track her down for a week: "Her tone strongly suggests that she'd prefer I go, but I don't feel that I can leave just yet."[64]

Davidson's case for why Dottie should just give in and answer her questions captures the essence of the "righteous mission" of the documentarian, the seemingly pure and progressive motives that inspire people to photograph and write about other people's lives yet nevertheless obscure the problems of power and ethics that lurk at the heart of every documentary encounter.[65] She told Dottie how *Famous Men* had inspired her own documentary project, "Recession Roadtrip," that portrayed "the lives of ordinary people struggling under extraordinary circumstances." She told her how Agee's description of her parents made her admire their "remarkable strength, endurance, and work ethic, their kindness and generosity, their grace and dignity in the face of almost unimaginable hardship." She told her how regrettable it was that her community had turned its back on its own history and the book, which had not been checked out of the Moundville library in more than a decade. She told her how unfortunate it was that the younger generation of her family seemed "unaware that their ancestors feature in the most significant historical documentation of Depression-era sharecropping and one of the greatest literary masterpieces of the 20th century." None of her appeals or lessons seemed to resonate with Dottie. One of Dottie's final statements summed up her position and that of so many others whose family legacy for the outside world takes the form of an unwanted documentary about poverty that also happens to be a literary masterpiece. "That was invading their privacy," she "emphatically" told Davidson. "They shouldn't have done that."[66]

One year later, a writer for the *New York Times*, Lawrence Downes, made the pilgrimage to Hale County. He had been there once before in 1993 when he met a farmer who knew the three families in *Famous Men* and took him to Mills Hill where they used to live. "I felt that sickly thrill of voyeurism that Agee and Evans had been so determined not to satisfy," he wrote. "The book imposed a strange and unwelcomed fame on Hale County, where many saw its unflinching depiction of poverty as exploitative and cruel. That is what makes the descendants there still so angry, quick to vent their frustration on the occasional reporter who arrives asking for names and directions." During his return trip to Hale County in the fall of 2011, he visited Mills Hill again, late in the evening. "The shadows grew as I watched the sun sink behind the pines. I thought about snakes and the persistence of poverty, and the beauty and menace of a place people think they understand, but don't." He drove past an abandoned house spray painted with a white "KKK" and swastika symbol. On a nearby post he saw a no trespassing sign: THERE WILL BE NO MORE WARNINGS.[67]

Conclusion

Seems a Land out of Time: Documentary's Enduring Legacy in the Twenty-First-Century South

Not long after Lawrence Downes walked among the ruins of Mills Hill, reflecting on the ethics of documentary work and the effects of *Let Us Now Praise Famous Men* on Hale County, Alabama, and the descendants of the families portrayed by Agee and Evans, the renowned novelist and travel writer Paul Theroux made his own pilgrimage to the county. Accompanied by photographer Steve McCurry, Theroux was then traveling through the rural South, making acquaintances and taking notes that would later appear in his book, *Deep South*.[1] One winter day Theroux sat in the home of Randall Curb in Greensboro, nineteen miles south of Mills Hill, explaining to him why he was in the area and how *Famous Men* had inspired him to do documentary work. Curb, a partially blind man in his sixties, is distinguished in Hale County for his cultural and literary refinement. Friends and acquaintances have described him as Greensboro's "blind sage." His roots in Hale County and his knowledge of its history have also made him its "unofficial historian," according to Theroux. "Hale County is unquestionably 'historic,' a word we often toss around vaguely, as if that said it all, but it is also uniquely valuable to Alabama and to America," Curb wrote in his 1989 book, *Historic Hale County*. "And to those of us who live there, it is a place to be cherished." Due to his reputation and generosity, Curb's house has served as a sort of salon for journalists, writers, photographers, and others following in the footsteps of Agee, Evans, Christenberry, and Mockbee.[2]

As they sat in his book-filled home, Curb asked Theroux why he was in Greensboro, a question posed, perhaps, out of politeness as much as curiosity, given the common, almost inevitable answers. Theroux first responded by referencing storied books in the history of documentary reportage. "A little like Orwell," he told Curb. "Think of *Road to Wigan Pier* or *Down and out in Paris and London*. I'm visiting the South, driving around, sticking to rural areas." Agee and Evans, however, provided the idea and inspiration for his book in progress. "It was *Let Us Now Praise Famous Men* that gave me the idea of looking at the South and visiting Greensboro," he said. "Oh, yes, other people say that," Curb replied. "They come here and they're disappointed that they don't find sharecroppers."[3]

Deep South, published in 2015, is Theroux's seventeenth travel book and his first to focus exclusively on the United States. It seems fitting to end this book by focusing on travel writing from the twenty-first century since the vivid descriptions and illustrations of nineteenth-century travel writers like Basil Hall, Frederick Law Olmsted, and others helped make the South into such an important, and continuous, site of documentary representation. Travel writing, of course, preceded professional ethnographic and sociological fieldwork, which distinguished itself from the work of "mere travelers" and "casual observers" by using the language, methodologies, and theories of modern social science while assuming an aura of detached objectivity. Historically, however, travel writing has shared a common documentary approach with those forms of professional fieldwork. "Fieldwork produces a kind of authority that is anchored to a large extent in subjective, sensuous experience," writes Mary Louise Pratt. "One experiences the indigenous environment and lifeways for oneself, sees with one's own eyes, even plays some roles, albeit contrived ones, in the daily life of the community." Documentarians, including travel writers, then use realist modes of representation to make their experiences and observations appear authentic and convincing for a public audience.[4]

In recent years, literary scholars have dissected and interpreted the unique stylistic devices and voices of travel writing, highlighting how it frequently weaves together fact, fantasy, autobiography, and ethnography—"often with a whimsical self-consciousness," write Patrick Holland and Graham Huggan. Travel writers are often at pains to prove they are not tourists flitting from place to place for pleasure alone, but rather are trenchant observers who make often distant places seem exotic and yet tantalizingly real and accessible to their audiences. The long history of travel writing and of documentary work in general, particularly in places like the South that have served as sites of realist representations for centuries, can result in repetitive images and tropes that eventually lapse into clichés. *Deep South* is a book "haunted by the specter of cliché." In such examples of travel writing, argue Holland and Huggan, "catalogs of anomalies are often recorded in remarkably similar terms. The same words and phrases crop up again and again, the same myths and stereotypes, the same literary analogies. One begins after a while even to recognize the same faces."[5]

Theroux has, of course, visited other similar sites of representation, places that rank near the top in what anthropologists Akhil Gupta and James Ferguson call the "hierarchy of purity," which has made them fieldwork destinations for generations of travel writers, ethnographers, and other documentarians. The repetition of realist representations produces what Holland and Huggan call "geographical-tropological regions," like the American South, that are defined by the "accumulation of lore," including ethnographic images and knowledge. In this regard, *Deep South* shares characteristics with other travel books by Theroux, particularly *These Happy Isles of Oceania* (1992), which details his travels in the South Pacific, including the Trobriand Islands where anthropologist Bronislaw Malinowski performed fieldwork that resulted in what many scholars regard as the first modern ethnographic text, *Argonauts of the Western Pacific*, published in 1922. As he did with *Famous Men*, Theroux read and used *Argonauts* to comprehend the area's culture. Just as Theroux longed for a foreign place inside America and found it in the "warm green states of the Deep South," so did he "want to see the *extreme* green isles of Oceania, unmodern, sunny, and slow"—a place far removed from "another big city," one "purified by water and wilderness."[6]

Deep South testifies to the power and influence of the long history of documentary work in the region and how books like *Famous Men* continue to inspire writers, photographers, filmmakers, and others to seek out a South made so seemingly real by past documentarians that they still imagine they will come upon sharecroppers, who disappeared from the landscape more than four decades ago. Adorned in denim overalls or a homespun cotton dress, wearing a broad-brimmed straw hat or bonnet, and living in a weathered board and batten "shack," the image of the sharecropper, which in the words of Alfred Kazin once "haunted the imagination," symbolizes the appeal of the rural South as a site of documentary representation. The sharecropper embodies both the premodern vernacular beauty and the endemic social pathology that made the South an enticing place to do documentary work. While Theroux had no illusions of seeing sharecroppers during his travels in the rural South, he did seek out the regional qualities they represent, the ones Agee and Evans made so evocative. "What I admired about [*Famous* Men]," he told Curb, "was the way it incorporated the vignettes of concentrated close-ups: the descriptions of people's clothes, the floorboards of the shacks, the frugal meals, the feral children with tangled hair and in rags. Walker Evans captured these in his images too." *Deep South* not only recycles old images and themes from the history of documentary work in the region but also replicates the conventions of the quintessential documentary book with its combination of words and photographs.[7]

By consciously following in the footsteps of his documentary predecessors, Theroux participates in what literary scholar Scott Romine calls "the self-fulfilling intentionality of southern travel, by which the South sought becomes the South found." The long history of documentary work in the region that purports to present a real South rooted in a rural culture makes such "self-fulfilling intentionality" possible. "It's as if Theroux consulted the classics of the South," Jack Hitt wrote in his less-than-favorable review, "the works that established many of the clichés: James Agee's *Let Us Now Praise Famous Men* . . . the photographs of Margaret Bourke-White . . . and then went to find exactly what he expected to see."[8]

Theroux began his search for the South made real by documentary art by leaving his New England home and descending into the "warm green states of the Deep South where [he] had longed to visit, where the 'past is never dead. It's not even past,'" he wrote quoting Faulkner's now-clichéd lines. To see that unchanging picture of the South, Theroux limited his itinerary to the poorest and most time-resistant places where a writer and photographer could find beauty in the blight: South Carolina's Lowcountry, the Mississippi Delta, and the Arkansas Ozarks. There he encountered poverty and an alluring primitivism that exceeded anything he had encountered in "distressed parts of Africa and Asia." Not only was the Deep South "utterly unlike the North," he wrote, but parts of it were "as odd and remarkable any I had seen in my traveling life." In addition to portraying the South as the nation's exotic colonial appendage, Theroux also captured another enduring theme in the long history of documentary work in the region: resistance to the "voyeuristic" romantic "gawping at the exotic." His experiences in places like Eutaw, Alabama; Glendora, Mississippi; and Allendale, South Carolina, bring out the often contentious interactional history of fieldwork. "Poor Americans, who have very little, still have their privacy—in many ways it is their last possession, and they resist losing it," he recognized.[9]

Just as he restricted his journeys to well-trodden places in the history of documentary work in the South, Theroux also narrowed his focus to common sites and signifiers of regional difference today: gun shows, evangelical churches, the poorest "flyspeck" towns, and their black and white residents. Even the presence of new immigrants, mostly the Indian motel and gas station owners Theroux interacted with, only reinforced the image of regional exoticism, leaving him again and again to compare the rural South with other distant places he had visited—often former colonial sites that

European travelers and ethnographers observed and wrote about during the nineteenth and twentieth centuries. "As I had noticed on my first visit, there was something weirdly colonial about the presence of Indians in the rural South, which reminded me of Africa: the Indian shop in the dusty upcountry town, the overpriced and grubby merchandise, the locals squatting under the trees, giving parts of the South an even more dramatic, sleepier, unfixable Third World appearance." Mary Louise Pratt has referred to such travel and ethnographic descriptions, including Theroux's in *The Old Patagonian Express*, which bear a family resemblance to Orientalism, as the "white man's lament" that "seems to remain uniform across representations of different places, and by westerners of different nationalities. It is a monolith, like the official construct of the 'third world' it encodes."[10]

Like other documentarians who came to the rural South out of a desire to fix or reform the region's problems, Theroux sought out community organizers, nonprofit workers, and clergy who dedicated their lives to reversing cycles of joblessness and poverty in their communities. He wondered why the federal government spent so much money on poverty abroad when such misery existed at home. Nevertheless, the rural South's poverty appeared more like a source of voyeuristic pleasure than a problem in need of radical change. Driving the roads near Allendale, South Carolina, he saw a "vision of ruin, of decay, of utter emptiness. . . . The main road was littered. The side streets, lined by shacks and abandoned houses, looked haunted. I had never seen anything quite like it, the ghost town on the ghost highway. I was glad I had come."[11]

Theroux seemed keen to see rural squalor firsthand, an eagerness that often resulted in resistance and hostility. He asked a black pastor who also ran a nonprofit agency in South Carolina to arrange visits to the homes of the poorest people he helped. "I put in a call," Pastor Wilbur Cave told Theroux after he requested to visit a family assisted by Cave's organization, Allendale County Alive. "We need permission if we're going to visit. Some people don't want visits or drop-ins. They're sensitive about their position." When Theroux finally arrived at one family's home, an old woman opened the door and "seemed dismayed that there were two of us. She knew Wilbur, but who was I"? Theroux writes. Though Theroux said he never felt "menaced" and found most people hospitable, his status as a well-to-do white man from the North gazing with wonderment, and often pleasure, at the poverty particularly of black southerners often resulted in what he described as "hostility." In Glendora, Tallahatchie County, Mississippi, near where Emmett

Till was murdered in 1955, "the vibration of hostility on this potholed road . . . was something that made me feel like an intruder and caused me to be watchful. Perhaps it was something simple, the shame of poor people, suddenly self-conscious in the presence of a stranger . . . the poor rooted in their decrepitude, hating to be observed, resenting me for having arrived, resenting me for so easily being able to depart."[12]

For Theroux, what made the rural Deep South an appealing place to observe and write about were the very things that made the region a site of documentary representation for generations. Its poverty made it accessible to a person of privilege who could leave home and travel into the field where he could knock on the doors or walk into the yards of the black and white poor who suddenly found themselves captive to a stranger. Poverty and defeat, he claimed, made the region and its people alternately suspicious and pliant. "Catastrophically passive, as though wounded by the Civil War, the South has been held back from prosperity and has little power to exert influence on the country at large, so it remains immune in its region, especially in its rural areas, walled off from the world," he observed. The source of its social and economic problems, of its "broken culture, perhaps unmendable," was also the source of pleasure for Theroux that inspired him to do documentary work.[13]

Indeed Theroux found "a melancholy pleasure" in the rural South's stasis and torpor. The region's repeated representation as a place of isolation and changelessness has made it a site of continuous return for documentarians, including travel writers. Its geographical and temporal distance from places like Theroux's native New England made it a place where the past was only a fourteen-hour road trip away. One morning while viewing the "ruination" of Allendale, South Carolina, Theroux discovered the rural South's source of allure: "It was then I realized that part of the appeal of my traveling in the South was that I could return and pick up where I left off, because in the rural parts where I had chosen to look, nothing changed." Sitting one day in a chicken restaurant in a small Alabama crossroads town, thinking about the "pockets of dereliction" he had just passed, the "decaying houses and some outright shacks—the obvious hunger and poverty in the beautiful pinewoods," Theroux wrote into his notebook: "*Seems a land out of time*."[14]

In one of his drafts of *Famous Men*, Theroux's inspiration, James Agee, made similar statements about the rural South as a place cut off from time's otherwise inexorable flow. While Agee's descriptions of the region did not appear in the book's final version, they capture a way of seeing the region that influenced him, one that his successors picked up and carried on well into the twenty-first century:

> For these people and this country, though they are of our century, and represent a great and ill-recognized weight not only in human existence but in history, do not belong to time as most cities and city people do. It would be no more correct to call them primitive, or medieval, or old-fashioned, than the call them modern: they simply do not belong to time, though they must take part in it; they belong to some other order of existence. . . . Moreover this is not just true of any part of the country: it is much stronger in the South and has a special quality there.[15]

McCurry's photographs, while compositionally compelling, reinforce Theroux's and Agee's image of a "land out of time" where beauty and blight blend. Many of his photographs also raise the same questions critic Dave Smith asked in a special issue on "New Southern Photography" of the photography journal, *Aperture*, twenty-six years earlier in 1989. "In recent photographs of the South," Smith asked, "why does it seem that everyone is black, poor, and sober of expression? Why are landscapes rural and abrasive? Why are people truncated, denied full physicality?" Turning to McCurry's photographs in the back of the book, readers see Allendale resident Melvin Johnson, a middle-aged black man, standing in front of his family's unpainted wood-framed and rusted tin-roofed "nineteenth century house" where he has lived for more than fifty years without plumbing and electricity. They meet the stare of Lester Carter, looking soberly into McCurry's camera while sitting "in front of his shack" in Cotton Plant, Arkansas, "penniless, unemployed, and hungry." His quote that accompanies the caption reads, "I got nothing to eat but some rice." A reader would be forgiven for thinking Erskine Caldwell somehow suggested the quote and caption to McCurry from beyond the grave or for wondering whether McCurry had simply slid in a couple of Caldwell's lines from *You Have Seen Their Faces*.[16]

These photographs all are clearly images McCurry made in the twenty-first-century South—the television satellite next to the "sharecropper's shack" and the black woman guarding the black male prisoners doing roadwork suggest as much. But they are also repetitions of photographs taken by Margaret Bourke-White and words written by Erskine Caldwell that appeared in *You Have Seen Their Faces* more than three-quarters of a century earlier; they are reiterations of photographs Walker Evans also took in the 1930s in some of the same places; they are refractions of the color photographs taken by William Christenberry and William Eggleston since the 1960s, many also from the same areas of the Alabama Black Belt and the Mississippi Delta. Given this history of documentary images of the region, one that has evolved into a kind of feedback loop, "it is no surprise" that "popular culture's representations of region, the South has become both an object of collective obsession and a thing to go looking for," writes musician and scholar Warren Zanes. Traveling through the rural South, many see a landscape created not by local residents but by visiting documentarians, particularly photographers like Evans, Christenberry, and even Bourke-White. A place like the crossroads country store and post office in Sprott, Perry County, Alabama, that Evans immortalized in the summer of 1936 becomes that "object of collective obsession" for those "On the Path of Walker Evans," as the title of a recent *New York Times* travel essay by Laura M. Holson phrased it. "This is one of the most photographed buildings in the country," Donna Hale, who owned the store in 2009 when it was an antique shop, told Holson. It is, of course, not surprising that one of the most photographed buildings in America sits in the rural South.[17]

The romantic fixation on the rural South's unchanging qualities, its "chronological lag," to quote Howard Odum, makes addressing the structural and political implications of its "dereliction" secondary to the aesthetic inspiration a documentarian can discover in the region's ruins. McCurry's photograph that appears on the cover of *Deep South* symbolizes the aesthetic appeal of finding ruins in a place that "seems a land out of time": it shows the abandoned "Pastime Theater" in Warren, Arkansas, with its rich red marquee wrapped around a weathered and scarred beige building. Why advocate for social and economic change in a place that appears so appealingly stuck in the past when you can take another photo for another book, magazine, or museum wall? Why address the structural issues that would allow a man to continue to live in a nineteenth-century house without plumbing and electricity or a family to still live in a former "sharecropper's shack" when those structures make for such beautiful documentary photographs?[18]

Walker Evans hinted at an answer to these questions in an interview he gave to folklorist and documentarian William Ferris in 1974. "The texture of unpainted wood is also very attractive to me; it's hard to say why," he told Ferris, "just an instinctive natural love. That's just America, and I'm deeply in love with traditional old-style America. Now, when I go out and see those houses painted over, I am dismayed. I don't want them to be painted." For Evans, an unpainted shack in Hale County represented a natural expression of the folk's aesthetic sensibility. Its beauty derived from its unpretentious

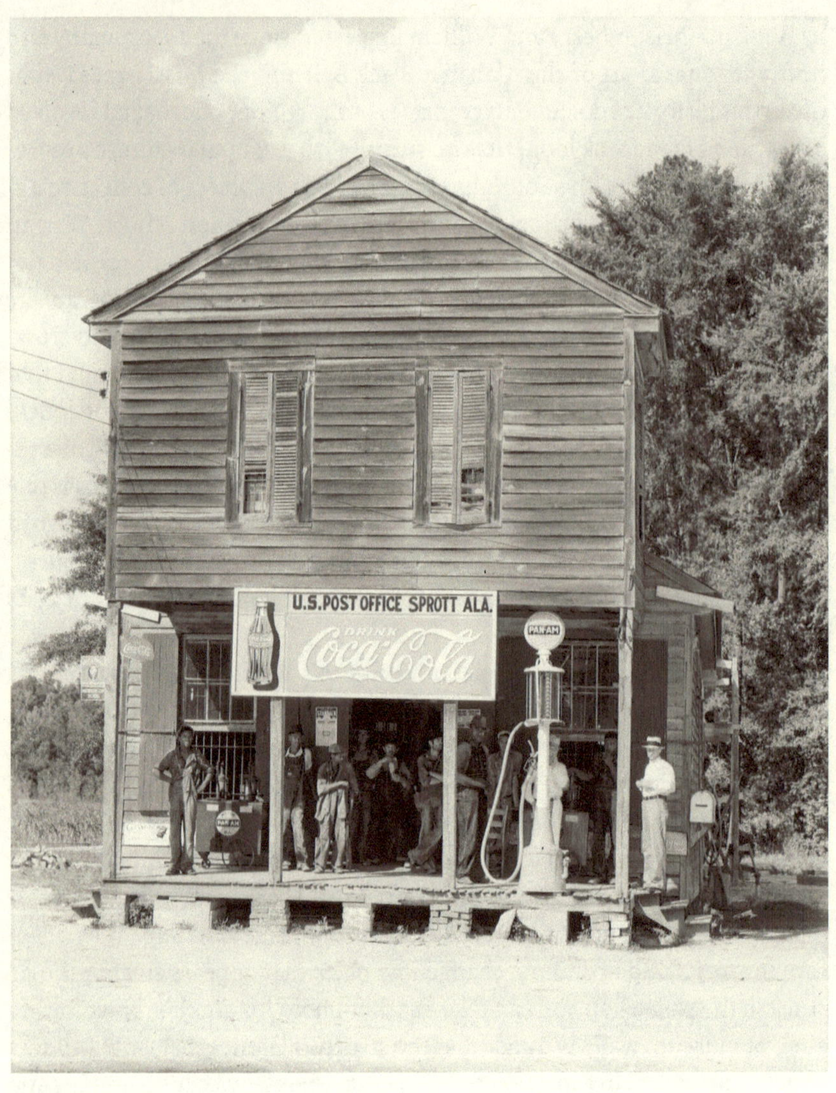

Walker Evans, *Crossroads Store, Sprott, Perry County, Alabama*, Summer 1936. Courtesy of the Library of Congress, Prints and Photographs Division, FSA/OWI Collection. LC-USF342-008158-A.

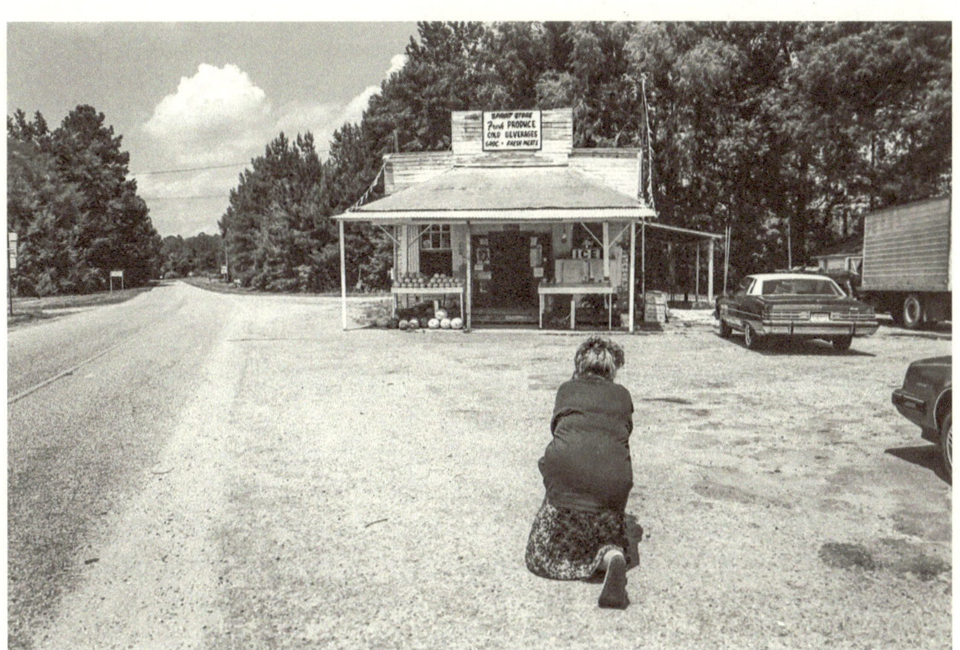

Bruce Jackson, *Sprott Country Store*, 1997. Courtesy of Bruce Jackson.

purity and its seeming rejection of slick mass culture, which the absence of paint conveyed. If Evans yearned for the sharecropper shacks to remain unpainted, then its stands to reason that he also, unconsciously, hoped that the sharecroppers would also remain poor and serve as subjects for his art. Agee also found immense aesthetic appeal in the tenant houses he saw in rural Alabama, lauding their "extraordinary beauty." That "beauty," however, did not exist in the eyes on the families themselves. "Oh, I do *hate* this house *so bad*! Seems like they ain't nothing in the whole world I can do to make it pretty," Agee recalls Allie Mae Burroughs [Annie Mae Gudger]," once saying. Perceiving beauty in an unpainted "shack" was a "class privilege," according to Agee, a "shameful" product of "their privilege of perception."[19]

The repetitions of these documentary representations of the rural South can also produce ideas of racial essence and purity or even an authentic regional ethnicity rooted in the region and visible in the faces and bodies of its black and white residents. As far back as the 1850s, travelers in the Lower South felt compelled to make sketches of the people they encountered because their apparently unique physical features seemed to signify and confirm the biological, rather than just political and economic, basis of regional difference in the nation. While on a business trip in Georgia in 1853,

Joseph Wharton, a Philadelphia industrialist and, later, founder of the Wharton School of Business at the University of Pennsylvania, found the South's economy inefficient but southerners' appearances fascinating. He took time to sketch the most intriguing individuals he saw and write to his family back home about the men's beards and mustaches, the "large proportion of aquiline and roman noses and of hawk eyes," and how the men appeared reminiscent of the "knights of a few centuries back." About the same time, a New Yorker named Ledyard Lincklaen longed to photograph rather than just sketch the people he saw in the South, "especially negros," since that new technology was the only way to make a "perfect representation."[20]

Eighty years later, Walker Evans spoke of a similar fascination for the unique physical features of rural southerners that suggested a racial purity unique to residents of a region uncorrupted by modernity. His image and ideas resemble common romantic tropes found in local-color literature about the rural South and southern Appalachia during the late nineteenth and early twentieth centuries. "I was a suburban city son of a Chicago business man, so I didn't really know a hell of a lot about what was [in the South]," he told Ferris in 1974. "But I had almost a blood relationship to what was going on in those people and understood the love for that kind of old, hard-working, rural southern human being. They appeal to me enormously from the heart and the brain. I saw [in them] Old America, which goes so far back that some of the people speak with something reminiscent to the Elizabethan days, and their faces are like that too. That sharecropper's wife [Allie Mae Burroughs] is a classic portrait of a real old pioneer, an American woman of English stock—and pure too."[21]

Forty-five years later, documentarian of the blues and photographer of the South, George Mitchell, traveled through the region, confining himself, like Theroux later did, to "rural areas and very small towns." There on the steps of crossroads stores and ancestral homes he saw people who retained vestiges of a unique vernacular culture that gave them a distinct physical appearance. "Indeed, I feel that in this age of growing mass culture, in which people increasingly look alike, talk alike, and act alike, Southerners—especially rural Southerners—have maintained a sense of individuality and cultural flavor that is reflected in their faces, the faces captured in these photographs," he wrote in his book of photography, *Southern Portraits* (1981). "Most importantly for me as a photographer, their faces, their dress, and their physical environment *look* Southern. The photographs in this book could have been taken nowhere else in the world." Forty years after Mitchell, Theroux traveled through many of the same places with McCurry, making similar observations and photographs that seemed to inscribe regional difference onto the bodies of rural southerners. "The mood of the South is powerful and the weight of its history is palpable in people's faces, their postures, their clothes, the houses and shacks, the look of abandonment," Theroux observed.[22]

Taken together such images of appealing primitivism and appalling pathology, and their manifestations on the bodies of rural southerners, make the realism of documentary work a critical part of the construction of "The South" and its endurance as a site of representation today. The region remains separate and different, seemingly immune to the forces of standardization, in part because documentarians continue to make it a compelling site of representation. It remains a place where it seems the faint traces of a regional folk culture can still be seen and salvaged, where the roots of our nation's enduring problems of poverty and racism and the legacy of slavery and the Civil War reach deep into the soil, requiring more chroniclers to dig them up, describe, and explain them. The documentary tradition therefore remains vibrant in the South's universities and publications and among its photographers, writers, and filmmakers. The University of Mississippi's Center for the Study of Southern Culture runs an institute called the Southern Documentary Project that produces films, photographs, and radio shows about the region. Duke University in Durham, North Carolina, is home to the Center for Documentary Studies (CDS) and offers rich and extensive course offerings in its documentary studies program, including "Documentary Photography and the Southern Landscape" and "The South in Black and White." A nonprofit known as the Southern Documentary Fund, also located in Durham, sponsors and "cultivates documentary projects made in or about the American South," including a PBS series called *Reel South* that showcases "the best non-fiction storytelling from the region" and "diverse Southern voices, topics, and points of view into millions of homes." And the press that Howard Odum helped found in 1922, the press that played a pivotal role in making the South perhaps "the most documented region in America," has its own book series, "Documentary Arts and Culture," which has published books of photography by important documentarians in the region's history such as Paul Kwilecki, Bruce Jackson, and William Ferris. It is also edited by photographer Tom Rankin, who has photographed extensively in the South for many years, written about the region's documentary tradition, and taught its practices and history as a professor at CDS.[23]

Journals and magazines that chronicle the region's history and culture have also focused on documentary expression. *Oxford American* has an ongoing photographic series called "Eyes on the South," curated by Jeff Rich, that spotlights the work of photographers documenting the twenty-first-century South. In 2014, *AINT-BAD MAGAZINE*, published in Savannah, Georgia, dedicated its summer issue to contemporary photography of the "American South" that addressed the region as "a reality and a fiction, a conceptual and cultural entity," wrote its editors. "As such, it has been famously challenged and perpetuated through photography in the form of singular iconic images in the work of photographers like William Eggleston and in the form of the photo-book essay, bridging journalism and fine art in the work of Walker Evans and James Agee." In 2009, the online journal *Southern Spaces* started a special ongoing series, "Documentary Expression and the American South" that features photo-essays, films, and interdisciplinary academic articles on the history of documentary work in and of the region. And in 2016, *Southern Cultures*, a journal associated with the University of North Carolina's Center for the Study of the American South (CSAS), published its own special issue on the topic, "Documentary Arts," which was edited by Rankin and featured his introductory essay, "Looking and Telling, Again and Again: The Documentary Impulse," that is suggestive of the South's status as "the most documented region."[24]

Record labels also carry on the documentary tradition established by Moe Asch and Folkways Records by releasing old and new recordings by southern artists and reissuing archival field recordings made in the South in collections that feature beautiful packaging, photography, and occasionally films from the region. In 2017, Smithsonian Folkways released *Spirituals and Shout Songs from the Georgia Coast: The McIntosh County Singers*, which contains new field recordings of the area's ring shout tradition by Art Rosenbaum and photographs of the singers by Margo Newmark Rosenbaum. Dust-to-Digital, an archival reissue label based in Atlanta, Georgia, and run by Lance and April Ledbetter, has released renowned collections of field recordings from the South in recent years, including work done by Art Rosenbaum, that have earned the label numerous Grammy nominations and awards. Two recent examples stand out in the label's rich catalog that highlight the enduring cultural influence and impact of the South's documentary tradition: *Parchman Farm: Photographs and Field Recordings, 1947–1959*, which features forty-four recordings and seventy-seven photographs made by Alan Lomax in the Mississippi Delta's notorious penitentiary and *Voices of Mississippi: Artists and Musicians Documented by William Ferris*, which includes recordings of black religious and blues music, stories and interviews as well as photographs and documentary films made by Ferris in his home state from the 1960s to the 1980s.[25]

DURING HIS TRAVELS in the rural South, Paul Theroux often heard locals make statements that assumed he would eventually return, in part, it seemed because of the paradox sociologist Howard Odum identified in 1942: the most documented region was also the least understood.

> I took it to mean that the traveler in the South, no matter who, would never light for any length of time, but keep returning, tumbling from one place to another. It was a conflicted assumption, perhaps the product of the aggrieved Southern feeling that the South was a place apart, deemed unworthy, weakened, misrepresented, hard to explain, but proud. The South was not a conventional destination, not a place where an outsider would fit in or a traveler would linger. The South was static, but gave the appearance of flux, offering a set of occasions to satisfy the wanderer's curiosity, and though the traveler might circle back for a bit, it was unthinkable that anyone would put down roots. We'd never understand the complexity of it. We were, all of us, just passing through, peering through windows.[26]

Perhaps fittingly, Theroux's last sentence here echoes W. E. B. Du Bois, the South's first professional fieldworker, specifically, his critique from *The Souls of Black Folk* of the early twentieth century "car-window sociologist . . . the man who seeks to understand and know the South by devoting the few leisure hours of a holiday trip to unravelling the snarl of centuries," but only ends up of misrepresenting and misunderstanding its problems and its people, particularly its poor black and white population, who embody the region for so many throughout the world. Writers, photographers, and other fieldworkers, it seems, have always seen the South and its people dimly, or darkly, through the spyglass of documentary—making another quixotic quest to confront it face to face, finally bring it into focus, and accomplish what Odum called "the well-nigh impossible task of interpreting to the public the realities of this regional culture."[27]

Theroux's *Deep South* demonstrates how the realist aesthetics and influence of documentary work from the twentieth century continue to make the South the "most documented region," an "object of collective obsession and a thing to go looking for" among documentarians in the twenty-first century. Documentary depictions of the region's folkways, the signifiers of an authentic indigenous culture, will also continue to resonate among audiences eager to see, read, and hear "the real thing" in a world of rootlessness, alienation, and artifice. At the same time, documentary portrayals of the region's people, particularly its poor black, white, and Latino populations, will remain controversial as photographers, filmmakers, and writers again look to the region to explain problems vexing the nation such as racial injustice, class identity, and immigration. Resistance and challenges to such documentary images made in the American South will persist in an era when the cultural politics of race and place, and the nature of reality itself, have become pivotal battles in the long fight to determine the nation's identity and destiny.

Notes

Introduction

1. Herring, *Southern Industry and Regional Development*, v.

2. Odum, "On Southern Literature and Southern Culture," 84; Odum, "Spirit of the New South," 7; Odum, "Patterns of Regionalism in the Deep South," 5; "Announcing the Old South Issue," 24; Dabney and Odum, "The Upper Old South: An Editorial," 3. For other statements made by Odum describing the South as the "most" or "best" documented region, see "Toward Regional Documentation," 302, and Odum, "The Way of the South," 260.

3. Reed, "Sociology of the South," 813. Reed has also described the South of the 1930s as "the most thoroughly documented society that has ever existed." See Reed, *Surveying the South*, 8. The quote by Ferris is from a class, Southern Literature and the Oral Tradition, I sat in on during the spring of 2011 while a postdoctoral fellow with UNC's Center for the Study of the American South.

4. I owe my conception of the South as a site of representation—both a geographic place where documentarians do their fieldwork and a place represented or imagined because of that fieldwork—to cultural geographer James Duncan and his phrase, "sites of representation." According to Duncan, his phrase "is intended to suggest to the reader both the site to be represented (a geographical place), and the site (the geographical, cultural, political, theoretical viewpoint) from which that representation emanates. The representation of places and regions," Duncan argues, "necessarily partakes this dualism." Duncan, "Sites of Representation," 39. Duncan's ideas, of course, resemble Edward Said's concept of Orientalism and what he calls the creation by the "Occident" of an "imaginative geography" of the mostly Muslim "Orient," the "notion that there are geographical spaces with indigenous, radically 'different' inhabitants who can be defined on the basis of some religion, culture, or racial essence proper to that geographical space." Said, *Orientalism*, 322.

5. For more on Odum's idea of various forms of regional "lag," see Odum, *Southern Regions of the United States*, 3, 47, 53; Odum, "The Way of the South," 252.

6. Hurley, "Documenting a Culture," 34.

7. Zanes, *Dusty in Memphis*, 91; Odum, "Patterns of Regionalism," 5.

8. Gupta and Ferguson, "Discipline and Practice," 8, 13.

9. Zanes, *Dusty in Memphis*, 49, 55, 59. The idea of a cultural eddy is one expressed by folklorist John Lomax and his son Alan while searching for folk music across the South in the 1930s. "Folk songs and folk literature flourish, grow—are created, propagated, transformed—in the eddies of human society, particularly [prisons] where there is isolation and homogeneity of thought and experience." John and Alan Lomax quoted in Porterfield, *Last Cavalier*, 523.

10. Duncan, "Sites of Representation," 42; Clifford, *The Predicament of Culture*, 228, 231; Clifford, "On Ethnographic Allegory," 112–13. The phrase "salvage ethnography" was originally developed by anthropologist Jacob Gruber. See Gruber, "Ethnographic Salvage and the Shaping of Anthropology," 1289–299. Anthropologist Johannes Fabian's book, *Time and the Other: How Anthropology Makes Its Object*, has also shaped my thinking about the meaning and message of documentary representations of the South, particularly the focus on the South as a premodern place impermeable to historical change. Fabian argues that anthropologists and ethnographers participate in a "denial of coevalness" with regard to the people and cultures they study. Observing and writing about the people as if they exist in a past order of time contradicts the authority of observations made in "the field," which rest upon observing and documenting people in "synchronous" or shared time. See Fabian, *Time and the Other*, xi, 31–32, 147–48. The South is hardly the only regional culture seen as threatened and in need of salvaging by ethnographers, folklorists, and photographers. The American West, particularly the Southwest, has for decades lured documentarians, including anthropologists, folklorists, photographers, and music recorders, eager to observe and preserve Native American cultures or document scenes of sublime natural beauty that seemed threatened by waves of white westward expansion. See Baker, *Anthropology and the Racial Politics of Culture*, and Zamir, *The Gift of the Face*.

11. Pratt, *Imperial Eyes*, 6, 136; Pratt, "Arts of the Contact Zone," 61–72; Clifford, *The Predicament of Culture*, 59; Holland and Huggan, *Tourists with Typewriters*, 98. For studies that address themes of resistance and "talking back" during and after fieldwork, see Brettell, ed., *When They Read What We Write*; Rosaldo, "When Natives Talk Back"; Sluka, "The 'Other' Talks Back," 175–82.

For a study that addresses the tensions that often existed between FSA photographers during the Depression and their subjects in the South, see Kidd, "Dissonant Encounters," 25–47. The murder of Canadian documentary filmmaker by Hobart Ison in eastern Kentucky in 1967 stands as a tragic example of how resistance to representation has turned violent. See Trillin, "A Stranger with a Camera," 193–201. For a documentary film that reflects on the O'Connor murder from the perspective of eastern Kentucky native and Appalshop documentarian Elizabeth Barret, see *Stranger with a Camera*. In 1969, eastern Kentucky natives began to counter outsiders' representations of their region and culture by creating their own community-based media organization, Appalshop, with funding from the War on Poverty's Office of Economic Opportunity. Local people took representational power into their own hands by creating films, theater productions, and records. For more on Appalshop see Williamson, "The Appalshop Filmmakers," 397–423.

12. Hall, "The Spectacle of the 'Other,'" 259, 261; Henninger, *Ordering the Façade*, 47–48; Gledhill, "Genre and Gender," 348; Rabinowitz, *They Must Be Represented*, 35–55.

13. Pratt, *Imperial Eyes*, 136; Scott, *Domination and the Arts of Resistance*, 154–56, 183, 199–200; Kelley, "'We Are Not What We Seem,'" 75–112; Gupta and Ferguson, "Culture, Power, Place," 19.

14. Mellow, *Walker Evans*, 213; Evans, "Lyric Documentary"; LaRocca, "Introduction: Representative Qualities and Questions of Documentary Film," 25–26; Hardy, ed., *Grierson on Documentary*, 13; Stott, *Documentary Expression and Thirties America*, 9.

15. Price, "Surveyors and Surveyed," 63; Rosler, "In, around, and Afterthoughts (On Documentary Photography)," 175–76; Coles, *Doing Documentary Work*, 262; Stott, *Documentary Expression*, 8, 1–62 (passim). For examples of historical studies of the social documentary tradition see Stange, *Symbols of Ideal Life*; Trachtenberg, *Reading American Photographs*; Willmann, *Lewis Hine as Social Critic*; Abbott, *Engaged Observers*; Klein and Evans, *The Radical Camera*; Yochelson and Czitrom, *Rediscovering Jacob Riis*.

16. Minh-ha, "Documentary Is/Not a Name," 76. The literature analyzing the discursive power and the rhetorical, semiological, and constructed nature of realist representations, including social science, photography, and film, is voluminous. Some of these critiques preceded postmodernism. Walter Benjamin questioned photography's claims to represent the real in 1931, quoting Bertolt Brecht: "less than at any time does a simple reproduction of reality tell us anything about reality." Benjamin quoted in Price, "Surveyors and Surveyed," 96. James Agee's writing in *Let Us Now Praise Famous Men* from 1941 also represented an early form of self-reflexive ethnography that anticipated postmodern critiques of realist representation by using bricolage, pastiche, and a collage of styles and voices. On *Famous Men's* postmodernist critique of and commitment to realism, see Reed, "Unimagined Existence and the Fiction of the Real," 156–76. For the seminal critique of ethnography's claim to represent reality see Clifford and Marcus, eds., *Writing Culture*. The essays of Roland Barthes and Victor Burgin in particular provided early and influential critiques of photography that highlight the rhetorical and semiological codes embedded in images. See Barthes, "The Photographic Message" and "Rhetoric of Image" in Barthes, *Image/Music/Text*, and Burgin, "Looking at Photographs." For books influenced by Foucault's ideas of power and surveillance, and how documentary functions as a form of power and control within the nation-state, see Tagg, *The Burden of Representation*; Tagg, *The Disciplinary Frame*; Stange, *Symbols of Ideal Life*.

17. Clifford, *The Predicament of Culture*, 22, 24, 26–27, 35, 37; Geertz, *Works and Lives*, 16. For a similar definition of documentary see Stott, *Documentary Expression*, 56. For a broad overview of fieldwork that also serves as a guide for doing fieldwork and is written by a documentarian who has done extensive fieldwork in the South, see Jackson, *Fieldwork*. Throughout this book, I use "documentarian," "documentary fieldworker," or "fieldworker" interchangeably. They are all intended to mean the same thing.

18. Cox, *Dreaming of Dixie*, 5; Woodward, *Origins of the New South*, 154–55; Silverman, *For the World to See*, 80.

19. Orvell, *The Real Thing*, x, xxvii. For Orvell's analysis of the legacy of *Famous Men*, see Orvell, *After the Machine*, 57–70.

20. Isenberg, *White Trash*, 47–54, 106, 112, 131. For Hall's written descriptions of his travels across America, including the southern states, see Hall, *Travels in North American in the Years 1827 and 1828*. Hall published the drawings he made during his trips in a separate publication. See Hall, *Forty Etchings*. For his description of the camera lucida and its purpose in his travels, see Hall, *Description of the Camera Lucida*. Ledyard Lincklaen quoted in Plaag, "'There Is an Abundance of Those Which Are Genuine'," 33.

21. Allen, Ware, and Garrison, eds., *Slave Songs of the United States*; Higginson, *Army Life in a Black Regiment*. On *Slave Songs* and *Army Life* as forms of "protoethnography" and a "scientific taxonomy" of black culture that anticipated modern fieldwork and folklore by whites who romanticized black music see Cruz, *Culture on the Margins*.

22. Olmsted, *The Cotton Kingdom*; Green, "The South in Reconstruction, 1865–1880," 3–125; Prince, *Stories of the South*, 25; Harrison, "Studies in the South," 198; Crimmins, "Frederick Law Olmsted and Jonathan Baxter Harrison," 138–40.

23. Kazin, *On Native Grounds*, 490.

24. Studies on documentary work during the 1930s, many of which focus on work from the South, emerged soon after the end of the decade and continue to the present day. Examples include Kazin, *On Native Grounds*, 485–518; Stott, *Documentary Expression*; Pells, *Radical Visions and American Dreams*, 194–251; Puckett, *Five Photo-Textual Documentaries from the Great Depression*; Noggle, "With Pen and Camera," 187–204; Peeler, *Hope among Us Yet*; Staub, *Voices of Persuasion*; McEuen, *Seeing America*; Böger, *People's Lives, Public Images*; Miller, "Inventing the 'Found' Object," 373–93; Raeburn, *A Staggering Revolution*; Allred, *American Modernism and Depression Documentary*; Retman, *Real Folks*.

Chapter One

1. "Toward Regional Documentation," 302–28; Odum, "From Community Studies to Regionalism," 245–46; "Official Reports and Proceedings," 556–57; Odum, "On Southern Literature and Southern Culture," 85; Vance, "The Twentieth-Century South as Viewed by English-Speaking Travelers, 1900–1955," 3–13. For a general history of the IRSS, written by two scholars Odum recruited to UNC and collaborated with in the 1920s, see Johnson and Johnson, *Research in Service to Society*.

2. "Toward Regional Documentation," 302.

3. Key studies of Odum's career and ideas include O'Brien, *The Idea of the American South*; Singal, *The War Within*; and Milligan, "The Contradictions of Public Service." The most in-depth biography of Odum, though it only covers the first two-thirds of his life, remains Brazil, *Howard W. Odum*. For an analysis of Odum's folk song collections, including his "Black Ulysses" trilogy, written by a folklorist, see Sanders, *Howard Odum's Folklore Odyssey*.

4. Odum, "From Community Studies to Regionalism," 246–47.

5. Odum, 246–47. Odum began using the phrase "folk background studies" in 1926. See Odum and Johnson, *Negro Workaday Songs*, iv, and Herskovits, "Negro Art: African and American," 291. In the 1920s, Odum's conception of the "folk" and "folk background studies" focused more on what he and Jocher referred to in *An Introduction to Social Research* as "the study of primitive and backward peoples," 409. Beginning in the 1930s, Odum provided a more nuanced, if still problematic, definition of the "folk" and "folkways" that drew from intellectual influences he encountered in graduate school, such as William Graham Sumner's *Folkways* (1906), Wilhelm Wundt's ideas of "folk psychology," and Ferdinand Tönnies's concepts of *gemeinschaft* and *gesellschaft*. For Odum, a "folk culture" was both an evolutionary process and a set of unique characteristics and "traits" that did not necessarily connote primitivism and

premodernity. Odum contrasted a folk society and its folkways; a state society and its stateways, including social interactions and processes influenced by government and laws; and a technological society and its technicways, habits and ways of living conditioned by new technology. At its base, Odum believed the South was a quintessential folk society made distinctive by the unique "historical" and "ethnological backgrounds" of the region's folk society. See Odum, "Folk Sociology as a Subject Field for the Historical Study of Total Human Society and the Empirical Study of Group Behavior," 204–5; Odum, "Notes on the Study of Regional and Folk Society," 171; Odum, "The Way of the South," 267.

6. Odum and Johnson, *The Negro and His Songs*; Odum and Johnson, *Negro Workaday Songs*; Metfessel, *Phonophotography in Folk Music*; Odum, *Rainbow Round My Shoulder*; Odum, *Wings on My Feet*; Odum, *Cold Blue Moon*. For a historical overview of sociological study in the South that distinguishes "sociology *for* the South" from "sociology *of* the South" and "sociology *in* the South" see Thompson, "Sociology and Sociological Research in the South," 356–65. Odum's career, in many ways, reflects each of these forms of regional sociology.

7. Du Bois, *The Souls of Black Folk*, 155. For more on how Du Bois's sociological work in the South preceded Odum's and his later marginalization in the history of regional sociology, see Wright, "W. E. B. Du Bois, Howard W. Odum and the Sociological Ghetto," 453–68; Green and Driver, "W. E. B. Du Bois: A Case in the Sociology of Sociological Negation," 308–33. For a recent book-length treatment on Du Bois's marginalization in the broader history of American social science see Morris, *The Scholar Denied*.

8. For a quote by Odum that captures his Progressive views on "practical community studies," see Sanderson, "The Teaching of Rural Sociology," 451.

9. Odum, "Standards of Measurement for Race Development," 375.

10. Odum, "From Community Studies to Regionalism," 248–49; Odum, "The Way of the South," 267; Odum, "Notes on the Study of Regional and Folk Society," 173.

11. Brazil, *Howard W. Odum*, 55–57.

12. Brazil, 61, 70–72; Odum, "On Southern Literature and Southern Culture," 97.

13. Brazil, 73–74.

14. Brazil, 75–76, 86–88, 104–7, 118; Bailey, "Children Differ in Environment," 300–302. Bailey published his main statement on the South's "Negro question" a few years after Odum left Oxford. See Bailey, *Race Orthodoxy in the South and Other Aspects of the Negro Question*.

15. Brazil, *Howard W. Odum*, 114–15; Odum, *American Sociology*, 153.

16. Odum, "From Community Studies to Regionalism," 246.

17. Odum, "From Community Studies to Regionalism," 246; Du Bois, "The Negroes of Farmville, Virginia," 1–38; Du Bois, "The Negro in the Black Belt," 401–17; Du Bois, "The Negro as He Really Is," 848–66.

18. DeVault, "Knowledge from the Field," 155–56; Breslau, "The American Spencerians," 59–60. For a useful overview of early sociological fieldwork that influenced W. E. B. Du Bois, see Morris, *The Scholar Denied*, 50–53. Odum wrote his own brief history of the "social survey" method in sociology that traces the tradition back to

Charles Booth's monumental multivolume study, *Life and Labour of the People of London*, first published in 1889, and to Jacob Riis's groundbreaking book published in 1890, *How the Other Half Lives*, that used photography and investigative journalism to document the plight of immigrant tenement dwellers in New York City's Lower East Side. See Odum, *American Sociology*, 153–54. Of course, sociology was not the only social science discipline to embrace fieldwork during the late nineteenth and early twentieth centuries. In the United States, Franz Boas emphasized inductive research methods that made ethnographic fieldwork a critical part professional anthropology's analysis of culture in discrete communities. Additionally, the Bureau of American Ethnology, which was founded in 1879, pioneered early participant-observation techniques in anthropology. Franklin H. Cushing, James Mooney, Matilda Coxe Stevenson, and Jesse W. Fewkes, among others, conducted fieldwork in Native American communities in the late nineteenth century and occasionally used new recording technology such as the phonograph to document Native American language and song. See Brady, *A Spiral Way*, 52–88.

19. Du Bois, "The Atlanta Conferences," 54. In an 1898 article Du Bois highlighted the shift from theorizing to fieldwork when he referred to the state of sociological study as "the period of observation." See Du Bois, "The Study of Negro Problems," 1–23.

20. McMurry, "A Black Intellectual in the New South," 339; Park quoted in Gilpin and Gasman, *Charles S. Johnson*, 35. On the local, national, and global collaboration between Park and Washington, see Zimmerman, *Alabama in Africa*, 218–47. For more on the sociological study of the "Negro Problem" before World War I, see Stanfield, "The 'Negro Problem' within and beyond the Institutional Nexus of Pre-World War I Sociology," 187–201.

21. Woodward, *Origins of the New South*, 352.

22. Baker, *Following the Color Line*; Hart, *The Southern South*.

23. Hart, *The Southern South*, 114; Brazil, *Howard W. Odum*, 117–18; Odum, "Religious Folk-Songs of the Southern Negro," 265.

24. Hamilton, *In Search of the Blues*, 29. For more on the invention and evolution of the graphophone and phonograph see Morton, *Sound Recording*, and Welch and Burt, *From Tinfoil to Stereo*.

25. Brady, *A Spiral Way*, 60, 62, 65, 71, 73, 85. Tragically, the cylinders amassed during Odum's recordings seem to have vanished. They are not part of his papers housed at the Southern Historical Collection at the University of North Carolina, Chapel Hill. Hamilton reports that Odum's daughter, Mary Frances, cannot locate the discs either, but can see them in her "mind's eye." Hamilton, *In Search of the Blues*, 45.

26. Hamilton, *In Search of the Blues*, 29, 45. Hamilton suggests that Odum's recordings "would make what seem to have been the first field recordings of African American song." Singal, *The War Within*, 116; Odum, "Religious Folk-Songs of the Southern Negro," 266.

27. Brazil, *Howard W. Odum*, 122–24; O'Brien, *The Idea of the American South*, 34–35; Bar-Tal, *Shared Beliefs in a Society*, 16–17; Gardiner, "Reviews of Books," 498.

28. Lears, *No Place of Grace*, 148; Hall, *Adolescence*, Volume I, vii.

29. Hall, "The Negro in Africa and America," 355–56, 358, 362–63; Thomas, "Howard W. Odum's Social Theories in Transition," 26.

30. Odum, "Religious Folk-Songs of the Southern Negroes," 265, 267. For an analysis of "Religious Folk-Songs" that "reveals many of the aspects that were generically shared by the psychological agenda of the period when analyzing aesthetic experience and activity," see Bernal-Marcos, Castro-Tejerina, and Loredo-Narciandi, "Psychological Keys in the Study of African-American Religious Folk Songs in the Early Work of Howard W. Odum," 28–49.

31. Winant, "The Dark Side of the Force," 548–49; Odum, *Social and Mental Traits*, 5, 15.

32. Fredrickson, *The Black Image in the White Mind*, 99–102; Singal, *The War Within*, 141. Odum fits into a long history of modernist fascination for the primitive, including ethnographic writing, which persists into the twentieth century. See Torgovnick, *Gone Primitive*, 3–41, 185–93, 244–49.

33. Odum, *Social and Mental Traits*, 54, 83.

34. Odum, *Social and Mental Traits*, 64.

35. Odum, "Religious Folk-Songs of the Southern Negroes," 280.

36. Odum, *Social and Mental Traits*, 82, 88–89.

37. Miller, *Segregating Sound*, 257; Odum, *Social and Mental Traits*, 19; Rosaldo, "From the Door of His Tent," 80–93.

38. Odum, *Social and Mental Traits*, 165–67.

39. Odum, *Social and Mental Traits*, 166–67, 220–21.

40. Odum, "Folk-Song and Folk-Poetry as Found in the Secular Songs of the Southern Negroes," 355. On the transformation from the trickster to the badman in black vernacular traditions, see Roberts, *From Trickster to Badman*.

41. Odum, *Social and Mental Traits*, 256–58; Baker, *Following the Color Line*, 39. On Du Bois's use of photography as a form of antiracist activism, including his 1900 Paris Exposition exhibit, see Smith, *Photography on the Color Line*.

42. Odum, *Social and Mental Traits*, 18–19. The phrase "everyday acts of resistance" comes from historian Robin D. G. Kelley, who has also used the term "infrapolitics" "to describe the daily confrontations, evasive actions, and stifled thoughts that often inform"—and precede—"organized political movements" among the black working class in the Jim Crow South. See Kelley, "'We Are Not What We Seem,'" 75–112. Kelley's conceptions of "everyday acts of resistance" and "infrapolitics" come from the work of anthropologist James C. Scott. See Scott, *Domination and the Arts of Resistance* and *Weapons of the Weak*.

43. Odum, "Folk-Song and Folk-Poetry," 259, 262; Odum, "Religious Folk-Songs," 5. Odum's difficulty in convincing black people to sing old religious folk songs for him resembles the struggle of Civil War era collectors of black sacred song such as William Francis Allen who, along with Lucy McKim Garrison and Charles Pickard Ware, published the first significant and systematized collection of black spirituals in 1867, *Slave Songs of the United States*. According to Allen, the old spirituals and jubilees were in jeopardy because former slaves increasingly refused to sing them. They represented the "relics" of oppression and were incompatible with a new identity as free people. "It is often, indeed, no easy matter to persuade them to sing their old songs, even as a curiosity, such is the sense of dignity that has come with freedom," Allen noted. See Allen et al., *Slave Songs*, i–iii.

44. Du Bois, "Study of the Race Problem: Review of Social and Mental Traits of the Negro," September 19, 1910. Du Bois Papers.

45. Hale, *Making Whiteness*; Du Bois, "The Study of Negro Problems," 16-17. Despite Du Bois's emphasis on the importance of quantitative methods, he also wrote some of his most important scholarship, including *The Souls of Black Folk*, in a distinctly poetic and impressionistic style. It again anticipated Odum's own descriptive style of writing he called "portraiture," which used poetic flourishes to heighten the drama and romance of his ethnographic descriptions.

46. Review of *Social and Mental Traits*, 1; Brazil, *Howard W. Odum*, 174-76.

47. Morris, *The Scholar Denied*, 19-20, 25, 27-28, 53, 59; Wright, "W. E. B. Du Bois," 464-65. After receiving his PhD from Columbia in 1910, Odum once again followed in the footsteps of W. E. B Du Bois. He spent two years working for the Bureau of Municipal Research in Philadelphia making comparative studies of the intelligence and performance of white and black schoolchildren in the city. He based his initial report, "The Problem of the Negro Child in the Public Schools of Philadelphia," in part on "comparative reference" to Du Bois's pioneering work of urban sociology, *The Philadelphia Negro* (1899). Odum's study, which was published in 1913 under a different title, seemed intended to justify a segregation policy in city public schools despite an 1881 state statute that prohibited it. The Bureau of Municipal Research never sanctioned Odum's report, deeming it too "controversial." Black resistance to Odum's work also continued apace in the urban North. Three years later, a group of black city leaders petitioned the Bureau to help them fund a new study to replace Odum's, but they were denied. The Bureau concluded that the "desire of the [black group] was doubtless to find flaws in Dr. Odum's report." See Brazil, *Howard W. Odum*, 198-99; Odum, "From Community Studies to Regionalism," 247-48.

48. Odum, "Some Studies in the Negro Problems of the Southern States," 185-86; Odum, "Standards of Measurement for Race Development," 377; O'Brien, *The Idea of the American South*, 38.

49. Johnson and Johnson, *Research in Service to Society*, 9-13; Singal, *The War Within*, 119.

50. Sosna, *In Search of the Silent South*, 45-46.

51. Williams, "The South as a Field for Sociological Research," 112.

52. Johnson and Johnson, *Research in Service to Society*, 14-26; Brazil, *Howard W. Odum*, 472; Reed, *Surveying the South*, 10; Odum, "From Community Studies to Regionalism," 248.

53. Johnson and Johnson, *Research in Service to Society*, 36, 133. Favor, *Authentic Blackness*, 1-23; Lamothe, *Inventing the New Negro*, 38-39.

54. Odum, "From Community Studies to Regionalism," 249.

55. Sondley quoted in Brazil, *Howard W. Odum*, 502-503; Odum, "From Community Studies to Regionalism," 257. For Odum's early statement on his concept of the "folk-regional society" and his emerging folk sociology, see Odum, "Notes on the Study of Regional and Folk Society." For a trenchant analysis of Odum's folk sociology see Milligan, "The 'Universal Constant in a World of Societal Variables,'" 5-25.

56. Odum, "From Community Studies to Regionalism," 249; Johnson and Johnson, *In Service to Society*, 131-43.

57. Sauer quoted in Johnson and Johnson, *In Service to Society*, 161–62.

58. Brazil, *Howard W. Odum*, 488; Johnson and Johnson, *Research in Service to Society*, 23, 132; Johnson quoted in Sanders, *Howard W. Odum's Folklore Odyssey*, 22.

59. Odum and Johnson, *The Negro and His Songs*, vii, 38.

60. Tindall, *The Emergence of the New South*, 307–8; Park, Book Review in *American Journal of Sociology*, 821; Davidson, "The Trend of Literature: A Partisan View," 190. For more on the social and literary history of racial mimicry in appropriation see Lott, *Love and Theft*, and Wonham, *Playing the Races*. Odum tells a story, possibly aprocryphal, in his 1930 book, *An American Epoch*, about a meeting between a "charming woman of wealth and position," presumably from the North, and a southerner in which she proceeded to ask a number of questions about the South, including "Are Paul Green [the UNC playwright, philosopher, and part-time folklorist] and Howard Odum really Negroes?" 75.

61. Du Bois, "Criteria of Negro Art," 259.

62. Johnson and Johnson, *Research in Service to Society*, 134; Odum, *American Epoch*, 64; Johnson quoted in Sanders, *Howard W. Odum's Folklore Odyssey*, 45.

63. Odum and Johnson, *Negro Workaday Songs*, 206, 252–55.

64. Odum and Johnson, *Negro Workaday Songs*, iv, xi, 7, 17, 19, 34.

65. Brazil quoted in Singal, *The War Within*, 134.

66. Odum and Johnson, *Negro Workaday Songs*, iii.

67. Odum and Johnson, *Negro Workaday Songs*, 9, 88–89.

68. Odum and Johnson, *Negro Workaday Songs*, 6; Wagner, *Disturbing the Peace*, 34–36.

69. Odum and Johnson, *Negro Workaday Songs*, 5–6; Baldwin, "Our Newcomers to the City," 170.

70. Odum and Johnson, *Negro Workaday Songs*, 11, 206–7, 221; Sanders, *Howard W. Odum's Folklore Odyssey*, 87–88, 154–55. Odum's transformation of Gordon into "Black Ulysses" follows a long tradition in Western writing, including ethnography that imagines supposed primitives as mythological figures. See Torgovnick, *Gone Primitive*, 10–11. Black writers during the 1920s also imagined rural black men from the South as Greek epic heroes. A year before Odum published *Rainbow Round My Shoulder*, black poet Sterling Brown published his poem, "Odyssey of Big Boy." While Brown romanticized the South's rural black folk, as did Odum and other white and black writers at the time, his poems depicted folk culture as a basis for black collective power and resistance against white supremacy. See, Lamothe, *Inventing the New Negro*, 101–2.

71. Johnson quoted in Sanders, *Howard W. Odum's Folklore Odyssey*, 53. On the romance of black folk figures by white folklorists and their attempts "to become black on symbolic and emotional levels to acquire greater understanding of African American folk culture and to satisfy their own psychological needs," see Mullen, *The Man Who Adores the Negro*. While Mullen does not address Odum, he does examine similar white folklorists and ethnographers such as Niles Newbell Puckett and John and Alan Lomax. Odum, and other whites of his generation were hardly alone in the 1920s in romanticizing the black wanderer. As Bryan Wagner has noted, "This ethnographic romance would also inform the works by artists associated with the Harlem Renaissance and the Popular Front." In *The New Negro*, published in 1925, Alain Locke

identified the "migrating peasant," the "'man farthest down' who is most active in getting up" as the model of black "self-determination" during the decade. See Wagner, *Disturbing the Peace*, 31.

72. Odum and Johnson, *Negro Workaday Songs*, 10, 16, 34, 214.

73. Metfessel, *Phonophotography in Folk Music*, 4, 20, 22.

74. Metfessel, *Phonophotography in Folk Music*, 17, 26, 28. Seashore and Metfessel's phonophotography and films anticipate Alan Lomax's use of sound recordings and film to document, classify, and analyze different singing and dance styles from across the globe, processes he called cantometrics and choreometrics, respectively, which linked a cultural group's performance style with the social structure in which they lived. See Szwed, *Alan Lomax*, 333–35, 345–47, 356–58, 372–77.

75. Metfessel, *Phonophotography in Folk Music*, vii, 16, 19; Odum and Johnson, *Negro Workaday Songs*, 253–54.

76. Odum to Chase, November 17, 1925. Odum Papers, Box 51, Folder—"Seashore Studies"; Johnson and Johnson, *Research in Service to Society*, 132; Odum and Johnson, *Negro Workaday Songs*, 264.

77. Bain, "A New Technique in Folk-lore," 299–300.

78. Metfessel, *Phonophotography in Folk Music*, 16, 178.

79. Metfessel, *Phonophotography in Folk Music*, 96–99; Odum and Johnson, *Negro Workaday Songs*, 243–244.

80. Odum and Johnson, *Negro Workaday Songs*, 13.

81. Hurston, *Mules and Men*, 2–3.

82. Odum and Johnson, *Negro Workaday Songs*, 13–14; Sanders, *Howard W. Odum's Folklore Odyssey*, 53; Brazil, *Howard W. Odum*, 179; Hurston, *Mules and Men*, 3; Odum, *Rainbow Round My Shoulder*, 309.

83. Odum and Johnson, *Negro Workaday Songs*, 94, 115, 171. In his early secular song collections, Odum also documented evidence of what he referred to as a "growing race feeling" in the songs of the younger generation that took the form of lyrics that flipped the balance of representational power and described whites in demeaning terms once reserved for blacks. Odum recognized the dangerous and subversive power of such songs. "There are apparently a good many sayings current among the negroes about the whites," he wrote. "Few of these, however, are heard by any save the negroes themselves. Likewise the songs of this nature would scarcely be sung where whites could hear them." One example was a song he recorded in Newton County, Georgia, "When He Gits Old—Old an' Gray," that was a "reply to the accusation that negroes are nothing more than apes of monkeys." Odum said the song originated after a young black man heard a white man call him an ape. See Odum, "Folk Song and Folk Poetry," 266–67.

84. Green, *Words and Ways*, 46. For more on Green, the role of folklore in his plays, and his relationship with Odum see Sanders, *Howard W. Odum's Folklore Odyssey*, 130–46.

85. Odum and Johnson, *The Negro and His Songs*, 3. The "white man settin'" songs seemed numerous, diverse, and adaptable. Odum gives another version in *Rainbow Round My Shoulder* as sung by "Left Wing" Gordon: "White man, white man settin' in shade/Laziest man that God ever made," 104. John Shelton Reed writes of another

version of the song Odum heard as "White man sitting on the wall/He don't work at all." Reed, *Surveying the South*, 3.

86. Odum and Johnson, *The Negro and His Songs*, 2–3.

87. Odum and Johnson, *Negro Workaday Songs*, 13–14.

88. Odum and Johnson, *The Negro and His Songs*, 9.

89. Kaplan, *Zora Neale Hurston*, 118–20, 126, 135, 151.

90. Hurston, *Mules and Men*, 1; Cotera, *Native Speakers*, 73–74, 79–80, 82, 93–94.

91. Singal, *The War Within*, 143; Odum, *Rainbow Round My Shoulder*, 316; Odum to Gerald Johnson, January 4, 1928, Box 12, Folder 157, Odum Papers; Lomax, *The Land Where the Blues Began*, 493, n.1.

92. Odum, *Southern Regions*, 245, 621–23; Rodgers, "Regionalism and the Burden of Progress," 10–11.

93. "Agencies Rendering Public Services in the Subregional Laboratory," 1941, Box 37, Folder 672, Odum Papers. For more on Odum and his Subregional Laboratory's collaboration with the FSA and Dorothea Lange in particular, see Spirn, *Daring to Look*, 90–139. While Odum collaborated with FSA photographers he also received inquiries about participating in a project to make documentary films and radio programs on regionalism and his research work in the South. A drama professor at Columbia University named Mack Gorham wrote to Odum indicating his interest in coming South to "make moving pictures," and Odum himself wrote to the American Film Center in New York expressing his desire to acquire documentary films about the South to show to different groups across the region. Though it seems nothing every came of these efforts, Odum continued to search for ways to maintain the South's status as the nation's "most completely documented region." Odum to David Slesinger, February 1, 1940, and Hazel Harvest to Odum, June 7, 1940. Box 77, Odum Papers; Odum and Jocher, *In Search of Regional Balance*, 60.

94. Odum, "From Community Studies to Regionalism," 256–57; Odum, *Southern Regions*, 237; Rodgers, "Regionalism and the Burdens of Progress," 18, 20.

Chapter Two

1. Singal, *The War Within*, 330; Alexander quoted in Dykeman and Stokely, *Seeds of Southern Change*, 121.

2. Raper, *Preface to Peasantry*, 183–91.

3. "Greene County, Georgia: The Story of One Southern County," 4–6, Folder 97, Raper Papers.

4. See 83 *Congressional Record*, H531–32 and 83 *Congressional Record*, H1737.

5. For Raper's memories of his work with Myrdal and Bunche in Greene County and other places in the South see, "Lest I Forget," Folder 172, Raper Papers.

6. Rodgers, "Regionalism and the Burdens of Progress," 23; Johnson, *Growing up in the Black Belt*.

7. Stoney, "Greene County Comes Back," *Atlanta Journal*, August 31, 1941, Folder 128, Raper Papers.

8. Earl Brown to Arthur Raper, December 15, 1941, Folder 97, Raper Papers. For more on Elisofon's work in Greene County see, Mazzari, *Southern Modernist*, 261–62.

9. Tidwell and Sanders, eds., *Sterling Brown's A Negro Looks at the South*, xi; Brown, "On the Government," in Tidwell and Sanders, eds., 81–89.

10. Raper and Raper, *Two Years to Remember and Other Writings*, 56–57. For Raper's recordings see, Volume I.2, "Audio Tapes and Slides, 1941–1979," Raper Papers.

11. *Historical Census Browser*. University of Virginia, Geospatial and Statistical Data Center. http://mapserver.lib.virginia.edu/collections/. Accessed September 20, 2016. Kidd, *Farm Security Administration Photography*, 192.

12. Raper, *Tenants of the Almighty*, 203–4, 211, 234. For more on the Unified Farm Program in Greene County see Summer, "The New Deal Farm Programs," 241–57, and Kuhn, "'It Was a Long Way from Perfect, but It Was Working,'" 68–90. Before his untimely death in 2015, Kuhn was working on what promised to be the definitive biography of Arthur Raper's life and career as a sociologist on the regional, national, and international stage. His research on Raper goes back to the 1970s when he began conducting oral interviews with him. See also Kuhn, "'A Mind-Opening Influence of Great Importance," 71–92.

13. According to the Library of Congress's online catalog of FSA/OWI photographs, Delano took 1,139 black and white photographs and 17 color photographs in Greene County in 1941. If one includes Maryland as part of the South, the distinction for most FSA photographs taken in one county in the region goes to Prince George's County, which has nearly 1,500 photographs in the archive. The large number of Prince George's County photographs was due in part to the creation of Greenbelt, Maryland, as a New Deal cooperative community in 1937. For black and white photographs, see www.loc.gov/pictures/collection/fsa/. For color, see www.loc.gov/pictures/collection/fsac/.

14. Maclachlan, Review of *Tenants of the Almighty*, 234. Historian Louis Mazzari published the first full-length biography of Arthur Raper and touches on his work with Delano and the making of *Tenants of the Almighty*. See Mazzari, *Southern Modernist*, 238–39, 241–43, 247–48. Mazzari has also published a separate essay on Raper's own documentary approach and sensibility while working in Greene County. See Mazzari, "Arthur Raper and Documentary Realism in Greene County." For Delano's thoughts on *Tenants* see Natanson, *The Black Image in the New Deal*, 242.

15. Stein, "In Pursuit of the Proximate," xviii.

16. Raper and Raper, *Two Years to Remember*, 49.

17. Delano, *Photographic Memories*, 19–20, 23.

18. Delano, 23–25; Maddow, "A Vision from Below," 52; Renov, "Towards a Poetics of Documentary," 33.

19. Delano, *Photographic Memories*, 23–30.

20. Stryker to Delano, November 1, 1939, Delano Papers, Box 2, Folder 5.

21. Delano, *Photographic Memories*, 30; Day, "Folklife and Photography," 124.

22. Trachtenberg, "From Image to Story," 58; Fleischhauer and Brannan, *Documenting America*, 1–3; Finnegan, *Picturing Poverty*, 41; Delano, *Photographic Memories*, 31; Peeler, *Hope among Us Yet*, 3, 60.

23. Oral history interview with Jack and Irene Delano.

24. Delano, *Photographic Memories*, 31–33.

25. Jack Delano to Clara Dean "Toots" Wakeham, March 28, 1941; Irene Delano to Wakeham, April 21, 1941; Roy Stryker to Jack Delano, April 3, 1941, Stryker Papers.

26. "Date Book 1941," Box 3, Folder 4, Delano Papers; Jack Delano to Roy Stryker, April 18, 1941; Roy Stryker to Jack Delano, April 30, 1941, Stryker Papers.

27. Oral history interview with Jack and Irene Delano.

28. Delano, *Photographic Memories*, 38-39.

29. Mazzari, *Southern Modernist*, 229-33; Delano, *Photographic Memories*, 38; Kidd, *Farm Security Administration Photography*, 193-94; Oral history interview with Jack and Irene Delano. Delano's journal also mentions Raper being "run out of town," which probably refers to his experiences in neighboring Putnam County, Georgia, in 1934 when he tried to use black fieldworkers for a research project for a federal program. Raper and the black fieldworkers were chased out of the county one night by hostile whites in their cars because Raper refused to cave to white demands to dismiss the black federal employees who dressed well and drove nice cars. See "Putnam County, Georgia—Oct 1-4, 1934," Folder 743, Raper Papers.

30. White, "Devil in de Cotton," 10-11; Kazin, *On Native Grounds*, 490; Rice, "Greene County, Georgia on Trial with Collier's as Prosecutor, the Nation as Jury and Owen P. White as the Star Witness," Folder 110, Raper Papers, 83; *Congressional Record*, "Greene County, GA," H1737. See also 83 *Congressional Record*, H531-32; Kidd, *Farm Security Administration Photography*, 123-25. For a full treatment of the controversy generated by "Devil in de Cotton," see Matthews, "'A Fierce Contest over Images.'"

31. Delano, *Photographic Memories*, 38; "Greene County Notes, June 1941," Folder 114, Raper Papers.

32. Untitled manuscript by George Stoney in reply to letter from historian Stuart Kidd, Folder 622, Stoney Papers; Delano, *Photographic Memories*, 55-56. A few months after meeting Delano and driving him around Greene County, George Stoney would publish a flattering photo-text story in the rotogravure section of the *Atlanta Journal* that promoted the beneficial changes occurring in the county because of the FSA. The story included photographs by Delano, Stoney, and Marion Post-Wolcott. See Stoney, "Greene County Comes Back," *Atlanta Journal*, August 31, 1941, Folder 128, Raper Papers. Raper hoped Stoney's story would not only promote the work of the FSA to a broad regional audience but would also increase respect for and give credence to his work for skeptical Greene County whites. Despite the positive and optimistic image Stoney wanted to spread about Greene County, he admitted to Delano in July 1941 that "things are so far from good in that county." For more on Stoney's photo-essay see Kidd, *Farm Security Administration Photography*, 194-95.

33. Jack Delano to Roy Stryker, May 7, 1941, Stryker Papers; Oral history interview with Jack and Irene Delano.

34. Jack Delano to Roy Stryker, May 7, 1941, Stryker Papers.

35. "Pictures for the Greene County Study," n.d. [Arthur Raper], Box 4, Folder 1, "Greene County, Georgia," Delano Papers.

36. Kidd, *Farm Security Administration Photography*, 63, 83-84. The late historian Stuart Kidd has written the most thorough and incisive analysis of the FSA's photographic work in the rural South, including overviews of the agency's bureaucratic demands and its representations of tenant farmers, African Americans, small towns,

and the landscape. For more on FSA photographers' portrayal of the rural South's landscape see Kidd, *Farm Security Administration Photography*, 63–91, and Kidd, "Art, Politics, and Erosion," 291–97.

37. Delano, *Photographic Memories*, 33; Oral history interview with Jack and Irene Delano; Raper, "Gullies and What They Mean," 203–5.

38. Roy Stryker to Jack Delano, April 30, 1941, Stryker Papers.

39. Delano to "Toots" (Clara D. Wakeham), May 20, 1940, Stryker Papers.

40. Quoted in Kidd, *Farm Security Administration Photography*, 89.

41. Stryker, "The FSA Collection of Photographs," 352; Oral history interview with Roy Stryker. While working in Greene County, Delano's artist wife Irene would often gaze on similar scenes and would feel compelled to set up her easel and begin painting. "Irene made quite a sensation," Delano told Stryker, "when she decided to sit in front of a general store in a little town and paint a landscape. I think the painting is pretty good although Irene doesn't." Jack Delano to Roy Stryker, May 29, 1940, Stryker Papers.

42. Jack Delano to Roy Stryker, June 11, 1940, Stryker Papers. Although dated 1940, this letter was most likely written in 1941.

43. "Date Book—1941," Box 3, Folder 4, Delano Papers; Jack Delano to Roy Stryker, May 7, 1941, Stryker Papers; Raper, *Tenants of the Almighty*, Plate 10.

44. Historian Maren Stange has argued that the demands of federal bureaucracy and the need to reach a wide public audience through mass media "mandated a new graphic rhetoric" that FSA photographers, under the direction of Roy Stryker, used to make "visually appealing images"; she refers to those images as "symbols of ideal life"—a phrase coined by John Dewey. My focus on Raper's and Delano's work in Greene County demonstrates how local demands and power structures played a more decisive role than institutional pressure from Stryker and the FSA in limiting the radical potential of New Deal documentary work and shaping its more idealistic image of rural life. See Stange, *Symbols of Ideal Life*, xvi, 104–5.

45. Jack Delano to Roy Stryker, May 7, 1941; Jack Delano to Roy Stryker, May 16, 1941, Stryker Papers.

46. Schmier and Montgomery, "The Other Depression," 134–35.

47. Day, "Folklife and Photography," 126. Irene Delano, who was an artist and brought brushes, paint, and an easel with her to the South, felt similarly inspired by the rural people she saw, particularly poor black southerners. During an interview Raper conducted with her in Greene County, he asked, "What were some of the things that you saw that you thought were worthy of painting?" She replied, "Well, mainly I was interested in painting Negroes and where they lived in Greene County and everything about their lives." See Audiotape T-03966/2, Raper Papers.

48. "Date Book—1941," Box 3, Folder 4, Delano Papers; Raper, *Tenants of the Almighty*, Plate 17.

49. "Pictures for the Greene County Study," Box 4, Folder 1, Delano Papers; Schmier and Montgomery, "The Other Depression," 140.

50. "Notes on Greene County Pictures, May 1941," and "Greene County Notes, June 1941," Folder 114, Raper Papers. The only reference to Thompson's attendance at Atlanta University comes from a caption from a photograph Delano took of him.

The caption was written either by Delano or Arthur Raper, www.loc.gov/pictures/collection/fsa/item/2017794658/, accessed May 21, 2018.

51. Blair, *Harlem Crossroads*, 78.

52. Wright, *12 Million Black Voices*, xix–xx; Raper and Reid, *Sharecroppers All*.

53. Wright, *12 Million Black Voices*, 10–11. In his book, *American Modernism and Depression Documentary*, Jeff Allred surmises that Thompson might be blind, suggests Wright's text "attributes blindness to the subject," and argues that Delano's photograph of Thompson in *Twelve Million Black Voices* confronts its mostly middle-class white audience "with the distortions inherent in its own habitual framing of blackness. In this context, the photograph provides readers not with a transparent representation of an other but with a mirror held up to their own blindness," 165. While I agree with Allred's reading of the photograph in the context of Wright's book, there is nothing in Raper's notes on Delano's photographs of Thompson, or in the captions for Delano's photographs, that indicates that Thompson was blind. See Allred, *American Modernism and Depression Documentary*, 162–65, 234.

54. Thompson, Review of *12 Million Black Voices*, 29.

55. It is worth noting that Jack Delano contributed the highest percentage of photographs of black people of any FSA photographer—a fact largely attributable to the influence of Arthur Raper. Of Delano's complete body of work for the FSA, 31.4 percent depicted black life. The next highest percentage came from two of the FSA's most respected female photographers: Dorothea Lange (31.1 percent) and Marion Post-Wolcott (23.6 percent.) Delano also produced a "day-in-the-life" chronicle of a young Greene County black child named Boyd Jones that mostly focused on his benefiting from FSA assistance in the form of better schools and a good home. The photographs, however, resemble the "required" shots Delano loathed and lack any of the artistic intent so many of his other images reveal. For more on the statistics and the Boyd Jones profile see Natanson, *The Black Image and the New Deal*, 72, 195–202.

56. Untitled manuscript by George Stoney in reply to letter from historian Stuart Kidd, Folder 622, Stoney Papers.

57. Natanson, *The Black Image in the New Deal*, 194; Delano, *Photographic Memories*, 39; Oral history interview with Jack and Irene Delano. My phrase, "righteousness of their mission," is a variation on a phrase by Trinh T. Minh-Ha—"righteous mission"—that she uses to describe the power and authority of the dominantly male voice-over in documentary film. See Minh-Ha, "Documentary Is/Not a Name," 84.

58. Schmier and Montgomery, "The Other Depression," 136. For a similar statement by Delano see Natanson, *The Black Image in the New Deal*, 193.

59. Kidd, "Dissonant Encounters," 32, 34.

60. Kidd, "Dissonant Encounters," 30–34.

61. Raper, *Tenants of the Almighty*, Plate 69.

62. "'Greene's Going Great' New Feature for Herald-Journal," Greensboro *Herald-Journal*, January 9, 1942, Folder 121, Raper Papers.

63. "List to whom *Tenants of the Almighty* has been sent in Greene County, Ga," Accession #: 1968-0606M, Raper Papers; "Dr. Raper to New Position," Greensboro *Herald-Journal*, September 1942, Folder 117, Raper Papers; "Dr. Raper to Leave," Greensboro *Herald-Journal*, August 7, 1942, Folder 117, Raper Papers.

64. Jack Delano to Roy Stryker, June 11, [1941], Stryker Papers; "Delano Photographs Greene County," Greensboro *Herald-Journal*, October 31, 1941.

65. Arthur Raper to Jack Delano, November 29, 1941, Folder 970, Raper Papers.

66. Arthur Raper to Jack Delano, November 29, 1941.

67. Raper and Raper, *Two Years to Remember*, 68.

68. Raper, *Tenants of the Almighty*, Plates 1–7.

69. Raper, Plates 19 and 20; Hawkins, "Case History of Cotton County Reveals Farm Life Difficulties," Folder 137, Raper Papers.

70. Mrs. C. M. Gooch to U. T. Miller, mid-July 1943, Folder 135, Raper Papers.

71. Raper, *Tenants of the Almighty*, Plate 18 and Plate 64.

72. Raper, 376–77.

73. Hayes, "Planning the 'Grass Roots,'" Folder 138, Raper Papers; Sherman, "Entrusted with a Portion of His Earth," 89; Lord, "A Place on Earth," 117.

74. Sherman, "Entrusted with a Portion of His Earth," 89; Lord, Review of *Tenants of the Almighty* in *Land Policy Review* (Fall 1943), Folder 138, Raper Papers.

75. Interview with Arthur F. Raper by Daniel Singal, January 17, 1971.

76. Natanson, *The Black Image in the New Deal*, 61–62, 178–83, 258. Gordon Parks later wrote that he thought Roy Stryker was loathe to bring him on as an FSA intern "because of the conditions that existed there at the time. It was an all-Southern laboratory." Esther Bubley, a photographer who worked for Stryker in the Office of War Information division when Parks was hired, described conditions in the FSA-OWI darkrooms that seemed to justify Stryker's fears: "The people in the darkroom were practically frothing at the mouth, they were so opposed to a black photographer. They sounded like a bunch of rednecks. It's amazing they didn't just destroy Parks's negatives." See Natanson, 61–62.

77. Tagg, *The Disciplinary Frame*, 179–84.

Chapter Three

1. Cohen, "Field Trip—Kentucky," 13; Cohen, "NLCR Reflections," 4; Pankake, "The New Lost City Ramblers," liner notes. This chapter first appeared in a different form in the journal *Southern Spaces* in 2008. See Matthews, "John Cohen in Eastern Kentucky."

2. Cohen, "Field Trip—Kentucky," 13.

3. Cohen, liner notes, *Mountain Music of Kentucky* CD, 29; Jean Ritchie's "good old boy" quote comes from an email exchange I had with her in 2006. Jean Ritchie to author, October 19, 2006; Shelton, "Folk Singer from the 'Source'," X22. The actual spelling of Roscoe Holcomb's last name is HALCOMB. I learned of the correct spelling while visiting Holcomb's friends and relatives in his native Perry County, Kentucky, during the summer of 2006. His nephew took me to his gravesite where I saw his name spelled "Rosco Halcomb" on his headstone. In his letters to John Cohen, Halcomb would also spell his first name "Roscoe" or "Rascal." The variety of spellings is due in part to Halcomb's handwriting. The spelling of his correct last name—Halcomb—is not in question. Cohen kept his last name as Holcomb for presentation purposes, believing Holcomb looked and sounded better than Halcomb. Throughout

this chapter, I refer to Halcomb as Holcomb to avoid confusion because that is how he is most widely known.

4. Cohen, liner notes, *Roscoe Holcomb: The High Lonesome Sound* CD, 10. For more on Holcomb's "Across the Rocky Mountain," including tuning and words see Cohen, "Roscoe Holcomb: First Person," 6. On Holcomb and the "high lonesome sound" in the context of bluegrass music see Cantwell, *Bluegrass Breakdown*, 129.

5. Cohen, "Roscoe Holcomb: First Person," 4. The myth of Appalachia as an isolated region in America has deep roots that reach back into the nineteenth century. Henry Shapiro and others have demonstrated how fiction writers beginning in the 1870s created the enduring myth of isolation and "otherness." As Shapiro notes, isolation was never just a "descriptive characteristic" but also a way to refer to "a state of mind, an undesirable provincialism resulting from a lack of contact between mountaineers and outsiders." Shapiro, *Appalachia on our Mind*, 77. Other Appalachian historians have in recent years produced probing histories that undermine ideas of the region's social and economic isolation from the rest of America. See Lewis, "Beyond Isolation and Homogeneity," 21-43.

6. Kephart, *Our Southern Highlanders*, 29-30. Harney and Frost's writings on the topic are collected in McNeil, *Appalachian Images in Folk and Popular Culture*. For more on the construction of the image of the Appalachian folk during the nineteenth and twentieth centuries, see Shapiro, *Appalachia on Our Mind*; Whisnant, *All That Is Native and Fine*; Batteau, *The Invention of Appalachia*; Becker, *Selling Tradition*.

7. Michaels, "Stranger in a Strange Land," 109; Pankake quoted in Cohen, liner notes, *Roscoe Holcomb: The High Lonesome Sound* CD, 2. For an incisive analysis of how Cohen straddled both the old-time music and avant-garde communities in New York and harnessed their ideas to inform his musical and documentary work see Jones, "Find the Avant-Garde in the Old-Time," 402-35.

8. Cohen, "NCLR Reflections," 4; Cohen, "A Reply to Alan Lomax," 32; Cohen, "Field Trip—Kentucky," 13.

9. Cohen, "NCLR Reflections," 5; Cohen quoted in Szwed, *Alan Lomax*, 337; Cohen, "The Folk Song Revival—A Historical Perspective Part I," 30.

10. Cohen, liner notes, *Roscoe Holcomb: An Untamed Sense of Control* CD, 8-9; Filene, *Romancing the Folk*, 5, 49. The mythic image of Holcomb that Cohen created in his documentary work, and the power of Holcomb's music, still captivates audiences across the globe. For a recent and evocative example, see Petrusich, "The Discovery of Roscoe Holcomb and the 'High Lonesome Sound'."

11. For Cohen's early recognition of the controversial ways in which Appalachia had been represented, see Cohen, "Field Trip—Kentucky," 13.

12. Oral interview with John Cohen conducted by author. Hereafter cited as Cohen interview; Radio interview with John Cohen, *All Things Considered*; Cohen, *There Is No Eye*, 22.

13. Cohen interview; Cohen, "A Visitor's Recollections," 115; Cohen, *There Is No Eye*, 24.

14. Montgomery, "The Folk Furor," 100.

15. Cohen, *There Is No Eye*, 42.

16. Cohen interview; Cohen, *There Is No Eye*, 82.

17. Cohen interview; Cohen, *There Is No Eye*, 81–82.

18. Cohen interview; Cohen, *There Is No Eye*, 82–83. For the distinction between Frank and Walker Evans, see Stott, "Walker Evans, Robert Frank, and the Landscape of Dissassociation"; Baier, "Visions of Fascination and Despair," 55–63; Papageorge, *Walker Evans and Robert Frank*; Bromfield, "'The Americans' and the Americans," 8–15.

19. Cohen, *There Is No Eye*, 82, 118; Cohen interview; Eskin, "His Worst Critic Proved Wrong," 38.

20. Pankake, liner notes, "The New Lost City Ramblers"; Goldsmith, *Making People's Music*, 259; Stekert, "Cents and Nonsense in the Urban Folksong Movement: 1930–1966," 96–97. Excellent histories of the New Lost City Ramblers include Gura, "Southern Roots and Branches"; Allen, *Gone to the Country*; and Malone, *Music from the True Vine*. For more on the popular and critical reception of Harry Smith's *Anthology of American Folk Music* during its release in 1952 and its reissue in 1997, see Skinner, "'Must Be Born Again,'" 57–75.

21. Cohen, "About Us," liner notes in *The New Lost City Ramblers*, 1.

22. Cohen, "The Revival," 23.

23. Cohen, "A Reply to Alan Lomax," 32–33.

24. Cohen, "A Reply to Alan Lomax," 32–33. On romanticism's rejection of universal truths and absolutes see Berlin, *The Roots of Romanticism*, 138, 140, 146–47.

25. Cohen, "Depression," liner notes in *The New Lost City Ramblers*, 1; Lund and Denisoff, "The Folk Music Revival and the Counter Culture," 400. For more on the unique social and cultural forces that shaped the character of America's postwar folk music revival see Cantwell, "When We Were Good" and *When We Were Good*.

26. Cohen, liner notes, *Mountain Music of Kentucky* CD, 6; Cohen, ed., *"Wasn't That a Time!"* 26; Braun, "On to Arcadia," 19; Cohen, "NLCR Reflections," 4. For the story of where Cohen came up with the title, "Gone to the Country," see Cohen, "Gone to the Country," liner notes in *The New Lost City Ramblers: Gone to the Country* LP, 1.

27. Montgomery, "Folk Furor," 99, 118.

28. Cohen, "A Visitor's Recollections," 116; Cohen interview. The digitized archive of Lomax's sound recordings and photographs from southern Appalachia made in August and September 1959 can be accessed at www.culturalequity.org/. For Shirley Collins's recollections of traveling and working with Lomax during his 1959 recording trip across the South, see Collins, *America over the Water*.

29. A website called *The Lomax Kentucky Recordings* provides extensive information about the Lomaxes' recording trips in the state as well as audio of the songs they recorded. The website is the product of a collaboration between the Association for Cultural Equity, Berea College, the Library of Congress, and the University of Kentucky. https://lomaxky.omeka.net/ (accessed May 23, 2018).

30. See for example, McGill, *Folk Songs of the Kentucky Mountains*; Wyman and Brockway, *Twenty Kentucky Mountain Songs*; Sharp and Karpeles, *English Folk Songs of the Southern Appalachians*. For a historical overview of these early collectors see, Whisnant, *All That Is Native and Fine*, and Shapiro, *Appalachia on Our Mind*.

31. Cohen, *There Is No Eye*, 120; Cohen, ed., *"Wasn't That a Time!"* 26; Cohen, "Field Trip—Kentucky," 13.

32. Cohen interview.

33. Cohen quoted in Bransford, "Trying to Make It Real," 232.

34. Cohen, *The High & Lonesome Sound*, 238; Cohen to Ross Grosman, June 1959. Letter in John Cohen's possession, photocopy made by author, January 2008.

35. Cohen to Grosman, second letter, [June 1959]. Letter in possession of John Cohen. Copy provided for author.

36. Cohen to Grosman, second letter; Cohen, liner notes, *Mountain Music of Kentucky* CD, 28.

37. Cohen interview; Cohen, *The High & Lonesome Sound*, 233. The dialogue between Cohen and the Halcombs comes from "Transcription of *Remembering the High Lonesome Sound*."

38. Quotes taken from Cohen, liner notes, *Mountain Music of Kentucky* CD, 29, and Cohen, liner notes *Roscoe Holcomb: The High Lonesome Sound* CD, 2.

39. Cohen, *The High & Lonesome Sound*, 234.

40. Cohen, liner notes, *Roscoe Holcomb: The High Lonesome Sound* CD, 3–4, 10.

41. Cohen, liner notes, *Roscoe Holcomb: The High Lonesome Sound* CD, 3, 4, 6; Cohen, "Interview with Roscoe Holcomb," *The High Lonesome Sound* LP, 1.

42. Cohen, liner notes, *Roscoe Holcomb: The High Lonesome Sound* CD, 1; Cohen, liner notes, *Mountain Music of Kentucky* LP, 3; Cohen, liner notes, *Roscoe Holcomb and Wade Ward* LP, 2.

43. Cohen interview; Cohen, ed., *"Wasn't That a Time!"* 38–39.

44. Cohen quoted in Guthman, *Strangers Below*, 122.

45. Cohen, "Field Trip—Kentucky," 14.

46. Cohen, liner notes, *Mountain Music of Kentucky* LP, 1–4.

47. Shelton, "Art of Folk Song in Festival Form," X14; *San Francisco Chronicle* reviewer quoted in Cohen, liner notes, *Mountain Music of Kentucky* CD, 34.

48. Cohen, liner notes, *Roscoe Holcomb: The High Lonesome Sound* CD, 8.

49. Cohen, "The Folk Music Interchange," 44.

50. Cohen, "Interview with Roscoe Holcomb," *The High Lonesome Sound* LP, 2; Cohen, liner notes, *Roscoe Holcomb: The High Lonesome Sound* CD, 12.

51. Cohen, "Field Trip—Kentucky," 13; Cohen, liner notes, *Mountain Music of Kentucky* CD, 24. The culmination of a decade of controversy over outside representations of Appalachia and its poverty occurred in 1967 with the murder of Canadian documentary filmmaker Hugh O'Connor by Hobart Ison in Jeremiah, Kentucky—just down the road and one county over from Daisy. For more on the murder and its legacy, see Trillin, "A Stranger with a Camera." The Hobart Ison case is also explored in more depth in a documentary film also titled *Stranger with a Camera* (2000) by Elizabeth Barrett of Appalshop.

52. Harkin, *Hillbilly*, 4, 171–76.

53. Wilgus, "On the Record," 96–97; *Mountain Life and Work*, 51.

54. Shelton, "Art of Folk Song in Festival Form," X14.

55. Deshin, "The Shows Are On: Five One-Man Exhibits among Season's First," X21.

56. Cohen, liner notes, *Roscoe Holcomb: The High Lonesome Sound* CD, 12.

57. Shelton, "Students Import Folk Art to Chicago," 11; Cohen, *The High & Lonesome Sound*, 238. Cohen's letter to Roscoe Holcomb is in Cohen's possession. I copied it during my visit in September 2006 while conducting my interview with him.

58. Cohen, liner notes, *Roscoe Holcomb: The High Lonesome Sound* CD, 2.

59. Quoted in Cohen, liner notes, *Roscoe Holcomb: The High Lonesome Sound* CD, 12.

60. Cohen, "Roscoe Holcomb at Zabriskie Point," 21.

61. Shelton, "Bountiful Area: Southern Highlands a Bottomless Well for Recordings of Folk Music," 126.

62. Cohen, liner notes, *Roscoe Holcomb and Wade Ward* LP, 1–2.

63. Shelton, "Bountiful Area: Southern Highlands a Bottomless Well for Recordings of Folk Music," 126.

64. Cohen interview; "A Transcription of *Remembering the High Lonesome Sound*"; Cohen, "A Visitor's Recollections," 117. Cohen's knowledge of documentary film at this time was limited. The documentary film Cohen recalled seeing before making his own in Kentucky was Helen Levitt's 1941 *In the Street*, a collaborative effort with James Agee. The film's unobtrusive and poetic depiction of daily life in Spanish Harlem bore all the hallmarks of Levitt's photography through its fleeting theatricality of children playing in the streets. He later met Levitt at the home of Robert and Mary Frank, his next-door neighbors on the Lower East Side, although he was familiar with Levitt's earlier work. It seems that Levitt was also familiar with Cohen's work: when a friend visited his apartment, he noticed a photograph of Cohen's from Peru and told him that Levitt had the same photograph on her mantel. For more on Cohen's documentary film influences, see Cohen, "Musical Documents," 460.

65. Cohen interview; Agee, "Killing a Turtle," 64.

66. Cohen interview; Oral history interview with Agee.

67. Cohen interview; Agee, "Killing a Turtle," 64; Cohen, "Musical Documents," 459.

68. Cohen, "Musical Documents," 459; Cohen interview; Cohen, "A Visitor's Recollections," 117.

69. Cohen, "Interview with Roscoe Holcomb," *The High Lonesome Sound*, LP, 2.

70. Cohen, "Musical Documents," 474; Cohen, *The High & Lonesome Sound*, 235.

71. In a 1968 interview Cohen conducted with Bob Dylan in *Sing Out!* Dylan referred to Holcomb as having an "untamed sense of control." This description later became the title of a CD of Holcomb's music released on Smithsonian Folkways and referred to throughout this article. Cohen, "Conversations with Bob Dylan," 6–23, 67.

72. Cohen would never again narrate his documentary films. "In my first film I was the narrator, but still feel discomfort at being the spokesman for people who don't need me as such," he told filmmaker Sharon Sherman. Cohen quoted in Bransford, "Trying to Make It Real," 230.

73. Sherman, *Documenting Ourselves*, 63–66.

74. Cunningham, "The High Lonesome Sound," 250–51.

75. Cohen, "Musical Documents," 459.

76. Cohen interview.

77. Cohen interview.

78. "A Transcription of *Remembering the High Lonesome Sound*"; Cohen interview.

79. Cohen interview.

80. Cohen interview.

81. Sherman, *Documenting Ourselves*, 232.

82. Cohen interview.

83. Bigart, "Kentucky Miners: A Grim Winter"," 1.

84. Quoted in Cohen, liner notes, *Roscoe Holcomb: An Untamed Sense of Control* CD, 10.

85. Cohen interview; Letter from Holcomb to Cohen, December 11, 1964. A second letter was read to me by Cohen during my first visit with him. I copied the December letter during my second visit.

86. Cohen, liner notes, *Roscoe Holcomb: The High Lonesome Sound* LP, 5; Luigart, "Roscoe Holcomb's Other World: Perry Folk Musician Finds Wide Audience."

87. Cohen, "Roscoe Holcomb at Zabriskie Point," 20.

88. Seeger, dir., *Rainbow Quest*, DVD 606.

89. Cohen, "Roscoe Holcomb at Zabriskie Point," 20–21.

90. Goldsmith, *Making People's Music*, 265–66; Holcomb's letter to Cohen in Cohen, *The High & Lonesome Sound*, 258. As Peter Goldsmith notes, Asch and Holcomb developed a "respect and fondness for another," and Asch would occasionally hand him a ten or twenty dollar bill when he saw him, an acknowledgment of the paltry return Folkways received from his and most of the label's records and a demonstration of Asch's "usual paternalistic style."

91. Cohen, liner notes, *Roscoe Holcomb: An Untamed Sense of Control* CD, 8.

92. Cohen interview; Cohen, liner notes, *Roscoe Holcomb: The High Lonesome Sound* CD, 8.

93. Cohen, "Roscoe Holcomb (1913–1981)," 41.

94. Cohen, "Field Trip—Kentucky," 13.

95. Cohen, liner notes, *Mountain Music of Kentucky* CD, 16, 24; Cohen interview.

96. Cohen, "A Visitor's Recollections," 117.

97. "A Transcription of *Remembering the High Lonesome Sound*."

Chapter Four

1. Bond, "Foreword," in Kelen, ed., *This Light of Ours*, 6, 15; Bond, "Foreword," in Lyon, *Memories of the Southern*, 6.

2. See https://deyoung.famsf.org/deyoung/exhibitions/world-not-my-home-photographs-danny-lyon (accessed February 3, 2017); Odum, *An American Epoch*, ix–x.

3. Raiford, *Imprisoned in a Luminous Glare*, 127. See also Raiford, "'Come Let Us Build a New World Together,'" 1129–57; Schmeisser, "Camera at the Grassroots," 105–25. Raiford's chapter on SNCC photography in *Imprisoned in a Luminous Glare* identifies three phases of SNCC photography from 1961–68: it demonstrates how its focus changed from envisioning the "beloved community" in 1961–64 to Black Power in 1965–68. Schmeisser's essay argues that SNCC photography "functioned as a corrective against slurs by racist media coverage," which helped SNCC create its own identity, secure personal and financial support, facilitate federal intervention, and record "movement culture from an engaged, activist point of view," 106–7.

4. Garner, *Disappearing Witness*, 43, 111; Bezner, *Photography and Politics in America*, 1–4, 217.

5. Cox, "Chasing down the Kid from Queens," 16.

6. Eskildsen, "Social Commitment as Personal Adventure," 36–42; Lyon, *Memories of Myself*, 6.

7. Eskildsen, "Social Commitment as Personal Adventure," 36–42.

8. Lyon, *Memories of the Southern Civil Rights Movement*, 20; Greenberg, *Circle of Trust*, 71–72; Hale, *A Nation of Outsiders*, 173.

9. Lyon, *Memories of the Southern Civil Rights Movement*, 20; Greenberg, *Circle of Trust*, 71–72; Hale, *A Nation of Outsiders*, 169.

10. Lyon, *Memories of the Southern Civil Rights Movement*, 23.

11. Lyon, 24.

12. Lyon, *Message to the Future*, 16; Lewis, *Walking with the Wind*, 29–43, 192, 263.

13. Lyon, *Memories of the Southern Civil Rights Movement*, 26; Hansberry, *The Movement*, 72, 118. Lyon, who wrote the brief photo captions that appeared in the back of *The Movement*, noted that "the pool was eventually closed." Hansberry, *The Movement*, 126.

14. Lyon, *Memories of the Southern Civil Rights Movement*, 26; Lewis, *Walking with the Wind*, 192; Raiford, *Imprisoned in a Luminous Glare*, 68; Blair, *Harlem Crossroads*, 203, 213; Hansberry, *The Movement*, 46; Ginocchino, "Not Quite Paradise, and Starting to Fall Apart," NJ9.

15. Lyon, *Memories of the Southern Civil Rights Movement*, 29–30.

16. Raiford, *Imprisoned in a Luminous Glare*, 70–71, 73–74; Forman, *The Making of Black Revolutionaries*, 244; Bond, "A Remarkable Time," 10. For a study of SNCC's communications department and its public relations work, see Murphree, *The Selling of Civil Rights*.

17. Greenberg, *Circle of Trust*, 38.

18. Bond quoted in Schmeisser, "Camera at the Grassroots," 110.

19. Lyon, *Memories of the Southern Civil Rights Movement*, 28–37.

20. Lyon, *Memories of the Southern Civil Rights Movement*, 35; Hayden quoted in Hale, *A Nation of Outsiders*, 175. For more on how activists in the New Left, under the influence of Christianity and existentialism, came to see social activism as the antidote to personal alienation and malaise, see Rossinow, *The Politics of Authenticity*.

21. Lyon, *Memories of the Southern Civil Rights Movement*, 38, 41; "Danny Lyon: Civil Rights Photographer," interview.

22. Greenberg, *A Circle of Trust*, 36–37.

23. Carmichael quoted in Visser-Maessen, *Robert Parris Moses*, 91. The phrase "Bob Moses mystique" is Visser-Maessen's, 92; Bond quoted in Schmeisser, "Camera at the Grassroots," 110. On Moses's recognition of the critical importance of creating ties between SNCC's movement in the South and sympathetic supporters in the North, see Visser-Maessen, *Robert Parris Moses*, 5, 135, 151.

24. Visser-Maessen, *Robert Parris Moses*, 34.

25. Dittmer, *Local People*, 102–106.

26. Visser-Maessen, *Robert Parris Moses*, 60, 92; Burner, *And Gently He Shall Lead Them*, 50–53; Newfield, *A Prophetic Minority*, 51–52.

27. Burner, *And Gently He Shall Lead Them*, 65–66; Hale, *A Nation of Outsiders*, 174–75; Lyon, *Memories of the Southern Civil Rights Movement*, 17.

28. Moses quoted in Hogan, *Many Minds, One Heart*, 78.

29. Payne, *I've Got the Light of Freedom*, 171; Lyon, *Memories of the Southern Civil Rights Movement*, 44, 55.

30. Visser-Maessen, *Robert Parris Moses*, 124–25.

31. Hansberry, *The Movement*, 109; King quoted in Burner, *And Gently He Shall Lead Them*, 2; Zinn, *SNCC: The New Abolitionists*, 5, 62.

32. Coles, *Doing Documentary Work*, 36–39.

33. Lyon, *Knave of Hearts*, 24.

34. Lyon, *Memories of the Southern Civil Rights Movement*, 38, 41; Fischer, "A Small Band of Practical Heroes," 20.

35. Lyon, *Memories of the Southern Civil Rights Movement*, 38, 41.

36. Hansberry, *The Movement*, 6.

37. Koningsberger, "Of Lenses and Literature," SNCC Papers, microfilm reel 27, frame 152.

38. Belfrage, *Freedom Summer*, 81–82. See also Hale, *A Nation of Outsiders*, 195–96.

39. Greenberg, *Circle of Trust*, 37; Hayden quoted in Ellis, "Romancing the Oppressed," 119. On the connection between the folk revival, the civil rights movement, and the romance of blacks in the rural South, see Hale, *A Nation of Outsiders*, 107–18.

40. Visser-Maeseen, *Robert Parris Moses*, 67, 215; Burner, *And Gently He Shall Lead Them*, 31; Hohle, *Black Citizenship and Authenticity in the Civil Rights Movement*, 117; Payne, *I've Got the Light of Freedom*, 101.

41. "Tamio Wakayama #8: Photographing the movement," www.youtube.com/watch?v=4POLTG4_Uoo (accessed January 7, 2017); Kelen, *This Light of Ours*, 19, 39; Lyon, *Message to the Future*, 19.

42. Lyon, *Memories of the Southern Civil Rights Movement*, 38.

43. Hansberry, *The Movement*, 22.

44. Hansberry, 32.

45. Hansberry, 32; Newfield, *A Prophetic Minority*, 68–69; Coles, *Doing Documentary Work*, 169.

46. Hale, *A Nation of Outsiders*, 88; Zinn, *SNCC: The New Abolitionists*, 15; Martinez, ed., *Letters from Mississippi*, 55–56. For similar statements made by white civil rights workers and black responses, see Coles, *Doing Documentary Work*, 56–57.

47. Lyon, *Memories of Myself*, 7.

48. Stott, *Documentary Expression*, 223; Raiford, *Imprisoned in a Luminous Glare*, 98–100.

49. Koningsberger, "Of Lenses and Literature," SNCC Papers, microfilm reel 27, frame 152.

50. Payne, "SNCC: An Overview Two Years Later," 88; Hale, *A Nation of Outsiders*, 118; Newfield, *A Prophetic Minority*, 69. Lyon's documentary style—his romantic realism that was influenced by the Beat movement and the New Left—represented only one way of portraying SNCC's work in the South during the early to middle 1960s. A fifty-year-old white filmmaker from California named Harvey Richards also produced documentary images of SNCC and rural South during the organization's early years. Richards made the first SNCC-sanctioned documentary film of the group's work in the rural South, *We'll Never Turn Back*, in 1963, and he made a second film for SNCC, *A Dream Deferred* one year later. Richards was a former Communist Party member and

labor organizer, and his documentary films for SNCC reflected the ideas of the Old Left, rather than the New. Instead of pastoral romanticism, his films emphasized agricultural exploitation and the role of violence in maintaining white supremacy while also foregrounding the heroic activism of local black people who worked with SNCC organizers like Bob Moses. See Richards, "Primary Source Documentaries."

51. Lyon, *Memories of the Southern Civil Rights Movement*, 135. Lyon's letter to his parents is dated February 12, 1964, and a copy is reproduced in full in the book.

52. Lyon, *Message to the Future*, 19, 73, 75; Lyon, *Memories of the Southern Civil Rights Movement*, 189. According to Lyon, *The Movement* "went into five editions in this country and another in England, where Penguin published it as *A Matter of Colour*."

53. Lyon, *Message to the Future*, 73; Hansberry, *The Movement*, 125–27; Betty Garman to Bob Gottleib, November 18, 1964. SNCC Papers, microfilm reel 27, frame 147. Sara Blair provides an incisive analysis of the text Hansberry wrote to accompany the photographs featured in *The Movement*. She argues that the "photo-text" allowed Hansberry "at a critical moment in the iconicity of black intellectuals, to begin imagining herself differently on the stage of public culture: as a writer of formally indeterminate texts rather than conventional well-made drama," 222. See Blair, *Harlem Crossroads*, 198–223.

54. Lyon, *Memories of the Southern Civil Rights Movement*, 149; Norris McNamara, "SNCC PHOTO: A PROPOSAL FOR MEETING THE NEEDS OF THE PHOTOGRAPHY DEPARTMENT OF THE STUDENT NONVIOLENT COORDINATING COMMITTEE," April 1964. SNCC Papers, microfilm reel 36, frames 47–49; Tom Wakayama, "Memo to Executive Committee Re: SNCC Photo," n.d., [late 1964?], SNCC Papers, microfilm reel 36, frame 667; Heron, *Mississippi Eyes*, 129; Lyon, *Knave of Hearts*, 28.

55. Lyon, *Memories of the Southern Civil Rights Movement*, 162–65.

56. Raiford, *Imprisoned in a Luminous Glare*, 71, 107–108, 118–19; Hale, *A Nation of Outsiders*, 207–208; Carson, *In Struggle*, 209.

57. Schmeisser, "Camera at the Grassroots," 115–16; Lester quoted in Raiford, *Imprisoned in a Luminous Glare*, 123.

58. "The Streets of Greenwood" pamphlet, no date, SNCC Papers, microfilm reel 36, frame 225.

59. Lyon later said that the recordings on *Movement Soul* "are the best I have ever heard." Lyon, *Memories of the Southern Civil Rights Movement*, 189. For more on Ribback, *Movement Soul*, and his recordings from the South during the civil rights movement, see http://sova.si.edu/record/NMAH.AC.0556. For more on ESP-Disk, including on Ribback and *Movement Soul*, see Weiss, *Always in Trouble*.

60. Hale, *A Nation of Outsiders*, 205; Turner, "Guy and Candie Carawan," 67.

61. Lester, "SNCC PHOTO NEWS," January 1967, SNCC Papers, microfilm reel 36, frame 441; Raiford, *Imprisoned in a Luminous Glare*, 121–23; Amaris, "Calendar Art," 180–81.

62. Raiford, *Imprisoned in a Luminous Glare*, 122–24.

63. Excerpts of the oral history of Julius Lester by Lián Amaris in 2008. Amaris, "Calendar Art," 182–86.

64. Lester, www.profotos.com/juliuslester/ (accessed March 19, 2017); Smith, "Thinking in Light."

65. "Danny Lyon, Civil Rights Photographer," interview; Amaris, "Calendar Art," 182–86. On the resistance and even "fury" Lyon faced from some of the black people he photographed, in particular during the funerals for the four black girls killed in the 16th Street Baptist Church bombing in Birmingham, Alabama, in 1963, see Raiford, *Imprisoned in a Luminous Glare*, 101.

66. Lyon quoted in Sussman, "The Story Was Destruction," in Lyon, *Message to the Future*, 33.

67. Lyon, *Danny Lyon: Photo-Film*, 42. Lyon published a collection of his photographs of biker gangs in 1968 in a book he titled *The Bikeriders*.

68. Lyon, *Message to the Future*, 77.

Chapter Five

1. Allie Mae Burroughs is her given name. James Agee referred to her as "Annie Mae Gudger" in *Let Us Now Praise Famous Men*. The aliases, intended to protect the families' privacy, lasted until the 1970s. Stories on the families have appeared during the last few years, and all use the families' given names. I use their given names in this chapter because they are already well known, because I write about many of them as individuals separate from Agee's book, and because the main people I discuss are no longer living. This chapter first appeared in a different form in 2016 in the journal, *Southern Cultures*. See Matthews, "Protesting the Privilege of Perception."

2. Agee and Evans, *Let Us Now Praise Famous Men*, 10; Lisle, "The Rural Studio."

3. Forgey, "Buildings with a Feeling of Belonging," C01.

4. Trachtenberg, "Walker Evans's Fictions of the South," 302. There are other important contributors to the history of documentary expression in Hale County whom I do not have space to include. In addition to Farm Security Administration photographers such as Walker Evans and Jack Delano who photographed in the county during the 1930s and 1940s, another group of government photographers, associated with the Historic American Buildings Survey (HABS), including Alex Bush, extensively photographed the county's antebellum architecture during the 1930s as did Francis Benjamin Johnston as part of the Carnegie Survey of Architecture of the South. Another important documentarian in Hale County's history is Frederic Ramsey, who traveled throughout the South, including Hale County, in the 1950s making recordings and taking photographs while in search of the origins of American music, particularly its "jazz backgrounds." His work resulted in the ambitiously titled *Music of the South*, a ten-volume anthology released on Folkways Records that featured recordings of music from the farms of the Alabama backcountry to the streets of New Orleans. In 1960, the same year *Let Us Now Praise Famous Men* was reissued and John Cohen released *Mountain Music of Kentucky* on Folkways, Ramsey published *Been Here and Gone*, a book of photographs and poetic descriptions of the people and places he encountered during his travels. Ramsey's work combined a salvage impulse with an aesthetic sensibility that poeticized and romanticized the seemingly premodern culture of black people in the rural South.

5. Pratt, *Imperial Eyes*, 136; Rosaldo, *Culture & Truth*, 245.

6. According to Agee, "To those who own and create it this 'beauty' is, however, irrelevant and undiscernible. It is best discernible to those who by economic advantage of training have only a shameful and thief's right to it: and it might be said that they have any 'rights' whatever only in proportion as they recognize the ugliness and disgrace implicit in their privilege of perception." Agee and Evans, *Let Us Now Praise Famous Men*, 178. Critics have long noted photography's ability to expose private life for publication consumption. In *Camera Lucida*, Roland Barthes highlighted how the advent of photography "corresponds precisely to the explosion of the private into the public, or rather into the creation of a new social value, which is the publicity of the private: the private is consumed as such, publicly." Barthes, *Camera Lucida*, 98.

7. Forney, "Reckoning the Land," 254. For an analysis of outside representations of "deeply othered places" in the American mind, such as Appalachia, that includes an overview of Hobart Ison's murder of Hugh O'Connor, see Cameron, "When Strangers Bring Cameras," 340–60.

8. Edwards et al., *Soil Survey: Hale County*, 1–2; Knight, *Mound Excavations at Moundville*, 1.

9. Baldwin, *A News and Complete Gazetteer of the United States*, 444.

10. Hubbs, *Guarding Greensboro*, 15, 17.

11. Hubbs, 20.

12. Olmsted, *Cotton Kingdom*, 551.

13. The fullest treatment of Young's life and work remains Hoole, *Martha Young*. For more on Otts, his work with Young, and an excellent overview of the history of photography in Alabama see Robb, *Shot in Alabama*, 164, 168–70.

14. Lott, *Love and Theft*; Culbertson, *Banjo Talks*. For more on Keipp, see Robb, *Shot in Alabama*, 164–65, 171–74. Dunbar did use a black photographer from Hampton, Robert Moton, to illustrate one of his poems, "A Hunting Song," from his 1896 book, *Poems of Cabin and Field*. See Moody-Turner, *Black Folklore and the Politics of Racial Representation*, 107–8. On Paul Laurence Dunbar's use of photographs made by the Hampton Camera Club in his volumes of dialect poetry see Sapirstein, "Out from behind the Mask," 167–203.

15. Henninger, *Ordering the Façade*, 47–48. For an examination of the cultural politics of the late nineteenth and early twentieth centuries when black educators, folklorists, and writers used folkloric and ethnographic styles and methodologies to challenge white representations of black identity see Moody-Turner, *Black Folklore and the Politics of Racial Representation*.

16. Ewell and Menke, *Southern Local Color*, xvii–xviii, xxxvi–xxxix, liv, lvii.

17. Hoole, *Martha Young*, 10–12; Young, "System for Story-Making—IV," *Birmingham Age-Herald*, Sunday, September 7, 1890. Box 1597.002/Folder 2, Young Papers.

18. Review of *Plantation Songs* in *The Era*, 888.

19. Young, *Minute Dramas—The Kodak at the Quarter*.

20. "Mammy's Photograph," Box 1597.005, Folder 4, Martha Young Papers.

21. Gibson, "The Alabama Black Belt," 20.

22. Dunbar, *Lyrics of Lowly Life*, 167.

23. Scarborough, *On the Trail of Negro Folk-Songs*, 15–16; Grider, "Scarborough, Emily Dorothy." For more on Scarborough's folk song collecting work, and this instance in particular, see Hamilton, *In Search of the Blues*, 53–90.

24. Young, *Minute Dramas*, 8.

25. Young, 43.

26. For a representative example of how Hale County became imagined as the embodiment of the Old South in the New South by travel writers, tourists, and photographers before James Agee and Walker Evans arrived in the summer of 1936 see Cleland, "The Alabama Black Belt," 375–76. According to Cleland, a science professor from Illinois, popular opinion among Alabamians confirmed that Greensboro in Hale County was the place most typical of the Old South.

27. Young, "Observations of Work among the Negroes of Hale County," undated. Martha Young Papers, Box 1597.006, Folder 9.

28. *Hale County News*, August 6, 1936.

29. Forney, "Reckoning the Land," 253; Sledge, "Hale County, Past the Present and into the Future," 260.

30. Cleland, "The Alabama Black Belt," 375–76.

31. Agee and Evans, *Let Us Now Praise Famous Men*, 319–20.

32. Agee and Evans, 23.

33. Michaels, *The Beauty of a Social Problem*, 136. On the difficulty of the "gaze" in the work of Agee and Evans in *Famous Men* and its role in producing relationships between documentarians, their subjects, and readers, see Olin, "'It's Not Going to Be Easy to Look into Their Eyes,'" 92–115.

34. Agee and Evans, *Let Us Now Praise Famous Men*, 321. For a recent study in German on resistance to Agee and Evans while working in Hale County that focuses on the Tingles, see Leicht, *Wei Katie Tingle sich weigerte ordentlich zu posieren und Walker Evans daruber nicht grollete*.

35. Agee and Evans, *Let Us Now Praise Famous Men*, 322; Maharidge and Williamson, *And Their Children after Them*, 39; Evans, *Walker Evans at Work*, 125.

36. Agee and Evans, *Let Us Now Praise Famous Men*, 323. Evans refers to Flora Tingle as Dora Mae Tengle in his captions for the FSA archive.

37. Sontag, *On Photography*, 4, 14–15; Spears and Cassidy, eds., *Agee*, 66.

38. Agee and Evans, *Let Us Now Praise Famous Men*, 326–27.

39. Michaels, *The Beauty of a Social Problem*, 122.

40. See in particular Stott, *Documentary Expression*.

41. Rabinowitz, *They Must Be Represented*, 53–54. In addition to Peter Cannon's work and Howell Raines's piece for the *New York Times*, "Let Us Now Revisit Famous Folk," other examples of rephotography and follow-up journalism on *Famous Men* during the late 1970s and 1980s include Jenkins, "Emma's Story: Two Versions," and Osbourne, "A Walker Evans Heroine Remembers," 70–73. Jenkins visited Hale County in November 1976 and interviewed Allie Mae Burroughs, her daughter Emma, and sons Junior, Squeaky, and Burt.

42. Rosler, "In, around, and Afterthoughts," 319.

43. Despite rumors that circulated among some people in Hale County that suggested Agee and Evans were communist spies, their documentary work garnered no

attention from local newspapers when they were in Alabama. The book's release in 1941 and reissue in 1960 also seemed to escape local notice. In 1941, the famed editor of the *Greensboro Watchman*, Hamner Cobbs, mentioned another influential book about the South written by a native son, William Alexander Percy. As one might expect from a member of the Black Belt elite, Cobbs praised Percy's paean to the noblesse oblige of the region's well-born whites in *Lanterns on the Levee*. "Fed as we have been on a diet of Erskine Caldwell and of Southerners of a similar ilk who have made a living out of fouling their nests, Mr. Percy's book comes even more as a refreshing personal study and even more as a fine presentation of the South of today," wrote Cobbs. For his editorials on the South in books and media in 1941, see *Greensboro Watchman*, June 12, 1941 and February 6, 1941.

44. Florence Thompson, like some of the people featured in *Famous Men*, would later express anger at how Lange's photograph of her and her children became a widely circulated work of art and iconic representation of America during the Great Depression without her consent or control. Thompson, like the Hale County families, interpreted the issue as one about power and rights. In 1958, Thompson wrote to *U.S. Camera* to complain about the appearance of the photograph in the magazine: "You would do Dorothea Lange a great Favor by Sending me her address That I may Inform her that should the picture appear in Any magazine again I and my Three Daughters shall be Forced to Protect our rights." Quoted in Gordon, *Dorothea Lange*, 241. Gordon acknowledges that Lange, in her mission to bring about social reform, never reflected on the ethics of documenting the poor and "never worried about potential harm to subjects," 243.

45. "Englishman Tracks down Subject of Evans,'" 28. For an extended analysis of Evans's photograph of Burroughs by one of Evans's former protégés, see Thompson, *The Story of a Photograph*.

46. "Resistance," Michel Foucault argued in an interview shortly before his death, "is not solely a negation but a creative process. To create and recreate, to transform the situation, to participate actively in the process, that is to resist. . . . To say no is the minimum form of resistance. But naturally, at times that is very important." Quoted in Shakespeare and Moody, eds., *Intensities*, 11.

47. "Englishman Tracks down Subject of Evans,'" 28.

48. *Art and Artists* 14 (1979): 50.

49. *Art and Artists* 14 (1979): 50; Bell, dir., *Let Us Now Praise Famous Men Revisited*.

50. Osbourne, "A Walker Evans Heroine Remembers," 70-73; Jenkins, "Emma's Story: Two Versions," 8-26; Bell, dir., *Let Us Now Praise Famous Men Revisited*; Spears, dir., *Agee*. Quote about the Agee film in Wolfe, "Just in Time," 215.

51. Raines, "Let Us Now Revisit Famous Folk," 31-32, 46.

52. Raines, 34.

53. Bell, dir., *Let Us Now Praise Famous Men Revisited*.

54. "Hale County Resident Drops Case," 4; "Decision on News Upheld," 2.

55. Bell, dir., *Let Us Now Praise Famous Men Revisited*.

56. Maharidge and Williamson, *And Their Children after Them*, 174, xxii.

57. Loke, "Harry Lunn, Jr., 65, Art Dealer Who Championed Photography"; Raines, "Let Us Now Revisit Famous Folk," 36.

58. Mitchell, *Picture Theory*, 293–94; Raines, "Let Us Now Revisit Famous Folk," 36; for more on the cultural politics and aesthetics of Evans's photographs, including his of Burroughs, see Michaels, *The Beauty of a Social Problem*, 122–27.

59. Raines, "Let Us Now Revisit Famous Folk," 36.

60. Maharidge and Williamson, *And Their Children after Them*, 139–40.

61. Davidson, "Let Us Now Trash Famous Authors." For other examples of twenty-first-century follow-up stories on the families, see Whitford, "The Most Famous Story We Never Told"; Downes, "Of Poor Farmers and 'Famous Men'"; Haughney, "A Paean to Forbearance (the Rough Draft)."

62. Maharidge and Williamson, *And Their Children after Them*, 206.

63. Edge, "Pie + Design = Change."

64. Davidson, "Let Us Now Trash Famous Authors."

65. The phrase "righteous mission" comes from Minh-Ha, "Documentary Is/Not a Name," 84.

66. Davidson, "Let Us Now Trash Famous Authors."

67. Downes, "Of Poor Farmers and 'Famous Men.'"

Conclusion

1. Theroux, *Deep South*, 21, 24, 78.

2. Theroux, 176–77; Journey, "Let Us Now Praise Greensboro, Alabama . . . (and Randall Curb)." The quote about Curb being the "blind sage" and his house serving as a "salon" is from Journey. He is an arts professor at Alabama A&M University in Huntsville and a Birmingham native who has known Curb for many years. Journey has also written about Walker Evans and William Christenberry for the *Encyclopedia of Alabama*. On Christenberry see www.encyclopediaofalabama.org/article/h-1624. On Evans see www.encyclopediaofalabama.org/article/h-1813 (accessed May 22, 2017). Curb is quoted in "Hale County, Alabama." See also Curb, *Historic Hale County*. Curb has also written about William Christenberry's photographic work from Hale County. See Curb, "The Literate Art of William Christenberry."

3. Theroux, *Deep South*, 178–83.

4. Hulme, "Traveling to Write (1940–2000)," 90; Pratt, "Fieldwork in Common Places," 27, 32.

5. Holland and Huggan, *Tourists with Typewriters*, vii–ix, xi, 2–3, 5–6.

6. Gupta and Ferguson, *Anthropological Locations*, 13; Theroux, *The Happy Isles of Oceania*, 19–22; Holland and Huggan, *Tourists with Typewriters*, 94, 110. For Malinowski's significance to the rise of modern ethnographic fieldwork see Stocking, "The Ethnographer's Magic," 12–59, and Kuper, *Anthropology and Anthropologists*.

7. Kazin, *On Native Grounds*, 490; Theroux, *Deep South*, 180–81; Garner, "In 'Deep South,' Paul Theroux Takes an Eye-Opening Road Trip."

8. Romine, *The Real South*, 61; Hitt, "Discovering the Deep South's Clichés All over Again."

9. Theroux, *Deep South*, 3, 5, 21, 24, 51.

10. Theroux, 148, 163; Pratt, *Imperial Eyes*, 220.

11. Theroux, 44–45.

12. Theroux, 205, 263, 265. Theroux has encountered the most resistance and resentment to his work as a travel writer in Hawaii. See Theroux, "Paul Theroux's Quest to Define Hawaii."

13. Theroux, *Deep South*, 38, 439–40.

14. Theroux, 155, 164, 284.

15. Agee quoted in Davis, *The Making of James Agee*, 133. Agee's quote here suggests what anthropologist Johannes Fabian calls the "denial of coevalness" that anthropologists and ethnographers engage in when writing about the people and cultures they have observed firsthand. Observing and writing about their subjects as if they occupy a past order of time contradicts the authority of observations made in "the field," which rest upon observing and documenting people in "synchronous" or shared time. See Fabian, *Time and the Other*, xi, 31–32, 147–48.

16. Theroux, *Deep South*; Smith, "Photography's New Southern Dream," 16.

17. Theroux, *Deep South*; Zanes, *Dusty in Memphis*, 87; Holson, "On the Path of Walker Evans."

18. Odum, "The Way of the South," 262.

19. Ferris, "Walker Evans, 1974," 32–34; Agee and Evans, *Let Us Now Praise Famous Men*, 177–78, 184, 277.

20. Plagg, "'There Is an Abundance of Those Which Are Genuine," 32–33; Yates, *Joseph Wharton*, 57–58.

21. Ferris, "Walker Evans, 1974," 32–34.

22. Mitchell, *Southern Portraits*; Theroux, *Deep South*, 216.

23. On the Southern Documentary Project at the University of Mississippi, see http://southdocs.org/ (accessed May 24, 2017). For information about Duke University's Center for Documentary Studies see https://documentarystudies.duke.edu/ (accessed May 24, 2017). Information about the Southern Documentary Fund and the *Reel South* series can be found at http://southerndocumentaryfund.org/programs/ (accessed May 24, 2017). For information about UNC Press's "Documentary Arts and Culture" series and a listing of its publications, see www.uncpress.org/series/documentary-arts-culture/ (accessed May 24, 2017).

24. The "Eyes on the South" series curated by the *Oxford American* can be found at www.oxfordamerican.org/itemlist/category/131-eyes-on-the-south (accessed May 24, 2017). The photo-essays, films, and articles published under *Southern Space's* "Documentary Expression and the American South" series can be accessed at https://southernspaces.org/series/documentary-expression (accessed May 24, 2017). Rankin, "Looking and Telling, Again and Again," 3–9.

25. For more information on these and other releases related to the South see https://folkways.si.edu/ and http://www.dust-digital.com/ (accessed May 21, 2018).

26. Theroux, *Deep South*, 91.

27. Du Bois, *The Souls of Black Folk*, 100; Odum, "Patterns of Regionalism in the Deep South," 5.

Bibliography

Manuscript Sources

Chapel Hill, North Carolina
  University of North Carolina, Chapel Hill, Southern Historical Collection
    Howard Washington Odum Papers
    Arthur Franklin Raper Papers
    George Stoney Papers
Tuscaloosa, Alabama
  University of Alabama, W. S. Hoole Special Collections Library
    Martha Young Papers
Washington, D.C.
  Library of Congress
    Jack Delano Papers

Digital Archives

Alan Lomax Collection, Association for Cultural Equity. www.culturalequity.org/.

Farm Security Administration—Office of War Information, Black and White Negatives, Library of Congress. www.loc.gov/pictures/collection/fsa.

Farm Security Administration—Office of War Information, Color Photographs, Library of Congress. www.loc.gov/pictures/collection/fsac/.

The Lomax Kentucky Recordings, Association for Cultural Equity, Berea College, the Library of Congress, and the University of Kentucky. https://lomaxky.omeka.net/.

University of Massachusetts, Special Collections and University Archives. W. E. B. Du Bois Papers. http://credo.library.umass.edu/view/collection/mums312.

Interviews

Oral history interview with Jack and Irene Delano, June 12, 1965. Archives of American Art, Smithsonian Institution. www.aaa.si.edu/collections/oralhistories/transcripts/delano65.htm. Accessed December 14, 2017.

Oral history interview with Roy Emerson Stryker, 1963-65. Archives of American Art, Smithsonian Institution. www.aaa.si.edu/collections/interviews/oral-history-interview-roy-emerson-stryker-12480#overview. Accessed December 14, 2017.

Interview with Arthur F. Raper by Daniel Singal, January 17, 1971 (B-0029), in the Southern Oral History Program Collection (#4007), Southern Historical Collection, Wilson Library, University of North Carolina at Chapel Hill.

Radio interview with John Cohen, *All Things Considered*. December 23, 2001. www.npr.org/templates/story/story.php?storyId=1135251. Accessed December 14, 2017.

Oral history interview with John Cohen conducted by the author at Cohen's home in Putnam Valley, New York, on September 1 and 2, 2006.

Oral history interview with Joel Agee conducted by the author at Agee's home in Brooklyn, New York, on September 3, 2006.

Cohen, John. "Interview with Roscoe Holcomb." *The High Lonesome Sound* Folkways Records FA 2368 (1965): 1–4.

"Danny Lyon: Civil Rights Photographer." Interview on *Weekend All Things Considered*, National Public Radio, February 20, 1993.

Email interview with Jean Ritchie and author, October 19, 2006.

Ferris, William R. "Walker Evans, 1974." *Southern Cultures* 13, no. 2 (2007): 29–51.

Weiss, Jason. *Always in Trouble: An Oral History of ESP-Disk, the Most Outrageous Record Label in America*. Middletown, CT: Wesleyan University Press, 2012.

Williamson, J. W. "The Appalshop Filmmakers." Interview with Herb E. Smith. In *Interviewing Appalachia: The* Appalachian Journal *Interviews, 1978–1992*, edited by Williamson and Edwin T. Arnold, 397–423. Knoxville: University of Tennessee Press, 1994.

Films

Baichwal, Jennifer, dir. *The True Meaning of Pictures*. 2003. Mercury Films.

Barret, Elizabeth, dir. *Stranger with a Camera*. 2000. Appalshop.

Bell, Carol, dir. *Let Us Now Praise Famous Men Revisited*. 1988. Blue Ridge Mountain Films.

Cohen, John, dir. *The High Lonesome Sound*. 1963. John Brandon Films, Inc.

Davenport, Tom, and Barry Dornfeld, dir. *Remembering the High Lonesome Sound*. 2003. Tom Davenport.

Seeger, Pete, dir. *Rainbow Quest: Johnny Cash & Roscoe Holcomb*. 2005. Shanachie DVD 606.

Spears, Ross, dir., *Agee*. 1980. Agee Films.

Records, CDs, and Liner Notes

Cohen, John. "About Us." Liner notes, *The New Lost City Ramblers* LP. Folkways Records, FA 2396 (1958).

———. "Depression." Liner notes, *The New Lost City Ramblers: Songs from the Depression* LP. Folkways Records, FH 5264 (1959).

———. "Gone to the Country." Liner notes, *The New Lost City Ramblers: Gone to the Country* LP. Folkways Records, FA 2491 (1963).

———. Liner notes, *Mountain Music of Kentucky* LP. Folkways Records, FA 2317 (1960).

———. Liner notes, *Mountain Music of Kentucky*. Smithsonian Folkways Recordings, SFW CD 40077 (1996).

———. Liner notes, *The Music of Roscoe Holcomb and Wade Ward* LP. Folkways Records, FA 2363 (1962).

———. Liner notes, *Roscoe Holcomb: The High Lonesome Sound*. Smithsonian Folkways Recordings, SFW CD 40079 (1998).

———. Liner notes, *Roscoe Holcomb: An Untamed Sense of Control*. Smithsonian Folkways Recordings, SFW CD 41044 (2003).

Pankake, Jon. "The New Lost City Ramblers: The Early Years, 1958-1962." Liner notes, *The New Lost City Ramblers, The Early Years, 1958-1962*. Smithsonian Folkways Recordings, SFW CD 40036 (1991).

Microfilm Collections

Student Nonviolent Coordinating Committee Papers, 1959-72. Sanford, NC: Microfilming Corp. of America, 1982.

Roy Emerson Stryker Papers, 1932-64. Archives of American Art, Smithsonian Institution.

Published Primary Sources

Agee, James, and Walker Evans. *Let Us Now Praise Famous Men*. New York: Houghton Mifflin, 2001.

Agee, Joel. "Killing a Turtle." *DoubleTake* 6 (Fall 1996): 64-66.

Allen, William Francis, Charles Pickard Ware, and Lucy McKim Garrison, eds. *Slave Songs of the United States*. Mineola, NY: Dover Publications, 1995.

"Announcing the Old South Issue." *Saturday Review of Literature*. January 9, 1943, 24.

Bailey, Thomas P. "Children Differ in Environment." In *Social and Mental Traits of the Negro: Research into the Conditions of the Negro Race in Southern Towns*, edited by Howard W. Odum, 299-302. New York: AMS Press 1968.

———. *Race Orthodoxy in the South and Other Aspects of the Negro Question*. New York: Neale Publishing, 1914.

Bain, Read. "A New Technique in Folk-Lore." *Social Forces* 5, no. 2 (December 1926): 298-300.

Baker, Ray Stannard. *Following the Color Line: An Account of Negro Citizenship in the American Democracy*. New York: Doubleday, Page & Co., 1908.

Baldwin, J. Thomas. *A News and Complete Gazetteer of the United States*. Philadelphia: Lippincott, Grambo & Co., 1854.

Belfrage, Sally. *Freedom Summer*. Charlottesville: University Press of Virginia, 1965.

Bigart, Homer. "Kentucky Miners: A Grim Winter." *New York Times*, October 20, 1963, 1.

Bond, Julian. "Foreword." In Danny Lyon, *Memories of the Southern Civil Rights Movement*, 6-7. Chapel Hill: University of North Carolina Press, 1992.

———. "Foreword." In *This Light of Ours: Activist Photographers of the Civil Rights Movement*, edited by Leslie G. Kelen, 13-17. Jackson: University Press of Mississippi, 2011.

———. "A Remarkable Time." In *Danny Lyon: Photo Film, 1959-1990*, 10. Heidelberg: Edition Braus, 1991.

Braun, Richard E. "On to Arcadia: Lead Belly's Last Sessions." *Generation* 7, no. 1 (1953): 19–22.

Brown, Sterling. "On the Government." In *Sterling Brown's* A Negro Looks at the South, edited by John Edgar Tidwell and Mark A. Sanders, 81–89. New York: Oxford University Press, 2007.

Cleland, Herdman F. "The Alabama Black Belt." *Geographical Review* 10, no. 6 (December 1920): 375–87.

Cohen, John. "Conversations with Bob Dylan." *Sing Out!* 18, no. 4 (October-November 1968): 6–23, 67.

———. "Field Trip—Kentucky," *Sing Out!* 10, no. 2 (Summer 1960): 13–15.

———. "The Folk Music Interchange: Negro and White," *Sing Out!* 14, no. 6 (December 1964-January 1965): 42–49.

———. "The Folk Song Revival—A Historical Perspective Part I: The Early Years." *Old-Time Herald* (Spring 1992): 27–32.

———. *The High & Lonesome Sound: The Legacy of Roscoe Holcomb*. Gottingen: Steidl, 2012.

———. "Musical Documents." *Visual Anthropology* 3, no. 4 (1990): 457–78.

———. "NLCR Reflections: The Bread Cast on the Waters Returns." *Old Time Music* 6 (Autumn 1972): 4–6.

———. "A Reply to Alan Lomax: In Defense of City Folksingers." *Sing Out!* 9, no. 1 (Summer 1959): 32–34.

———. "The Revival." Part of a symposium titled "Folk Music Today." *Sing Out* 11, no. 1 (February-March 1961): 22–24.

———. "Roscoe Holcomb (1913-1981)." *Sing Out!* 29, no. 1 (January-February 1983): 41.

———. "Roscoe Holcomb: First Person." *Sing Out!* 16, no. 2 (April-May 1966): 3–7.

———. "Roscoe Holcomb at Zabriskie Point." *Sing Out!* 20, no.1 (September-October 1970): 20–21.

———. *There Is No Eye*. New York: powerHouse Books, 2001.

———. "A Visitor's Recollections." In *Long Journey Home: Folklife in the South*, edited by Allen Tullos. *Southern Exposure* 5, nos. 2–3 (1977): 115–18.

Cohen, Ronald D., ed. *"Wasn't That a Time!" Firsthand Accounts of the Folk Music Revival*. Metuchen, NJ: Scarecrow Press, 1995.

Collins, Shirley. *America over the Water: A Musical Journey with Alan Lomax*. London: SAF Publishing, 2004.

83 *Congressional Record*, H531–32 (February 8, 1938) (statement of Representative Paul Brown).

83 *Congressional Record*, H1737 (February 9, 1938) ("Greene County, GA").

Culbertson, Anne Virginia. *Banjo Talks*. Indianapolis: Bobbs-Merrill, 1905.

Cunningham, Keith K. "*The High Lonesome Sound* by John Cohen and Patricia Jaffe." Review of *The High Lonesome Sound: Kentucky Mountain Music*, directed by John Cohen. *Journal of American Folklore* 90, no. 356 (April-June 1977): 250–51.

Dabney, Virginius, and Howard W. Odum, "The Upper Old South: An Editorial." *Saturday Review of Literature*, January 23, 1943, 3.

Davidson, Christina. "Let Us Now Trash Famous Authors," *The Atlantic*, April 2010. www.theatlantic.com/magazine/archive/2010/04/let-us-now-trash-famous-authors/307994. Accessed July 15, 2015.

Davidson, Donald. "The Trend of Literature: A Partisan View." In *Culture in the South*, edited by W. T. Couch, 183–210. Chapel Hill: University of North Carolina Press, 1935.

Day, Greg. "Folklife and Photography: Bringing the FSA Home." *Southern Exposure* 5, nos. 2–3 (1977): 122–33.

"Decision on News Upheld." *Tuscaloosa News*, August 21, 1982, 2.

Delano, Jack. *Photographic Memories*. Washington, DC: Smithsonian Institution Press, 1997.

Deshin, Jacob. "The Shows Are On: Five One-Man Exhibits among Season's First." *New York Times*, October 25, 1959, X21.

Downes, Lawrence. "Of Poor Farmers and 'Famous Men.'" *New York Times*, November 26, 2011, SR10.

Du Bois, W. E. B. "The Atlanta Conferences." In *W. E. B. Du Bois on Sociology and the Black Community*, edited by Dan S. Green and Edwin R. Driver, 53–60. Chicago: University of Chicago Press, 1987.

———. "Criteria of Negro Art." In *The New Negro: Readings on Race, Representation, and African-American Culture, 1892–1938*, edited by Henry Louis Gates and Gene Andrew Jarrett, 257–59. Princeton, NJ: Princeton University Press, 2008.

———. "The Negro as He Really Is." *World's Work* 2 (June 1901): 848–66.

———. "The Negro in the Black Belt: Some Social Sketches." *Bulletin of the Department of Labor* 4 (May 1899): 401–17.

———. "The Negroes of Farmville, Virginia: A Social Study." *Bulletin of the Department of Labor* 3 (January 1898): 1–38.

———. *The Souls of Black Folk*. New York: W. W. Norton & Co., 1999.

———. "The Study of Negro Problems." *Annals of the American Academy of Political and Social Science* 11 (January 1898): 1–23.

Dunbar, Paul Laurence. *Lyrics of Lowly Life*. New York: Dodd, Mead and Co., 1920.

Edge, John T. "Pie + Design = Change." *New York Times Magazine*, October 8, 2010. www.nytimes.com/2010/10/10/magazine/10pielab-t.html. Accessed June 30, 2015.

Edwards, M. J., et al., *Soil Survey: Hale County*, Series 1935, No. 4. Washington, D.C.: U.S. Department of Agriculture, 1939.

"Englishman Tracks down Subject of Evans.'" *Youngstown Vindicator*, March 29, 1979, 28.

Eskin, Blake. "His Worst Critic Proved Wrong." *New York Times*, November 18, 2001, 38.

Evans, Walker. "Lyric Documentary: An Illustrated Transcript of a Lecture by Walker Evans Presented at Yale University, March 11, 1964." http://isites.harvard.edu/fs/docs/icb.topic867995.files/Evans%20Lyric%20Documentary.pdf. Accessed August 27, 2014.

Evans, Walker, and Jerry L. Thompson. *Walker Evans at Work*. New York: Harper & Row, 1984.

Fischer, John. "A Small Band of Practical Heroes." *Harper's Magazine*, October 1963, 16–28.

Forgey, Benjamin. "Buildings with a Feeling of Belonging." *Washington Post*, May 22, 2004, C01.

Forman, James. *The Making of Black Revolutionaries*. Seattle: University of Washington Press, 1997.

Gardiner, H. N. "Reviews of Books." *Philosophical Review* 11, no. 5 (1902): 498.

Garner, Dwight. "In 'Deep South,' Paul Theroux Takes an Eye-Opening Road Trip." *New York Times*, September 22, 2015. www.nytimes.com/2015/09/23/books/review-in-deep-south-paul-theroux-takes-an-eye-opening-road-trip.html?_r=0. Accessed May 20, 2017.

Gibson, J. Sullivan. "The Alabama Black Belt: Its Geographic Status." *Economic Geography* 17, no. 1 (January 1941): 1–23.

Ginocchino, Benjamin. "Not Quite Paradise, and Starting to Fall Apart." *New York Times*, May 25, 2003, NJ9.

Green, Paul. *Words and Ways: Stories and Incidents from My Cape Fear Valley Folklore Collection*. Special issue of *North Carolina Folklore Journal* 16, no. 4 (December 1968).

Greenberg, Cheryl. *Circle of Trust: Remembering SNCC*. New Brunswick, NJ: Rutgers University Press, 1998.

"Hale County Resident Drops Case." *Tuscaloosa News*, November 6, 1982, 4.

Hall, Captain Basil. *Description of the Camera Lucida: An Instrument for Drawing in True Perspective*. London: Gaulter, 1830.

———. *Forty Etchings from Sketches with the Camera Lucida in North America in 1827 and 1828*. Edinburgh: Cadell & Co., 1830.

———. *Travels in North American in the Years 1827 and 1828*, vol. 3. Edinburgh: Cadell & Co., 1830.

Hall, G. Stanley. *Adolescence*, vol. 1. New York: D. Appleton and Co., 1904.

———. "The Negro in Africa and America." *Pedagogical Seminary* 12, no. 1 (March 1905): 350–68.

Hansberry, Lorraine. *The Movement: Documentary of a Struggle for Equality*. New York: Simon & Schuster, 1964.

Hardy, Forsyth, ed. *Grierson on Documentary*. Berkeley: University of California Press, 1966.

Harrison, Jonathan Baxter. "Studies in the South." *Atlantic Monthly*, August 1882, 194–204.

Hart, Albert Bushnell. *The Southern South*. New York: D. Appleton and Co., 1910.

Haughney, Christine. "A Paean to Forbearance (the Rough Draft)." *New York Times*, June 3, 2013, C1.

Herring, Harriet. *Southern Industry and Regional Development*. Chapel Hill: University of North Carolina Press, 1940.

Herron, Matt. *Mississippi Eyes: The Story and Photography of the Southern Documentary Project*. Jackson: University Press of Mississippi, 2014.

Herskovits, Melville J. "Negro Art: African and American." *Social Forces* 5, no. 2 (December 1926): 291–98.

Higginson, Thomas Wentworth. *Army Life in a Black Regiment*. Mineola, NY: Dover Publications, 2002.

Hitt, Jack. "Discovering the Deep South's Clichés All over Again," *Washington Post*, October 2, 2015. www.washingtonpost.com/opinions/discovering-the-deep-souths-cliches-all-over-again/2015/10/02/ff43c3 B.C.-45c9-11e5-8e7d-9c033e6745d8_story.html?utm_term=.0ddfa388e494. Accessed May 20, 2017.

Holson, Laura M. "On the Path of Walker Evans," *New York Times*, April 23, 2009. www.nytimes.com/2009/04/24/travel/escapes/24alabama.html. Accessed May 25, 2017.

Hurston, Zora Neale. *Mules and Men*. New York: Harper Perennial, 2008.

Jenkins, Bradford L. "Emma's Story: Two Versions." *Southern Exposure* 2, no. 1 (Spring 1979): 8–26.

Johnson, Charles S. *Growing up in the Black Belt: Negro Youth in the Rural South*. Washington, DC: American Council on Education, 1941.

Journey, Edward. "Let Us Now Praise Greensboro, Alabama . . . (and Randall Curb)." https://professionalsoutherner.com/2015/10/13/let-us-now-praise-greensboro-alabama-and-randall-curb. Accessed May 22, 2017.

Kaplan, Carla. *Zora Neale Hurston: A Life in Letters*. New York: Doubleday, 2007.

Kazin, Alfred. *On Native Grounds*. New York: Harcourt Brace & Co., 1995.

Kelen, Leslie G. ed., *This Light of Ours: Activist Photographers of the Civil Rights Movement*. Jackson: University Press of Mississippi, 2011.

Kephart, Horace. *Our Southern Highlanders*. New York: Outing Publishing Co., 1913.

Koningsberger, Hans. "Of Lenses and Literature." *The Reporter*, January 14, 1965, 42.

Lange, Dorothea, and Paul S. Taylor. *An American Exodus: A Record of Human Erosion*. New York: Reynal and Hitchcock, 1939.

Lewis, John. *Walking with the Wind: A Memoir of the Movement*. New York: Simon & Schuster, 1998.

Lisle, Andrea. "The Rural Studio: *Architecture That Empowers*, One Building at a Time." *Paste*, November 15, 2005.

Loke, Margaret. "Harry Lunn, Jr., 65, Art Dealer Who Championed Photography." *New York Times*, August 24, 1998. https://www.nytimes.com/1998/08/24/arts/harry-lunn-jr-65-art-dealer-who-championed-photography.html. Accessed May 23, 2018.

Lomax, Alan. *The Land Where the Blues Began*. New York: New Press, 1993.

Lord, Russell. "A Place on Earth." Review of *Tenants of the Almighty* by Arthur F. Raper. *New Republic*, July 26, 1943, 117.

Luigart, Fred W., Jr. "Roscoe Holcomb's Other World: Perry Folk Musician Gaining Audience." Louisville *Courier-Journal*, September 17, 1962, 15.

Lyon, Danny. *The Bikeriders*. San Francisco: Chronicle Books, 2003.

———. *Danny Lyon: Photo Film*. Heidelberg: Edition Braus, 1994.

———. *Knave of Hearts*. Santa Fe, NM: Twin Palm Publishers, 1999.

———. *Memories of Myself: Essays*. New York: Phaidon Press, 2009.

———. *Memories of the Southern Civil Rights Movement*. Chapel Hill: University of North Carolina Press, 1992.

———. *Message to the Future*. New Haven: Yale University Press, 2016.

Maclachlan, John. Review of *Tenants of the Almighty* by Arthur Raper. *Social Forces* 22, no. 2 (1943): 234.

Maharidge, Dale, and Michael Williamson. *And Their Children after Them—The Legacy of* Let Us Now Praise Famous Men: *James Agee, Walker Evans, and the Rise and Fall of the Cotton South*. New York: Pantheon Books, 1990.

Martinez, Elizabeth, ed. *Letters from Mississippi*. Brookline, MA: Zephyr Press, 2007.

McGill, Josephine. *Folk Songs of the Kentucky Mountains: Twenty Traditional Ballads and Other English Folk-Songs*. New York: Boosey Co., 1917.

Metfessel, Milton. *Phonophotography in Folk Music: American Negro Songs in New Notation*. Chapel Hill: University of North Carolina Press, 1928.

Michaels, Mike. "Stranger in a Strange Land." *No Depression* (September-October 2002): 100-109.

Mitchell, George. *Southern Portraits*. Bear Creek, LA: Bear Creek Books, 1981.

Montgomery, Susan. "The Folk Furor." *Mademoiselle*, December 1960, 98-100, 117-19.

Mountain Life and Work: Magazine of the Southern Mountains, 36, no. 3 (Fall 1960): 51.

Newfield, Jack. *A Prophetic Minority*. New York: Signet Books, 1966.

Odum, Howard W. *An American Epoch*. New York: Henry Holt, 1930.

———. *American Sociology: The Story of Sociology in the United States through 1950*. New York: Greenwood Press, 1969.

———. *Cold Blue Moon: Black Ulysses Afar Off*. Indianapolis: Bobbs-Merrill, 1931.

———. "Folk Sociology as a Subject Field for the Historical Study of Total Human Society and the Empirical Study of Group Behavior." *Social Forces* 31, no. 3 (March 1953): 193-223.

———. "Folk-Song and Folk-Poetry as Found in the Secular Songs of the Southern Negroes." *Journal of American Folklore* 24, no. 93 (July-September 1911): 255-94, and 24 no. 94 (October-December 1911): 351-96.

———. "From Community Studies to Regionalism." *Social Forces* 23, no. 3 (March 1945): 245-58.

———. "Notes on the Study of Regional and Folk Society," *Social Forces* 10, no. 2 (December 1931): 164-75.

———. "On Southern Literature and Southern Culture." In *Southern Renascence: The Literature of the Modern South*, edited by Louis Rubin Jr. and Robert D. Jacobs, 84-100. Baltimore: Johns Hopkins University Press, 1953.

———. "Patterns of Regionalism in the Deep South." *Saturday Review of Literature*, September 19, 1942, 5.

———. *Rainbow Round My Shoulder: The Blue Trail of Black Ulysses*. Indianapolis: Bobbs-Merrill, 1928.

———. "Religious Folk-Songs of the Southern Negroes." *American Journal of Religious Psychology and Education* 3 (July 1909): 265-365.

———. *Social and Mental Traits of the Negro: Research into the Conditions of the Negro Race in Southern Towns*. New York: AMS Press 1968.

———. "Some Studies in the Negro Problems of the Southern States." *Journal of Race Development* 6, no. 2 (October 1915): 185-91.

———. *Southern Regions of the United States*. Chapel Hill: University of North Carolina Press, 1936.

———. "Spirit of the New South." *Saturday Review of Literature*, April 4, 1942, 7.

———. "Standards of Measurement for Race Development." *Journal of Race Development* 5, no. 4 (April 1915): 364–83.

———. "The Way of the South." *Social Forces* 23, no. 3 (March 1945): 260.

———. *Wings on My Feet: Black Ulysses at War*. Indianapolis: Bobbs-Merrill, 1929.

Odum Howard W., and Katharine Jocher. *An Introduction to Social Research*. New York: Henry Holt, 1929.

Odum Howard W., and Guy Benton Johnson. *The Negro and His Songs: A Study of Typical Negro Songs in the South*. Chapel Hill: University of North Carolina Press, 1925.

———. *Negro Workaday Songs*. Chapel Hill: University of North Carolina Press, 1926.

"Official Reports and Proceedings." *American Sociological Review* 10, no. 4 (August 1945): 524–57.

Olmsted, Frederick Law. *The Cotton Kingdom*. Edited by Arthur M. Schlesinger with an introduction by Lawrence N. Powell. New York: Modern Library, 1984.

Osbourne, Scott. "A Walker Evans Heroine Remembers." *American Photographer*, September 1979, 70–73.

Park, Robert E. Book Review. *American Journal of Sociology* 31, no. 6 (May 1926): 821–24.

Payne, Bruce. "SNCC: An Overview Two Years Later." In *The New Student Left: An Anthology*, edited by Mitchell Cohen and Dennis Hale, 79–96. Boston: Beacon Press, 1967.

Raines, Howell. "Let Us Now Revisit Famous Folk." *New York Times Magazine*, May 25, 1980, 31–36, 38, 40, 42, 46.

Ramsey, Frederic. *Been Here and Gone*. Athens: University of Georgia Press, 2000.

Raper, Arthur F. "Gullies and What They Mean." *Social Forces* 16, no. 2 (December 1937): 201–7.

———. *Preface to Peasantry: A Tale of Two Black Belt Counties*. Chapel Hill: University of North Carolina Press, 1936.

———. *Tenants of the Almighty*. New York: Macmillan, 1943.

Raper Arthur F., and Martha J. Raper. *Two Years to Remember and Other Writings*. Oakton, VA: n.p., 1977.

Raper, Arthur F., and Ira de Reid, *Sharecroppers All*. Chapel Hill: University of North Carolina Press, 1941.

Review of *Plantation Songs for My Lady's Banjo* by Martha Young [Eli Shepperd] in *The Era: A Monthly Magazine of Literature* 8, no. 12 (December 1901): 888.

Review of *Social and Mental Traits* by Howard W. Odum. *New York Times*, July 30, 1910, 1.

Sanderson, Dwight L. "The Teaching of Rural Sociology: Particularly in the Land-Grant Colleges and Universities." *American Journal of Sociology* 22 (July 1916–May 1917): 451.

Scarborough, Dorothy. *On the Trail of Negro Folk-Songs*. Cambridge, MA: Harvard University Press, 1925.

Sharp, Cecil, and Maud Karpeles. *English Folk Songs of the Southern Appalachians*. London: Oxford University Press, 1932.

Shelton, Robert. "Art of Folk Song in Festival Form," *New York Times*, April 24, 1960, X14.

———. "Bountiful Area: Southern Highlands a Bottomless Well for Recordings of Folk Music," *New York Times*, June 2, 1963, 126.
———. "Folk Singer from the 'Source.'" *New York Times*, April 24, 1966, X22.
———. "Students Import Folk Art to Chicago," *New York Times*, February 12, 1961, 11.
Sherman, Caroline. "Entrusted with a Portion of His Earth." Review of *Tenants of the Almighty* by Arthur Raper. *The Land* (1943): 89–90.
Smith, Dave. "Photography's New Southern Dream." *Aperture* 115 (Summer 1989): 16–30.
Spears, Ross, and Jude Cassidy, eds. *Agee: His Life Remembered*. New York: Holt, Rinehart and Winston, 1985.
Spirn, Anne Whiston. *Daring to Look: Dorothea Lange's Photographs and Reports from the Field*. Chicago: University of Chicago Press, 2008.
Stryker, Roy Emerson. "The FSA Collection of Photographs." In *Photography in Print: Writings from 1816 to the Present*, edited by Vicki Goldberg, 349–54. New York: Simon & Schuster, 1981.
Sumner, William Graham. *Folkways*. New York: Ginn and Co., 1906.
Theroux, Paul. *Deep South: Four Seasons on Back Roads*. Boston: Houghton Mifflin Harcourt, 2015.
———. *The Happy Isles of Oceania: Paddling the Pacific*. Boston: Houghton Mifflin, 2006.
———. "Paul Theroux's Quest to Define Hawaii." *Smithsonian Magazine*, May 2012. www.smithsonianmag.com/travel/paul-therouxs-quest-to-define-hawaii-61158475/. Accessed May 22, 2018.
Thompson, Edgar T. "Sociology and Sociological Research in the South." *Social Forces* 23, no. 3 (March 1945): 356–65.
Thompson, Ralph. Review of *12 Million Black Voices* by Richard Wright. *New York Times*, November 18, 1941, 29.
Tidwell, John Edgar, and Mark A. Sanders, eds. *Sterling Brown's* A Negro Looks at the South. New York: Oxford University Press, 2007.
"A Transcription of *Remembering the High Lonesome Sound*." www.folkstreams.net/film-context.php?id=92. Accessed February 8, 2018.
Trillin, Calvin. "A Stranger with a Camera." In *Appalachia in the Sixties: Decade of Reawakening*, edited by David S. Walls & John B. Stephenson, 193–201. Lexington: University of Press of Kentucky, 2014.
"Toward Regional Documentation." *Social Forces* 23, no. 3 (March 1945): 302.
White, Owen P. "Devil in de Cotton," *Collier's Weekly*, January 1, 1938, 9–11, 42.
Whitford, David. "The Most Famous Story We Never Told." *Fortune*, September 19, 2005. http://archive.fortune.com/magazines/fortune/fortune_archive/2005/09/19/8272885/index.htm. Accessed December 14, 2017.
Wilgus, D. K. "On the Record," *Kentucky Folklore Record* 6, no. 3 (July–September 1960): 96–100.
Williams, L. A. "The South as a Field for Sociological Research." *Social Forces* 1, no. 2 (January 1923): 112–14.
Wright, Richard. *12 Million Black Voices*. New York: Thunder Mouth's Press, 1988.

Wyman, Loraine, and Howard Brockway. *Twenty Kentucky Mountain Songs*. Boston: Oliver Ditson Co., 1920.

Young, Martha [Shepperd, Eli]. *Plantation Songs for My Lady's Banjo and Other Negro Lyrics and & Monologues*. New York: R. H. Russell, 1901.

Young, Martha. *Minute Dramas—The Kodak at the Quarter*. Montgomery, AL: Paragon Press, 1921.

Zinn, Howard. *SNCC: The New Abolitionists*. Boston: Beacon Press, 1965.

Secondary Sources

Abbott, Brett. *Engaged Observers: Documentary Photography since the Sixties*. Los Angeles: J. Paul Getty Museum, 2010.

Allen, Ray. *Gone to the Country: The New Lost City Ramblers and the Folk Music Revival*. Urbana: University of Illinois Press, 2010.

Allred, Jeff. *American Modernism and Depression Documentary*. New York: Oxford University Press, 2010.

Amaris, Lián. "Calendar Art: How the 1968 SNCC Wall Calendar Brought Activism Indoors." In *Modern Print Activism in the United States*, edited by Rachel Schreiber, 179–92. Burlington, VT: Ashgate, 2013.

Baier, Leslie. "Visions of Fascination and Despair: The Relationship between Walker Evans and Robert Frank." *Art Journal* 41, no. 1 (Spring 1981): 55–63.

Baker, Lee D. *Anthropology and the Racial Politics of Culture*. Durham, NC: Duke University Press, 2010.

Bar-Tal, Daniel. *Shared Beliefs in a Society: Social and Psychological Analysis*. Thousand Oaks, CA: Sage, 2000.

Baldwin, Davarian L. "Our Newcomers to the City: The Great Migration and the Making of Modern Mass Culture." In *Beyond Blackface: African Americans and the Creation of American Popular Culture, 1890–1930*, edited by W. Fitzhugh Brundage, 159–89. Chapel Hill: University of North Carolina Press, 2011.

Barthes, Roland. *Image/Music/Text*. New York: Macmillan, 1978.

———. *Camera Lucida: Reflections on Photography*. New York: Hill and Wang, 1981.

Batteau, Allen. *The Invention of Appalachia*. Tucson: University of Arizona Press, 1990.

Becker, Jane S. *Selling Tradition: Appalachia and the Construction of an American Folk, 1930–1940*. Chapel Hill: University of North Carolina Press, 1998.

Berlin, Isaiah. *The Roots of Romanticism*. Princeton, NJ: Princeton University Press, 1999.

Bernal-Marcos, José Marco, Jorge Castro-Tejerina, and José Carlos Loredo-Narciandi. "Psychological Keys in the Study of African-American Religious Folk Songs in the Early Work of Howard W. Odum." *History of Psychology* 20, no. 1 (February 2017): 28–49.

Bezner, Lili Corbus. *Photography and Politics in America: From the New Deal into the Cold War*. Baltimore: Johns Hopkins University Press, 1999.

Blair, Sara. *Harlem Crossroads: Black Writers and the Photograph in the Twentieth Century*. Princeton, NJ: Princeton University Press, 2007.

Böger, Astrid. *People's Lives, Public Images: The New Deal Documentary Aesthetic*. Tubingen, Germany: Narr, 2001.

Brady, Erika. *The Spiral Way: How the Phonograph Changed Ethnography*. Jackson: University Press of Mississippi, 1999.

Bransford, Stephen Henry. "Trying to Make It Real: The Documentary Imagination of American Roots Music." PhD diss., Emory University, 2008.

Brazil, Wayne D. *Howard W. Odum: The Building Years, 1884–1930*. New York: Garland Publishing, 1988.

Breslau, Daniel. "The American Spencerians: Theorizing a New Science." In *Sociology in America: A History*, edited by Craig Calhoun, 39–62. Chicago: University of Chicago Press, 2007.

Brettell, Caroline B., ed. *When They Read What We Write: The Politics of Ethnography*. Westport, CT: Bergen and Garvey, 1993.

Bromfield, John. "'The Americans' and the Americans." *Afterimage* 8, no. 1/2 (Summer 1980): 8–15.

Burgin, Victor. "Looking at Photographs." In *Thinking Photography*, edited by Victor Burgin, 142–53. New York: Macmillan, 1982.

Burner, Eric. *And Gently He Shall Lead Them: Robert Parris Moses and Civil Rights in Mississippi*. New York: New York University Press, 1994.

Cameron, Ardis. "When Strangers Bring Cameras: The Poetics and Politics of Othered Places." In *Looking for America: The Visual Production of Nation and People*, 340–460. Malden, MA: Blackwell, 2005.

Cantwell, Robert. "When We Were Good: Class and Culture in the Folk Revival." In *Transforming Tradition: Folk Music Revivals Examined*, edited by Neil V. Rosenberg, 35–60. Urbana: University of Illinois Press, 1993.

———. *When We Were Good: The Folk Revival.* Cambridge, MA: Harvard University Press, 1997.

———. *Bluegrass Breakdown: The Making of the Old Southern Sound*. Urbana: University of Illinois Press, 2003.

Carson, Clayborne. *In Struggle: SNCC and the Black Awakening of the 1960s*. Cambridge, MA: Harvard University Press, 1981.

Clifford, James. "On Ethnographic Allegory." In *Writing Culture: The Poetics and Politics of Ethnography*, edited by James Clifford and George Marcus, 98–121. Berkeley: University of California Press. 1986.

———. *The Predicament of Culture*. Cambridge, MA: Harvard University Press, 1988.

Clifford, James, and George Marcus, eds. *Writing Culture: The Poetics and Politics of Ethnography*. Berkeley: University of California Press, 1986.

Cohen, Ronald D. *Rainbow Quest: The Folk Music Revival and America Society, 1940–1970*. Amherst: University of Massachusetts Press, 2002.

Coles, Robert. *Doing Documentary Work*. New York: Oxford University Press, 1997.

Cotera, María Eugenia. *Native Speakers: Ellen Deloria, Zora Neale Hurston, Jovita González, and the Politics of Culture*. Austin: University of Texas Press, 2008.

Cox, Julian. "Chasing down the Kid from Queens." In *Message to the Future*, edited by Danny Lyon, 15–31. New Haven, CT: Yale University Press, 2016.

Cox, Karen. *Dreaming of Dixie: How the South Was Created in American Popular Culture*. Chapel Hill: University of North Carolina Press, 2011.

Crimmins, Timothy J. "Frederick Law Olmsted and Jonathan Baxter Harrison: Two Generations of Social Critics of the American South." In *Olmsted South: Old South Critic/New South Planner*, edited by Dana F. White and Victor A. Kramer, 137–54. Westport, CT: Greenwood Publishing, 1979.

Cruz, Jon. *Culture on the Margins: The Black Spiritual and the Rise of American Cultural Interpretation*. Princeton, NJ: Princeton University Press, 1999.

Curb, Randall. *Historic Hale County*. Greensboro, AL: Preservation Committee of the Alabama Reunion, 1989.

———. "The Literate Art of William Christenberry." *Oxford American*, January/February 1999. www.oxfordamerican.org/magazine/item/1051-the-literate-art-of-william-christenberry. Accessed May 23, 2017.

Davis, Hugh. *The Making of James Agee*. Knoxville: University of Tennessee Press, 2008.

DeVault, Marjorie L. "Knowledge from the Field." In *Sociology in America: A History*, edited by Craig Calhoun, 155–82. Chicago: University of Chicago Press, 2007.

Dittmer, John. *Local People: The Struggle for Civil Rights in Mississippi*. Urbana: University of Illinois Press, 1994.

Duncan, James. "Sites of Representation: Place, Time and the Discourse of the Other." In *Place/Culture/Representation*, edited by James Duncan and David Ley, 39–56. New York: Routledge, 1993.

Dykeman, Wilma, and James Stokely. *Seeds of Southern Change: The Life of Will Alexander*. Chicago: University of Chicago Press, 1962.

Ellis, Richard J. "Romancing the Oppressed: The New Left and the Left Out." *Review of Politics* 58, no. 1 (Winter 1996): 109–54.

Eskildsen, Ute. "Social Commitment as Personal Adventure," In Danny Lyon, *Danny Lyon: Photo Film, 1959–1990*, 36–42. Heidelberg: Edition Braus, 1994.

Ewell, Barbara C., and Pamela Glenn Menke, eds. *Southern Local Color: Stories of Region, Race, and Gender*. Athens: University of Georgia Press, 2002.

Fabian, Johannes. *Time and the Other: How Anthropology Makes Its Object*. New York: Columbia University Press, 1983.

Favor, J. Martin. *Authentic Blackness: The Folk in the New Negro Renaissance*. Durham: Duke University Press, 1999.

Filene, Benjamin. *Romancing the Folk: Public Memory and American Roots Music*. Chapel Hill: University of North Carolina Press, 2000.

Finnegan, Cara A. *Picturing Poverty: Print Culture and FSA Photographs*. Washington, DC: Smithsonian Institution Press, 2003.

Fleischhauer, Carl, and Beverly W. Brannan, eds. *Documenting America, 1935–1943*. Berkeley: University of California Press, 1988.

Forney, John. "Reckoning the Land." In *Rural Studio at Twenty*, edited by Andrew Freear and Elena Barthel, with Andrea Oppenheimer Dean, 252–54. New York: Princeton Architectural Press, 2014.

Fredrickson, George M. *The Black Image in the White Mind: The Debate on Afro-American Character and Destiny, 1817–1914*. Middletown, CT: Wesleyan University Press, 1987.

Garner, Gretchen. *Disappearing Witness: Change in Twentieth-Century American Photography*. Baltimore: Johns Hopkins University Press, 2003.

Geertz, Clifford. *Works and Lives: The Anthropologist as Author*. Stanford, CA: Stanford University Press, 1988.

Gilpin, Patrick J., and Marybeth Gasman. *Charles S. Johnson: Leadership beyond the Veil in the Age of Jim Crow*. Albany: State University of New York Press, 2003.

Gledhill, Christine. "Genre and Gender: The Case of Soap Opera." In *Representation: Cultural Representations and Signifying Practices*, edited by Stuart Hall, 337–86. London: Sage, 1997.

Goldsmith, Peter. *Making People's Music: Moe Asch and Folkways Records*. Washington, DC: Smithsonian Institution Press, 1998.

Gordon, Linda. *Dorothea Lange: A Life beyond Limits*. New York: W. W. Norton, 2010.

Green Dan S., and Edwin D. Driver, "W. E. B. Du Bois: A Case in the Sociology of Sociological Negation." *Phylon* 37, no. 4 (1976): 308–33.

Green, Fletcher. "The South in Reconstruction, 1865–1880." In *Travels in the New South: A Bibliography. Vol. 1, The Postwar South, 1865–1900: An Era of Reconstruction and Readjustment*, edited by Thomas D. Clark, 3–125. Norman: University of Oklahoma Press, 1962.

Grider, Sylvia. "Scarborough, Emily Dorothy." *Handbook of Texas Online*. www.tshaonline.org/handbook/online/articles/fsc01. Accessed December 5, 2017.

Gruber, Jacob W. "Ethnographic Salvage and the Shaping of Anthropology." *American Anthropologist* 72, no. 6 (December 1970): 1289–99.

Gupta, Akhil, and James Ferguson, eds. *Anthropological Locations: Boundaries and Grounds of a Field Science*. Berkeley: University of California Press, 1997.

———. "Culture, Power, Place: Ethnography at the End of an Era." In *Culture, Power, Place: Explorations in Critical Anthropology*, edited by Akhil Gupta and James Ferguson, 1–29. Durham, NC: Duke University Press, 1997.

———, eds. *Culture, Power, Place: Explorations in Critical Anthropology*. Durham, NC: Duke University Press, 1997.

———. "Discipline and Practice: 'The Field' as Site, Method, and Location in Anthropology." In *Anthropological Locations: Boundaries and Grounds of a Field Science*, edited by Akhil Gupta and James Ferguson, 1–46. Berkeley: University of California Press, 1997.

Gura, Philip F. "Southern Roots and Branches: Forty Years of the New Lost City Ramblers." *Southern Cultures* 6, no. 4 (Winter 2000): 58–81.

Guthman, Joshua. *Strangers Below: Primitive Baptists and American Culture*. Chapel Hill: University of North Carolina Press, 2015.

Hale, Grace Elizabeth. *Making Whiteness: The Culture of Segregation in the South, 1890–1940*. New York: Vintage, 1998.

———. *A Nation of Outsiders: How the White Middle Class Fell in Love with Rebellion in Postwar America*. New York: Oxford University Press, 2011.

Hall, Stuart. "The Spectacle of the 'Other.'" In *Representation: Cultural Representations and Signifying Practices*, edited by Stuart Hall, 223–90. London: Sage, 1997.

Hamilton, Marybeth. *In Search of the Blues*. New York: Basic Books, 2009.

Harkin, Anthony. *Hillbilly: A Cultural History of an American Icon*. New York: Oxford University Press, 2003.
Henninger, Katherine. *Ordering the Façade: Photography and Contemporary Southern Women's Writing*. Chapel Hill: University of North Carolina Press, 2007.
Hogan, Wesley C. *Many Minds, One Heart: SNCC's Dream for a New America*. Chapel Hill: University of North Carolina Press, 2009.
Hohle, Randolph. *Black Citizenship and Authenticity in the Civil Rights Movement*. New York: Routledge, 2013.
Holland, Patrick, and Graham Huggan. *Tourists with Typewriters: Critical Reflections on Contemporary Travel Writing*. Ann Arbor: University of Michigan Press, 2000.
Hoole, William Stanley. *Martha Young: Alabama's Foremost Folklorist*. Tuscaloosa, AL: Confederate Publishing, 1982.
Hubbs, G. Ward. *Guarding Greensboro: A Confederate Company in the Making of a Southern Community*. Athens: University of Georgia Press, 2003.
Hulme, Peter. "Traveling to Write (1940–2000)." In *The Cambridge Companion to Travel Writing*, edited by Peter Hulme and Tim Youngs, 87–104. Cambridge: Cambridge University Press, 2002.
Hurley, F. Jack. "Documenting a Culture." In *Southern Mind, Southern Eye: A Photographic Inquiry*, edited by Jack and Nancy Hurley and Gary Witt, 34–35. Memphis, TN: Memphis Academy of Arts, 1981.
Isenberg, Nancy. *White Trash: The 400-Year Untold History of Class in America*. New York: Viking, 2016.
Jackson, Bruce. *Fieldwork*. Urbana: University of Illinois Press, 1987.
Johnson Guy Benton, and Guion Griffis Johnson. *Research in Service to Society: The First Fifty Years of the Institute for Research in Social Science at the University of North Carolina*. Chapel Hill: University of North Carolina Press, 1980.
Jones, Brian. "Finding the Avant-Garde in the Old-Time: John Cohen in the American Folk Revival." *American Music* 28, no. 4 (Winter 2010): 402–35.
Kelley, Robin D. G. "'We Are Not What We Seem': Rethinking Black Working-Class Opposition in the Jim Crow South." *Journal of American History* 80, no. 1 (June 1993): 75–112.
Kidd, Stuart. "Art, Politics, and Erosion." *Revue Francaise D'Etudes Americanes*, nos. 48–49 (April–July 1991): 291–97.
———. "Dissonant Encounters: FSA Photographers and the Southern Underclass, 1935–1943." In *Reading Southern Poverty between the Wars, 1918–1939*, edited by Richard Godden and Martin Crawford, 25–47. Athens: University of Georgia Press, 2006.
———. *Farm Security Administration Photography, the Rural South, and the Dynamics of Image-Making, 1935–1943*. Lewiston, NY: Edwin Mellen Press, 2004.
Klein, Mason, and Catherine Evans. *The Radical Camera: New York's Photo League, 1936–1961*. New Haven: Yale University Press, 2011.
Knight, Vernon James, Jr. *Mound Excavations at Moundville: Architecture, Elites, and Social Order*. Tuscaloosa: University of Alabama Press, 2010.
Kuhn, Cliff M. "'It Was a Long Way from Perfect, but It Was Working'": The Canning and Home Production Initiatives in Greene County, Georgia, 1940–1942." *Agricultural History* 86, no. 2 (Spring 2012): 68–90.

———. "'A Mind-Opening Influence of Great Importance': Arthur Raper at Agnes Scott College." *Southern Cultures* 18, no. 1 (Spring 2012): 71–92.

Kuper, Adam. *Anthropology and Anthropologists: The Modern British School*. New York: Routledge, 2006.

LaRocca, David. "Introduction: Representative Qualities and Questions of Documentary Film." In *The Philosophy of Documentary Film*, 1–54. Lanham, MD: Lexington Books, 2017.

Lamothe, Daphne. *Inventing the New Negro: Narrative, Culture, and Ethnography*. Philadelphia: University of Pennsylvania Press, 2009.

Lears, T. J. Jackson. *No Place of Grace: Antimodernism and the Transformation of American Culture, 1880–1920*. Chicago: University of Chicago Press, 1981.

Leicht, Michael. *Wei Katie Tingle sich weigerte ordentlich zu posieren und Walker Evans daruber nicht grollete*. Bielefeld, Germany: Transcript, 2006.

Lewis, Ronald L. "Beyond Isolation and Homogeneity: Diversity and the History of Appalachia." In *Back Talk from Appalachia: Confronting Stereotypes*, edited by Dwight B. Billings, Gurney Norman, and Katherine Ledford, 21–43. Lexington: University Press of Kentucky, 1999.

Lott, Eric. *Love and Theft: Black Face Minstrelsy and the American Working Class*. New York: Oxford University Press, 1993.

Lund, Jens, and R. Serge Denisoff. "The Folk Music Revival and the Counter Culture: Contributions and Contradictions." *Journal of American Folklore* 84, no. 334 (October–December 1971): 394–405.

Maddow, Ben. "A View from Below: Paul Strand's Monumental Presence." *American Art* 5, no. 3 (Summer 1991): 48–67.

Malone, Bill C. *Music from the True Vine: Mike Seeger's Life and Musical Journey*. Chapel Hill: University of North Carolina Press, 2011.

Matthews, Scott L. "'A Fierce Contest over Images': *Collier's* Magazine and the Fight against Documentary Reportage in Greene County, Georgia, during the Great Depression." In *Reassessing the 1930s South*, edited by Karen L. Cox and Sarah E. Gardner, 154–71. Baton Rouge: Louisiana State University Press, 2018.

———. "John Cohen in Eastern Kentucky: Documentary Expression and the Image of Roscoe Holcomb During the Folk Revival." *Southern Spaces* (August 2008). https://southernspaces.org/2008/john-cohen-eastern-kentucky-documentary-expression-and-image-roscoe-halcomb-during-folk-revival. Accessed December 21, 2017.

———. "Protesting the Privilege of Perception: Resistance to Documentary Work in Hale County, Alabama, 1900–2010." *Southern Cultures* 22, no. 1 (Spring 2016): 31–65.

Mazzari, Louis. "Arthur Raper and Documentary Realism in Greene County, Georgia." *Georgia Historical Quarterly* 87, no. 3/4 (Fall/Winter 2003): 389–407.

———. *Southern Modernist: Arthur Raper from the New Deal to the Cold War*. Baton Rouge: Louisiana State University Press, 2006.

McEuen, Michelle A. *Seeing America: Women Photographers between the Wars*. Lexington: University Press of Kentucky, 2000.

McNeil, W. K., ed. *Appalachian Images in Folk and Popular Culture*. Knoxville: University of Tennessee Press, 1995.

McMurry, Linda O. "A Black Intellectual in the New South: Monroe Nathan Work, 1866–1945." *Phylon* 41, no. 4 (1980): 333–44.

Mellow, James. *Walker Evans.* New York: Basic Books, 2008.

Michaels, Walter Benn. *The Beauty of a Social Problem: Photography, Autonomy, Economy.* Chicago: University of Chicago Press, 2015.

Miller, Karl Hagstrom. *Segregating Sound: Inventing Folk and Pop Music in the Age of Jim Crow.* Durham: Duke University Press, 2010.

Miller, James S. "Inventing the 'Found' Object: Artifactuality, Folk History, and the Rise of Capitalist Ethnography in 1930s America," *Journal of American Folklore* 117, no. 466 (Autumn 2004): 373–93.

Milligan, Michael J. "The Contradictions of Public Service: A Study of Howard Odum's Intellectual Odyssey." PhD diss., University of Virginia, 1994.

———. "The 'Universal Constant in a World of Societal Variables': Howard Odum's Use of the Folk Concept in Folk Sociology, 1930 to 1953." *Folklore Historian* 8 (1991): 5–25.

Minh-ha, Trinh T. "Documentary Is/Not a Name." *October* 52 (Spring 1990): 76–98.

Mitchell, W. J. T. *Picture Theory: Essays on Verbal and Visual Representation.* Chicago: University of Chicago Press, 1995.

Moody-Turner, Shirley. *Black Folklore and the Politics of Racial Representation.* Jackson: University Press of Mississippi, 2013.

Morris, Aldon. *The Scholar Denied: W. E. B. Du Bois and the Birth of Modern Sociology.* Berkeley: University of California Press, 2015.

Morton, David. *Sound Recording: The Life Story of a Technology.* Baltimore: Johns Hopkins University Press, 2004.

Mullen, Patrick B. *The Man Who Adores the Negro: Race and American Folklore.* Urbana: University of Illinois Press, 2008.

Murphree, Vanessa. *The Selling of Civil Rights: The Student Nonviolent Coordinating Committee and the Use of Public Relations.* New York: Routledge, 2006.

Natanson, Nicholas. *The Black Image in the New Deal: The Politics of FSA Photography.* Knoxville: University of Tennessee Press, 1992.

Noggle, Burl. "With Pen and Camera: In Quest of the American South in the 1930s." In *The South Is Another Land: Essays on the Twentieth-Century South,* edited by Bruce Clayton and John A. Salmond, 187–204. New York: Greenwood Press, 1987.

O'Brien, Michael. *The Idea of the American South, 1920–1941.* Baltimore: Johns Hopkins University Press, 1979.

Olin, Margaret. "'It's Not Going to Be Easy to Look into Their Eyes': Privilege of Perception in *Let Us Now Praise Famous Men.*" *Art History* 14, no. 1 (March 1991): 92–115.

Orvell, Miles. *After the Machine: Visual Arts and the Erasing of Cultural Boundaries.* Jackson: University Press of Mississippi, 1995.

———. *The Real Thing: Imitation and Authenticity in American Culture, 1880–1940.* Chapel Hill: University of North Carolina Press, 2014.

Papageorge, Tod. *Walker Evans and Robert Frank: An Essay on Influence.* New Haven: Yale University Art Gallery, 1981.

Payne, Charles. *I've Got the Light of Freedom: The Organizing Tradition and the Mississippi Freedom Struggle.* Berkeley: University of California Press, 1995.

Peeler, David P. *Hope among Us Yet: Social Criticism and Social Solace in Depression America*. Athens: University of Georgia Press, 1987.

Pells, Richard H. *Radical Visions and American Dreams: Culture and Social Thought in the Depression Years*. New York: Harper & Row, 1973.

Petrusich, Amanda. "The Discovery of Roscoe Holcomb and the 'High Lonesome Sound'." *New Yorker*, December 17, 2015. www.newyorker.com/culture/culture-desk/the-discovery-of-roscoe-holcomb-and-the-high-lonesome-sound. Accessed December 21, 2015.

Plaag, Eric W. "'There Is an Abundance of Those Which Are Genuine: Northern Travelers and Souvenirs of the Antebellum South." In *Dixie Emporium: Tourism, Foodways, and Consumer Culture in the American South*, edited by Anthony Joseph Stanonis, 24–49. Athens: University of Georgia Press, 2008.

Porterfield, Nolan. *Last Cavalier: The Life and Times of John A. Lomax, 1867–1948*. Urbana: University of Illinois Press, 2001.

Pratt, Mary Louise. "Arts of the Contact Zone." In *Mass Culture and Everyday Life*, edited by Peter Gibian, 61–72. New York: Routledge, 1997.

———. "Fieldwork in Common Places." In *Writing Culture: The Poetics and Politics of Ethnography*, edited by James Clifford and George Marcus, 27–50. Berkeley: University of California Press, 1986.

———. *Imperial Eyes: Travel Writing and Transculturation*. New York: Routledge, 1992.

Price, Derek. "Surveyors and Surveyed: Photography out and About." In *Photography: A Critical Introduction*, edited by Liz Wells, 9–54. New York: Routledge, 1998.

Prince, K. Stephen. *Stories of the South: Race and the Reconstruction of Southern Identity*. Chapel Hill: University of North Carolina Press, 2014.

Puckett, John R. *Five Photo-Textual Documentaries from the Great Depression*. Ann Arbor: University of Michigan Research Press, 1994.

Rabinowitz, Paula. *They Must Be Represented: The Politics of Documentary*. New York: Verso, 1994.

Raeburn, John. *A Staggering Revolution: A Cultural History of Thirties Photography*. Urbana: University of Illinois Press, 2006.

Raiford, Leigh. "'Come Let Us Build a New World Together': SNCC and Photography of the Civil Rights Movement." *American Quarterly* 59, no. 4 (December 2007): 1129–57.

———. *Imprisoned in a Luminous Glare: Photography and the African American Freedom Struggle*. Chapel Hill: University of North Carolina Press, 2011.

Rankin, Tom. "Looking and Telling, Again and Again: The Documentary Impulse." *Southern Cultures* 22, no. 1 (Spring 2016): 3–9.

Reed, John Shelton. "Sociology of the South." In *The Companion to Southern Literature: Themes, Genres, Places, People, Movements, and Motifs*, edited by Joseph M. Flora and Lucida H. Mackethan, 813. Baton Rouge: Louisiana State University Press, 2002.

———. *Surveying the South: Studies in Regional Sociology*. Columbia: University of Missouri Press, 1993.

Reed, T. V. "Unimagined Existence and the Fiction of the Real: Postmodernist Realism in *Let Us Now Praise Famous Men*." *Representations* 24 (Autumn 1988): 156–76.

Renov, Michael. "Towards a Poetics of Documentary." In *Theorizing Documentary*, 12–36. New York: Routledge, 1993.

Retman, Sonnet. *Real Folks: Race and Genre in the Great Depression*. Durham: Duke University Press, 2011.

Richards, Paul. "Primary Source Documentaries: The Making of *We'll Never Turn Back* (1963) and *A Dream Deferred* (1964) by Harvey Richards." Unpublished article. https://hrmediaarchive.estuarypress.com/wp-content/uploads/2013/01/The-Making.pdf. Accessed May 22, 2018.

Robb, Frances. *Shot in Alabama: A History of Photography, 1839–1941*. Tuscaloosa: University of Alabama Press, 2017.

Roberts, John W. *From Trickster to Badman: The Black Folk Hero in Slavery and Freedom*. Philadelphia: University of Pennsylvania Press, 1989.

Rodgers, Daniel T. "Regionalism and the Burden of Progress." In *Region, Race, and Reconstruction: Essays in Honor of C. Vann Woodward*, edited by J. Morgan Kouser and James M. McPherson, 3–26. New York: Oxford University Press, 1982.

Romine, Scott. *The Real South: Southern Narrative in the Age of Cultural Reproduction*. Baton Rouge: Louisiana State University Press, 2008.

Rosaldo, Renato. *Culture & Truth: The Remaking of Cultural Analysis*. Boston: Beacon Press, 1993.

———. "From the Door of His Tent: The Fieldworker and the Inquisitor." In *Writing Culture: The Poetics and Politics of Ethnography*, edited by James Clifford and George Marcus, 77–97. Berkeley: University of California Press, 1986.

———. "When Natives Talk Back: Chicano Anthropology since the Late Sixties." In *The Renato Rosaldo Lectures, 1985*, 3–20. Tucson, AZ: Mexican-American Studies and Research Center, 1986.

Rosler, Martha. "In, around, and Afterthoughts (on Documentary Photography)." In *Decoys and Disruptions: Selected Writings, 1975–2001*, 151–206. Cambridge, MA: MIT Press, 2004.

Rossinow, Doug. *The Politics of Authenticity: Liberalism, Christianity, and the New Left in America*. New York: Columbia University Press, 1998.

Said, Edward. *Orientalism*. New York: Vintage, 1979.

Sanders, Lynn Moss. *Howard Odum's Folklore Odyssey: Transformation to Tolerance through African American Folk Studies*. Athens: University of Georgia Press, 2003.

Sapirstein, Ray. "Out from behind the Mask: Paul Laurence Dunbar, the Hampton Institute Camera Club, and Photographic Performance of Identity." In *Pictures of Progress: Early Photography and the Making of African American Identity*, edited by Maurice O. Wallace and Shawn Michelle Smith, 167–203. Durham, NC: Duke University Press, 2012.

Schmeisser, Iris. "Camera at the Grassroots: The Student Nonviolent Coordinating Committee and the Politics of Visual Representation." In *The Civil Rights Movement Revisited: Critical Perspectives on the Struggle for Racial Equality in the*

United States, edited by Patrick B. Miller, Therese Frey Steffen, and Elisabeth Schafer-Wunsche, 105–25. Hamburg: LIT, 2001.
Schmier, Louis, and Denise Montgomery. "The Other Depression: The Black Experience in Georgia through an FSA Photographer's Lens." *Georgia Historical Quarterly* 78, no. 1 (Spring 1994): 811–22.
Scott, James C. *Domination and the Arts of Resistance: Hidden Transcripts*. New Haven: Yale University Press, 1990.
———. *Weapons of the Weak: Everyday Forms of Peasant Resistance*. New Haven: Yale University Press, 1985.
Shakespeare, Steven, and Katharine Moody, eds. *Intensities: Philosophy, Religion and the Affirmation of Life*. London: Ashgate, 2012.
Shapiro, Henry D. *Appalachia on Our Mind: The Southern Mountains and Mountaineers in the American Consciousness, 1870–1920*. Chapel Hill: University of North Carolina Press, 1978.
Sherman, Sharon. *Documenting Ourselves: Film, Video, and Culture*. Lexington: University Press of Kentucky, 1998.
Silverman, Jonathan. *For the World to See: The Life of Margaret Bourke-White*. New York: Viking Press, 1983.
Singal, Daniel Joseph. *The War Within: From Victorian to Modernist Thought in the South, 1919–1945*. Chapel Hill: University of North Carolina Press, 1982.
Skinner, Katherine. "'Must Be Born Again': Resurrecting the *Anthology of American Folk Music*." *Popular Music* 25, no. 1 (2006): 57–75.
Sledge, William. "Hale County, Past the Present and into the Future." In *Rural Studio at Twenty*, edited by Andrew Freear and Elena Barthel, with Andrea Oppenheimer Dean, 259–60. New York: Princeton Architectural Press, 2014.
Sluka, Jeffrey A. "The 'Other' Talks Back." In *Ethnographic Fieldwork: An Anthropological Reader*, edited by Antonius C. G. M. Robben and Jeffrey A. Sluka, 175–82. Malden, MA: Blackwell, 2007.
Smith, Jessamyn. "Thinking in Light: The Art of Julius Lester." *Tupelo Quarterly*. www.tupeloquarterly.com/thinking-in-light-the-art-of-julius-lester-by-jessamyn-smyth. Accessed March 19, 2017.
Smith, Shawn Michelle. *Photography on the Color Line: W. E. B. Du Bois, Race, and Visual Culture*. Durham, NC: Duke University Press, 2004.
Sontag, Susan. *On Photography*. New York: Picador, 2001.
Sosna, Morton. *In Search of the Silent South: Southern Liberals and the Race Issue*. New York: Columbia University Press, 1977.
Stanfield, John H. "The 'Negro Problem' within and beyond the Institutional Nexus of Pre-World War I Sociology." *Phylon* 43, no. 3 (1982): 187–201.
Stange, Maren. *Symbols of Ideal Life: Social Documentary Photography in America, 1890–1950*. Cambridge: Cambridge University Press, 1989.
Staub, Michael E. *Voices of Persuasion: Politics of Representation in 1930s America*. Cambridge: Cambridge University Press, 1994.
Stein, Sally. "In Pursuit of the Proximate: A Biographical Introduction." In *Photographic Memories* by Jack Delano, ix–xxiv. Washington, DC: Smithsonian Institution Press, 1997.

Stekert, Ellen J. "Cents and Nonsense in the Urban Folksong Movement: 1930–1966." In *Transforming Tradition: Folk Music Revivals Examined*, edited by Neil V. Rosenberg, 84–106. Urbana: University of Illinois Press, 1993.

Stocking, George W. "The Ethnographer's Magic: Fieldwork in British Anthropology from Tylor to Malinowski." In *The Ethnographer's Magic and Other Essays in the History of Anthropology*, 12–59. Madison: University of Wisconsin Press, 1992.

Stott, William. *Documentary Expression and Thirties America*. Chicago: University of Chicago Press, 1986.

———. "Walker Evans, Robert Frank, and the Landscape of Disassociation." *Arts Canada* 31 (December 1974): 83–89.

Summer, Mary. "The New Deal Farm Programs: Looking for Reconstruction in American Agriculture." *Agricultural History* 74, no. 2 (Spring 2000): 241–57.

Sussman, Elisabeth. "The Story Was Destruction." In Danny Lyon, *Message to the Future*, 33–41. New Haven: Yale University Press, 2016.

Szwed, John. *Alan Lomax: The Man Who Recorded the World*. New York: Penguin Books, 2011.

Tagg, John. *The Burden of Representation: Essays on Photographies and Histories*. Minneapolis: University of Minnesota Press, 1993.

———. *The Disciplinary Frame: Photographic Truths and the Capture of Meaning*. Minneapolis: University of Minnesota Press, 2009.

Thomas, William B. "Howard W. Odum's Social Theories in Transition." *American Sociologist* 16 (February 1981): 25–34.

Thompson, Jerry L. *The Story of a Photograph: Walker Evans, Ellie Mae Burroughs, and the Great Depression*. Venice, CA: Now and Then Reader, 2012.

Tindall, George. *The Emergence of the New South, 1913–1945*. Baton Rouge: Louisiana State University Press, 1967.

Torgovnick, Marianna. *Gone Primitive: Savage Intellects, Modern Lives*. Chicago: University of Chicago Press, 1990.

Trachtenberg, Alan. "From Image to Story: Reading the File." In *Documenting America, 1935–1943*, edited by Carl Fleischhauer and Beverly W. Brannan, 43–75. Berkeley: University of California Press, 1988.

———. *Reading American Photographs: Images as History, Mathew Brady to Walker Evans*. New York: Hill and Wang, 1990.

———. "Walker Evans's Fictions of the South." In *Lincoln's Smile and Other Enigmas*, 299–314. New York: Hill and Wang, 2007.

Turner, Kristin Meyers. "Guy and Candie Carawan: Mediating the Music of the Civil Rights Movement." MA thesis, University of North Carolina, Chapel Hill, 2011.

Vance, Rupert B. "The Twentieth-Century South as Viewed by English-Speaking Travelers, 1900–1955," In *Travels in the New South: A Bibliography, vol. 2*, edited by Thomas D. Clark, 3–13. Norman: University of Oklahoma Press, 1962.

Visser-Maessen, Laura. *Robert Parris Moses: A Life in Civil Rights and Leadership at the Grassroots*. Chapel Hill: University of North Carolina Press, 2016.

Wagner, Bryan. *Disturbing the Peace: Black Culture and the Police Power after Slavery*. Cambridge, MA: Harvard University Press, 2009.

Welch, Walter L., and Leah Brodbeck Stenzel Burt. *From Tinfoil to Stereo: The Acoustic Years of the Recording Industry, 1877–1929*. Gainesville: University Press of Florida, 1994.

Whisnant, David E. *All That Is Native and Fine: The Politics of Culture in an American Region*. Chapel Hill: University of North Carolina Press, 1983.

Willmann, Kate Sampsell. *Lewis Hine as Social Critic*. Jackson: University Press of Mississippi, 2009.

Winant, Harry. "The Dark Side of the Force: One Hundred Years of the Sociology of Race." In *Sociology in America: A History*, edited by Craig Calhoun, 535–71. Chicago: University of Chicago Press, 2007.

Wolfe, Charles. "Just in Time: *Let Us Now Praise Famous Men* and the Recovery of the Historical Subject." In *Fugitive Images: From Photography to Video*, edited by Patrice Petro, 196–217. Bloomington: Indiana University Press, 1995.

Wonham, Henry B. *Playing the Races: Ethnic Caricature and American Literary Realism*. New York: Oxford University Press, 2004.

Woodward, C. Vann. *Origins of the New South, 1877–1913*. Baton Rouge: Louisiana State University Press, 1981.

Wright, Earl, II. "W. E. B. Du Bois, Howard W. Odum and the Sociological Ghetto." *Sociological Spectrum* 34 (2014): 453–68.

Yates, Willard Ross. *Joseph Wharton: Quaker Industrialist Pioneer*. Bethlehem, PA: Lehigh University Press, 1987.

Yochelson, Bonnie, and Daniel Czitrom. *Rediscovering Jacob Riis: Exposure Journalism and Photography in Turn-of-the-Century New York*. Chicago: University of Chicago Press, 2014.

Zamir, Shamoon. *The Gift of the Face: Portraiture and Time in Edward Curtis's* The North American Indian. Chapel Hill: University of North Carolina Press, 2014.

Zanes, Warren. *Dusty in Memphis*. New York: Continuum, 2007.

Zimmerman, Andrew. *Alabama in Africa: Booker T. Washington, the German Empire, and the Globalization of the New South*. Princeton, NJ: Princeton University Press, 2012.

Index

www.ingramcontent.com/pod-product-compliance
Lightning Source LLC
LaVergne TN
LVHW050954080826
845145LV00006B/1498